MAN AND THE SOCIAL SCIENCES

TWELVE LECTURES
delivered at the London School of
Economics and Political Science
tracing the development of
the social sciences during
the present century

EDITED BY
WILLIAM A. ROBSON

Professor Emeritus of Public Administration
London School of Economics
and Political Science

SAGE PUBLICATIONS
Beverly Hills

First American Edition—1974

© 1972
*The London School of Economics
and Political Science*

For information address:

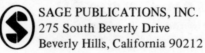 SAGE PUBLICATIONS, INC.
275 South Beverly Drive
Beverly Hills, California 90212

Printed in the United States of America

International Standard Book Number 0-8039-0355-3(cloth)
0-8039-0375-8(paper)

Library of Congress Catalog Card No. 73-91352

FIRST PRINTING

CONTENTS

INTRODUCTION

WILLIAM A. ROBSON

Ph.D., LL.M., B.Sc. (Econ.) Lond.

Professor Emeritus of Public Administration
The London School of Economics
and Political Science

Barrister-at-law of Lincoln's Inn. Reader in Administrative Law at the L.S.E. 1934–46. Former President of the International Political Science Association. Vice-President of the Political Studies Association, and of the Royal Institute of Public Administration. Has received honorary degrees from the Universities of Lille, Grenoble, Paris, Algiers, Durham, Manchester, and Birmingham. Honorary Fellow, L.S.E. Author of many books and articles in learned publications. Founder and Joint Editor of *The Political Quarterly*. Has advised the Governments of Lebanon, Nigeria, Turkey, and Tokyo.

INTRODUCTION

One of the most significant movements in the world of learning in the twentieth century has been the growth of the social sciences. They have outstripped the older arts subjects in many respects and now rival the physical and natural sciences in their appeal. But despite a vast expansion of teaching and research, an immense increase in the numbers of students and staff devoting themselves to these subjects, and a veritable torrent of publications of all kinds, attempts are seldom made to trace and evaluate the developments which have taken place during a specified period. An opportunity to carry out an exercise of this kind occurred in May 1971, when Sir Walter Adams, Director of the London School of Economics and Political Science, invited me to organize a course of public lectures tracing the development of the social sciences in the twentieth century and the part which the School had or had not played in that development. This was the genesis of the lectures published in this book. They were delivered in the Michaelmas and Lent terms of the 1971–2 session and attracted large audiences both from inside and outside the University.

I

The social sciences can most easily and accurately be defined as the disciplines devoted to the study of man in society. Some people of a pedantic turn of mind object to the use of the word 'science' in this connection on the ground that such studies do not have the same degree of accuracy, certainty, universality, or ability to formulate general laws as physics or chemistry. This objection is based on a misunderstanding of the word science, which is derived from the Latin *scientia*. The word signified knowledge, and according to the *Shorter Oxford English Dictionary*, its meanings include knowledge acquired by study; acquaintance with or mastery of any department of learning; or a particular branch of knowledge or study, a recognized department of learning. The restricted meaning given to the word as referring only to the exact, experimental, natural, or physical sciences is quite modern and has no special claim to validity.

Can we be equally confident about the use of the word 'discipline'? The term suggests a rigorous mode of thought, a specialized language, and a common set of assumptions shared by those claiming to understand or exercise the discipline. Economics is clearly a discipline judged by these tests; and so too are law and mathematical statistics. Political science, which usually includes political theory, the history of political thought, government, political parties, groups and associations, elections and public opinion, is more dispersed, less integrated, and lacks a technical vocabulary. But political science is recognized today in every British university (with the possible exception of Cambridge) as a major social science. Sociology is even more diffused and complex, and is divided into a large number of sectional studies; and for the most part it uses the language of everyday speech. After forty years of neglect and hostility in almost all British universities except London, sociology has recently been rising rapidly in the firmament of higher education, and seems now to be regarded as the example *par excellence* of a social science: indeed, as the queen of the social sciences. Professor MacRae refers to 'the history of the discipline' (p. 43 below) without inquiring whether it is a discipline. Professor Goodwin, in tracing the emergence of the much younger subject of international relations, writes of the 'recognition and affirmation of international relations as a discipline with a unity and focus of its own' (p. 95 below). In a later passage, however, he remarks that the L.S.E.'s main contribution in the teaching realm has been to secure widespread acceptance of international relations 'not necessarily as a distinct discipline but as a subject with a distinctive concern, namely, political activity at the level of international society, . . .' (p. 101 below).

Professor Roberts traces the pedigree of the equally new subject of industrial relations. He does not refer to it as a discipline but as 'an area of human activity of fundamental importance to the welfare of mankind' (p. 255 below). A serious interest in various aspects of labour questions had for long been shown by the Departments of Law, Economics, Economic History, and Social Administration, but a Department of Industrial Relations was set up to co-ordinate interdisciplinary activities, to develop specialized knowledge and analytical techniques.

I think we should reject any attempt to distinguish between social sciences which claim to be disciplines in the strict sense of the term and those which do not. Whether we regard the concentrated study of a particular sphere or aspect of human activity as an area of study, or as a subject, or as a discipline, is not important. In the future as in the past, new areas of study are likely to emerge either because of their intellectual interest or because of their practical importance. These areas of study will be manned at first by teachers from existing established subjects and, in the course of time, by scholars who have been educated in the new field. After a certain point of development has been reached, an academic department may be created for the new subject, chairs and lectureships established, and a place found for it in the regular curriculum. This has happened in the present century at the L.S.E. and elsewhere, in regard to sociology, anthropology, geography, social statistics, international relations, industrial relations, social administration, public administration, operational research, and several other subjects.

I have mentioned law as a recognized discipline. What is of infinitely greater importance than its status as a discipline is whether law may properly be regarded as a social science. In the past, law has been regarded as a study of the rules, principles, doctrines, or standards emanating from recognized sources of authority to determine norms of conduct, or to establish rights and duties in specified circumstances. In universities this study has usually been supported by teaching in the history and philosophy of law. But this approach does not make legal studies a social science because it fails to take account of the causes and consequences of legislation or common law doctrines or judicial decisions. The causes of law and its consequences must be sought in economic, social, political, or psychological phenomena, if we are to treat legal studies as a social science.

The law schools in Britain have been traditionally concerned in the main with the lawyer's view of law, meaning by that the professional lawyer. He is necessarily concerned with the particular interests of his client, which may concern property rights or a civil dispute or a contravention of the criminal law. Whatever the issue may be, it is only the individual case which concerns him, not the broader interest of society. Moreover, the broader social consequences of the law are reflected less in the marginal or pathological cases which form the subject matter of litigation and criminal trials, than in the effects of legal provisions on the conduct of businessmen or parents or motor-car manufacturers or civil servants or investors or newspaper proprietors or doctors in the ordinary business of life.

At the L.S.E. legal studies have for long been regarded as one of the social science; but this does not mean that it is not taught in a way which provides a good professional training. Indeed, the very opposite may be true, for to an increasing extent the practising lawyer is expected to possess some insight into the broader effects of legal arrangements, particularly in such spheres as labour law, the law of restrictive practices, company law, the law of taxation, the law of town and country planning, and family law.

The social sciences may be said to comprise economics, politics and public administration, sociology, social administration, law, anthropology, international relations, industrial relations, social psychology, human geography, statistics, demography, management, together with the relevant branches of history. The scope and magnitude of the corpus of knowledge varies greatly among these subjects, depending to some extent on the length of time during which they have developed.

II

There are several ways in which a course of lectures on the social sciences could be devised. One way would be to take each academic department in turn and to survey its progress or shortcomings. I rejected this because the organization of university departments and even faculties, and the distribution of subjects among them, is sometimes the result of historical accidents or the influence of particular individuals rather than the application of rational criteria. But a more important consideration was my desire to see how far, or whether, developments in the social sciences have succeeded in throwing light on some of the most important problems which are confronting civilized society at the present time. It is for this reason that I called the course, and this book, *Man and the Social Sciences*. Another reason was the growing evidence that some of the most intractable problems cut across the boundaries of individual disciplines and I wanted the lecturers to feel free to cross the boundaries if they wished; and some of them have done so. It was evident, however, that each lecture would have to have its main focus in a more or less specialized field of study.

For the reasons set out above, I proposed that the lectures should be related to a number of themes. All but one of the lecturers accepted the themes I had suggested; and despite a considerable variation in the treatment of the themes, as a whole they clearly reveal the degree of awareness prevailing among eminent scholars of the challenges which these themes present to the social sciences, and how effective the response is likely to be.

Many readers will be struck by the close interrelations between many of the themes and the problems which underlie them. I will illustrate this with some examples.

The twentieth century has been one in which many upheavals and catastrophes have occurred: the two world wars, and the wars in Korea, Vietnam, the Middle East, and India; the civil wars in Spain and Nigeria; the revolutions in Russia, China, and many smaller countries; the termination of the British, French, and Dutch empires, and the emergence of many new independent states; the Great Depression of the 1930s. These events and their aftermath have left a heritage of violence and conflict, which has been and is being manifested all over the world. Protest and demonstration have become almost daily events in many countries, often linked with demands for freedom or autonomy, or better treatment of one kind or another. Such protests and demonstrations often erupt into violence. Every government facing such confrontations is forced to seek ways of maintaining and enhancing the degree of unity in the nation over which it rules. In many countries social cohesion can no longer be taken for granted in the old easygoing way: it must be consciously safeguarded and nurtured. The vulnerability of the nation to disruption, fragmentation, and conflict are among the facts of life of which most governments are unpleasantly conscious.

We look primarily to sociologists to explain 'how society is possible and how it coheres'. Professor MacRae tells us something of their approach in terms of institutional relationships, roles and status-systems, socialization and communication. We know that there are many factors which bind men together in a community, such as ethnic and family ties, language, religion, law, economic interest, fear, and the need for security. But we have also learned by the kaleidoscope of events that 'social structures are less coherent than we have believed' (p. 56 below).

Wide-ranging analysis of this subject may be the special concern of the sociologist, but important aspects of it also fall within the province of other social sciences. No great insight is needed to realize that the malfunctioning of industrial relations can at the extreme lead to a kind of civil war within the economy. It can produce feelings of injustice, oppression, disloyalty, irresponsibility, resentment, vindictiveness, malevolence, not only in the parties or groups concerned in industrial disputes, but in the wider public who are adversely affected. Such feelings inevitably undermine the degree of social cohesion existing within the community.

Then again we must consider the social ills which the modern state attempts to remedy or prevent. The social services are methods of providing help for the sick, the unemployed, the aged, the blind, the incapacitated, the handicapped and disabled, the homeless, those living in slums or overcrowded conditions, orphans and deprived children. A state which ignored the needs of those suffering the vicissitudes of life, the underprivileged and handicapped, would be not merely lacking in compassion but neglecting to perform an integrating function. For beyond the object of providing a remedy for the social ills from which particular indivduals or groups suffer, is the purpose of making the less fortunate feel that the community cares for them and this in turn may lead them to identify with the society or at least to prevent their alienation. Thus social administration has a contribution to make to social cohesion.

Reference to the social services immediately raises the question

what is or what should be the provinces of state action in this and related spheres. Academic teachers of social administration have felt impelled to inquire into this matter for several reasons. One is that private remedies as well as public remedies are available to deal with some social ills, and it would be absurd to consider public policies concerning the latter without taking account of the alternative remedies. Voluntary and statutory services exist side by side in relation to the care of the aged, orphans and deprived children, the blind and the physically handicapped, and many other categories of those in need of help. There is also the question of 'the appropriate and desirable balance between the market and the state in meeting the individual's needs for insurance against adversity, education, or health care' (Parker, p. 121 below). As many kinds of help provided by the state are also provided by commercial or charitable agencies, why is the state also involved? Is it possible to discover any valid principles in allocating responsibility to the public and private sectors respectively? One basis of distinction depends on whether social justice or the price mechanism is accepted as the guiding principle of allocation. But Professor Parker insists that preferences of this kind derive ultimately from political conviction (p. 122 below).

Increasing interest in taxation policy as an instrument of redistribution has also led to comparisons between the benefits accruing to the poor or the lower income groups through cash benefits and the allowances given to the better-off through the income-tax system. Some of the work in this field has been carried out by eminent teachers of social administration such as Professor Titmuss and Professor Abel-Smith, and some of it by economists specializing in public finance.

Political scientists have not provided a satisfactory theory, or indeed any theory at all, of the proper province of state action in the contemporary world. Professor Self began his lecture by drawing attention to the failure of political theory to keep up with the growth of collectivism in the modern democratic state. We have, he pointed out, little more than the traditional liberalism of Locke and John Stuart Mill combined with the socialistic framework set out in Laski's *Grammar of Politics* as a political philosophy for an era in which the functions and aims of the state have widened almost beyond recognition. The term welfare state offers no guide

to the proper limits of individual freedom or governmental action. The stagnant condition of political theory is partly due to the rise of logical positivism in the schools of philosophy, and partly to the relegation of value judgements to the status of mere personal preferences without rational validity. The rise of political behaviourism, political sociology, and doctrines about political systems, have contributed little or nothing to our understanding of the proper role of the state in today's industrialized, urbanized, democratic society.

Can we turn to the economists for guidance on this fundamental question? If economics can be defined as 'the scientific study of choice, both individual and collective' (Johnson, p. 4 below) it follows that choices exercised by public authorities at all levels of government form part of this study; but the question of which choices should be made by individuals or non-governmental bodies and which by government would not necessarily be included in the study.

Professor Johnson identifies various conditions in which the inferior performance of an economic system may call for government intervention. They concern defects in market prices which do not adequately reflect social benefits or social costs; competition failing to produce an ethically equitable distribution of income; the aggregate of individual choices leading to high unemployment or inflation; and an unacceptable balance of payments deficit or surplus. Moreover, he remarks, there may be social objectives in the economic field which transcend or differ from those which would result from unfettered individual choice in a free market. Recognition of such social objectives is in sharp opposition to the doctrines and outlook of the classical economists but it reflects the mood of those contemporary ecnomists who seek by state action to increase economic growth or to level down the inequalities of income of different regions. The widespread belief in the need for a regulated economy and the immense increase in the economic and social functions of the state are due in his view to the historical events of the past half-century.

The vast expansion in the role of the state in regulating the economy has led a group of American economists to attempt an analysis of the political process and political decisions by methods similar to those used in the private sector.

A fuller description of this new trend is given by Professor William G. Mitchell in a recent essay entitled 'The Shape of Political Theory to Come: From Political Sociology to Political Economy'. (1) Mitchell declares that a new era of inquiry embracing political science and economics is emerging.

The new political economy is mainly focused on how collective choices are made by non-market institutions in various political systems using different processes. The political economists pursuing this area of study regard politics as a type of exchange operation analogous to economic exchanges in the market. The political decision-makers are assumed to exercise rational choices in an environment in which all the persons or organisations are seeking to promote their own self-interest. This approach differs basically from the economists' traditional view which takes public policies for granted and seldom becomes involved in the political consequences of economic policy or the economic consequences of political policy.

The main subject-matter of the new American school of political economists is resource allocation, which obviously lends itself most easily to the techniques of economic analysis. While this is of great importance it by no means comprises the whole field of state activity. Such areas of government as international relations, the liberties of the citizen, law and order, public morals, family relationships, the status of women, race relations, local government, and many others are matters in which questions of resource allocation are only of remote or slight importance in determining public policy. Professor Mitchell welcomes the new movement, because it may lead to a theory of resource allocation that will explain how rational decisions can be made concerning the appropriate share of the G.N.P. to be administered by government, the optimum priorities about the allocation of that share among public goods and services; and the optimum choice between current consumption and investment in the future.

The great dilemma of our times arises from the conflict between the incessant demands for more state action of many different kinds put forward by a multitude of pressure groups and interest groups and the decline in governmental authority and respect for law and order. The problem which faces governments is to obtain from the mass of citizens and organizations the co-operation, the

consciousness of consent, the acceptance of high levels of taxation, and the obedience to regulation which are required for an effective response to these demands.

The present situation is a dangerous one because more is demanded of government than it can achieve without more support of the kinds mentioned above: the recent past in Britain is littered with example of this in such matters as 'prices and incomes policy', economic growth, industrial relations, Rhodesia, Northern Ireland, full employment, and the control of inflation. If government is unable to fulfil popular expectations, no matter whether they are reasonable or not, there is a danger of disillusion and cynicism spreading among the people, and if that continues unabated the stability of any regime is weakened. One of the causes of the decline in authority and diminished respect for law and order may be, as Professor Self suggests, that the present working of the political process hardly enlarges the citizen's understanding or draws attention to his responsibilities (p. 84 below). The emphasis today is almost exclusively on rights, seldom on duties.

The difficulties of formulating a logically coherent political philosophy suited to our era are shown in the essay 'Social Knowledge and the Public Interest'. In this, Professor Watkins calls in aid what he describes as the distinctive methodological tradition developed at the L.S.E. by Robbins, Hicks, Hayek, and other economists powerfully reinforced by Popper, to reject classical utilitarianism and any form of comprehensive collectivism. This tradition does not conflict with the gradualist aspect of the Webbs' collectivism (one remembers Sidney Webb's famous phrase about 'the inevitability of gradualism') because this is consonant with Popper's view that piecemeal engineering is the only acceptable mode of reform and his explicit rejection of utopian engineering involving a complete reshaping of society. Watkins argues strongly against the Webbs' belief in collectivism without, perhaps, appreciating the fact that they were advocates of decentralization rather than believers in the centralized state. What worries him most is the assumption that the central authority in a collectivized regime could discover and promote the best interest of the society over which it exercises power (p. 185 below).

In formulating the tasks of government, Professor Watkins

proposes that we should begin by classifying functions into those which can be performed only by governments; those which can be much better done by government than by other bodies; those which governments should or should not do according to our political views; and at the other end of the spectrum the functions which government cannot perform. But no matter how the classification may work out, a guiding principle is that state action should seek to minimize suffering and not to maximise happiness. This is the doctrine of negative utilitarianism. It postulates that the appropriate aim of a government is to reduce suffering, leaving the pursuit of happiness to private initiative. The statesman's goal, one might say, is to achieve full employment, but not full enjoyment (pp. 192–3 below).

Such a doctrine might provide clear rules in regard to some existing functions such as the maintenance of art galleries, national libraries, and museums. They do not reduce suffering but increase wellbeing and perhaps promote happiness, so they should be discontinued. But if we consider the public education service, at what point do we decide that the government is trying to reduce suffering by eliminating illiteracy or, by contrast, seeking to increase happiness by providing deserving students with higher education or training? Difficulties of this kind crop up all along the line. However, Professor Watkins concludes by quoting an encouraging remark by Stigler to the effect that the classical economists were at their best when dealing with issues posed by concrete problems of the day; and he thinks that social ills present a challenge to social scientists, which may evoke advances in knowledge and stimulate new constructive ideas.

In no sphere of knowledge and action is this more urgently needed than in relation to the human environment. In his talk on 'Man and his Environment' Professor Wise shows that the study of the interaction between man and his habitat was a deeprooted concern of Sir Halford Mackinder, the founder of 'the new geography', and a Director of the L.S.E. from 1903 to 1908. Mackinder was a man of genius in the intellectual sphere, and anyone who heard him lecture will never forget the experience. His pioneering work gave an impetus to the study of societies and their environment which has been pursued continuously at the L.S.E. by a number of distinguished geographers. It implies no

detraction from the value of their contributions to say that in our own day the subject has acquired new dimensions, new aspects, and a new importance.

Some of these aspects are concerned with the degradation of the environment by pollution of the air, the sea, rivers, and the land itself by noxious fumes, persistent pesticides, or toxic waste. There is the threat caused by noise, whether on the ground or overhead. There is the threat to the countryside, where development so often means destruction. There is the threat to urban amenity caused by motorways and the torrent of motor-cars on roads of all classes. Below these surface symptoms are deeper biological manifestations, particularly the escalating growth of population, the destruction of the ecosphere, and the reckless use of natural resources. These aspects all point to the need to fend off or prevent the consequences flowing from man's irresponsible or ignorant activities affecting the environment.

But there is another and more positive side to the new concern with the environment. Very belatedly there has arisen in many countries a new emphasis on 'the quality of life'. The expression is at present vague but it clearly means something very different from the accumulation of household durables, the universal ownership of motor-cars, full employment regardless of job satisfaction or the social value of the product; a plethora of betting shops and bingo halls; and economic growth as the supreme good.

The task of discovering what 'the quality of life' signifies, how it can be achieved and at what cost, will involve an immense intellectual effort involving all the social sciences and many of the natural sciences. Professor Wise is in no doubt that history, economics, sociology, social administration, social anthropology, government, social psychology, and law are all relevant to environmental questions. That these disciplines will require extending and adjusting if they are to focus effectively on these problems is also not open to doubt. Above all, interdisciplinary co-operation will be required not only among the social sciences but between the social and the natural sciences (p. 241 below).

It must be admitted that interdisciplinary studies have not as yet made great progress in the social sciences. Several of the authors in this book refer to contributions made by colleagues in other disciplines. For example, Professor Roberts mentions the

work of Bowley and Sir Roy Allen in developing the techniques and methods of presenting labour statistics, of Professor Kahn-Freund in the field of labour law, of Sir John Hicks and others on the economic problems of industrial relations. Labour history has for long attracted many able historians, and more recently sociologists have been working in the industrial field. International relations has been studied by historians, international lawyers, economists, political scientists, and others. But the multi-disciplinary approach is not the same at interdisciplinary study and research. The former results in a series of separate studies dealing with particular aspects of the subject, whereas the latter aims at an integrated and co-ordinated view of the whole. Professor Kendall ends his essay with an eloquent plea for more crossing of the intellectual and practical barriers which confine the disciplines into neat compartments (pp. 146–7 below). Economics, he remarks, can no longer be left to the economists or sociology to the sociologists; and the same could be said of politics and other social sciences. He pleads for teams of behavioural scientists, mathematicians, statisticians, psychologists, systems analysts, and numerical data handlers, to study complex interactive systems.

A special case of the interaction between disciplines occurs when the methodology or the outlook of a particular subject permeates that of others. Sociology is everywhere, observes Professor MacRae, 'in the sense that, to an extraordinary extent and not always fully aware, the social and historical sciences and the public consciousness of political and social affairs have become sociologized' (p. 42 below). Certainly sociology has had a marked influence in sociologizing several other areas of thought and action. Political sociology, the sociology of crime and punishment, the sociology of religion, of medicine, of education, are examples.

The interactions between the social sciences and the world of action are strong. The academic study of international relations in Britain began with the creation of the Wilson Chair of International Politics at Aberystwyth, followed soon afterwards by the Cassell Chair of International Relations at the L.S.E. The creation and endowment of these chairs 'reflected the widespread sense of revulsion at the long drawn-out blood letting of the First World War' (Goodwin, p. 92 below). The substantial development of the

study in British universities has no doubt increased our understanding of the complex relations between nation states and the working of international institutions. It would be difficult to show that it has made the world a more peaceful place or prevented the outbreak of war or increased the amount of international co-operation. In the area of industrial relations, the other great sphere of conflict and co-operation, a similar situation prevails, for industrial conflict has been on the increase in all the pluralist countries (Roberts, p. 266 below). Although our understanding of the causes of industrial disputes is very much greater, Professor Roberts frankly admits that the total impact of the courses on British industrial relations has not been great enough.

Recognition of the limited effect of these disciplines on the world of action must not be regarded as a criticism either of the social science studies or those who direct them. They are concerned with areas of human behaviour in which passions are easily aroused, in which conscious and unconscious motivations are extremely strong, and irresponsible and shortsighted action often triggered off without full consideration of the consequences. In any event I would maintain that the fundamental aim of academic study is to enable us to understand the world in which we live; or at least to understand it better than we otherwise would. It is highly gratifying when an eminent scholar in a particular discipline can point the way to the solution of an intractable problem, in the manner of Maynard Keynes. A breakthrough of this kind is rare in any field of knowledge. The influence of the social sciences has been of a more pervasive kind. It has modified the attitudes of responsible persons in the world of action rather than provided them with specific remedies or doctrines. The attitude towards the treatment of convicted criminals, for example, has been substantially modified by the work of criminologists and psychologists; attitudes of ministers, civil servants and business men towards taxation have been greatly changed by the work of economists, and so on. Professor R. M. Titmuss and other leading thinkers have had a notable influence on social policy; and the Greater London Group of the L.S.E. made a substantial contribution to the reorganization of London government. (2) Influence on practical affairs has often been exerted by university teachers serving on royal commissions or

government committees, or by presenting evidence to such bodies, or acting as consultants to them.

III

Three of the lectures dealt with themes which have a bearing on the whole range of the social sciences. They are 'Time and Change', 'Measurement in the Study of Society', and 'Models of Man'.

The paper by Professor Kendall discusses the most important methodological development of the present century: the introduction of measurement in varying degrees in virtually every one of the social sciences. A major device used nowadays for a great variety of purposes is the sampling method which was pioneered at the L.S.E. by Bowley. The astonishing accuracy of the laws of averages and aggregates has become so commonplace that it is a positive relief when a general election prediction turns out to have been wrong! Public opinion polls, market research, social surveys, and a hundred other forms of inquiry now employ increasingly sophisticated sampling techniques. And this is only one strand in the thread. The spectacular rise of econometrics and the spread of quantitative methods in economics, sociology, political science, geography, and other disciplines for purposes of analysis as well as for purposes of measurement, has transformed the study of society.

In view of the prevailing mood it is easy to assume that only measured knowledge can be deemed to have objective validity. Professor Kendall warns us against some of the pitfalls implicit in that assumption. We are currently using many concepts and expressions, such as welfare, democracy, participation, equity, social justice, motivation, confidence, incentives, alienation, culture, which are difficult or impossible to quantify in our present state of knowledge. We should not abandon these words on the ground that the things or notions they represent cannot be measured. To do so would be to leave us without a vocabulary. Moreover, these words represent ideas and aspects of social life of great importance. The effort to push forward the frontiers of quantified knowledge will continue, and doubtless much progress will be achieved by the end of the century. In addition to measure-

ment there are several other approaches which rely on quantified knowledge in one form or another, such as computerized simulation, mathematical analysis of complex situations, systems analysis, operational research, and model-building. All of them are useful in appropriate circumstances. The one fundamental danger is that we should cease to think and care about ultimate ends and purposes on the ground that often they cannot be measured.

The most novel theme in the course is 'Models of Man'. What led me to propose this theme was the belief that every social science assumes, and must assume, that man in society has certain characteristics. The social scientist cannot operate without a conceptual framework about the nature of man even though reflection and research may show that some or all of the assumptions on which it is constructed are wholly or partly wrong. The classic theory of democracy assumed that men and women when performing the ordinary voting function would act in an entirely rational manner and take decisions only after a lengthy process of ratiocination. Graham Wallas's book, *Human Nature in Politics*, blew this notion skyhigh.

Economists assume that economic man is a creature whose actions are normally informed by enlightened self-interest. He is supposed to be endowed with a propensity to save or to spend, to do this or do that, in response to certain stimuli or constraints. The common law assumes that people intend the consequences of their acts and are deemed to know what they are likely to be. Man in society is assumed by the lawyer to be a rational creature. The concept of the reasonable man is fundamental to the law of torts and criminal law. Negligence, for example, involves behaving in a manner in which no reasonable man would behave in those circumstances; and liability in many kinds of accident is determined by whether the parties behaved in a reasonable manner or not.

Few of these assumptions concerning the nature of men have been seriously challenged either by exponents of the subjects which produced them, or by outside critics. Yet many of them are untested and at least some are false. The assumptions of the criminal law about men and women being fully responsible for their actions appear very questionable in the light of Freudian and

post-Freudian psychology, even when mental illness is not pleaded. What is the model of economic man which can be accepted as valid today? Is he a creature whose conduct is substantially influenced by the carrot and the stick? And how does the carrot work in an industrial environment in which a workman who exceeds the 'stroke' laid down by his union will be severely dealt with by the union or by fellow workmen on the shop floor; while the impact of the 'stick' is scarcely visible if supplementary benefits are payable to the wife and children of a man on strike, and he himself is able to obtain temporary employment in another occupation during the dispute. What do we really know about the vital question of incentives to work, about the effects on such incentives of direct and indirect taxation, of death duties, and other compulsory obligations concerning which dogmatic assertions are frequently made? All this is a little-explored area of great significance.

Professor Leach discusses some conceptual questions which are even more fundamental than these. He accepts that all the major sociological theorists have been model-builders, and many celebrated examples are scattered through the pages of his essay. But he selects four specific models which raise in one form or another the basic question of the relation between the observer and the observed. 'Is it possible', he asks, 'in social science to distinguish subject from object?' (Leach, p. 157 below). Since virtually all social sciences are focused on the behaviour of human beings conditioned to a particular culture, and since they are capable of behaving in a manner which is fundamentally different from the flora and fauna, or any of the other components of the natural world, does this not distinguish social science from natural science? The unique characteristic of cultured man is his ability to alter the environment by deliberate and conscious effort, and to lie; the deliberate deceit of a man being quite different from the camouflage of the butterfly which resembles a leaf. Such considerations lead to the question whether the student of social science can ever hope to arrive at objective truth.

The Provost concludes that because all who work at the L.S.E. regard themselves as social scientists they tend to use the models of Descartes, of Darwin, and of Comte, which distinguish sharply the observer and the observed, man and the natural world. These

models are borrowed from the natural sciences, and from the beginning of the twentieth century we have taken it for granted that 'a value-free sociology is a possibility and that the attainment of value-free objectivity is the primary justification for all social science methodology' (p. 170 below). He warns us that we ought to be more open minded, for it may well be the case that there is an area of human science to which the principles of non-human science cannot be applied. I have already tried to show the difficulties facing some social studies which seek to develop while avoiding value judgements.

History occupies an ambiguous position among the social sciences. The great tradition in English, and indeed European, education has been the belief that we can learn from history. This was the explanation for the view which prevailed in the seventeenth, eighteenth and nineteenth centuries that a classical education was the best possible preparation for the future leaders of the nation in nearly every walk of life. History, and particularly the history of the ancient world, was firmly established at the older universities long before the social sciences emerged as subjects of higher education. But as soon as political thought found its way into the curriculum, the history of political ideas from Plato and Aristotle onwards became an indispensable part of the course. Economic history took its place side by side with economic theory; international history with international law and international relations, and similar associations occurred in other fields.

Professor Postan draws attention to the fact that it was Darwin who extended to all living matter the concept of society and social existence as a time-sequence which the continental historians—especially the Hegelians—had imposed on virtually every department of social and political thought. It was largely due to the publication of *On the Origin of Species* that social scientists sought for the origins of institutions and ideas and tried to trace stages of their evolution. Herbert Spencer joined in this search, for he shared the Darwinian faith. Karl Marx also joined in the hunt, for he too was a Darwinian.

It was his avowed intention to do for social sciences what *On the Origin of Species* did for biology, and to establish in the former an evolutionary doctrine as firm and all-embracing as Darwin's. Above

all, he was an historian. He invariably presented the state of the world in which he lived solely as a product of historical change. Economic systems, those of tribal society, feudalism or capitalism, were presented as phases of historical development (Postan, p. 28 below).

The names of Darwin, Comte, and Marx figure not only in Professor Postan's essay as formative influences in the conceptual approach to social studies, but they occur prominently also in Dr. Leach's four basic models of man (Leach, p. 152 below).

The historical approach to social science strongly influenced some of the most famous L.S.E. teachers in the first half of the twentieth century. Professor Postan mentions Graham Wallas, Harold Laski, the Webbs, Charles Webster, R. H. Tawney, and Eileen Power. They were, of course, a very diverse group, and the last three were professional historians. The Webbs wrote many volumes of history, but they also engaged in many other activities, both literary and practical, directed to social or political reform. But none of them were guilty of the sins of historicism which Sir Karl Popper has denounced so strongly (3).

IV

I shall not attempt to summarize the contribution which the London School of Economics has made to the social sciences during the present century. This has been described by the authors of the various essays as they see it. No one who takes the trouble to read these pages can doubt that the L.S.E. has been the principal centre in the United Kingdom, and indeed in Europe, for the development of the social sciences as a whole during the twentieth century. In certain subjects, such as economics, its achievements have covered only part of the field, and in other parts the most distinguished work has been done elsewhere (Johnson, p. 21 below). Broadly speaking, the most outstanding achievements of the L.S.E. during the present century have taken place in geography, statistics, social administration, economics, sociology, social anthropology, logic and scientific method, demography, industrial relations, law, and government. The historians mentioned above were the most eminent in their own fields not only in their own day but at any time. The work of the L.S.E. in politics and government is lightly touched on by Professor

Self, but it can be said without hesitation that the L.S.E. has been a leading centre for many years, especially in the field of graduate studies. Here it has shared the honours with Oxford and Manchester. In international relations the L.S.E.'s main achievement until recently was to get the subject established as a recognized field of study.

It is well to remember that the role of an academic institution is to be assessed not only in terms of the famous teachers which it includes on the faculty, nor on whether some of them have produced new ideas or methodologies or written books which have penetrated the world of thought at home and abroad. We must consider also the extent to which the institution has established and nourished certain subjects which were neglected or unrecognized elsewhere; the extent to which those subjects have grown roots and flourished, and above all the extent to which large numbers of students have been attracted from the corners of the earth to imbibe the knowledge offered by that institution. The L.S.E. has attracted far more graduate students than any other European centre from almost every civilized country. A few figures will show the growth of the Graduate School. In 1938–9 there were 265 full-time and part-time students doing graduate work. In 1955–6 the number was 421; in 1966–7, 1,095 (of whom 688 came from overseas); in 1970–1, the total was 1,449 (of whom 703 came from overseas). It has done more to spread knowledge and understanding of the social sciences throughout the world, than any other academic institution. The name of the L.S.E. is widely known and respected throughout the world, as I have found in the course of my travels in North America, Asia, Africa, the Middle East, the Far East, and most parts of Europe.

V

The social sciences have grown enormously in scope and depth during the twentieth century. Moreover, they have become much more complex and technical. Economics in particular has become highly technical, and the current literature contains many articles and books full of mathematical reasoning which would be beyond the understanding of most economists of an earlier generation.

Several of the other social sciences have developed their own jargon and techniques.

There has been a greatly extended use of empirical methods and of quantitative research. Applied statistics have transformed many branches of study. Market research and public opinion polls are everyday examples of sampling methods. Social surveys based on similar methods are widely used by the Government and other public authorities. These sampling methods are devised by mathematical statisticians, the questions to be asked are drawn up or approved by psychologists, the operations require the use of teams of interviewers and supervisors, and the resulting data involves tabulation, machining, and computerization. The interpretation of the results often demands considerable knowledge and experience. Such investigations thus need skilled personnel and expensive equipment, and require expenditure on a substantial scale. Research of this kind is far removed from the purely literary research carried on by scholars working in libraries.

Sir Karl Popper states that all theoretical or generalizing sciences make use of the same method, whether they are natural sciences or social sciences. There are certain differences in method appropriate to particular sciences, whether natural or social, but there is a basic unity of scientific method applicable to all theoretical studies which transcends these relatively minor variations. (3) It is obvious, however, that research in the social sciences yields knowledge of a different kind from that which the chemist, the physicist, the astronomer, or the geologist acquires.

The principal difference is that the physical and natural sciences are able to formulate laws or general principles which are presumed always to hold good in the specified circumstances regardless of time and place, whereas the doctrines or conclusions of social scientists cannot claim a similar universality. Propositions about human society, however carefully supported by factual observation, are normally limited in time and place, and are not of universal application. Moreover, such propositions are valid only so long as the observed behaviour continues unchanged; and human conduct in every department of life is subject to immense variations at different times and in different countries. It is difficult to think of any institution, any body of received ideas, any pattern of conduct, which is found in broadly similar form in all societies at any given moment of time, or in any one society during the whole course of its history.

I will illustrate the point with a practical example. One may be able to state approximately the number of persons who will be killed in road accidents next month in any country for which accurate statistics exist, but no one can predict what the mortality rate on the highways will be twenty years from now, for this depends on the extent to which existing methods of transportation and equipment continue to be used, the highway system and its safety devices, etc., and no one can foresee the future when the creative powers of the human mind are involved.

Comte considered that from an objective point of view a unity of method is the only unity we should ask for, meaning by that the positive method in its completed application. (4a) Outside that unifying element we must be satisfied if the doctrines relating to the different branches of knowledge are homogeneous and convergent, which would not be the case if, for example, doctrines or laws in one department were positive, in another metaphysical, and in a third theological. Hence, positivism must prevail as a method throughout the entire realm of knowledge.

When we consider scientific knowledge from the subjective point of view the position is quite different, since we are now looking at human theories as originating in ourselves, as the result of mental evolution both in society and in individuals, and as having for their aim the satisfaction of our cravings of every kind. When thus regarded in relation to mankind, the diverse branches of real knowledge have an evident and natural tendency towards a complete systemization both logical and scientific. From this subjective point of view there is at bottom but one science, the human or, more accurately, the social science. (4b) In short, Comte contends that the human mind is the unifying element which binds together all the various branches of knowledge which we are accustomed to call subjects or disciplines. In one of his early essays Comte divided natural science into the four main categories of Celestial Physics; Terrestrial Physics, Mechanical and Chemical; Vegetable Physics; and Animal Physics. An additional science which he called Social Physics was needed to complete the natural sciences which would make possible a truly positive philosophy capable of satisfying every real requirement of our intelligence. Thereafter we could escape from theological or metaphysical methods. (5a)

Comte explained that by social physics he meant the science which is engaged in the study of social phenomena, considered in the same light as astronomical, physical, chemical and physiological phenomena, and thus subject to natural and invariable laws. It would seek to explain the development of the human race in order to understand the present and to provide a general indication of the future. Social science would be concerned only with the observation of social facts, their mutual relations and their influence on human development. It would eschew any attempt at admiration or criticism, and would thus be value-free. A fundamental principle of the method appropriate to social science is that in investigating social laws we must proceed from the general to the special. One therefore begins by apprehending the entire development of the human race in its totality, distinguishing only a very few successive stages. Subsequently one would gradually proceed to a numbr of intermediate steps, ultimately reaching intervals of only a single generation. (5b).

It cannot be said that in the century and more since Comte's death progress has been made towards a single unified social science. The several social sciences go their respective ways and sociology appears not to have attempted an integration of economics, anthropology, politics, and the rest. Progress has, however, taken place towards a unity of method, most notably in the use of measurement and quantitative methods. Comte wanted to see not only a developed social science but also a positive philosophy which would assist mankind to rise from the state of degradation into which it had fallen. He thought the absence of any common intellectual bonds had resulted in the licence which is caused by unregulated individualism. He saw an entire absence of public morality, the universal spread of egotism, materialism, and corruption for which the only remedy could be to bring society back to mental unity by the formation of a positive philosophy. (5c) This aspiration seems today to be even further away from the achievement of the social sciences and one could almost add even to their aims or goals. And the evils which Comte observed are still with us.

VI

Despite the increasing tendency towards differentiation among the social sciences, and the absence of a unified positive philosophy based on a single social science, there has been a notable increase of professionalism in several spheres. Economics has been ahead in this progression, and economists are employed in substantial numbers in the civil service, in industry, commerce, finance, trade unions, and in professional and vocational organizations of many kinds. Statisticians are also so widely employed in these and other spheres that they are in short supply. It was not until 1946 that statisticians were recognized by the Civil Service, and economists only in 1965, as belonging to the professional class alongside scientists, engineers, architects, and others. Sociologists are now regularly employed in planning teams, in the development of new towns, in the social services, in dealing with the causes of crime and penal methods, in the study of drug addiction, vandalism, hooliganism, and other areas of social concern. Social administration is essentially a training for professional work of some kind. The chief area of employment is in the administration of the statutory social services, but there are also opportunities in voluntary social organizations, in hospitals and clinics, in advising ministers on policy, etc. Geographers have now attained an important role in town and country planning work. Anthropologists were formerly in great demand in the colonial service, where their knowledge of tribal habits or primitive customs were supposed to be able to save colonial governments from taking decisions or actions which would be offensive to the native population. Today, anthropologists are more often employed as members of teams sent to developing countries to advise or assist in industrialization or urbanization projects likely to disrupt the traditional pattern of life. Technical assistance teams also frequently include economists, sociologists, social administrators, and other experts. Political scientists and public lawyers were in considerable demand during the period of decolonization after the Second World War, when their advice was sought on constitutional matters, various forms of franchise and the machinery of government. More recently the principle demand for political scientists has been for those specializing in public administration, who could assist developing countries to establish training programmes for their civil servants, or to help them raise the efficiency of government organization and management.

This brief description of the outlets for professional skills in the social sciences is by no means exhaustive and gives no indication of the scale of the demand. Figures are not available, but it is certain that the demand for economists, statisticians, social workers, sociologists, and anthropologists has greatly increased.

I have not so far made any reference to what are probably the largest fields of employment: teaching and research. The social sciences occupy a prominent place in the old, the newer, and the newest universities. Social studies are taught in the polytechnics, in technical and commercial colleges, in evening institutes, in extramural courses, in secondary schools of all kinds, in public schools both day and boarding. Social science research is carried on not only in universities and university institutes but by such bodies as the Royal Institute of International Affairs, the Royal Institute of Public Administration, Political and Economic Planning, the Centre for Environmental Studies, the National Institute of Economic and Social Research, the Acton Society Trust, and others. Government departments have research staffs which often include men and women trained in the social sciences. Research is also carried on by large industrial and commercial firms, nationalized industries, banks, stockbrokers, and other enterprises.

This widespread expansion in the employment opportunities available to men and women holding degrees in the social sciences is clearly a gain in terms of their growth and the support which they receive in universities and other institutions. But this has its dangers.

Professor Johnson points with unconcealed disdain to the contrast between the 'ideal' function of the economists in government service, which is to use their knowledge of the economic system to assist the Government in deciding its collective economic policy, and the reality of what happens all too frequently when they succumb to political pressure to produce politically acceptable advice. He mentions several examples, including the one in which a large group of economists who worked on the Labour Government's national plan 'were seduced into bending their assumptions systematically so as to establish the feasibility of a politically pre-determined high rate of national economic growth' (Johnson, p. 10 below).

Here we see the wheel turning full circle. Economists and some other social scientists have been asserting that (1) they are professionals and (2) they are not qualified in that capacity to express any view on ends, their competence extending only to the choice of means for the attainment of given ends. In practice, however, their acceptance of the given ends is alleged to be so unqualified that their professional integrity is impaired. Such a state of affairs is indeed sad in view of the fact that government service is probably the largest field of employment for economists. But is it typical or of frequent occurrence?

However that may be, we are now confronted with the fact that something called the 'Policy Sciences' has appeared and claims to be able to fill the gap left by the refusal of some social scientists to prescribe ends or to make value judgements. A number of American universities have set up centres or programmes for the study of the policy sciences and a new international journal bearing the title *Policy Sciences* has been started. It has an advisory board drawn from many different countries and including scholars specializing in numerous subjects.

A printed memorandum setting out the scope and purpose of this journal begins with the statement that it is devoted to policy analysis, systems approaches, and decision-making. It then states that in recent decades such tools of management as operations research, systems analysis, simulation, gaming, linear programming, and computers have transformed people's ideas about the nature of policy and how it should be made. Their success has, however, been limited particularly in public policy areas where political and social considerations are dominant and the private sector exercises strong influence. The aim of the policy studies is therefore to blend the management and decision-making techniques with what the behavioural and political sciences have to offer, thereby evolving a new interdisciplinary activity focused on policy making and its improvement.

The specific mission of the policy sciences, the statement declares, is to comprehend the policy-making process and to evaluate and design policy and policy-making systems. In undertaking this mission they will call on systems analysis, management science, decision theory, programme budgeting, operations research, organization theory, strategic analysis, general systems theory, computer science, economics, political science, public and business administration, sociology, psychology, history, law, and philosophy. All these disciplines are regarded as 'relevant to the policy sciences and contribute to them' but no one of them can by itself fulfil their specific mission mentioned above.

This *omnium gatherum* of a vast collection of subjects into a single net is both formidable and intimidating: it implies that by bringing together all the knowledge and the methodologies and insights which these different disciplines or techniques can provide, we shall somehow discover the right policies to choose in any given situation and the right methods of determining policies. One needs a very cool head to keep one's feet on the ground when faced with such a grandiose plan.

It is doubtful whether merely bringing together a number of value-free disciplines will by itself throw any light on policy-making in the sense of indicating what the policy should be in any specific matter. It is clear that many management techniques can indicate what is the most efficient, or quickest, or cheapest method of attaining a given end, and what are the probable consequences of using alternative methods. Cost-benefit analysis can be useful in assessing the advantages and disadvantages of particular choices, though one should not accept the valuations placed on non-market factors or aspects without the greatest caution and reserve. But the result of a cost-benefit analysis does not necessarily decide which policy is the best one. Moreover, in determining priorities a wise government will recognize that the 'right' policy in any particular matter may involve striking a balance between political, economic, and social considerations, and therefore those with knowledge of these aspects should have an opportunity to express an opinion.

The danger in abstracting 'policy' from the rest of a subject matter or field of activity and segregating it to a special area of 'policy sciences' could lie in the assumption that one can understand and make the correct policy decisions without knowing anything about the subject matter as a whole. It recalls the old notion which prevailed for so long that policy can be separated from administration. To arrive at a sound public policy in public health or education or town planning requires a considerable knowledge of these fields of activity. The techniques of management and the 'policy sciences' may help, but they will not go far by themselves. Finally, what is the significance of the term 'policy sciences' in the plural? Does it signify that each of the constituent techniques or social sciences mentioned above is itself a policy science? And if so, how can this be the case if those who profess these subjects are at pains to avoid committing themselves to the pursuit of particular ends or values? For policies are in fact decisions to pursue courses of action intended to achieve prescribed ends.

I have posed these awkward questions because I believe that the invention of 'policy sciences' is an American device for escaping from the attempt to develop the social sciences as though they were branches of technology, capable only of recommending means but not ends, of specifying *how* but not *what*.

VII

The social sciences comprise a group of disciplines which can be distinguished from the physical sciences on the one hand and the traditional arts subjects on the other. The fact that they are using quantitative methods and observational techniques in studying human behaviour does not mean that they can be lumped together with physics or chemistry or astronomy, any more than their concern with man in society justifies their assimilation to the life sciences.

The social sciences are in a dynamic and vital stage of development, but they are nonetheless passing through a critical phase. We live in an age of technology, in which the cry for more and better machines is sweeping everything before it. There are tendencies at work which could eventually transform social scientists into technologists. This would mean that they would concentrate entirely on finding out how to do things more efficiently and ignore trying to discover what are the things worth doing.

It would be a major misfortune if the social sciences were to develop exclusively on these lines. We live in an era which has witnessed a series of remarkable discoveries in the physical, biological, and medical sciences and which has provided the great majority of the nation with a much higher standard of living than they had previously enjoyed; yet contemporary society is marked by manifest discontent, frustration, anger, and violence. We are confronted by alarming increases in crime, juvenile delinquency, illegitimacy, marital failure, hooliganism, vandalism, maladjustment, a holocaust of unnecessary highway deaths, drug addiction, and other symptoms of unhappiness, alienation, irresponsibility, and frustration. If we are to create a happier, more contented, and more peaceful world, we must discover much more than we now know about the nature of man in society, about his aims and aspirations, his needs and emotions, the sources of his satisfaction and dissatisfaction. Surely it is social scientists who could throw most light on these dark recesses of our society. Their willingness and ability to do so will greatly influence the future of western civilization.

REFERENCES

1. LIPSET, Seymour Martin (ed.), *Politics and the Social Sciences*, pp. 103–4 (New York: Oxford University Press, 1969).
2. RHODES, Gerald, *The Government of London: The Struggle for Reform*, pp. 53–9, 71–3, 80–4 (London: L.S.E. and Weidenfeld & Nicolson, 1970).
3. POPPER, Karl R., *The Poverty of Historicism*, pp. 130, 137, and 143 (London: Routledge and Kegan Paul, 1957).
4. COMTE, August, *Discourse on the Positive Spirit*, translated by E. S. Beesly, (a) p. 38, (b) p. 39 (London: W. Reeves, 1903).
5. —— *Early Essays on Social Philosophy*, edited by Frederic Harrison, (a) pp. 236–7, (b) p. 239, (c) pp. 250–1 (London: Routledge).

INDIVIDUAL AND COLLECTIVE CHOICE

HARRY G. JOHNSON

HARRY G. JOHNSON

M.A. (Toronto, Cantab., Manchester),
Ph.D. (Harvard), F.B.A.

Professor of Economics
The London School of Economics
and Political Science

Harry G. Johnson is Professor of Economics at
both the London School of Economics and Political
Science and the University of Chicago. Previously,
he was Lecturer and Fellow of King's College,
Cambridge, and Professor of Economic Theory at
the University of Manchester. He is author of
fourteen books, the most recent being *Macro-
economics and Monetary Theory*, and co-author
or editor of over twenty-five others. He received
his Ph.D. from Harvard University, and has been
awarded six honorary degrees by universities in
Britain and Canada, as well as the Prix Mondial
Nesim Habif by the University of Geneva.

INDIVIDUAL AND
COLLECTIVE CHOICE

It is appropriate that economics should have been selected as the first of the social sciences for examination in this series of public lectures on *Man and the Social Sciences*, for it is the first-established of the social sciences in the sense of being both the first to have embraced scientific methods of inquiry and reasoning, and the first, though by a much shorter lead, to have gone in for empirical measurement of relationships and testing of hypotheses on a large scale as a normal aspect of its activities. Nevertheless, although the main lines of contemporary economic science may be said to have been fairly well established by the end of the nineteenth century, the subject has been evolving very rapidly in the present century. Indeed, the emphasis on empirical measurement just mentioned, while recommended by such great nineteenth-century figures as Alfred Marshall and responsible for the unique place in the social sciences in this country occupied by the study of economic history, has achieved practical fulfilment only in the period since the Second World War; and in so doing has been heavily dependent both on the emergence of a new generation trained in mathematics and quantitative methods rather than in philosophy, history, and the classics, and on the rapid development of computer technology. Apart from this evolution towards more consciously and more conscientiously quantitative method, there have been important changes in both the approach and the content of economics over the past seventy-five years and especially over the past fifty.

It is the purpose of this lecture to survey these developments, with particular but by no means exclusive attention to the part that economists at the London School of Economics and Political Science have played in them or failed to play in them. As a prelude, however, some rather extensive remarks are required on the general nature and contours of economics as a social science.

As a social science, economics may be broadly and briefly defined (following the classic work by Lionel Robbins on *The Nature and Significance of Economic Science*, to which I shall be referring in more detail later) as the scientific study of choice, both individual and collective, and of the implications of choice in welding man's economic activities into a coherently organized system. Economics begins from the assumption that people, either as individuals or as organized groups, are subject to a resource constraint on the satisfaction they can achieve, and choose among the alternatives available to them under this resource constraint so as to maximize the satisfaction they achieve. This makes their behaviour in the aggregate determinate, in the sense of involving predictable responses to changes in the resource constraint or in the terms attaching to the available alternatives; and the interactions of the economic behaviour of different individuals or groups with different objectives and different resource constraints and determinate behaviour patterns produces an organized economic system which tends towards a general equilibrium of prices and quantities produced and consumed.

There are three points worth remarking on about this system of thought at this stage, since it is frequently misunderstood, even by economists themselves. First, contrary to what was widely asserted by economists in the 1930s, and is still asserted by some people nowadays, the linking of individual economic activities into a coherent system of economic organization depends in no way on the fulfilment of a variety of highly unrealistic assumptions generically describable as 'perfect competition'; coherence follows from the assumption of maximizing activity and the existence of the resource constraints, and is independent of market structure. Secondly, there is the issue of freedom versus determinism, economics often being criticized for being inhumanly deterministic; on the contrary, determinacy in the aggregate is a deduction from the freedom of the individual, coupled with the assumption that he will use his freedom to his own best advantage. Thirdly, there is the question of the origins of the wants that individuals and groups are assumed to be trying to satisfy. This question, at least in any fundamental sense, economists leave to the other social sciences to answer, though one school of thought likes to take the view, which in my opinion is both superficial and mistaken, that in the modern world these wants are the mere frothy creations of the advertising men, and that people would be better off if they either practised austerity or had their consumption habits dictated by their intellectual superiors; a post for which the school in question is eager to volunteer its services.

Given the hypothesis of an economic system organized by the exercise of choices subject to constraints, the next question is how understanding of this system fits into man's knowledge of his society and can serve his efforts to control and govern it in the broad sense of those terms. The Marxist view on this question is familiar and simple: the social, political, and ideological superstructure is determined by the technological and economic substructure, and specifically by the distribution of property rights associated with the system of production *and* the economic system contains an internal contradiction between the social nature of production and the private appropriation of the product that will inevitably lead to economic breakdown, political revolution, and the establishment of socialism. This position is clearly inadequate, not merely because of the failure of its empirical predictions but because the allegedly determinate superstructures react back on and change the economic substructure, and also because the technological substructure itself evolves as a result of human efforts to change and improve it, and with it evolve the property rights in, and social relations of, production. Some contemporary social critics among professional economists, such as J. K. Galbraith of Harvard and E. J. Mishan of the L.S.E., have been attempting in effect to apply elements at least of Marx's method of analysis to a contemporary economic system radically transformed from that of the nineteenth century about which Marx wrote. More conventional contemporary economists have been attempting to capture the essence of modern industrialism within the conventional framework of economic analysis through the development of new concepts such as 'human capital' (i.e. educated skill as a form of capital) and the treatment of industrial knowledge as a form of capital and a factor of production.

In the Marxist view, economics is a complete social science, embracing politics, sociology, anthropology, and economic history as well as economics in the classical sense, and a deterministic science in a much more sweeping and fundamental sense than conventional or mainstream economics as described earlier. Mainstream economics has been more modest in its claims to usefulness and importance as a social science, though its claims have recently been becoming much bolder, as will be elaborated on later. The broad position of contemporary economics (which has emerged gradually over the period under review) is that the economic system, as a system organized by individual choices seeking to maximize satisfaction subject to a resource constraint, may not for various reasons result in the achievement of the maximum possible social benefit attainable within society's over-all resource constraint; and that in such cases governmental intervention or control is necessary to improve on the economy's performance. This position, it should be noted in passing, is essentially Benthamite or Fabian in its view of the governmental process, and is considerably more naïve about that process than the views that Graham Wallas of the L.S.E. reached in his classic *Human Nature in Politics*.

Specifically, there are three major possibilities of inferior performance of the economic system requiring governmental intervention and management, which I shall describe briefly in the chronological order of their emergence in the theory of economic policy.

First, the workings of the competitive system may not produce socially optimal results, in two senses. First, private choices may produce socially inefficient results, because the prices set in private markets do not capture for the private individual all the social benefits of the goods he sells or impose on him all the social costs of the goods he buys. Secondly, the competitive system may not produce an ethically equitable distribution of income. These possibilities and the policies required to correct or prevent them were analysed in A. C. Pigou's essentially pre-First World War work on *The Economics of Welfare* (which I shall later take as the reference-point for the evolution of economic science in our own age.

Secondly, the sum total of individual choices, and particularly of choices to purchase goods in the market place, may be inconsistent with the attainment of the maximum possible collective satisfaction. Specifically, these choices may produce undesirably high unemployment on the one hand, or inflation on the other, and in an open economy may produce an unwanted and unsustainable balance-of-payments deficit or surplus. In such cases, it is the obligation of the government to employ the various levers of control over market decisions that it has at its disposal (fiscal policy, monetary policy, and the exchange value of the currency) to ensure that these decisions add up to a socially satisfactory outcome in terms of employment, inflation, and the balance of payments. Recognition of this problem, analysis of it, and prescription for it were of course the contribution of J. M. Keynes's *General Theory of Employment, Interest and Money*, published in 1936.

Thirdly, there may be social objectives in the economic field, transcending or at variance with what would result from the free play of individual choices under competition. Recognition of this possibility as a legitimate occasion for governmental intervention is, of course, sharply at variance with the general orientation of classical and neo-classical economics, which viewed the functions of the state as the provision of a framework for private competition within which the individual would have the maximum possible degree of economic liberty and freedom to pursue his own economic ends; but it is the mood, or the implicit assumption, of much of contemporary economics, as reflected for example in the concern to accelerate economic growth, reduce regional disparities of incomes, and promote 'technological leadership'. In contrast to the first two possibilities sanctioning governmental economic intervention, this one cannot be identified with the name of any particular great economist, except possibly in the special field of development economics where the name of Gunnar Myrdal springs to mind. It is instead a response to the political and economic history of the world since the 1920s: the great depression and the resulting conviction of the need for governmental management of the economy, the vast expansion of the economic and social role of the state during and after the Second World War, and the emergence of nationalism in response to the domination of the western world by the United States of America.

Acceptance of the concept of the state as having economic objectives transcending the welfare of its citizens is particularly characteristic of contemporary economics in this country, owing both to the stubborn determination on national survival that has carried this country successfully (though at tremendous economic cost) through two world wars, and to the extreme centralization of the society and the culture in the capital city, and the concentration of its attention on the governmental process, inherited from its imperial past. But it is also characteristic of the other major European ex-imperial powers (which makes the idea of Europe attractive to the European nation-states but ominous for the rest of the world) and of the less-developed countries, which have taken over from European thought the concept of the nation as an entity transcending the private interests of its citizens and indeed implicitly or explicitly regarding the citizens as mere resources for the service of the state.

This concept of the state is a very dangerous one for economics as a social science, since it not only turns economic language into political rhetoric but also casts economists as both interpreters of the political will and eager servants of their own interpretation of it, and elevates them into political powers in their own right; and for neither of these roles have they been properly trained and proven competent. The much-enlarged role of the state as manager of the economic system with transcendent objectives of its own has produced a reaction among a small but growing group of economists, in the form of economic theories of the political process and of political decisions, based on treating government like private economic actors as trying to maximize a preference function subject to a budget constraint of popular support. Most of this work has been done by American economists of orthodox or right-wing persuasion. It has had little impact on or follow-up among economists in this country, apart from the brief sojourn at the L.S.E. of the Canadian public finance specialist Albert Breton and various visits to the School by the American pioneer in the field James Buchanan. The main reason in my judgement is that British economists have been too corrupted by their culture to be able to look at either government or capitalism in objective non-political terms. This is ominous for the prospects of the survival of British academic economics as a live scientific subject, since the great British economists of the past either could assume that Britain's problems were the archetypical problems of capitalism, or were sufficiently independently placed in relation to the governmental process to be able to criticize its decisions in terms of fundamental economic principles, and not merely in terms of the rhetoric of vulgar political mythologies about economics; and neither is true any longer.

Be that as it may, both developments (the majority of economists gladly throwing themselves into the service of politics, and the minority attempting to apply economic analysis to the processes of political decision) do exemplify the growing boldness of economists mentioned above, though it is boldness in two quite contrasting senses. In the first case it is social boldness, expressed in the claim to have discovered through economic science the key to society's problems and therefore to deserve a special position in the government of society; in the second case it is scientific boldness, expressed in the intrusion into the fields of the other social scientists, especially politics and to a lesser extent sociology, on the grounds that economics is superior in its capacity both to recognize relevant problems and to employ sophisticated techniques in solving them. It is no wonder that the other social scientists resent the economists as much as they do!

To return to the main line of the argument, in respect of all three possible occasions for governmental intervention, inefficiency and inequality, depression and inflation, and national policy objectives transcending individual desires, the accepted function of the economist ideally is to use and develop his theoretical and empirical knowledge of how the economic system works, a knowledge based on the theory of private choices, in order to assist government in choosing among alternative ways of achieving its socio-economic objectives, whatever they may be: i.e. to assist in the making of collective economic choices. I use the adjective 'ideally' because when it comes down to hard cases of actually advising governments, economists only too frequently yield to the political pressure to produce politically satisfactory advice. The political process relies heavily on two contra-social-scientific notions: that because the political public would like to get something for nothing, it must be possible to find an expert who can deliver it; and that it is possible to repeal the laws of economics by political means if they become an intolerable constraint on the desire to get something for nothing.

British economists, for reasons discussed earlier, have been particularly prone to succumb to the temptations of these two political notions, to the detriment of the progress of economic science in this country. As evidence, I may cite on the one hand the endless search for panaceas to promote the country's economic growth, including the advocacy of demand inflation to stimulate investment and the simplistic theory that manufacturing and not services is strategic to growth that produced the Selective Employment Tax; and on the other hand the persistent recommendation by Oxbridge (and some L.S.E.) economists of an income policy as a painless way of resolving the political dilemma between inflation and unemployment. A more insidious example is the way in which the large subsample of the country's ablest economists who worked on the preparation of the ill-fated National Plan were seduced into bending their assumptions systematically so as to establish the feasibility of a politically pre-determined high rate of national economic growth.

The purpose of this lecture, however, is not to furnish a critique of contemporary, and particularly contemporary British, economics (my colleagues in the other social sciences who will lecture later need no help from me in that endeavour) but to provide a survey of the development of economic science in this century. My remarks so far, though intended as a broad résumé of the current state of economic theory, have implicitly performed part of the task. It remains to trace the specific evolution more explicitly. This would, as all of us participating in this lecture series are fully aware, really require a large-volume study in the history of thought; treatment of the subject within the confines of a general lecture must necessarily be sketchy and impressionistic.

Speaking very broadly and loosely indeed, one can describe the period since the beginning of the century in terms of three historical phases: consensus, revolutionary transformation, and consolidation; the revolutionary transformation occurring in a relatively short space of years in the 1930s.

Before the First World War, economics had digested the so-called 'marginalist revolution' (which was not really a revolution at all, but an improvement on and elaboration of the core theory of the English classical economics of Smith, Ricardo, and Mill, based on the introduction into economics of the differential calculus and resulting in what has been variously called neo-Ricardian, neo-classical, or 'orthodox' economics) and had arrived at a fair consensus on what the subject was about and where it fitted into the universe of knowledge and into the structure of society. The consensus was embodied in two monumental books, Marshall's *Principles of Economics* and Pigou's *Economics of Welfare*, which were widely used as textbooks in the better universities well up towards the beginning of the Second World War, and in some places (including Cambridge) well past its ending. It involved certain basic ideas about the scope and method of economics that I shall describe briefly, and rather selectively, in order to provide a background for discussion of subsequent developments.

Some of these ideas reflected the personalities of the economists concerned and the fact that they had come to economics through a concern about the problems of poverty and inequality. The same motivation, it should be noted, attracted many of the young economists who emerged eminent from the revolutionary period of the 1930s, and has been attracting young people to the subject again in the past few years, though one of the major contrasts between contemporary economics and the economics of the pre-Second World War period is that the modern economist is a middle-class professional man rather than a detached social philosopher, which is one reason why relics of the 1930s revolutionary fervour like Joan Robinson rail so vehemently against modern 'scientific' economics, especially as practised in the United States. But the strong personal imprint that both very small numbers with correspondingly high average quality, and arrival in the subject through idiosyncratic personal experience and motivation, enabled Marshall and Pigou and later eminent figures such as Keynes, Robertson, Robbins, Harrod, Henderson, and Joan Robinson to impress on the subject, is no longer possible in an era of professionalism and large academic numbers; there is only one eminent figure in contemporary economics whose economic writing and research is strongly personal, Milton Friedman, and there are many who regard him as an obnoxious anachronism.

Some of the central ideas of what may be termed the pre-First World War consensus were that economics was neither an intellectually challenging nor a socially very important subject; that its main justification was the assistance it may give to social improvement; and that anyway it was difficult and not very promising. A classic quotation from Pigou's *Economics of Welfare* (fourth edition, p. 4) illustrates the point:

If it were not for the hope that a scientific study of men's social actions may lead, not necessarily directly or immediately, but at some time and in some way, to practical results in social improvement, not a few students of these actions would regard the time devoted to their study as time misspent. That is true of all social sciences but especially of economics. For economics 'is a study of mankind in the ordinary business of life' [Marshall's definition]; and it is not in the ordinary business of life that mankind is most interesting or inspiring. One who desired knowledge of man apart from the fruits of knowledge would seek it in the history of religious enthusiasm, of martyrdom, or of love; he would not seek it in the market-place.

Or again (p. 5)

Wonder, Carlyle declared, is the beginning of philosophy. It is not wonder, but rather the social enthusiasm which revolts from the sordidness of mean streets and the joylessness of withered lives that is the beginning of economic science.

Moreover, Pigou draws a very careful distinction between economic welfare and total welfare, and points out that total welfare may fall while economic welfare rises; a point ignored by the growthmen of the post-Second World War period until recent concern about congestion, pollution, and the quality of the environment recalled it to contemporary attention. As regards economic welfare, Pigou and his neo-classical predecessors regarded it as virtually axiomatic that a more equal distribution of income would improve social welfare, though Edgeworth at least was aware that this assumption lacked any scientific theoretical foundation, and that therefore income-redistributing policies were socially desirable.

The general orientation of the consensus, then, was towards humility about the intellectual pretensions of economics, and insistence both on its practical usefulness and on the difficulty of empirical quantification of economic relationships. In fact (a strong impetus derived from the tastes and views of Marshall) the consensus looked to economic history, in contrast to the contemporary emphasis on econometrics, to provide the skeleton of theory with empirical flesh. Moreover it was Marshall who insisted that the body should be decently clad in verbiage that the ordinary literate reader could understand (a mis-selection of audience still appealed to in order to put down the technically ambitious young) and that any mathematical work underlying a complex piece of analysis should be decently shrouded or concealed from the reader's view. This in turn implied heavy reliance on the sometimes treacherous tools of partial equilibrium analysis and particularly their geometrical representation by demand and supply curves. Finally, uncertain and failing health prevented Marshall from working out a full-dress version of his theory of money and of the relation between the real theory expounded in the *Principles* and the monetary aspects of the economy. The consensus was therefore critically weak on this crucial question, and in particular inclined to make the fatal error of attempting to treat monetary disturbances as attributable to real causes, because it understood the latter but not the former. This, of course, provided the golden opportunity for the Keynesian Revolution, when the great depression of 1929 erupted and the orthodox school attempted to explain it away by the satiation of wants and rejected proposals to remedy it by public works and monetary expansion.

The pre-war consensus remained the definition of the subject of economics after the interruption of the First World War and well into the late 1920s: the periods immediately after wars appeared at the time to be periods of great intellectual ferment, and probably are so as regards manners and morals, but in retrospect one is struck by the tameness of the actual retreat into the scientific modes of thought and conceptions of problems of the pre-war period. The 1920s now appear as a stiflingly dull period in economics, in which those economists who were not preoccupied with the post-war problems of the British economy, particularly the difficulties of British industry, were concerned with adding footnotes and qualifications to the pre-war consensus, notably making good some ambiguities and logical shortcomings of Marshall's theory of the firm (which was an uneasy compromise between the strict logic of the mathematics and his own knowledge of economic history and observations of industrial competition in practice), and attempting to construct the monetary theory that was missing from the pre-First World War consensus. While important work was done on the latter problem by Robertson and Keynes in Cambridge and subsequently by Hayek at the L.S.E., it had the fundamental defect of assuming an economy that remained in full employment, so that monetary disturbances resulted in inflationary or deflationary movements of prices, rather than of fluctuations in output and employment, and (in the work of Hayek) the costs of monetary mismanagement appeared as distortions in the allocation of resources between consumption and investment and in inappropriate choices of productive techniques. It therefore fell a helpless victim to the Keynesian Revolution: unjustly so, I think, because much of recent theorizing about both money and economic growth has been working its way back to conceptions and formulations already embedded in fairly sophisticated form in that hastily discarded literature. On this subject, I should call attention to the important influence on English-language monetary economics of the work of Knut Wicksell and his followers on the analysis of the conditions for 'monetary equilibrium'. I should also remark that the situation of economics elsewhere, apart from Sweden and Austria but including the United States, was as dull as in this country.

But while the 1920s appeared to be dull, the seeds of transformation were germinating under the surface, to flower in the 1930s. They grew because the soil was fertile: a new generation was emerging, more technically competent and professional than their seniors, and more numerous, who found the weight of the authority of the neo-classical consensus increasingly confining and the obligation to respect it increasingly onerous, especially as it seemed so irrelevant to Britain's problems in the 1920s and the world's problems after the onset of the great depression. It was a generation, moreover, which found the study of economics intellectually challenging in its own right and not requiring the apology of social usefulness, and which saw no need either to limit itself to the tools specified by the limited mathematical competence or personal taste of the neo-classical greats, or to disguise their use in order to make their work accessible to an amateur rather than a professional audience.

The result was a transformation of the subject through a related series of what may be loosely described as 'revolutions'; though the adjective 'related' is not strictly correct, since some of them, notably the general equilibrium revolution and the Keynesian Revolution, were initially in conflict with one another and a synthesis had later to be worked out. The 'revolutions' referred to, and which I think are the most important for the evolution of the subject, are six in number. I list them not in chronological order but in the order most convenient for discussion. They are the professional revolution, the revolution in welfare economics, the general equilibrium and mathematical economics revolution, the imperfect or monopolistic competition revolution, the Keynesian Revolution, and the empirical revolution.

The L.S.E., which as Lord Robbins has reminded us in his recent *Autobiography* was an extremely active and productive centre for economic theory and research in the 1930s, participated in or was aware of them all, but aside from the writings of a few junior staff members and/or students, notably Nicholas Kaldor, Abba Lerner, and Tibor Scitovsky, it can be credited with significant contributions only to the first three. The imperfect/ monopolistic competition revolution, though at the American end of it the work of E. H. Chamberlain, a pupil of Allyn Young, who was for a brief period Professor at the School, made little impression on the School's thinking. This was probably a wise reaction, since as Hicks pointed out at the time, the main implications of market imperfections lay in the field of welfare economics rather than positive economics; and even there the implications of welfare loss were far more doubtful than the Cambridge economists claimed them to be. On the other hand, the failure of the leading figures at the School (Hayek and Robbins) to understand what Keynes was driving at in the arguments and discussions that led up over a protracted period of time to the writing of the *General Theory* was a major intellectual catastrophe, the result of trusting to and elaborating on theory while refusing to check its assumptions and conclusions against the facts of everyday, more accurately nearly a decade's, economic experience; and it led, or so the oral tradition has informed me, to both estrangement between the School and Cambridge, the two active centres of economic thought in this country at that time, and (more productively) to the undertaking by graduate students in the two places to found the *Review of Economic Studies*, which has been described not altogether inaptly by Joan Robinson as 'the children's newspaper'. In its early days the *Review* kept alive largely by feeding on the controversies generated by J. R. Hicks's concept of 'the elasticity of substitution', a concept thrown up by Hicks's pioneering work at the School on *The Theory of Wages*. The School played a negligible part also in the empirical revolution, except to the extent that mathematicization can be regarded as a form of quantification; but the reasons for that were endemic (and still are) in the structure of the British approach to economics rather than peculiar to the School.

In the first three revolutions (professionalization, welfare economics, and general equilibrium through mathematicization) the School played an important part. The first two were linked in Lionel Robbins's classic *An Essay on the Nature and Significance of Economic Science*, though that book played a more direct part in the welfare economics revolution than in the process of professionalization. Essentially, the book was directed against two major aspects of the orientation of the pre-First World War Marshall-Pigou, consensus. The first was that economics is concerned with a narrow and rather ignoble aspect of human existence, and must justify its existence in terms of serving ethical values as applied to that aspect. By making choice subject to constraint, whatever the ethical quality of the objects and motivations of choice, and regardless of whether those objects and motivations were economic or materialistic or not, Robbins freed the subject from the need for defensive apologetics, the burden of which it had been carrying since it first became known as 'the dismal science'. The full effects of this liberation have only been felt in the past decade or so, however, as preoccupation with material ends and material choices was socially urgent in the 1930s, 1940s, and 1950s of mass depression, war, and post-war reconstruction, and those who understood these matters were socially valuable and had no need to apologize for themselves; and it is only subsequently, as described earlier in this lecture, that economists have begun to apply their science of choice to such matters as the theory of government or the assessment of the amenity values inherent in the choice of location of airports.

The second aspect of the neo-classical consensus that Robbins attacked had a much more immediate impact on the development of economic theory: it was the assumption that economics has a scientific basis for the proposition that greater equality of income distribution improves the social welfare. Robbins asserted, to the contrary and correctly, that there is no scientific basis for the assumed interpersonal comparability of utility on which such a proposition has to rest. This was nihilism of a breath-takingly large order; and nearly twenty years were spent by the ablest theorists in trying to find a way around Robbins's point by means of various so-called 'compensation tests' (i.e. tests of whether after an economic change it would be possible by suitable income redistributions to make everyone at least as well off as he was before the change) before welfare theory settled for Samuelson's proposition that such tests involve propositions about the potential and not the actual welfare effects of economic changes, and that ethical neutrality requires that they be satisfied for every potential distribution of welfare among the members of the community. Nihilism, however, even the most elegant and sophisticated nihilism, prevents the economist from making any policy prescriptions whatsoever; and since the public and the politicians demand such prescriptions, and since economists as human beings find it as difficult as anyone else to refuse to impress their fellow-citizens by offering free advice based on expert inside knowledge, most economists nowadays are content to pay lip-service to the principle of nihilism when they have to (and they mostly have to only when attacked by fellow-economists) before continuing happily on to make their policy pronouncements. Suffice it to say that economists working at the L.S.E. or closely connected with it played a leading part in the successive stages of evolution of welfare economics up to the immediate post-Second World War period, and that the School has continued to play a leading part in the development of the successor to theoretical welfare economics, the practical art of cost–benefit analysis.

The third revolution involved the conscious application of mathematical methods to economic theory, and the introduction into English-language economics of the methods of general equilibrium analysis pioneered by the continental neo-classical masters, Walras and Pareto. While mathematical economics and general equilibrium analysis had reared their heads in English economics at a much earlier stage, in the works of Jevons, Edgeworth, and the early works of Marshall himself (and also of Arthur Bowley of the School), they had been more or less deliberately stamped out single-footed by Marshall, whose motives for doing so do not appear entirely reputable in the most dispassionately scientific light, so that those who used mathematical techniques that now would be regarded as within the competence of a normal undergraduate found their work dismissed and shelved as both esoteric and eccentric. The revolution in question consisted essentially in making mathematics, up to the level of the differential and integral calculus, a part of the normal and expected professional equipment of the economic theorist. It was pioneered at the School in J. R. Hicks's *Theory of Wages*, which introduced and used the concept of the production function to rework and clarify a number of problems in classical distribution theory, including the famous Ricardian problem of whether technical progress could ever redound to the disadvantage of the working class. The basic theory was shot down in a review by the Cambridge economist Gerald Shove, on the basis of the neo-classical recognition that capital is a produced and not an original factor of production, and as a result the book stayed out of print for some thirty years. (Cambridge University, in the persons of Joan Robinson, Nicholas Kaldor, Piero Sraffa, and their younger disciples, has been trying throughout the post-war period to repeat this victory over the mathematical reformulation of neo-classical theory by means of insisting on the same point, the theoretical complexity of capital as a produced means of production, though their fire has been directed against the mathematical general equilibrium theorists at the Massachusetts Institute of Technology rather than at L.S.E. economists.) Despite this basic error, the *Theory of Wages* is still an important book, which has influenced much of the modern theory of distribution. More important still, however, was the work that Hicks undertook jointly with R. G. D. Allen on the mathematical theory of general equilibrium, which laid the foundations of Hicks's later classic work *Value and Capital* and of Allen's important series of works in mathematical economics (from the first of which, *Mathematics for Economists*, I taught myself what little mathematical economics I know during two long summers of learning-by-doing at Harvard and Cambridge). These two were the pioneers; but general equilibrium analysis in either mathematical or geometrical form was also developed and applied to a variety of fields of economic inquiry by other junior members of the School, including Kaldor, Scitovsky, and the incredibly ingenious theoretician, Abba Lerner.

The other three revolutions, in which the School played little part, can be treated briefly. The imperfect-monopolistic competition revolution solved a problem left unsettled by Marshall, why competition is consistent with finite size of the individual firm, by postulating a downward-sloping demand curve for the individual firm; having been a student of both the protagonists in this development, Joan Robinson and Edward Chamberlin, and read both works very carefully in my youth, I can state my judgement that the American version contained more real economics and far less fudging of important issues such as product differentiation and advertising than the English one, though the latter contains some brilliant chapters on such matters as price discrimination and economic rents. However, I think that both books missed the central point of the phenomena under analysis: they were attempting to force these phenomena into the realm of analysis of static equilibrium theory, whereas their essence is the problem of industrial strategy in a world of rising and changing living standards. The Keynsian Revolution needs no gloss before an audience such as this; or if it does it needs another lecture. The empirical revolution, however, does merit some comment. This revolution, based on the development of statistical techniques, started with an insistence on the desirability of measuring economic relationships, and later, after the war, switched its emphasis from measurement to the testing of empirical hypotheses. In spite of the flowering of statistics in the United Kingdom in the first decade of the century, in the hands of Karl Pearson and others, the empirical revolution has been almost entirely an American creation, and has tended to remain so until the present day.

I would briefly venture two explanatory hypotheses. The first is that, ever since the time of Marshall and his prize pupil Clapham, the broad historical scholarship expected of the economic historian has commanded far more respect than the apparently mechanical but actually exactingly intellectual work required of the researcher employing the methods of statistical inference from very unsatisfactory data; the telling of a satisfactorily literate and scholarly tale also appeals far more than the competent performance of technical work requiring a high degree of scientific expertise, to the British governmental tradition of the gifted amateur in charge and the expert 'on tap but not on top'. The second hypothesis is that, given the European tradition that Britain shares, of the professoriate as a miniscule intellectual élite who must perforce be all-rounders in their subject, there is a high premium on the ability to marshal easily available statistics in the defence of a clever but superficial argument, and a very low premium indeed on the input of work required to know what those statistics really are and what they mean in terms of theory. One symptom of the difference between Britain and the United States in this regard is that whereas in the United States the econometricians are almost invariably members of an economics department or business school, obliged to co-operate with their non-econometric economist colleagues in the structuring of courses and in the training of undergraduate and graduate students, in the United Kingdom they typically have, *de facto* or *de jure*, their own department and their own teaching programme. Another symptom is that the best work in econometrics done in the United Kingdom (and the best of it has been done at the L.S.E., whose econometrics division ranks among the world's best) has been on the theory of econometrics and not on what econometrics is supposed to be about, namely, superior analysis and solution of important economic problems based on a combination of economics, mathematics, and statistics.

As mentioned earlier in explaining the structure of this lecture, the ferment of the 1930s has been followed in the post-Second World War period by a phase of consolidation and extension of the new ideas and new knowledge acquired so rapidly and explosively in that period, a phase in which the essentially conservative nature of the endeavour has been disguised from most of the participants by the memory of the lively intellectual battles for big stakes that occurred in the antecedent period. The big battles (sometimes sham battles) have been concerned on the one hand with the reconciliation of the Keynesian Revolution with the preceding orthodoxy of monetary theory and with the general equilibrium and empirical revolutions; and on the other hand with the rediscovery and the mathematical and empirical elaboration of Pigouvian welfare economics, in so far as it concerns failures in the efficient social functioning of the private competitive system, rather than the achievement of an ethically just distribution of income. The latter question was disposed of once and for all by Lionel Robbins, despite the continued hankering of many economists after a scientific basis for the primitive Christian belief in the innate equality of man. British economists, including the economists at the L.S.E., have not been pioneers in these developments: leadership in the development of the subject has passed to the United States, at least temporarily, and most British economists have been intellectually satisfied enough with participation in an American-based international community of scholars from which they can draw techniques, problems, and a sense of direction and intellectual involvement not available in the hierarchical, Oxbridge-based, and politically dominated academic structure of this country. The dissenters are naturally enough the Oxbridge establishment and the self-styled radical young, both of whom can derive an artificially self-flattering pseudo-impression of intellectual superiority by placing themselves in the position of passing judgement on the work the Americans have been doing and they have not.

Nevertheless, the work that has been done at the L.S.E. in the phase of consolidation has been impressive, both judged by a world standard and judged by comparison with other British universities. The L.S.E. has been respectively the place of delivery and the intellectual origin of the only two really original economic ideas generated in Britain in the post-Second World War period that have had a genuinely world-wide impact on economics: Harrod's dynamic Keynesian economics, expressed in his growth equation; and the Phillips curve, which encapsulated in empirical form the Keynesian policy dilemma between full employment and inflation. In addition, the L.S.E. has made noteworthy contributions to the work of consolidation of the results of the revolutions of the 1930s: notably James Meade's work on the theory of economic policy in an international economy, which both transcended American work on the theory of the foreign trade multiplier and led to the new welfare economic theory of the economics of second best, and stimulated his students W. M. Corden and T. M. Rybczynski, as well as myself, to elaborate the theory of the interrelations between international trade and economic growth; A. W. Phillips's work on the electrical engineering mathematics of stabilization policy; Archibald and Lipsey's contribution to the evolution of the Patinkinian synthesis of monetary and value theory; and in a somewhat different sphere, Richard Sayers's marshalling of recent developments in Keynesian theory into the intellectual foundations of the *Radcliffe Report*, one of the great British reports on the working and control of the British monetary system. Other contributions of School economists could be mentioned, including Henry Phelps Brown's perhaps unwitting contributions to the emergence of cliometrics (the application of econometrics to economic history) and the support that Alan Walters and myself and other School staff have given to the revival of the quantity theory approach to monetary policy as an alternative to the prevailing Keynesian orthodoxy.

But I would not want to claim too much for the School; the essential thing is that it is the one centre of economic teaching and research in this country that is genuinely international in its orientation, in the sense that it is not merely an established British university that allows itself the luxury of a few foreign staff-members and students for the sake of variety and balance, but a world university that tries both to keep in touch with whatever of intellectual importance is going on elsewhere in the world, and to admit to its scholarly fellowship students of quality whatever their origin may be. The School has made misjudgements and mistakes in scholarly strategy, the most important of which I have retailed to you in this lecture. It has also scored some brilliant scholarly successes in economics. But the most important thing about the School is its recognition that it has to live in an international world of economic scholarship. It has consistently done its best according to its lights to make the best of that world available to its students and its professional colleagues in this country.

TIME AND CHANGE

MICHAEL M. POSTAN

MICHAEL M. POSTAN
M.Sc. (Lond.), M.A. (Cantab.), F.B.A.

Professor Emeritus of Economic History
University of Cambridge

Michael M. Postan is a Fellow of Peterhouse. He graduated at the London School of Economics and Political Science and took his Master's Degrees at London and Cambridge. He was Official Historian of War Production at the Cabinet Office 1942–55. He was editor of the *Economic History Review* 1933–58 and is editor and contributor to the Cambridge Economic History of Europe. He is the author of *The Economic History of Western Europe 1946–64* and many other publications. He is the Honorary President of the International Association of Economic History.

TIME AND CHANGE

I

In the history of all thought, *ergo* in the history of history itself, all periods are periods of transition. However, some are more transitional than others, and none perhaps more so than the beginning of the present century when the L.S.E. was founded. At that juncture in Britain the battle of methods in which the social scientists and historians had been locked abroad for nearly a century, that between time-oriented historical procedures on the one hand and the analytical or theoretical ones on the other, still remained what it always had been in this country, a mere cold war. In this as in many other respects British philosophy and scholarship exhibited that imperfect insularity (peninsularity would perhaps be a better word) which characterizes British intellectual life as a whole. On the one hand British thinkers appeared to share most of the foreign fashion: in fact they gave birth to many of the ideas which propelled the intellectual movement abroad. On the other hand they did not take sides so clearly or irrevocably as their opposite numbers in Germany and France. As a result the intellectual traffic in social studies appeared at times to flow in opposite directions and not along the one-way roads the same traffic took on the continent.

The paths trodden by social scientists and historians abroad in the course of the nineteenth century are easily traced. Until the closing decades of the century European thought moved in response to several impulses, all of them historical in inspiration or effect: that of the so-called Romantic reaction, that of Hegelian dialectic, and that of the Darwinian evolution.

The Romantic impulse was a reaction from the French Revolution. The lawyers turned to legal history as an alternative to what they, as it turns out erroneously, believed to be the abstract jurisprudence of Montesquieu or Napoleon. The economists sought to substitute the lessons of past economic development for what they thought were purely theoretical constructions of Adam Smith, Say, and the Physiocrats. The French eulogists of monarchy and catholicism, men like Bonald or de Maistre, appealed to the ancient wisdom of hereditary royalty and of the historical Church; while at the other end of the political spectrum the German liberals who were engaged in the struggle for individual freedom drew their ammunition from the historical legend of *Urfreiheit*, the erstwhile equality and freedom of tribal societies at the dawn of European history. In this way the entire universe of social and political thought came to be shared out by historical schools of every kind: those of law, economics, politics, material culture, ethnology, and linguistics. Both thinkers and practical reformers turned to history for lessons, and for their part historians tried to oblige them by looking for lessons and finding them. Hence the remarkable progress of historical studies. The historians flourished in the role of intellectual goldminers, prospecting the past for mintable metal.

Underlying these immediate and largely practical preoccupations of the various historical schools were certain trends in the philosophy of the time, above all in the Hegelian theory of history. It is perhaps symptomatic of the spirit of the time that since Vico, or perhaps since Aristotle, Hegel should have been the first important philosopher to construct a general theory of history and, in doing so, to impose a philosophical system upon the time-sequences of history. But it is even more symptomatic of the spirit of the time that he should have done the obverse: imposed a scheme of historical sequences on the very process of philosophical thought. Shorn of its poetic excrescences the Hegelian dialectic is little more than a view of the social and intellectual processes as chains of sequences. In this sense it is purely historical. To relate situations to their antecedents, is to account for them historically, i.e. to derive them from the situations which preceded them. It matters not that Hegel believed that successive situations descended from each other not harmoniously but by opposition and contrast. What matters is that events, configurations of events, indeed entire societies in their complexity, should have been explained by their order of *ante-* and *post-*: which is a pure time order even when it happens to be presented as one of thesis and antithesis.

The view of society and social existence as a time-sequence was soon to be extended to all living matter by Darwin. The Darwinians may have been innocent of both history and philosophy, and, if at all philosophical, were anything but idealistic. Yet what they did was to reveal in the life processes a chain of sequences parallel to that which the Hegelians had imposed upon social facts and the philosophical thought about them. That the Darwinian system of ideas should have fitted so well to the common denominator of contemporary outlooks is not surprising. We now know that various evolutionary notions had been current before the *Origin of Species* came out. Geographers and geologists, in the first place the great Lyell, had occupied themselves for some time with the origins and transformations of continents and oceans, and were thereby drawn into speculation about the concomitant changes in live matter. The British sociologists, above all Herbert Spencer, appear to have discovered for themselves, and may even have anticipated, some of the most characteristic formulae of the Darwinian system. Nevertheless the publication of the *Origin of Species* and the subsequent speculation it provoked were turning points in the intellectual life of Europe. They helped to spread the assumptions of evolution and the modes of evolutionary thought to fields well outside that of biology proper. It is very largely due to the Darwinian infection that the search for origins and for stages of development came to dominate all human studies. In every field of study men tried to map out the stages by which things reached their Victorian perfection. Like Topsy, everything just growed, and as it grew, it got progressively finer; or to use the favourite Darwino-Spencerian circumlocution, it attained ever-greater co-ordination through ever-greater differentiation.

Somewhat earlier than Darwin and the Darwinists and therefore independently of them, August Comte started in France a train of ideas which, in the subsequent intellectual history of Europe was destined to feed some of the deepest channels of Darwinian and post-Darwinian thought. The central ideas of Comte's system were not conspicuously historical or time-oriented, although a sequential order can be discerned in the ascending ladder of complexity and perfection in which he arranged the various scientific disciplines. But his essential idea was the unity and universality of knowledge: an idea which later generations would have described as that of 'unity of scientific method'. All scientific knowledge aims at the discovery of the general laws of nature; and in this respect the knowledge of society, or sociology, shares both the objects and ambitions of other sciences. The pan-scientific, or positivist, assumptions helped to carry into social and political thought the presupposition of biology and physical sciences and thereby helped to reinforce the dominance of evolutionary ideas in the studies of humanity.

At the risk of harping on the obvious, I must recount how in an apparent independence of most of his predecessors and in avowed opposition to Comte, Karl Marx merged all the variants of time-oriented and 'scientistic' thought: the Romantic of the earliest 1800s, the Hegelian of the 1830s and 1840s, and the evolutionary of the mid-century. As we all know so well, Marx was a Hegelian. By converting the idealist dialectic of Hegel into one of his own, he merely reaffirmed its sequential, time-oriented nature, while reinforcing it by a science-oriented (he called it materialist) argument. Marx was also a Darwinian, perhaps the most ambitious Darwinian there ever was. It was his avowed intention to do for social sciences what the *Origin of Species* did for biology, and to establish in the former an evolutionary doctrine as firm and all-embracing as Darwin's. Above all, he was a historian. He invariably presented the state of the world in which he lived solely as a product of historical change. Economic systems, those of tribal society, feudalism, or capitalism, were presented as phases of historical development. Indeed his reliance on historical explanations was whole-hoggish and exclusive to the point of bigotry. I consider Marx and Marxism as the final stage in the progress of the nineteenth-century empirical time-oriented and history-dominated thought.

II

This, the furthest point in the development of history-dominated thought, was also its climacteric. By the time the third volume of *Das Kapital* was published reactions against the historical ~pproaches were erupting all over the place. In one or two fields human study the historical point of view may never have suc- ͺeded in wholly repressing the currents of pure theory. Even in ͺermany the historical school of political economy never succeeded in rubbing out the economics of the *a-priori* school. The latter were to make a triumphant comeback at the end of the century in Vienna where Menger and the Marginalists conjured up a body of doctrine and a technique more abstract than anything the British classical economists had ever dreamt of. From Vienna, the new, or the renewed, testament of pure economics spread, and founded its apostolic seats in several countries, above all in Sweden, Switzerland, and Italy. In England the gospel was not always followed to the letter. The prevailing tendency was to graft it on to the old testament of classical economics, as transmitted by John Stuart Mill, and to produce a typical Anglican compromise. Thus Alfred Marshall, while taking up a 'marginalist' position in his short-term analysis, still adhered to principles and methods of the English classical school in his treatment of long-term problems. He went even further in his avowedly empirical volumes on industry and trade, but these were in every way untypical exercises, which even his worst critics did not suspect of being truly historical or sociological. Some British economists however (Jevons and perhaps Wickstead) were marginalists pure and simple; and elsewhere in Europe (in Stockholm, Lausanne, Milan, and Turin) in fact wherever the marginalists established a hold, its highly theoretical and near-mathematical points of view prevailed.

The reaction against the historical orientations was equally pronounced in political and social studies. In political and social philosophy the reaction was mainly directed against historical determinism. It was the Marxian dialectic which was first and foremost to come under fire. Surprisingly enough, much of the fire came from quarters which still officially ranked as Marxist.

The German social democrats were the first and so far the only great legalized party to build its programme on Marxist foundations, and in the first place on the Marxist belief in the historical inevitability of proletarian socialism. But its experience of two decades of legal politics proved highly destructive to the most fundamental of Marxist expectations. The historical inevitabilities of Marxian dialectic were not turning out to be at all inevitable. The peasants and the petty bourgeois were not being proletarized; the proletariat itself was not being impoverished and crushed; the entire capitalist system showed fewer and fewer signs of succumbing to the play of historical forces; on the contrary the clearest sign of economic change, clearer in Bismarckian Germany than anywhere else, was the mounting strength of the capitalist order. A very large section of German social democrats, those commonly described as Revisionists, were therefore bound to conclude that if socialism was to triumph, and if its triumph was to be advanced, the case for it could not rest on its historical inevitability. The hope for socialism as an inevitable outcome of historical evolution had to be somehow replaced, and replaced it was, by other ideas which were not historical and did not invoke the irresistible social forces. Of these ideas none was a more obvious alternative and lay nearer to hand than the Kantian philosophy. Its usefulness to the Revisionists was in its clear distinction between pure and practical reasons. The world of practical reason to which all human affairs belong is governed by the categorical imperatives, the moral desiderata and the will of God, and not by the objective categories of the physical world and of our knowledge of it. This aspect of Kantian philosophy as brought out by the neo-Kantians provided an alternative to Marxian dialectic. It enabled the Revisionists to switch the argument for socialism from historical necessity to ethical preference: from 'it will' to 'we shall'.

In spite of their constant invocation of the Old Man of Königsberg the neo-Kantians were, from our point of view, true innovators. Their object and their achievement were to provide real alternatives to time-oriented or quasi-biological thought. Soon after their birth in Germany the neo-Kantian ideas crossed the Rhine and the Channel and by the turn of the century established themselves firmly in every branch of social study. Max Weber was perhaps the only epigone of Marx whose divergencies from dialectical materialism did not carry him to an unhistorical view of society. Perhaps equally untouched with anti-empirical bias was the other co-founder of modern sociological theory, Emile Durkheim. His main input, however, was to be found in the psychological theories round which he grouped his empirical data. The data itself was mainly ethnological and did not in any way affiliate him to the historical or even to the Darwinian tradition of nineteenth-century anthropology.

Weber and Durkheim apart, the intellectual fashions in all countries moved strongly against historical, and indeed all empirical, study of society. To this country they came somewhat belatedly, but having come, imposed their remarkable uniformity on the prevailing points of view and language. The manner in which this particular fashion was, and still is, worn in Britain may not have done British philosophy much good. In its British version the argument against history and empirical social science wears an air of provincial innocence. The writers who have most recently given it expression, Collingwood, Stebbing, or even Isaiah Berlin, do not avow their allegiance to Dilthey, Rickert, or other founders of the neo-Kantian school; for all I know some of them may not even be aware of the fathers who begot them. But this may have made them appear even more British than they are and more acceptable to the simple minds than they might otherwise have been. So acceptable they indeed have been that their views of history have reached even the ears of historians.

In fact the recoil from the earlier pursuit of historical lessons went furthest of all in the study of history itself. The main reasons for the recoil were of a kind which I understand are described on the Stock Exchange as 'technical'. The lessons of history had been overproduced; their market value fell. Like all other thinking Europeans, the historians who still considered it their business to think had come to be discouraged by the paucity of cogent historical lessons. After more than half a century of study and propaganda the various historical schools produced a harvest of lessons not only meagre but also poor in quality. They were bound to fall out of favour with the new generation of historians. For as historical researches proceeded, the standards of scholarly accuracy and circumspection rose; and judged by these standards, the performance of lesson-hunting historians were bound to appear to the lesson-shy historians as very shoddy : marred by premature generalization and by cavalier use of evidence.

The mounting distrust of historical lessons found in neo-Kantians a very good philosophical justification. It would, of course, be unduly flattering to the profession of historians to assume that in their rejection of historical lessons they were strongly moved by philosophical arguments, neo-Kantian or other. Most of them could not have been so moved simply because academic history had by then been drained of ideas not related to the actual techniques of historical investigation. The profession of academic historians had developed an impenetrable indifference not only to the scientific purposes of their study, but also to the philosophical arguments about them. Nevertheless there were still left a few historians who tried to rationalize their attitudes, and they liked to be told that their repugnance to lessons was good philosophy. They found it only too easy to accept the anti-positivist argument that a science of society in the image of natural sciences was impossible and unnecessary, and that it was least possible and least necessary in the study of historical events. They were told and believed that historical events defied scientific generalization since, being events and being historical, they were all essentially biographical, i.e. unique, individual, and unrepeatable.

III

I have dwelt on the anti-historical reaction on history itself at somewhat greater length than all the other actions and reactions in social studies. I have done so because in England the historian's revulsion from historical lessons continued longer and was more widespread than any of the other intellectual fashions with which I have so far dealt. All the other fashions, with the sole exception of Darwinian evolution, never occupied the intellectual scene as entirely as they did abroad, and seldom abandoned it equally completely. The result was that at the turn of the nineteenth and twentieth centuries, when the idea of the L.S.E. was born and the School itself was formed, the intellectual scene was composed of (or shall I say littered with?) fragments of doctrines of early nineteenth-century design, as well as with ideas more recently formed. Political philosophy in the country in general was still largely represented by men like Green or Bosanquet whose roots were obviously in the earlier idealist philosophies of Germany. Yet at the same time, at the L.S.E., Graham Wallas, and after him Laski, stood for a more empirical, historically inspired, version of their subject. Wallas's *Social Heritage* might not perhaps pass muster as a work of history, yet his thesis was unequivocally historical. The Webbs were students of history pure and simple. They contributed to the science of government by compiling detailed histories of its various branches since the Middle Ages; and this is precisely what political scientists of the historical schools had tried to do in early nineteenth-century Germany. The Webbs may even have intended to present historical lessons of government, though in fact the lessons do not emerge at all clearly from their histories. On the other hand the L.S.E. sociology, as represented by Hobhouse, was wholly rooted in philosophical ethics, some of it very ancient indeed. It did not in any material sense depend on social evidence, historical or other. Curiously enough, it was economics, wholly or largely theoretical elsewhere, that was fact-bound, and frequently reproduced the best and the worst features of the German historical school. Least affected by the pretentions of the historical school was Edwin Cannan, the main purveyor of economic theory at the L.S.E. Yet even he taught economics in the way he wrote it, as a march-past of old economic writings. His underlying system of economic theory had to be distilled from his strictures of the economists of long ago. Even more time-oriented and nearer the German tradition was the applied economics represented by Hewins, a Director of the School. He, like Sir William Ashley and Archdeacon Cunningham, the economic historians of Birmingham and Cambridge, tried to do for conservative politics, above all for Chamberlain's tariff reform, exactly what List and Roscher had done for nationalistic policies in Germany. It was not until the mid 1920s, when Beveridge was Director, and Allyn Young succeeded Cannan, and Robbins and Hayek succeeded Allyn Young, that the teaching and writing on economics at the School finally shed its connections with the historical schools, whether German or British.

While the argument for and against the historical approaches peacefully occupied and then equally peacefully evacuated the field of L.S.E. economics, a veritable conflict on the same issue broke out among the School's anthropologists. In anthropology the intellectual bias had been vaguely evolutionary. Westermarck harked back to the topics and methods of Victorian ethnology, though Seligman, with his Andaman background, to some extent anticipated the emphasis which his successors were to lay on fieldwork and on direct access to evidence. But the main controversy centred round the historical pre-occupations of the so-called diffusionist school of anthropology at University College. The fountain-head of this school, Elliot Smith, tried to locate the origin of western civilization, and believed to have discovered it in the same place in which Pharaoh's daughter found the infant Moses: in the bullrushes of the Nile. Malinowski, who led the attack against U.C.L. from L.S.E., objected to the very search for origin or for routes of diffusion. In doing so he enunciated what he thought was the true antidote to Elliot Smith's historical anthropology. His own 'functional' anthropology endeavoured to relate social phenomena not to their antecedents but to their concomitants: the concomitants which in combination formed societies, social structures, or cultures in their entirety.

On their part, the L.S.E. historians were also at some variance with historians elsewhere. In all other universities at the beginning of the twentieth century, the study and the writing of history conformed very closely to the German ideal of pure and mindless scholarship. The sole exceptions were perhaps the diplomatic historians, especially Charles Webster and Harold Temperley, whose work was dominated by their intimate concern with world order and the principles of international relations. In all other branches of history, research and teaching were conducted in proud independence of outside interests and above all apart from the social sciences. In these as in many other respects, the L.S.E. historians were a law unto themselves. Until the late 1920s history (and at the L.S.E. that meant economic history) was in the hands of Lilian Knowles. She was a pupil of William Cunningham, shared Cunningham's conservative and protectionist ideas, and more generally stood for the same view of economics and history which had been earlier represented at the L.S.E. by

Hewins. Her study of Burleigh's economic policy in Cunningham's great treatise, her lectures and textbooks on British and
European history, were charged with historical lessons of the
kind the continentals had tried to teach in the 1830s. To this
extent she was something of an anachronism and, not surprisingly, left behind her little intellectual progeny.

It was left to the historians who succeeded her, Tawney and
Eileen Power, more particularly Tawney, to establish at the L.S.E.
and through the L.S.E. in the country as a whole, a current of
thought which, though still a small tributary, flowed very abundantly. It is flowing strongly in our own day. Tawney is known
and esteemed as a historian and as a social reformer or a social
moralist. To those who did not know him, or have read him
superficially, Tawney may therefore appear as a split personality,
or as the Germans would have put it, a man of two souls: that
of an economic historian and that of a social moralist. The split
was not, of course, there. All his social and political tracts, above
all *The Acquisitive Society* and *Equality*, were rooted in his historical studies and directly emanated from what he knew and
thought of the earliest and the latest stages of England's industrial
civilization. His historical work correspondingly centred on the
problems which his social tracts laid bare: above all, the origin,
the limits and the consequences of the market economy and the
unlimited profit motive which actuated it. It was as problem-
oriented a history as there ever was, and it reached to propositions
and conclusions as general as social science could ever hope to
establish.

This has also been the attitude of most of Tawney's pupils or
his pupils' pupils. It matters not that nowadays their extra-
historical preoccupations do not always happen to be those of
Tawney. Most of them nowadays try to establish links with
theoretical economics and theoretical sociology: fields of study
which Tawney rated somewhat lower than we do now, and which
in his day did not perhaps deserve much higher rating. Indeed,
so different are nowadays the theoretical links of economic history
from Tawney's preoccupations with profit and equality that
some modern economic historians may be surprised at being
bracketed with Tawney and still more at being advised, as I am

going to do presently, that they could do much worse than be so bracketed.

The historians I have specially in mind are those who wish to be known as the New Economic Historians. The New Economic Historians want to be considered first as a group, secondly as economic historians, and thirdly as new. The ground on which their case is based is that they believe themselves to be the sole advocates of a close linkage between economic history and economic theory, and that they try to forge that link by interpreting historical situations with the aid of economic theory at its most refined and of econometric techniques at their most advanced. For all its occasional stridency, their case fits neatly with the present-day tendency to connect economic history with economic theory, and also with the anciently established predilection of economic historians for quantitative methods. Indeed, so well does New Economic History, considered broadly, go with the established points of view that people like myself may feel not a little surprised that the New Economic Historians should have found it necessary to describe themselves as new. If an adjective was wanted, economic history 'resurrected', or 'rejuvenated', or even 'ever-green' would have been a much more accurate appellation as well as a more modest one.

If, however, the claims and above all the performances of the New Economic Historians are considered not broadly but closely, they may turn out to be less acceptable. To employ economic theory and econometric tests in the interpretation of famous historical events such as the emancipation of the Negro slaves, or the decision to open up the American interior by railway construction, is a useful but perhaps an over-modest enterprise. It is over-modest not only because it tries to do what economists could always do without the assistance of historians, but also because it concerns itself more with historical episodes than with economic problems. For this and other reasons it does not offer to economists the kind of collaboration which, whether they know it or not, they most need. What economists require or ought to require from the social scientists nearest to them, and especially from economic historians, is not that they should verify the established propositions of economics or use them to illuminate episodes of general history, but that they should help to make economic propositions verifiable and applicable. These propositions are as a rule arrived at by a process of abstraction, i.e. by eliminating for the purposes of analysis a wide range of social conditions which would complicate the analysis, or even make it impossible. The results of analysis so conducted cannot be used as a basis for policy, as a key to the understanding of real phenomena, or even as verifiable hypotheses until, and unless, they are reincorporated into the totality of the situation from which they have been abstracted. This is the work which the more broadly based social scientists, and above all the economic and social historians, can do best. An economic historian ought to know and employ his economic theory not in order to be able to use it in reinterpreting historical situations, but in order to uncover in it those vacant points into which historical matter has to be pumped.

It is from this point of view that New Economic History may, even if it does not yet, offer a compromise between the time-oriented and time-allergic thought. What discredited the early nineteenth-century search for lessons was an excess of ambition. It was obviously impossible to derive from history and history alone an entire system of generalized propositions capable of explaining and helping to manage the world around us. The historical schools failed, like Aesop's frog, from over-inflated conceit. But it was and is equally hopeless for the theoretical economists to offer their theorems, so to speak stripped, and to parade them in the nude as reliable guides for economic policy and economic expectations. There are many reasons why the most recent economic predictions and economic advice should have failed to bite, as they obviously have, but to my mind the main reason is that economic propositions as fashioned by economists are woefully incomplete and need clothing with social or historical matter. If it is over-ambitious of historians to try to derive a complete economic theory from historical experience, as List tried to do 150 years ago, it is also insufficiently ambitious of them to refuse to study social experience with the view to making economic propositions fuller, more relevant, and better capable of representing and impressing the world we live in.

THE BASIS OF
SOCIAL COHESION

DONALD G. MacRAE

DONALD G. MACRAE

M.A. (Glasgow and Oxon.)

Professor of Sociology
The London School of Economics
and Political Science

Donald G. MacRae has also been visiting Professor of Sociology in the University of California at Berkeley and at the University of the Gold Coast in Ghana. He was a Fellow of the Centre for Advanced Studies in the Behavioural Sciences at Stanford. He is author of *Ideology and Society* and edits Heinemann books on sociology. He has served on a number of commissions and Government bodies in this country and abroad. He is a member of the Council for National Academic Awards and chairman of its Committee of Arts and Social Sciences.

THE BASIS OF
SOCIAL COHESION

Let me begin where perhaps I should end. Let me say what I think has been the achievement of sociology at the London School of Economics, what I believe is the truth about sociology, what are the primary modalities of the sociological endeavour, what are its difficulties and who are its enemies, above all what is at the heart of sociological activity and inquiry. Throughout I shall try to keep in mind a simple truth: one does not exhaust one's account of a subject or science when one says what its practitioners know and what they do, but one can only falsify if one does not keep in mind that a discipline is its practice and that it lives only in action. Sociology is sociologizing, is sociologists.

The achievement of sociology at L.S.E. is threefold. First, it began here in the eighth year of the School's existence and has had an unbroken history here since 1903. Our founders always intended that sociology should hold a strong place in the School. The first chairs in the subject were established here in 1907, held by Westermarck and Hobhouse, and for nearly forty years sociology in Britain *was* L.S.E. Second, sociology survived here despite thin support, indifference, and hostility. This survival was not easy, but it was never bought at the cost of low standards nor of compromise with fashion. Third, sociology is now everywhere. It is everywhere in two senses. It exists throughout nearly all our universities, polytechnics, and colleges of education, is a popular subject of both undergraduate and graduate study, and sociologists are increasingly employed as such in an ever-widening number of vocations and sources of gain. This has been in no small measure owing to the endurance and example of sociology at the School. This success, indeed, although recent, a matter of just over a decade, has not been, as we shall see, accidental, but involved a costly choice of role by sociologists in L.S.E.

But sociology is also everywhere in the sense that, to an extraordinary extent and not always fully aware, the social and historical sciences and public consciousness of political and social affairs have become sociologized. One may regard this double success as regrettable. Certainly many elements in it do not please me: in some ways the victory of sociology is like the shirt of Nessus; a torment to its wearer but a glory to those who behold it. But that, however it may be, is not our concern here at this time or in this place.

If then that is something of the achievement of sociology at the L.S.E., let me turn to what I take to be some fundamental truths about the character of the discipline. Sociology is the endeavour to answer, at large or in detail, the questions: How is society possible? How can men bear each other? By what devices can this stupid, timorous, invidious animal, man, yet somehow, sometimes co-operate, and limit his desires, indolence, and rage? Why is sin so universal and so constant, yet not altogether ruinous to each and every relationship? (If you don't like the word sin, then the psychologists will provide you with plenty of periphrastic but equivalent terms.) Is it conceivable that these questions can be answered with rigour and accuracy?

Sociology is a mirror, blotched, flawed, and distorting, but the mirror in which we can see the face of social man. Society is the medium in which we are human as truly as the sea is the medium in which fish have their being. Sociology is in endless tension. It is adopted and sought by radicals, revolutionaries, and those to whom the burden of public injustice or their own private suffering is intolerable and demands both hope and a cure. But sociology is essentially conservative. Pursued with honesty and patience it shows how precarious are our social achievements and how difficult their attainment, how little can be done, at what cost and often with what uncertain, surprising, and daunting consequences. It breeds scepticism and thus, in affairs of practical decision, often yields irresolution. It throws, as do the historical sciences, its practitioners into endless complexities. Its generalizing and simplifying ideas (unlike those of economics, perhaps?) are felt by those with any sociological imagination to do violence, for all their power, to the subtle tissues of reality and thus the sociological quest is as endlessly unsatisfying as it is endlessly tempting.

But if for these reasons sociology is in some way always conservative, yet it is also always subversive. The mirror for all its imperfections is a truth-teller. The truths of sociology are often very uncomfortable or worse. For hope, for fear, in order to have a good conceit of itself, the world has always wished to be deceived. Sociology is undeceiving. And thus sociology, caught by this tension, is a rope-dancer. One of its delights is that it involves both vertigo and danger.

It thus seems to me that the modalities of sociologizing are, or ought to be irony, pity, an irenic temper, a sustenance of constant ambiguity, a recognition that our best endeavours at science will usually yield a both, not an either-or; probability, not certainty. All of which, I believe, should be very educative, but none of which is very consoling for the sociologist nor, indeed, for society. Certainly it raises difficulties for someone whose given subject is 'The Basis of Social Cohesion'. Nevertheless we shall come closer to grips with that theme which is in part a mere restating of our already stated problem of how society, all society or any society, is possible.

How have sociologists attempted to deal with this question? Remembering that sociology is sociologizing, then we can look at this problem in the light of the somewhat odd history of the discipline both in the world and in the L.S.E. and hope to gain something from the exercise. I say 'odd history' because of the quite remarkable separation of two central strands in the development. On the one hand there is the intellectual history of sociology which is no insignificant part of the larger history of ideas in the last two centuries and of the lesser history of the development and refinement of social science research techniques. On the other hand, going back for only about a century, there is the story of the institutionalization of the subject. The intellectual history is above all European. The institutional history is primarily American. I propose to say something first of this latter, rather queer American tale.

Sociology is, of course, a French word, the bastard issue, half Latin, half Greek, of August Comte. It was first anglicized, replacing such earlier usages as 'social physics', in 1843 by J. S. Mill and an anonymous writer on Comte in *Blackwood's Magazine*. In the southern states of the ante-bellum United States the word and the idea were taken up by a number of writers in obscure reviews and in at least one book, *Sociology for the South* by George Fitzburgh (Richmond, Va., 1854). The author was intelligent, gleefully malignant, and an able defender of slavery. Unjustly his work was soon forgotten. But in the middle of the war between the states something very important took place. By the Morrill Act of 1862, at least as significant for the growth of American higher education as was the Robbins report a century later for Britain, Congress established the land-grant system whence arose an extraordinary proliferation of universities throughout the Union. This supplemented the private universities, great or petty, which had already flourished and multiplied on a scale unknown in our staider societies, less persuaded of the possibilities and virtues of the democratic intellect.

The war over, the devout, sectarian, and fanatical Americans were confronted by an industrialization, an urbanization, a mechanization, and a population growth new to the experience of mankind. Wealth and poverty, crass luxury and squalor, culture and ignorance (the ignorance of the immigrant) subsisted in juxtaposed extremes. The Christian conscience in America embraced the polarities of comfortable pharisaism and burning charitable zeal. And the universities were dominated by the churches and some of the churchmen were preaching, to use their own term, the Social Gospel. Sociology was a magniloquent word, chairs of the subject were established, students arrived, professors professed : what?

There was the rub, and there, for the moment we shall leave it. One consequence was that by 1900 all over America there were departments, virtuous and energetic, of sociology. The new University of Chicago, one of the greatest of all the world's schools of the social sciences, set its imprimature on sociology by sponsoring the *American Journal of Sociology*. A large sociological establishment, teaching, researching, writing, preaching, existed with a solid institutional base. Whatever might be the vicissitudes of specific departments, Columbia is a good instance of trial and triumph, sociology in America was a great educational fact with a solid economic and institutional base. But what to build on these foundations remained in large part problematic.

But in the cis-Atlantic world the situation was very different. Talent and even that inconvenient thing, genius, there was in plenty. Long before Comte, the brilliance of Montesquieu, the solid genius of Ferguson, the dry patience of Sinclair, the talent of Quetelet had made sociology though they had neglected to name it. When L.S.E. was founded in 1895 Pareto was in his forties, and Durkheim, Simmel, Weber, and Hobhouse were in their vigorous thirties. But there was no real sociological establishment in the simple sense of numerous ongoing institutions paying salaries, conducting research, instructing students. The researches of Le Play or Booth were personal and specific. Herbert Spencer, by this time in his seventy-sixth year, had been financed by the kindness of J. S. Mill, the united efforts of some American admirers and, in his last period, by the beneficence of Andrew Carnegie.

Consider these names more closely. Spencer, Pareto, and Le Play had all been engineers. Pareto indeed became a professor, but of economics, which he adorned, not sociology. Weber only consistently began to refer to himself as a sociologist about 1908 after more than twenty years of academic preferment in other subjects. Durkheim, too, was long employed as educationalist and Simmel as philosopher. When Hobhouse and Westermarck became professors here in 1907 they were members of a group of fewer than twenty people in university employment in all Europe, including the Russia of Mikhailovski, unequivocally bound by the terms of their appointment to the endeavour of sociology.

The American sociological establishment, comparatively rich, could and did pursue any of four courses singly or in combination. It could pursue other activities, history, philosophy, etc., and call this sociology. It could teach what the Europeans had done or were doing, and first Spencer, then Simmel (surprisingly), then many others were soon speaking with an American accent. It could, in the tradition of the Social Gospel and Bliss's *Encyclopaedia of Social Reform*, preach and practise social welfare and research into specific problem areas; a sort of proto-social administration influenced among other things by the odd English journal

Meliora, and our Social Science Association. Or it could begin to do new things, or as one might have said a year or two ago, to do its own thing.

Now what that thing was is very complex and not central to our attempt to look at the basis of social cohesion. Basically, particularly at Chicago, it was to document the varieties of American life, particularly in its extremes: in *The Gold Coast and the Slum* as one of its most famous books was called. Of course it moved in from the slums, the criminal, the migrant and immigrant, the ethnic and the peasant, more to the core of what was involved in being American. But the two great *Middletown* studies are late arrivals. The deviant was the norm of American sociological study: I do not use the word *deviant* as a euphemism for *criminal*. A certain theoretical element, arising out of these researches, did indeed come into being and was specifically American. Cooley's *primary group* was not grand theory, but a useful concept. Concern with the direct contacts of men gave rise to the earliest elements of what is now called interactionism. So far as there is a theory of urban sociology, of what is urbanism as a way of life, it is American. And so I could go on, but the truth is that although there is quantitatively quite a lot, yet for large integrated theoretical systems as for heuristically important concepts down to the 1930s one had to turn to Europe.

More significant, indeed, was the refinement of the tools of research into concrete situations and the development of quantitative treatments of sociological data in the United States. Yet survey methodology was largely British. Sampling had been reintroduced early in this century by Bowley, later of this School. Field methods of another kind were developed more by Radcliffe-Brown and by Malinowski here than by American sociologists or anthropologists. And the brutal extremes of American sociology's 'radical empiricism', focused in a narrow beam on social facts but never asking that minatory question 'What is a fact?' has cursed a great deal of subsequent sociology, and not just in the United States.

The great age, in some senses exemplary and classical in American sociology, runs from about 1935 to about 1955. A new paradigm of the sociological was produced in one of the great efforts of the human mind addressing itself to social understanding. It is usual to ascribe this to the emigration of scholars, fleeing the tyrannies of Europe, to the charity and profit of America. Refugees carried their intellectual luggage in their heads whatever they left behind in the way of material goods. One was not asked to declare one's knowledge of Max Weber on the quays of New York. No doubt this was important. Something else was more important. Professor Talcott Parsons, who had studied at the L.S.E., was introduced to Weber by Tawney (not, surprisingly enough, by Ginsberg; I have it on Parson's own authority) and to Durkheim by Malinowski. He wrote well in the 1920s on both Sombart and Weber. In the mid 1930s he produced the *Structure of Social Action*.

As recently as fifteen years ago that book was perhaps overpraised. Today it is condemned. Any bright undergraduate can give you a quasi-Marxist explanation of its faults and vices without having to do anything so radical as read it. To phenomenological and ethnomethodological sociologists it is the arch example of the endistancing of the sociologist from the social by a sort of pantograph of reified abstractions. So be it. What concerns us here is twofold. Parsons saw that quite certainly both Durkheim and Weber were saying complementary and convergent things which looked vastly unlike because the languages, the special vocabularies, the thought worlds of France and Germany disguised this possible unity. In this complementarity Pareto, too, was implicated, along with Alfred Marshall and some others. The result was a general theory of society built on the atom of a unitary social act, and this theory was at once Parson's discovery in his sources and his personal creation. It seemed, too, capable of being large enough to include the psychology of socially shaped personality, and yet also detailed enough to yield confirmable propositions for empirical researchers.

In all this, what else can one do so briefly? I simplify brutally, and I am unjust not only to the many names and themes I do not mention but also to those I use for my purposes. If I am right in stressing the role of Parsons it is not to put down others, least of all the refugees. It is to give the overture to the triumphal symphony of American sociology before its decline and transformation in the last decade or so. In this symphony theory and research seemed to operate in as strict a counterpoint as they are ever likely to find in our imperfect world. Society was not problematic and it cohered because cohesion was its mode. Of course I parody what was done, but I think that, essentially and allowing for all the diversity of real men doing real things, I do not falsify. Certainly American sociology could be condemned as a huge tautology, a reinforcement of each segment by each, a chain linked to itself, a Midgard Serpent with its tail in its mouth. But this condemnation applies to Newtonian physics or Marshallian economics if I grasp them aright. It is a vulgar error to think that in knowledge all circles are vicious.

In an impoverished, perplexed Europe where murder for insensate secular ideology and defence against such murder dominated society, sociology did not flourish. With the peace of 1945 American sociology seemed splendid in itself and uniquely splendid in the European void. Germans and Frenchmen alike turned to it, and paid it the sincere flattery of imitation. For ten or fifteen years American or American-style sociology was nearly, but not quite, all there was. After the death of Stalin and, particularly, after the Polish October of 1956 one even found it rooted in the western marches of the Soviet imperium. The American sociological establishment had absorbed and transformed the work of the European mind. The new European establishment imitated the American.

And while all this was going on, what of our domestic concerns at the L.S.E.? After all, for much of the century the sociology department of the L.S.E. quite simply was British sociology. The story is idiosyncratic, parochial perhaps, but not discreditable.It also, rather like the best of the silent films, is full of temptations and at least one hairbreadth escape. It begins with Herbert Spencer who was keenly interested in the new institution and physically bequeathed us his upright piano. But intellectually he left us something more important, an outlook which combines some of the most typical features of the British mind over the last two centuries. In Hobbes, Smith, Darwin, and Spencer the world is seen as composed of discrete, atomic units, constantly competitive. In Smith, Darwin, and Spencer it is seen as developmental: the clash of the primary competitive units produces unintended consequences. Out of this matrix arise new species, new institutions. The world is process, and has a history which can rationally be understood and which is in one sense organic in that its process has a shape in time. Biological nature and society are not like machines that can be run as well forward as backward. Each moment results from its past and is irreversible. To believe this makes it easy, of course, to believe in progress, but the ascription of an increasing valuation to temporal change is no necessary part of this kind of thought any more than is a romantic historical pessimism.

Spencer's sociology is one in which from human interaction there develops a heterogeneity of devices by which men attain their ends better, or attain a larger number of their ends, mainly through what we would today call a multiplication of occupational and other social roles along with an institutional structure and variety to sustain and assign these roles. These institutions have functions, otherwise they would not exist. As roles, institutions and functions all multiply, the specialization of each increases. As this specialization increases so does the mutual interdependence of constituent parts of society increase. Thus the specialized heterogeneity that is society is a system of interconnected, interdependent parts. Some of these are conscious social inventions. Most of them are the unconsicous, unintended consequence of self-seeking action. Spencer is an evolutionary utilitarian. He welcomes the process, but recognizes its costs in individual and social failure, disappointment and the extinction of the unsuccessful or superseded. Society is possible at the price of endless change.

Leonard Hobhouse, who dominated sociology at the L.S.E. for about a quarter of a century, seems at first sight hardly to be in the Spencer tradition. Without the genius of Durkheim in France he failed to seize on the essential in Spencerian sociology, the analysis of social structure, and Hobhouse's social evolutionism is deliberately expressed in new terms and with new emphasis. He was, one is universally assured, a moving and gripping lecturer. He conveyed intimations to his listeners of high seriousness and higher moral purpose. Perhaps this is what is mysterious about him. We have our own moral cant: it is not that of the Edwardians. In a way he has suffered from having as disciple and successor a greater sociologist in Morris Ginsberg. Just as one may say that the Max Weber of Talcott Parsons is

different from, and in the sense of system-building, better than
the actual chaos of learning and intelligence and muddle that is
the real Weber, so Ginsberg's Hobhouse seems to me a more
formidable figure than the reality to be found in Hobhouse's
own specifically sociological works. I do not mean by this to
criticize what Hobhouse did in, for example, political philosophy
or in other areas, but these other writings of his are not his
sociology. Of that sociology only his *Social Development* seems
to me a permanent monument.

This sociology combines three elements: an evolutionism
which sees moral institutions (i.e. patterns of social control and
the sanctions which enforce and legitimate them) as the main
content of that evolution; a weak[1] historical functionalism
derived from Spencer but without his rigour or grim acceptance
of the brutality of social life; and a belief that it was increasingly
by the constant and growing rationality and self-consciousness of
mankind that the course of social development was shaped. His
learning was ample. The detail was often admirable: for example,
he is one of the major pioneers of a comparative sociology of
law. He refined and improved sociological usage: for example,
again, his discussion of the word 'institution'. And he was
responsible for what seems to me one of our hairbreadth escapes.

The founders of the L.S.E., Sidney and Beatrice Webb, were
fond of the word sociology and often referred to themselves as
sociologists. In fact they were radical empiricists of a kind valuable indeed to society and social policy, but absolutely divorced
from the central effort of sociology. Their world was one of hard,
accurately ascertained, discrete facts. It was a world without real
people, quirky and strange, and without society as the medium
in which people live, and without ideas. The truth was to them
the simple, the immediate, and the obvious. Only deliberate vice
could conceal the plain stuff of reality and political morality;
and all their morality is political. Sociology was a perfect card
index of all unique social facts. From this barren philistinism (to
which we yet owe so much that makes our society not quite intolerable) Hobhouse's concerns saved the subject at the L.S.E. and
to some extent in Britain. He perhaps made social cohesion too
much a moral matter. But he did see that social cohesion is largely

1. I use 'weak' as opposed to 'strong' and rigorous; not as condemnation.

in very truth a function of morals treated as facts of social existence. Values are facts; unfortunately perhaps Hobhouse confused their factuality with their transcendent claims to command our reasons and our wills. He accepted, indeed, something of the brutality and privation of existence, but his vision of rational moral harmony in society while certainly amiable is very unconvincing and not sociology nor scholarship.

I said that Hobhouse's learning was ample. Whatever is true of his work is psychology and in political philosophy he does not seem to me to have commanded as a sociologist the rigour, the scepticism, the critical spirit that are three-fifths of the equipment of a scholar. Morris Ginsberg, whose death in 1970 we still mourn, was rigorous, sceptical, critical, and on all specific issues a pessimist. He did his great work despite that particularistic pessimism because he could still believe it rational to cherish a thin universal hope. He knew everything. He did not parade his learning but it was ever at his command. His power of synthesis was so bound to his clarity and concision that very often his readers and his less able students found him easy and obvious, just as the effortless appearance of a dancer's skill may delude us into underestimating her painful and unrelenting art. The lessons his studies taught him were daunting, but the facts that somehow society was possible and that critical thinking actually occurred sustained him.

He was a great communicator. He knew the best of continental European sociology and what he wrote in the 1920s on Durkheim, Pareto, and Weber is still worth reading. All his criticisms and reservations are sound, yet perhaps there is something missing. He was a great teacher; by his modesty, his intelligence, his integrity, his goodness he impressed without a display of enthusiasm or the more obvious platform arts. He was a researcher in three senses. The comparative method, however much one may be told by methodologists of its unsoundness (or of the unsoundness of Book Six of Mills's *Logic*, which is the same point) or instructed in its impossibility by anthropologists and historians afraid of the violence that comparison does to the ethnographically or temporally unique, is unavoidable in sociology and I believe in all the social sciences. (Everyone uses it, including its critics, but the critics do not realize what they are up to.)

Hobhouse, Wheeler, and Ginsberg's *Material Culture and Social Institutions of the Simpler Peoples* remains one of its classics. So does Ginsberg's great Huxley lecture *On the Diversity of Morals* written more than a generation later. But his pioneer quantitative studies of the processes of social mobility belong to a different, equally important tradition of research, broken, in his life, by the greater demands of the 1930s and 1940s on his energy and conscience. And, almost forgotten, he conducted scholarly inquiries of a kind that cannot concern us here, as in his work of Malebranche, as well as in drawing from the writings of Hobhouse and Westermarck more, I think, than these men ever knew was there.

And, in worse times than those of Hobhouse and Westermarck, he kept sociology going and earned for it a respect which was also personal. Now, outside of London, sociology began tentatively to take root, aided by that remarkable dying institution, the London external degree system, and by the new provincial university colleges. (How often, how easily, the role of London as a mother of universities is forgotten!) Ginsberg did not create a school; of such things he disapproved, but his pupils were to be found carrying on as best they could his concerns throughout England and the world.

Yet, as I said, perhaps something was missing. Of no man can it be said that there is nothing in his life or work not deserving praise. Yet it is nearly true of Ginsberg. But his fear of enthusiasm may have concealed an ultimate lack of sociological creativity and the ability to recognize it in others. I can think of only one theoretical concept we owe to him. At the last in all areas of science and scholarship major discovery involves major risks of haste and error. By capacity or temperament (or by mere ill fortune?) Ginsberg was not ultimately creative as a sociologist in this rare sense.

Like Hobhouse, however, he was more than a sociologist. He was a social philosopher. Like so many of the greatest figures in the L.S.E. he was a liberal socialist. It is a vulgar error to assume that there is a contradiction in this position, so central in the spirit of Wallas, of Tawney, of Beales, of Hobhouse, and so many others in so many departments of our life. But Ginsberg uniquely thought it out. Here he was creative and quietly bold. I cannot believe everything that he believed. I wish I could, but my vision is darker. In talking of social cohesion and the L.S.E. this is a theme to which I must recur. Our achievements and failures are incomprehensible without it.

Let us now widen our perspective again. In the decade after 1945 the dominant influence in sociology was American and at the L.S.E. we were fortunate in having for some years the benign influence of Edward Shils. He brought to us knowledge of what had been and was being done in the United States with the authority of one who was a major contributor to that achievement. He stressed for us the importance in making society possible of the functions of primary bonds, seldom articulated, working at the most fundamental level of the social. He inspired our new students of sociology, ever more numerous, with a belief in their endeavours and the desirability of sustained empirical inquiry. He perhaps failed to communicate to all of them his sense of the dangerous in social life. But to all his students sociology became not only a discipline, but a commitment, and from him many learned a quirky tolerance and a resigned moralism.

In a way he continued in slightly better times the work begun by the to me puzzling figure of Karl Mannheim who had brought as a refugee a commitment to our studies which was immensely serious, publicly influential, and cut short by his early death. Certainly both Mannheim and Shils made real to our sociology certain aspects of Central European sociology which Ginsberg's dry light had illuminated but thrown into no sharp relief. Without losing its own character L.S.E. sociology, almost unwittingly, became ecumenical.

It was also a time of division. T. H. Marshall preached and, better, practised the virtues of a *via media* in theory and research and illuminated in a way better understood today in Harvard than here, how our kind of society was possible not in despite, but in a way because of social stratification and the historical growth of statuses and the super-ordinate role of citizenship. But at the same time certain bonds were being dissolved: the alliance of sociology with social administration, as we now call it, might continue but the institutional links were cut. Now not all the sociologists at the L.S.E. were to be found in the departments of sociology and anthropology, and after social administration, social psychology broke away into its own department. The uniting interest in social philosophy, in the attempt to establish a defensible casuistry of distributive justice for industrial societies, was perhaps the major victim of this change, and I regret it. So I suspect does Richard Titmuss who succeeded Marshall in his responsibilities to the conduct of virtue by public policy and bureaucracy. One can after all dream that a visible social justice might aid a society to a desirable cohesion.

And it was a time of a major expansion of factual social knowledge all over the world. To the richly exotic data provided by our anthropological friends was added the kind of solid information that Carr-Saunders, David Glass, and our succession of demographers have given us, so that until recently a serious population study was an all but unique L.S.E. speciality. More widely social statistics, variously sound, useful or illuminating became enormously available and their compilation and processing seemed, and still seem, to many the proof of sociological virtue. Much of this work was of the order which shows a strong positive correlation between hands and gloves. Some was not: for example, the great social mobility survey under Glass in the early 1950s which established international standards for the study and understanding of who got where and of how roles are allocated in our societies. This in turn gave rise to studies by Mrs. Floud and others which, for good or ill, have profoundly influenced English attitudes to the schools. Thirty years later, indeed, that work of Glass is now being replicated (in the social sciences one is too proud merely to *repeat* something) in Oxford.

Yet it would be idle to contend that the L.S.E. has contributed to the massing of quantitative social data on the scale that its size and primacy might lead one to expect. One can explain this in part by a certain proud parsimony bred in us by the long years in which one of our boasts was to have survived. More strongly there was a missionary spirit: sociology we believed was a good widely to be distributed; our task was to train undergraduates and graduates (we had faith in 'conversion courses', an odd usage) to teach and research elsewhere. There was also a kind of cosmopolitanism, not, alas, always well-based, which turned our eyes too much beyond these islands. And there was a hatred for the meretricious, the slipshod, the mimicry of physical science, and the making of great claims for trivial researches. There was also sheer over-work, for sociology is demanding and our department in the 1960s was not merely less than half the size of the largest of the new departments in other universities, but much smaller than those of several polytechnics and at least one regional technical college. Yet I know that the L.S.E. educated more undergraduates, produced far more graduates, and published more than any other sociology department in Britain at this time. I must not exaggerate these things. After all we have done much of this work of mapping the social. But if we do not have a good sociography of British society, and we do not, it is in part our fault as well as the fault of some of the exarchs who control the funding of researches and whom it is easy and consoling to blame.

And now I have come nearly to the present. In the last ten or so years for reasons that can be explained, though not in this lecture, the prestige, the confidence, and the content of American sociology have all declined. The sociological scene internationally is full of new arrivals and discordant voices. At the L.S.E. I think we flourish modestly, but it would be invidious for me to bring my sketch too close to the moment. And if ideologues, various fanatics, and panacea-mongers make life difficult for us by claiming to be sociologists at least we have the comfort of knowing that our name is worth the stealing. What is perhaps worrying is rather that the expansion of our subject at the breakneck speed of the last decade has produced a certain dilution of quality in British sociology. Time will remedy that. It may even convert some of those who have jumped on the bandwagon into citizens of the sociological republic.

What can we now say about how society is possible and how it coheres? I think we have for the moment nearly exhausted what can be said with present knowledge and understanding about social structure. We basically know how to analyse the major relationships of men which take institutional form, to show how roles in these institutions are distributed and assigned and how status-systems adhere to these roles. We have indeed, as a former student of the L.S.E. Dr. Dahrendorf puts it, now got a clear picture of *homo sociologus* to set beside that odd anthropoid, *homo oeconomicus*: man as a role player and role victim. We can combine and compare our analyses of structure to enable us to embark with new confidence on the old task of comparative sociology and I expect and hope we shall do so.

But what seems to me clear is that social structures are less coherent than we have believed. Individual life is, thank God, made possible by this fact. We can say a great deal, for example, about class and the wider issues of social stratification, differentiation, and mobility, and say it with precision. We are being forced to realize that some of every social life, much of most, and all of some, is lived outside of the structure of class. We are being forced to accept the fact that all social structures are formally incomplete and that the lacunae in them occur in different places, at different times, in each society. We have learned that there are important asymmetries and intransivities in social structure. By this I mean that the relations of our institutional responses to the inescapable fundamentals of society, communication, economic action, the specific socialization of the individual, and social (including political) control, are not relations of equality of differential power nor of equivalent strength on each dimension of social action. We are learning to wonder if the pursuit of a social atom, a unit action, relation or role, is sensible. I suspect that an image of the physical world, built up on fundamental particles, may mislead us here, and that society may even best be understood as having its constituent units, whatever they may be, dependent on its larger structures and on things which are not structural at all.

We do not see society as static, but as constant patterned motion. In doing so we can learn from Durkheim and his predecessors something of the major patterns of this motion and from Weber and Pareto something of how this imperfect patterning is sustained and legitimated and enforced. Not much of this would have surprised Ginsberg, although the total emphasis, I think, would have perturbed him. But he would have been very unsurprised that we are again concerned by questions, large and small, as to how this patterning has evolved.

All this, formal and abstract, must be brought to the bar of fact. Here we need more and better ethnography or sociography of societies, industrialized and pre-industrial, than we have. We need this both in the form of minute researches, which may be as long and tedious as, say, minute research in genetics, and also synthetically and on a large scale. I would like to be able to speak as confidently of England as, following Firth or Evans-Pritchard, I may about Tikopia or the Nuer; and I would, where possible, like to put quantities to my statements.

But what is becoming overwhelmingly clear is that none of this is enough. *Homo sociologus* is the man who makes social structure possible, but social structure is only in part self-explanatory. This is not because of the problems arising out of the facts of social change, which seem to me not difficult although most interesting, nor because we need, though we do, more concrete, specifically sociological (i.e. not merely social) researches. It is because of something that is central to the history of sociology and particularly exemplified here at the L.S.E. Sociology is the child of the enlightenment in its assumptions, methods, programme, and hope. The rationally accessible world of formal relations and the melioristic impulse are central to its history. If it deals with the irrational, as it must, it does so with a sigh and by a kind of rationalistic fable. If it deals with conflict, and it does, it deals with it in the hope of harmony whether in Comte's positive polity or Hobhouse's humane and altogether rational, tolerant welfare state: and how much real good that latter ambition has produced! An occasional sociologist like Weber has been haunted by the insights, the passions and alarms of romanticism, but has not quite known what to do about them. One solution, belonging to the minor tradition of the enlightenment, is Pyrrhonism, as in Hume or Pareto. But that is to ignore or treat with irony, while admitting their existence, certain realities. I personally find this Pyrrhonism very attractive.

But the other course is to take seriously what the enlightenment tradition avoided and yet try to subject it to the dry light of empirical rationality. This is to develop a sociology of culture and a theory, yielding confirmable propositions, of the relations of culture to structure. This is beginning to emerge, often in an infuriating form, in the untidy, needlessly obscure, but very important work of French anthropologists, sociologists, and semiologists. (The word semiology is an old one: the science of signs. I use it very loosely here to stand for the sociology of symbolic orders.) It is also to be found in Britain in the growing body of studies of great originality, fundamentally Durkheimian, into the sociology of language which Professor Bernstein, a student of the L.S.E., has created, and in the field of the sociology of religion which centrally concerns so many of my immediate colleagues. These are, as yet, beginnings, but they are already more than promises. They are all congruent with the continuing tradition of sociology.

Denying that tradition are the new arrivals of phenomenology and ethnomethodology. Sociology is, they say, a cultural device whose theories and methods endistance us from the everyday, the apparently trivial, the shifting, fine-grained, tricky existence of actual people experiencing and creating reality in the minute contexts of personal fleeting social intercourse. Yet it is at this level that cohesion (and disjunction) are most fundamentally found. The denial seems to me absurd. The insight seems to me expensive and the results small. Yet it is early to say this, and it may be that here too is one way of getting at the fundamental workings of the cultural. I can see nothing in the programme of ethnomethodology that is incongruous with traditional sociology, and this domestic quarrel in the subject is, I suspect, merely one of ideological misidentification. It is in the study of the cultural, answering the question (which is not a psychological one) of how society enters and is the mind, that I expect to find in the next generation the most illumination as to the basis of social cohesion.

It may be, too, that ethological studies will play their part in this. Hobhouse and Ginsberg would have liked this thought, but the biology of their day could not yield what they needed. So far inter-species comparisons of behaviour seem to me far less rigorous and much less illuminating than inter-societal ones. But the endeavour is surely correct, and perhaps the L.S.E. should reinvest in the chair of social biology we lost when Hogben left us. I leave that thought to the Director and the Court.

Perforce this has all been very abstract. I would have wished to fill it with concrete instances, but time does not allow. Let me then say, to those who are worried about costs and benefits, and do not think the endeavour of systematic knowledge a sufficient good in itself (which it is in my view) that it is by these concerns that sociologists can in the daily life of policy and administration find out social facts with an accuracy and relevance that simple empiricism or bureaucratic priority cannot give. Much of our special sociologies (industrial, urban, medical, educational) can at least teach men of power to avoid certain errors, question certain assumptions, and delimit the areas of ignorance in which choice must be made. But sociology to be an aid to policy should not be the mere servant of power, however benign, nor should it encourage or excuse those who want to enter too minutely into the daily life of the citizen even for his own good. One lesson of sociology is that the burden of society, legally rational and statistical, can become so great that men will destroy their own, unintended cohesion and take to paths of action both desperate and irrational. Social cohesion is tough, subtle and various: it is a sad paradox that the abuse of its study may lead to its destruction and to the reign of tyrannous emotion yielding in turn to those sentimental tyrannies of secular idolatory from which our century has so deeply suffered.

THE STATE
VERSUS MAN

PETER J. O. SELF

PETER J. O. SELF

M.A. (Oxon.)

Professor of Public Administration
University of London

He was the first Director of Administrative Studies
at the British Government's Centre for Administrative Studies (1969–70); author of *Cities in Flood*
(2nd edition, 1961), (with H. Storing) *The State
and the Farmer* (1962), *Metropolitan Planning*
(1971), and *Administrative Theories and Politics*
(1972); has been active in urban and regional
planning as both Chairman and Vice-Chairman of
the Town and Country Planning Association and
as a member of the South-East Region Economic
Planning Council.

THE STATE VERSUS MAN

Introduction

My title reverses Spencer's famous book, first published in 1884. The collectivism he so deplored as inimical to individual liberty and social progress has developed enormously. What would Spencer say today?

Few people appear to question in principle the still expanding role of government, despite much argument about methods and resistance to providing the financial resources and legal authority that government needs. Thus, one might say that the question today is whether individuals will furnish government with financial, legal, and moral support essential for the achievement of agreed collective ends: a paradoxical reversal of Spencer's thesis.

But a greater paradox still is the failure of political theory itself to develop and keep up with the growth of collectivism within democratic societies. There is much talk of government planning but hardly a book which gives a good analysis of the process and rationale of such planning. In this era of collectivism the hardiest theoretical plant, using theory in its normative sense, is traditional liberalism. Under new names such as polycentricity or disjointed incrementalism the ancient dream of a harmonious, self-regulating order, powered by individual will and choice, continues to exercise its sway. The rational individualism of classical economics and utilitarianism lives on in some strange new guises, and notable teachers in the L.S.E., one thinks particularly of F. A. Hayek, have helped to keep this particular grass green. By contrast, the theory of government action remains as inchoate, piecemeal, and pragmatic as the growth of such action itself. At the level of theory even Spencer might still feel quite at home.

My task now will be to develop my view along several lines. First I will consider very briefly the development of political science in this century, so as to reveal some of the difficulties and prospects of theorizing about the State. Next I turn to the much less charted sea of administrative politics, and then compare the actual functioning of the administrative system with possible theories of modern democracy. I conclude by suggesting some possible reforms of political and administrative institutions, which seem to me necessary if democracy is to support the now (to my mind) inevitably vast scale of public collective action. Thus the discussion moves downwards by stages, from the heights of theory and methodology to current policy issues broadly treated.

Political science

My review starts, appropriately, with Graham Wallas. In *Human Nature in Politics,* Wallas stressed the inadequacy of rationalist explanations of political behaviour. People in the mass do not vote according to careful calculations of either public or individual interest, but are influenced by cruder and vaguer emotional attitudes. Wallas and his contemporary (but very different) American thinker, Arthur Bentley, paved the way for modern political psychology and sociology. The psychological approach revealed the importance of group and family loyalties for voting patterns; the influence of vaguely formed (and now deliberately cultivated) party 'images' as opposed to specific programmes; and the relationship between types of personality (authoritarian, permissive, etc.) and political behaviour. By contrast the sociological approach of Arthur Bentley laid the foundations of interest group studies.

Wallas's thought reduced the practical influence of deliberately chosen goals or ideals in favour of often unconscious emotional and psychological factors. In so doing he formed part of the whole movement of thought, originated in different spheres by Darwin, Marx, and Freud, which reduced the zone of human rationality and freedom through elucidation of biological, sociological, and psychological determinants of individual action. It could not be expected that politics would escape this process, nor has it. The result has been an increasing separation between supposedly hard-headed, factually based studies of sociological or psychological variety, and theorizing about political values which at least until very recently has become more constricted, limited, and defensive.

Wallas himself certainly did not desire this result. On the contrary, he saw psychological realism as a pathway towards a more broad-based form of political idealism forged out of self-conscious recognition of the emotional and irrational elements in human behaviour. His successors, whether as empirical social scientists or as theorists, have mainly judged otherwise.

The rationalist tradition of political thought proceeds through the analysis and prescription of regulative ideals or principles which should govern political relations, in particular the political rights and duties of individuals, and the relationships between individuals, organized groups, and the organs of government. This tradition informed the approach of Wallas's equally famous successor at the L.S.E., Harold Laski, who sought to redefine political principles so as to meet the conditions and problems of modern economic organization. There are actually two Laskis, the exponent of basic democratic rights and the Marxist, and the two elements do not cohere easily. In the later Laski, the Marxist element became much more dominant. However my point is that he carried on the rationalist exploration of political values, notably in A *Grammar of Politics*.

Since Laski's day the treatment of political values has narrowed, despite a few notable contributions in the older tradition including books by Reginald Bassett and Richard Greaves. The reasons for this development are fairly familiar. Modern philosophy became absorbed with linguistics and methodology. Logical positivism insisted upon an absolute distinction between facts and values, and one influential school of ethics reduced value statements to unarguable expressions of emotional preferences. Although the philosophic climate has now changed, a narrowly linguistic and relativist view of political values, evinced by such a book as Weldon's A *Vocabulary of Politics*, contributed to a temporary vacuum in political theory.

Increasingly, political thought was related to its historical context, and discussed in terms of the special conditions and institutions of its particular period. This historical treatment is itself most desirable, especially when treated as brilliantly and carefully as by Laski's successor Michael Oakeshott. But there is no easy resting point in the pendulum movement of academic bias. Excessive rationalism commits the sin against history of supposing that Plato, Machiavelli, and J. S. Mill can be presumed to be discussing the same subjects; excessive historicism reverses the error by supposing that no real dialogue across the ages is possible at all. Wherever the balancing point is found, if it can be, there seems no doubt that historical and ethical relativism has seemed to undermine the point of rationalist theorizing.

The philosophic treatment of political values has also become more logically cautious. These views from the mountaintop are refreshing if rare, but reveal the large unoccupied ground between philosophy and political issues. One such example is *Social Principles and the Democratic State*, in which Stanley Benn and Richard Peters base their analysis of equality, liberty, and justice upon a minimal requirement of rational ethics, the treatment of individuals as ends in themselves. More venturesomely, Brian Barry in *Political Argument* resurrects classical Utilitarianism in such a way as to suggest that some substantive rules can perhaps be found for the calculation of public interest.

Meanwhile empirical political studies have proliferated but have become very entangled with doubts about their methodology. Modern political scientists are keen to make their discipline genuinely scientific, and have an inferiority complex because they seem less successful than economists, psychologists, or anthropologists. I believe myself that the same basic problems of methodology are common to all the social sciences, including economics, but it is true enough that these problems seem particularly intractable in politics, and that attempts to solve or bypass them lead easily to pretentious but unconvincing forms of theorizing.

Modern social science has not overcome the ancient treadmill of how to describe the relations between the individual and society or State. Much political, like sociological, analysis is conducted in terms of description of roles and/or of situational logic, which excludes variations in individual personality and aims. For example, it makes sense to say that any leader of the British Labour Party, any Foreign Secretary, or any chairman of the Gas

Council will be constrained to act in certain ways whatever his personal preferences (if the strain is too great he may, of course, resign). But a close look at any situational description reveals it to be a minefield for logical analysis. The multiple influences that bear upon the Labour leader, for example, can be analysed in a diversity of ways. There are aspects of his behaviour which can be explained in terms of theories about the logic of choice or of games and this is possible because, for example, certain fairly predictable relations exist between the end of winning an election and the functioning of the British electoral system. But the Labour leader is guided simultaneously by procedural requirements such as parliamentary and party rules; by programme or policy commitments whose binding effect may actually be very uncertain; and by elements of political acculturation which will, of course, have shaped to some extent his own personality; although this is not to deny the existence of a residuum of individual personality which could not be socially explained. (One could, of course, reverse the analysis, and explain behaviour in terms of personal goals into which would have to be built a variety of social or cultural elements, leaving some concept of situational logic as the unexplained or separately explained residuum.)

It would not be unreasonable to conclude that the only general explanations of the behaviour of Labour leaders are to be found in biographies or party histories. These explanations can be objectively grounded in the sense of utilizing certain broad rules of evidence, but not of producing causal or predictive hypotheses. Still, even a biographical or descriptive analysis would by implication push into the methodological territory of what influences upon the Labour leader to include, how to weight them, and how to relate them.

Now economics, in so far as it offers causal and predictive hypotheses, must deal with the same problems of situational logic. The behaviour of markets can only be predicted to the extent that consumers and producers have standardized reactions. Predictions are possible because behaviour is channelled according to a fairly specific and narrowly defined situational logic, and can be measured through a great number of separate transactions. But some constraints in human behaviour must still be assumed; men who burnt their own banknotes would defeat predictions. However, where responses are unexpected or idiosyncratic, as for example are those of many farmers to changes in the prices of their products, economics too must investigate the cultural elements in decision-making, as can indeed be seen in the emergence of a separate subject of agricultural economics.

I am aware that economic theories have been deliberately purged, so to speak, of their cultural and ethical connotations. Marginal utility theory, for example, has been restated so as to exclude the idea that consumers are or should be receiving equal units of pleasure or satisfaction from their marginal outlays. Incidentally it is curious that while these classical links between economics and psychological or ethical Utilitarianism have been snapped, economists in the United States of America such as Gordon Tullock and Anthony Downs are busy explaining political behaviour in terms of Utilitarian axioms or assumptions. The old wine, it seems, is right for politics, but too polluted with values for economic bottling.

But to the extent that economic theory becomes axiomatic, and excludes consideration of social values, the scope of its explanatory power is inevitably much reduced, even if what remains is explained more rigorously. Economic behaviour can, of course, be measured after the event, but it can only be predicted to the extent that constant human reactions to possible economic situations actually occur.

The interest of this point is that all social sciences might proceed (as they are sometimes popularly supposed to proceed) through the identification of separate elements in human behaviour which can be predicted and preferably measured. In the case of economics the analysis concerns logical choices over the use of scarce resources, usually as mediated through standardized units of exchange (money); and behaviour is predictable to the extent that the logical assumptions do in fact hold. What would be the political equivalent to this kind of reasoning? The obvious and frequently given answer is logical analysis of the uses of power or, better, of influence. Up to a point I believe that the analogy holds. For example, the influence which a politician can command is usually a scarce commodity in relation to the ends which he would like to achieve. He may often only be able to achieve one goal through incurring 'debts' towards supporters and unpopularity among opponents which lessen his capacity to achieve another goal.

The basic notion of opportunity costs can thus be broadly applied in the same way to politics as to economics, referring in each case to the costs that must be paid (of foregone resources or of foregone influence) to achieve some result. Moreover both subjects must in a sense cope with the same problem; namely, that to predict or explain behaviour at all closely, the analysis must descend from purely logical assumptions into investigations of institutional and sociological factors; for example, exactly how mobile are specified resources, or exactly how malleable are political opinions, in some specified situation? But I would, of course, concede that political exchanges cannot be analysed or measured with anything like the precision of economic exchanges.

This brief dive into the comparison between economics and politics is intended to illuminate what I believe to be a central dilemma in the efforts of modern students of politics to be 'scientific'. The models of the other social sciences pull them in two opposite directions. The example of economics points towards basing the subject upon the logic of choice in given political situations, and thence going on to investigate to what extent and why political choices are 'irrational', for example by departing from the most logical method of achieving a presumed end. One obvious answer to this problem is that the ends of politics are extremely diverse and heterogeneous, which partly explains why 'trade-off values' cannot be measured in the way that is possible for goods in a shop. In some cases indeed the goals appear to be completely irreconcilable. On the other hand some political goals are extremely simple, for example, winning an election, and this is where methods of logical and mathematical analysis can prove quite powerful, to the extent that politicians really do prize an election victory above all else.

Opposed to the methodology of economics is that of social anthropology. Here a typical aim is to explain behaviour in terms of the requirements of roles, which are in various ways interrelated and mutually supportive. Underlying these roles are culturally supported values which sustain the whole system in terms of its productive functions, social relations, collective methods of defence, and so on. The analysis here is much broader than in the case of economics, it extends to all aspects of behaviour, and behaviour is required not in terms of individual choice but of the requirements of the whole system, however this is defined. Whether or not it is possible (and I confess to being sceptical) it is the hope of some political scientists to isolate and analyse a 'political sytem', which can then be explained in terms of interrelated institutions, roles, and values.

Curiously it is arguable that law provides the nearest equivalent to a separable and predictable (but certainly not measurable) element in political behaviour. Law provides a series of guidelines and constraints which normally will be followed and cannot be quickly changed, and which also have a *prima-facie* claim to moral respect. Often law is the most unchallengeable and determinate element in a policy decision, where all else are matters of opinion and guesswork. Still it must be admitted that law provides a very narrow and inadequate explanation of political behaviour as normally understood and that its traditional importance as a basis for political and especially administrative studies has declined, although remaining far more important in European countries than in Britain.

But to return to my main theme. An intellectual gulf exists between traditional political philosophy and modern political sociology. Partly this is the fault of philosophy for becoming too abstract, limited, linguistic, or purely historical. Partly it arises through the wish of empirical political science to eschew any kind of idealism and to concentrate upon discovering the facts of political behaviour. In itself this may be a healthy aspiration, the problem being to identify and order the relevant facts.

Political behaviouralism, using the phrase broadly to imply only a concentration upon explanations of behaviour, has many varieties. One interesting distinction, which mirrors age-old discussions about relations between individual and State, is between theories which explain political behaviour as an open-ended contest between separate elements (which may be individuals, groups, or organizations), and theories which derive behaviour from the properties of the political or social system as a whole. The former sphere includes group interest theories such as Bentley's and Truman's, some branches of organizational theory, and egoistic theories such as those of Tullock and Downs. These theories differ as to whether it is the individual, the formal organization, or the latent interest which is the effective unit of political competition and conflict, but in any event the State itself merely provides limited rules of arbitration.

The second batch of theories includes the Parsonian social system, the Eastonian political system, the input–output analysis of Almond and Coleman, and (more doubtfully) various system theories derived from biology or mathematics. These theories tend to describe political behaviour in terms of the requirements of the system as a whole; although system here has many meanings. It may be viewed as an abstracted element within a broader system (Parsons), as a unified system in its own right (Easton), or as a series of Chinese boxes.

Here one is not dealing directly with concrete systems or entities, but with abstracted systems; intellectual maps which purport to plot aspects of behaviour which are hard to detect unambiguously 'on the ground' and in some cases are even declared untraceable by the makers.

I cannot do justice here to these various theories, but would make three points. First, some of them can be viewed as no more than heuristic devices for investigating or organizing data, and the relationships which they posit may be of a purely logical and analytic kind. This might be said of Easton's original model, and of some models of political bargaining between groups or individuals. The theory in question is useful to the extent that it genuinely can help to abstract and explain meaningful aspects of political behaviour. The results have hardly been spectacular, but the method itself is respectable.

Secondly, though, many theorists are determined to unearth the 'real' sources of political power or the determinants of political action in some specified (if usually unobservable) location. This source is variously run to ground in some attempted definition of group interests, organizational needs, or the needs of some total system. No evidence, either of observation or introspection, convincingly supports these hypotheses which are curiously metaphysical. They stand witness to the continuing occupational temptation to conspiracy theories in politics.

But thirdly the line between fruitful empirical observation and an alleged social law is a subtle one. For example, Banfield contends that the policy decisions which he studied in Chicago arose from the maintenance and enhancement needs of large formal organizations. They were not caused by the efforts of politicians to win votes, by differences of ideology or group interest, or by the machinations of a power élite, although once someone had started an issue, other actors came on the scene. As Banfield himself says, this is only a limited theory about aspects of Chicago politics, it cannot be generalized; but as an insight into the political conditions in that city at a particular time, it could be broadly true and interesting.

And one might go further. I believe that the most fruitful approach to studying political behaviour is through examining the structure of influence. One must use hypotheses, but they should be empirical ones which relate the interplay of political roles within and between different kinds of organization. Within modern democracies, the most significant units of analysis seem to be large productive or service organizations (both public and private), political parties, and pressure groups. We have rather few studies of this kind for Britain as yet, but I believe that as they appear they will show that many conventional assumptions about the political process are erroneous.

I prefer this approach to the systems one because it is more realistic to build upwards than downwards. Viewed as a set of mutually supportive relations or functions, the concept of system has some utility. But one has to recognize that any hypothesized system tends to be too artificially bounded, too open-ended, and too unstable to be described very accurately, while the enormous variety of interpersonal and intergroup relations in political society cannot be plausibly explained as the resultant of 'system needs'. System theories are not necessarily dedicated to some assumption about equilibrium or stability, they can explore the conditions of change, they can recognize the number and diversity of system components. But it is hard for systems analysis to recognize the full diversity and spontaneity of political life, which a more empirical approach can recognize without difficulty. Also, in so far as there is a choice of ethical philosophies implicit in these sociological methods, between a belief in social determinism on the one hand and in rational individualism on the other (as I believe in fact there is), my preference is for the latter; but only because it accords with a sounder epistemology.

Political sociology and philosophy interact on the subject of values. Crude behaviouralism which ignores motivation completely is simply dumb, for there is nothing to explain (it can only be kept going through postulating some predetermined cause, as in Bentley's use of 'interest', thus rescuing hardheaded realism by metaphysics). Otherwise one is dealing with a system of reflecting mirrors. The sociologist describes the values which appear to be implicit in the behaviour he observes, but his outward gaze has to be guided by his own determinations of what is important or significant, subject to the checkpoint provided by the observations and interpretations of other sociologists. Conversely, the philosopher analyses principles or ideals in a largely introspective manner, but his conclusions have little interest unless they have some appeal as guides to political behaviour, and his checkpoint is the opinion of other reasoning men.

I mentioned that the puzzle of the relations between the individual and society is unsolved. The systems theorists who stress the 'integration' requirements of some total system differ from theorists of group or individual conflict in much the same kind of way as collectivist philosophic thinkers differ from individualist ones. One may suspect by now that the choice of approach is influenced by temperamental factors, but it remains empirically as well as ethically important.

Be this as it may, the assumption that political life consists simply of 'demands' or 'inputs', or of half-conscious impulses and responses, seems to me to have been carried unreasonably far. Admittedly the number of people who consciously reason about political values and ideals may be small, but values also exist implicitly in the rules and assumptions of political activity without being recognized as such by participants. The importance of such values is indeed explicitly recognized in sociological studies of political acculturation and socialization. One point of a philosophic statement of regulative ideals is to enable reflective men to debate the adequacy of the 'fit' between actual political institutions and those regulative ideals which appear to them to be intrinsically desirable and feasible. In this sense, political philosophy provides a practically limited but intellectually essential platform for the contemplation of political change. It is my contention that the operative ideals of modern democracy are urgently in need of reconsideration, as these relate to the enlarging sphere of government.

The administrative system

The administrative system is still a neglected aspect of politics, for several reasons. The political process, as normally defined, is bathed in publicity, and appears important and glamorous, whereas the administrative process is relatively obscure. It is in the interest of political leaders to exaggerate their control of policy decisions, and officials (in Britain at least) are not expected to contradict them. The public may suspect the deception, but political scientists have not yet helped out with more realistic accounts of the policy process. Public administration is a tough field of study; pretty inaccessible in European countries (not in the United States), very diverse and concrete, not susceptible to the quantitative kind of analysis used in electoral studies.

There is a subject called organization theory. But most of its material and its models are drawn from the activities of large business corporations. Administrative behaviour is actually and necessarily quite unlike that which occurs inside even I.C.I. or Shell. But the fact is hidden by what I would call the efficiency fallacy. True enough, some methods of business efficiency are applicable inside the government, but the goals of government are much more diverse and far-ranging, methods of decision-making and resource allocation are very different, and concepts of efficiency have to be related to these conditions. For example, while Drucker tells us that the first rule of business is market innovation, the government equivalent could be said to be market compression; keeping the totality of public demands within some acceptable global sum. This is too simple no doubt, but perhaps it is suggestive.

Administrative theories and politics are still the Cinderella both of political science and organization theories. I have attempted elsewhere to remedy this deficiency a little.

The modern democratic State is, of course, not at all the towering monolith pictured by Spencer and by many contemporary exponents of political protest. On the other hand it is not a welfare state either, if that concept implies a high measure of egalitarianism or close attention to the needs of the unfortunate. A government which did much less in general could achieve (if it wished) much more in these respects.

The term 'administrative state' is fairly neutral, and helps to draw our attention to certain points. First, government consists of a great number of agencies performing diverse tasks. The system is pluralist in the sense that each agency has some (though varying) autonomy, and that their respective policies are frequently conflicting or contradictory. Some reasons for this situation are:

(a) Inconsistent political demands become routinized and frozen in administrative action. Often the inconsistency is unforeseen, sometimes it can be deliberate. For example, the Government has offered £50 million to mineral companies to explore for deposits in remote (and consequently beautiful) parts of Britain, but is simultaneously trying to channel funds to amenity societies who will fight to the death these same companies; or again, local authorities usually lead the fights against development proposals by public corporations or government departments.

(b) Each agency must to some extent adjust its activities to specific sources of support and opposition. For example the Department of Trade and Industry has to persuade or coerce determinate individuals (industrialists) on behalf of a latent clientele (the unemployed in development areas); it must strike a workable balance between the two groups.

(c) Each agency is influenced not only by its history, organization, and balance of tasks but also by its professional resources. An agency always becomes more confident or aggressive when to departmental interest is added strong professional interest and training. British examples are difficult to name, but agencies dominated by engineers or architects are often of this kind. The results may be good as well as bad; this depends on the desirability of the goals, and the breadth and competence of the training. The U.S. Army Corps of Engineers is the stock warning to quote of narrowly partisan behaviour, but dedicated and even dogmatic forestry or conservation services in any country are frequently admired.

The opposite fact to administrative pluralism is administrative co-ordination. This is a very curious phenomenon indeed. The whole of the system is linked together in multiple ways, both vertically (i.e. between different geographical or hierarchical levels) and also horizontally (for example, between parallel agencies or departments). So much so that it becomes exceedingly difficult to define organization within government at all realistically, or to plot the system at all accurately. Perhaps we can identify Millett's basic work units: for example in individual schools, hospitals, crime squads, or State forests. But the work unit is buried, so to say, beneath a heavy superstructure of organizational co-ordination.

This integrative framework results from two basic factors: first the unifying features of modern politics which administration must mirror; secondly the centralization of financial resources which has occurred for a mixture of political and technical reasons. The two modes of co-ordination are policy control and resource control. The logic of these processes often differs. Thus resource planning theoretically works systematically from the top downwards and up again, while policy planning works outwards more indeterminately but intensively from analysis of some policy problem. The present fashion in co-ordination is heavily biased towards resource planning. Sir Richard Clarke's new book represents this as the main rationale for recent government reorganization; it is also interestingly the rationale for parliamentary reorganization of select committees; it is the rationale too of such techniques as P.P.B.S. But I believe that there are strict limitations to the possibilities of rational resource planning in government, that business analogies and economic theorizing have unduly raised expectations, and that in some respects these trends are inimical to effective forms of policy analysis and co-ordination. But I cannot pursue this theme here.

Administrative pluralism and integration are continually in conflict or tension. Political forces pull both ways, financial ones favour integration. Professional forces tend to favour vertical integration (so as to strengthen specialization and career ladders) but horizontal division (so as to emphasize the distinctive nature of the profession). But there are also gropings towards more broadly based professions: for example in physical planning,

social services, health. They face formidable difficulties. Administrative co-ordination is not the same as integrated planning,
although the two seem often to be confused. Co-ordination of
itself cannot produce positive results *unless* there is a parallel
movement of unifying goals (based on a common 'appreciative
judgement' in Sir Geoffrey Vickers's sense) and of professional
techniques. An enormous load of administrative effort is ex-
pended, rightly or wrongly, upon making marginal adjustments
to decisions up and down the system, and upon maintaining at
least the formal appearances of consistent action.

Whether all this effort is well spent seems to me very questionable indeed. As already said, administrative co-ordination is
partly the product of political pressures; of the need of any government to appear 'to speak with one mind', or to be able to
assure questioners that 'national' considerations have been fully
borne in mind in some local decisions; but in addition administrators then acquire an interest of their own in further developing the refinements of the system.

It is true that an 'unco-ordinated' system can exact a very
heavy price through duplication of public services, conflict of
goals, etc.; and from this standpoint the stress placed upon the
desirability of administrative co-ordination (and the wickedness
of non-co-ordination) in British and European systems is doubtless well placed. But we should look much more closely at the
meanings of administrative co-ordination; where it stands for a
lengthy process of minor adjustments which are intended to (but
usually cannot) remedy the contradictions or ambiguities of the
political process, there may not be a lot to say for it. The problem
here is that the administrative implications and costs of political
behaviour are so little understood or considered.

Modern democratic theories

How do these features of the administrative state correspond to
modern theories of democracy? Not very easily or obviously
perhaps. Ideas about democratic *legitimacy* are subtly changing.
Twenty years or so ago, typical British opinion (if one may dare
use that phrase) accepted the right of duly elected political leaders
to make all policy decisions of importance, subject of course to

rights of criticism and eventual dismissal at the polls. But today pluralism (the right of organized groups to contribute to public decisions) has gained greater legitimacy although its limits are vague.

More significantly, perhaps, there is an increase of populism : meaning by this the rights of citizens to have their preferences considered over particular issues. The classic forms of populism (the referendum and recall, for example, or annual parliaments) have not, it is true, much currency. But there is a new stress upon rights of consultation or participation (the distinction is hazy), as in the Skeffington Report on town planning. Then again, officials are becoming more concerned with the direct ascertainment of the wishes of administrative consumers or clients, either for their intrinsic relevance or as a check upon the claims of organized groups. These wishes can be inspected through the relatively straightforward methods of social surveys and opinion polls, or via the esoteric mysteries of cost-benefit analysis.

There is a fashionable theory of democracy which may be called the new Utilitarianism. Espoused particularly by such American writers as Downs, Tullock, and Buchanan, the doctrine is rooted in the thought of Bentham and of classical economics. It assumes rationalism and egoism, for example, that the individual will consult his own interests, order his preferences rationally, and act accordingly. Political parties are assumed, for example in Downs's *Economic Theory of Democracy*, to be concerned primarily with maximizing their support, so that they will endeavour to please the greatest possible number of voters on the greatest possible number of issues. Public agencies, by an extension of this approach, could be assumed to try to maximize their support, and thus also their funds and their size. My earlier description of *one* factor in administrative pluralism here would become the dominant explanation : for example the Department of Trade and Industry must seek to minimize its nuisance to industrialists while maximizing satisfactions to the unemployed. In a subtle variant it might, of course, concentrate upon pleasing the industrialists as an administrative bulwark against more radical measures, although this conservative ploy would only work if the few industrialists were more powerful than the many unemployed; a possible situation.

All this is a market theory of politics. Voters are consumers, public agencies are firms, parties are a species of merchant bankers mobilizing and distributing resources. Whether intended as description or prescription (like classical economics it seems to be both), these theories are much cruder than their economic equivalents. For example, the economic consumer balances his outlay among a variety of goods but the political consumer must concentrate a variety of purposes into single acts such as voting. If one attempts to ascertain in more sophisticated ways the detailed preferences of citizens, one is up against all the questions about relevance of interests, intensity of demands, and rules of distribution which seem to block any plausible summation of the results. The attempt can be made, but as the work of the Roskill Commission perhaps showed, there is no sure way of identifying relevant interests, very much less so of measuring and aggregating them. And while the atomistic subdivision of the individual's interests may be helpful up to a point, it must reckon with the biologically unified responses of single individuals; which are apt to surprise the atomistic analysts.

It would seem that, imperfect as they are, economic markets are still much more accurate than political markets. None the less, according to W. J. Mackenzie, the results of the economic market proved so deplorable (at least in the 1930s) that some economists preferred to try to resurrect, within the more intractable conditions of political activity, the kind of welfare calculus which had eluded them in their natural home. But I cannot follow this fascinating question further.

Skipping the logical problems of the new Utilitarianism, I must say a word about its ethics. Rationalism is often deplored on the Graham Wallas argument that political behaviour is largely irrational, but the objection is not a good one. Democracy surely presupposes *some* capacity for rational reflection and the need to encourage it, for after all if the individual cannot order his own preferences, who is to do it for him? David Butler wonders at the unrealistically rationalist style in which elections are still conducted, but this style is the now reduced tribute that vice pays to virtue, and at least serves to *encourage* rational behaviour.

But egoism is another matter. Egoism may seem refreshingly realistic and free of the alleged cant that politics is about ideals.

Sociologically this is not true because of the influence of group loyalties and mores. Still, the mixture of egoist and rationalist assumptions can have limited explanatory force in certain situations; as in the theory of games applied to voting in committee or to international conflicts. And it may also be claimed to be a valid prescription: why should the individual not vote for his own interest as he understands it?

Unfortunately a thoroughgoing egoism would seem to make the machinery of modern government pretty unworkable. The new Utilitarians themselves have demonstrated this point in their discussion of bureaucracy. Thus Gordon Tullock contends that there is no feasible way of securing the compliance of officials with organizational objectives in the face of conflicting individual interests. For example, he claims that the emissaries of the U.S. State Department are supposed to influence foreigners but that it pays them much better to influence Americans. Downs gives an alarming picture of the egoistic roots of bureaucratic expansion, and the attractions to various agencies of climbers, conservatives, zealots, and other species of individual: some of whom, admittedly, are not wholly egoistic. There are echoes here of Parkinson's law, Peter's principle, and many other simplified bureaucratic laws. Such plausibility as these theories possess, and it sometimes seems to be considerable, must be derived from constant individual reactions to different institutional situations, as in theories of economic man. But the plausibility is limited, cultural factors are ignored, and the postulates or axioms remain a curious mixture of dubious psychology and ethics; as perhaps in the old Utilitarians.

The public interest

Lacking in these theories is an adequate concept of public interest. Now interests are not the same as wants. As Barry points out, a solicitor can look after my interests perfectly well without knowing much about my personal wants or preferences. In an extended way the State can be conceived as meeting the interests of its citizens through maintaining minimal conditions for a tolerable existence. How far it should go further and offer educational, cultural, and recreational opportunities contributive to individual development or 'the good life' is matter for argument. I believe that it should, but time is lacking to explore the issue.

Public interest differs from any summation of private interests through implying rules of generality, impartiality, reciprocity. Generality is hard to state. It cannot be that an interest is more 'public' just because it is more widely shared, because intensity of need is also important. Everyone requires good roads, but the interest of a minority in finding work may be just as important. Public interest is often rightly distinguished from special interests, but the interest of a special group (say of very underpaid workers) may on occasion rightly prevail over the broader interests of consumers or taxpayers. Sometimes a true general public is said to consist of a category of indeterminate individuals. It was on this basis that Hayek drew his famous distinction between legitimate general laws, which are directed towards no particular individual or firm, and discriminating actions whose use paves 'the road to serfdom'. The distinction has value, and probably is right where individuals are concerned, but not in relation to large firms or organizations.

The principles of impartiability and of reciprocity of rights and duties are implicit in the values of democracy as described by Sir Karl Popper and by Benn and Peters. The notion of 'reasonableness' which is a necessary part of democracy implies that I will concede to others in similar situations any claim made for myself, listen to arguments, recognize a diversity of interests, etc. The citizen then is logically required, if he is a reasonable being, to modify his egoism by reference to these principles. This modest doctrine is poles apart from another alternative to Utilitarianism that is often advanced, namely that special or exclusive weight should be put upon the ideals advanced by individuals in contrast to their wants. The imposition of ideals upon society, on the premise that they are other-regarding, can be tyrannous. By contrast the notion of public interest here preferred remains based in rational individualism.

But this argument cannot overcome the fact that public interest necessarily has many aspects. Consider a central area redevelopment by a local authority. The valuers' department wants the scheme to be profitable, the highways and housing departments want land for their purposes on favourable terms, the architects' department wants an aesthetic design, the planning department wants a variety of shops and pedestrianization, and so on. All these views can be traced back to interests: ratepayers', the underhoused, motorists, shoppers, etc. Can any view express the interest of the whole citizen or community? All that can be done is to weigh up these claims in terms of their breadth, intensity, and relevance to the project; to consider alternative opportunities for their realization or compensation; and to try to harmonize on the ground in design terms those claims finally accepted as relevant and legitimate (for example, through a plan).

For these reasons public interest must primarily be a procedural rather than substantive concept. It refers to a series of relevant principles and procedures, for example, that all relevant interests were considered fairly, that channels for their expression were open, that decision-makers were sensitive to concepts of impartiality and reciprocity, etc. Beyond this public interest is only an always arguable principle of harmony between *relevant* interests.

Democracy cannot be adequately defined as a device for aggregating interests through majoritarian or other rules. Rather does it imply a series of institutional balances whereby the notion of public interest is successively articulated and adapted. The numerical superiority of the electorate is balanced against the greater concern and involvement of elected representatives; the democratic legitimacy of these representatives is balanced against the professional legitimacy (for example, superior knowledge) of officials; centralized is balanced against localized decision-making; and generalized decision-making (for example, in Cabinet or Treasury) against specialized (for example, in particular organs concerned with agriculture and education). Reverting to the redevelopment scheme, the local authority departments are controlled by council committees, themselves controlled in various ways by central departments and ultimately by ministers, while professional bodies, voluntary organizations, etc., jump on and off the sidelines.

All this looks like a simple endorsement of pluralism, and of the Braybrooke–Lindblom theory that public policy should proceed by small changes and on the basis of mutual adjustment between conflicting interests. But this is not so. In terms of the structure of power and influence, modern systems *are* pluralist and I have accepted that democratic theory endorses some of the procedural principles that underlie pluralism, at least as it works in Britain. But pluralism is an elastic concept. It is also possible to inquire into the weak points of the system: points of social tension or of ethical doubt. I can only indicate briefly the grave problems of this kind which I believe to exist.

The comprehensive state

Much as government already does, it seemingly needs to do a great deal more. For one thing labour will need to shift from the manufacturing sector where productivity is rapidly rising to the labour-intensive social and personal services; additionally it can be claimed that public social services are 'underdeveloped' in terms of their due contribution to social welfare and justice. Given possible developments in medical science, the scope for fruitful, some would say essential, growth of the health service is enormous. Then again, the serious varieties of pollution which increasingly afflict human health and natural resources call inescapably for more stringent, broad-based measures of public regulation.

One cannot build too much on any list. But my belief is that we have completely to reverse Spencer's thesis. In other words the political and administrative order must be viewed as comprehensive not minimal in its coverage of the requirements of a civilized and just society. I am well aware of the dangers of tyranny and totalitarianism thus conjured up. But these results are not a function of the *extent* of the State's concerns, but of its aims and methods. In pluralistic societies, the greater danger may be that citizens will not provide government with sufficient inputs of support, in terms of finance, interest, co-operation, participation, and aid with law enforcement, to sustain the necessary framework of collective action. A resurgence of the practice and teaching of civics could also prove the best defence against the undoubted latent dangers of tyranny.

This view may seem naïve, and undoubtedly requires qualifications as well as elaboration. For example, a likely result of administrative pluralism is that a government agency may itself contribute to the very problems that collective action is required to rectify. Officials in Britain are generally disinterested but they are not always wise and they may be over-influenced by special interests. An example might be official encouragement for the use of certain artificial fertilizers, which can now be seen to have led to short-sighted farming practices and considerable pollution of rivers.

Then again, too little attention is given to the possibilities of removing and reshaping old functions of government as new ones are added. Administrative activity has accumulated over time in the manner of successive layers of geological deposits, but the attention of politicians and even top officials is almost exclusively directed towards the top of the heap. Possibly systematic inquiries of this kind would do more for general efficiency and economy than the other methods currently in vogue.

The present workings of the political process hardly enlarge the understanding of the citizen or draw attention to his responsibilities. In Britain the revolving of party and electoral politics around the key issue of the management of the economy is both restrictive and curious when actual performance is considered. A sophisticated view might contend that other major issues (such as health, education, the environment, or scientific development) are better handled through the specialized circles of opinion which in a pluralist system increasingly proliferate. Still, the citizens' view of what government involves is grievously narrowed save where he has specialized knowledge, a situation which cannot help towards obtaining adequate inputs of public support for laws and services.

Political parties often promise to enlarge the rights of citizens but rarely mention their duties; which was a danger of democracy known to Aristotle. Given the load of public action, it may well be desirable to bring its implications more closely and directly home to those affected. One example is finance. Given again the strong case for more expenditure on some public services and the resistance to this offered by general taxpayers, the case for more direct charges for public services becomes a very strong one. Now that so many services are available to all citizens, this policy is in fact quite compatible with measures (if such be desirable) to achieve greater equality of incomes; although one must admit that each particular adjustment changes the political starting-line for further change. Again the appropriate treatment for an indirect cost imposed by one citizen upon others is surely to charge the offender. Although I would be the first to argue that the calculation can only be notional, rough justice in such cases need hardly matter if the offence is serious. Then again, the modern practice of continually compensating citizens or firms for complying with standards which have been publicly agreed is surely both financially wasteful and injurious to civic spirit, as, for example, in the case of the clean-air regulations in Britain.

The applications of this same approach to administration are too diverse to explore here. In general it would favour greater decentralization so as to fix responsibilities more closely and clearly. Some degree of central supervision, some measure of professional specialization, some fraction of possible economies of scale would have to be sacrificed for this purpose. But it is curious how those who deplore the remoteness and complications of administrative action seem reluctant to draw the obvious conclusions; and curious too that a Reith lecturer should be prophesying the end of the centre-periphery type of organization when the modern State provides such gigantic examples to the contrary.

Finally the most crucial of the institutional balances described as implicit in modern democracy is that between the politician and the career official. The effective fusion of these contributions is now more important and difficult because of the increased knowledge and experience necessary to policymaking; and in this respect government certainly suffers by comparison with the integrated management pattern of business. Some government systems try to meet this problem through the use of hybrid types, not wholly successfully. The American political executive integrates policy skills with administrative experience, but lowers the quality and initiative of the civil service. The French high officials achieve a comparable fusion of skills within a bureaucratic framework, but their lack of political legitimacy certainly contributes to the detached 'politics of protest' that is a feature of French society; and that is probably growing in Britain.

The ancient partnership of non-specialized ministers and generalized administrators is wearing thin in Britain. Since in this country the differentiation of politicians and officials seems likely to continue, and can be conceded to have many advantages, the way ahead is to focus the energies of both these partners more effectively upon basic policy issues. Surely there should be more British politicians (at present there are only a handful in each case) who have a reasonably adequate grasp of the problems of environmental pollution or town planning or scientific research? To realize this modest aim calls for ladders of political advancement which depend less closely upon the M.P.'s utility to his party within a very generalized and combative political arena. If there were a distinctive legislative career ladder, so that it was really worthwhile for the M.P. to become expert in Select Committee work, this aim would have more chance of realization. There are obvious dangers of futile conflict between ministers and committees, but the division need not be taken to American lengths. Alternatively, perhaps preferably, parties must change their perception of their own policymaking requirements so as to encourage and accommodate the greater depth of relevant knowledge within their ranks. Within the Civil Service the same aim calls for replacing the old distinction between narrow specialist and very broad generalist with intermediate fusions of scale and experience of a broad-based professional type.

These are broad, lightly sketched reforms to end on. I intend them more as suggestions than dogmas, yet I am sure that they refer to serious deficiencies in the fit between a viable system of democracy and modern government institutions. Spencer's thesis has been reversed and the pluralist administrative state will continue to grow. But how are we to work it democratically and well?

I end this discussion with a brief reference to the traditions of the L.S.E. Sidney Webb was always convinced that the completely unfettered pursuit of social knowledge would uphold the desirability of Fabian Socialism. In itself this view is mistaken or at any rate utopian, as the substantial contribution of many eminent teachers in the L.S.E. to policy conclusions of a different kind demonstrates

In other ways, though, the beliefs of the founders of the L.S.E. have been justified. One such was their strong interest in the study of administration, a tradition carried on by the many contributions of my eminent predecessor William Robson, the L.S.E.'s first Professor of Public Administration. Contemplating the scale and character of the administrative activities it is surely now obvious that what may be called administrative politics constitutes a very large part indeed of the total political process.

But additionally, I suggest that the nature of modern administration prompts questions about the meaning of democracy which are too rarely asked. The need for democratic concepts and devices which can adequately *sustain*, and not merely *criticize*, the requisite degree of collective action would certainly be apparent to the Fabian founders of the L.S.E. And in viewing the growth of the State, not with anger or incomprehension, but with what Morris Finer termed an ironic sympathy, I am also carrying on these older traditions.

REFERENCES

Introduction

HAYEK, F. A., *The Constitution of Liberty* (London: Routledge, 1960).
SPENCER, Herbert, *The Man versus the State* (London, 1884; new edition, ed. D. MacRae, Penguin Books, 1969).

Political Science

ALMOND, G. A., and COLEMAN, J. S. (eds.), *The Politics of the Developing Areas* (Princeton N.J.: Princeton University Press, 1960).
BANFIELD, E. C., *Political Influence* (London: Free Press, 1965).
BARRY, Brian, *Political Argument* (London: Routledge, 1965).
BASSET, Reginald, *The Essentials of Parliamentary Democracy* (London: Macmillan, 1935; new edition, Cass, 1964).
BENN, S. I., and PETERS, R. S., *Social Principles and the Democratic State* (London: Allen & Unwin, 1959).
BENTLEY, A. F., *The Process of Government* (Chicago: University of Chicago Press, 1908).
EASTON, David, *The Political System* (New York: Knopf, 1953).
GREAVES, H. R. G., *The Foundations of Political Theory* (London: Allen and Unwin, 1958; 2nd edition, Bell, 1966).
LASKI, Harold, *A Grammar of Politics* (London: Allan & Unwin, 1925; 4th edition, 1938).
PARSONS, Talcott, *The Social System* (London: Tavistock, 1952; new edition, Routledge, 1970).
TRUMAN, David, *The Governmental Process* (New York: Knopf, 1951).
WALLAS, Graham, *Human Nature in Politics* (London: 4th edition, Constable, 1948).
WELDON, T. H., *The Vocabulary of Politics* (London: Penguin Books, 1953).

The Administrative System

CLARKE, Sir Richard, *New Trends in Government* (London: H.M.S.O., 1971).
DRUCKER, Peter, *The Practice of Management* (London: Heinemann, 1955; new edition, Pan Books, 1968).

MILLETT, John D., *Organisation for the Public Service* (Princeton N.J.: Van Nostrand, 1966).

SELF, Peter, *Administrative Theories and Politics* (London: Allen & Unwin, 1972).

VICKERS, Sir Geoffrey, *The Art of Judgment* (London: Chapman & Hall, 1965; new edition, Methuen, 1968).

Modern Democratic Theories

BUCHANAN, J. M., and TULLOCK, C., *The Calculus of Consent* (Ann Arbor: University of Michigan Press, 1962).

BUTLER, D. E., *The Study of Political Behaviour* (London: Hutchinson, new edition, 1966).

COMMITTEE ON PUBLIC PARTICIPATION IN PLANNING, *People and Planning* (London: H.M.S.O., 1969).

DOWNS, Anthony, *An Economic Theory of Democracy* (New York: Harper, 1957).

—— *Inside Bureaucracy* (Boston: Little, Brown, 1967).

MACKENZIE, W. J. M., *Politics and Social Science* (London: Penguin Books, 1967).

PARKINSON, C. N., *Parkinson's Law* (London: Murray, 1958; Penguin Books, 1970).

PETER, L. J., and HULL, R., *The Peter Principle* (London: Souvenir Press, 1969; Pan Books, 1971).

ROSKILL REPORT, *Report of the Commission on the Third London Airport* (London: H.M.S.O., 1971).

TULLOCK, Gordon, *The Politcs of Bureacracy* (Washington D.C.: Public Affairs Press, 1965).

The Public Interest

BRAYBROOKE, D., and LINDBLOM, C., *A Strategy of Decision* (New York, Free Press, 1963).

HAYEK, F. A., *The Road to Serfdom* (London: Routledge, 1944).

The Comprehensive State

SCHON, Donald A., *Beyond the Stable State* (London: Temple Smith, 1971).

CONFLICT AND CO-OPERATION

G. L. GOODWIN

G. L. GOODWIN

B.Sc. (Econ.)

*Montague Burton Professor
of International Relations
The London School of Economics
and Political Science*

Educated at Marlborough College; the Royal Military College, Sandhurst; L.S.E. Regular Army officer 1936–43 (the Suffolk Regiment; Army Physical Training Staff; Combined Operations; major commanding Independent Company, **Gibraltar). Foreign Office, 1945–8. L.S.E. 1948– ; Principal, St. Catharine's, Windsor Great Park; Commissioner on International Affairs, World Council of Churches.** Publications include *Britain and the United Nations; The University Teaching of International Relations* (editor); articles in *International Affairs, International Organisation; Political Studies,* etc.

CONFLICT AND
CO-OPERATION

The School has grown up in what our late colleague, Frank Chambers, once aptly called 'This Age of Conflict'. It would have been surprising, therefore, if it had not, from the outset, paid heed to that particularly intractable social problem, the problem of war, and to means of alleviating its incidence through such devices for international co-operation as the League of Nations and the United Nations Organization. In fact, the study of conflict and co-operation at the international level, the study of relations, that is, between sovereign states and peoples, whether from the political, legal, historical, or economic point of view, has been an integral part of the developing intellectual life of the L.S.E. from its earliest days. Lowes Dickinson, author of that seminal work *The International Anarchy*, published in 1926, was an occasional lecturer in political science from as early as 1896 until 1920; Paul Mantoux, author of several major works bearing on relations between states, and later a distinguished Co-Director of the Graduate Institute of International Studies in Geneva, held the Chair in French History and Institutions from 1912 to 1914; Graham Wallas, in his *The Great Society*, helped to illuminate the springs of the external behaviour of states. Above all, I believe that it was while he was Lecturer in International Law at the School that Oppenheim, in 1905–6, published volumes I and II of the first edition of his famous treatise on international law.

What might be called international studies was therefore well established from an early date in the L.S.E.'s history. The academic subject of international relations did not take root, however, until 1924 when, for five years only in the first instance and then only on a part-time basis, there was instituted the Sir Ernest Cassell

Chair of International Relations. Philip Noel Baker was the first occupant.

This was not the first chair in the subject in this country. The first was the Wilson Chair of International Politics, created at Aberystwyth through the generosity of the Davies family. The institution of both these chairs and the terms of their endowment reflected the widespread sense of revulsion at the long-drawn-out bloodletting of the First World War. This monstrous outrage against humanity, which seemed to have burst on a world habituated to peace, instilled in many of the finest minds of the generation that survived in this country the deep sense, so poignantly expressed by Wilfred Owen, of 'the pity of war, the pity war distilled' and imbued them with a determination to do what they could, in the words later to be found in the Charter, to 'save succeeding generations from the scourge of war'. This determination was often matched by a deep-rooted scepticism (not shared, one should add, at the official level) about the capacity of traditional practices and institutions (such as the balance of power or the Concert system) to form a secure basis for the future international order, and an often rather facile optimism about the capacity of new institutions such as the League of Nations and the International Labour Organization to refashion the world along more co-operative lines. It was an optimism which stemmed from the almost unquestioned assumption of the solidarity, or at least the potential solidarity, of the states comprising international society. This in turn reflected a view of man, collective as well as individual man, as essentially peace-loving, a view which encouraged the belief that whatever propensity he had to conflict could be curbed by appropriate institutional improvements.

These beliefs were fortified by the widespread conviction that Europe was still the centre of the diplomatic scene; that the diplomatic world was still 'Europe and its periphery' and that Britain's leadership could be decisive not only in shaping European attitudes, but also in influencing for good the general course of world events. Moreover, as democracy came to replace despotic and dynastic regimes, and 'open covenants, openly arrived at' came to replace the intrigues of secret diplomacy, so the peace-loving voice of the common man would come to be more effectively heard. Physical force, it was true, was recognized to be lurking in the background, but it was the force of public opinion which was widely expected to serve as the most reliable, and not merely the only available, sanction behind the Covenant's security system. Consequently, it was the responsibility of the academic world, so Charles Webster claimed in his inaugural lecture at Aberystwyth, to ensure that young men and women were trained to become not just 'citizens of democratic communities' but also 'members of the community of nations'; the 'whole mass of the people' had indeed to be 'informed of the nature of the world in which they live and [of] the countless ties which bind all the nations together.' (1)

Philip Noel Baker shared and, indeed, in his writings vividly reflected this approach to world problems. He was, and happily is, a scholar with an acute and searching mind, as his books on the *Geneva Protocol* and *The Juridical Status of the British Dominions in International Law* witness. But much of his energy and skill, both then and since, were devoted to rallying support for the institutions of the League of Nations which he claimed in 1926 provided 'a sound foundation upon which international co-operation can in the future be built up'. Nor, at the time, did this seem altogether too bold a claim. The League was firmly established. The League Council meeting in Geneva brought together the leading world statesmen, from both victors and vanquished, while at the Café Bavaria on the other side of Lac Léman Briand, Austen Chamberlain, and Stresemann foregathered in an atmosphere of cordiality which suggested that old animosities had been finally set to rest. In such a world the regulation and limitation of armaments no longer seemed altogether an ideal dream, so that when in a more prophetic vein Noel Baker alerted the public to the threat from the private manufacturers and traders in arms (*The Hawkers of Death*) and through his 1926 study on *Disarmament*, to the possible future perils of air bombardment and the dire need for a 'world-wide scheme for reduction and limitation of armaments', he had a ready and attentive audience.

Noel Baker brought to his work the political experience he had gained at the Paris Peace Conference as secretary to Lord Robert Cecil as well as the zest of the political reformer. (He was later to become, in 1929, a Labour M.P. and Parliamentary Private

Secretary to Arthur Henderson, Foreign Secretary in the second Labour government.) His invigorating influence was such as to lead to a marked growth of interest within the L.S.E. in international studies. A Stevenson Chair in International History was created in 1926 (the first holder was Arnold Toynbee), a distinct Department of International Studies formed in 1927 'having a unity of its own, though closely in touch with all the rest of the School', and a full-time Chair of International Law established the same year.

The 1930s were far more turbulent than the 1920s. They were to witness the successful challenge to the Versailles settlement by the revisionist powers (Germany, Japan, and Italy), the virtual demise of the League, the near collapse of the world economy with the advent of the Great Depression, and the coming of a Second World War even more damaging than the first. At the L.S.E., however, it was a period in which the academic study of international relations became firmly established. Two major developments occurred in 1930. The first was the appointment of Charles Manning to succeed Noel Baker to the Chair of International Relations, now put on a full-time basis. Manning had been Personal Assistant to Sir Eric Drummond, the first Secretary-General of the League of Nations, and later in the diplomatic division of the International Labour Office. The second was the institution of international relations, in conjunction with international law, as a special subject within the B.Sc. (Econ.). Now for the first time international relations emerged as an academic subject with a distinctive focus of its own. This did not portend a weakening of its links with cognate disciplines such as international law or economics, links which were incidentally a valuable check on a growing tendency towards the fragmentation of knowledge within the universe of the social sciences. On the contrary, Manning's own legal background and, for instance, S. H. Bailey's concern with the political as well as the economic aspects of international relations, brought some strengthening of these links, while conversely international lawyers and economists (particularly Hersch Lauterpacht and Lionel Robbins) were making major contributions respectively to the study of the legal and economic aspects of international relations.

But it did greatly contribute to the identification and

development of a 'hard core' of the subject, namely, the study of the relations between states in an international society characterized by the absence of government.

This was in contrast to the view taken at Oxford by Sir Alfred Zimmern where international relations was seen as 'not a single self-contained subject or study, but a whole bundle of subjects— like a faggot held together by a string'. Manning, on the contrary, argued that there was a unitary concern which gave the subject unity and focus: 'every one of us lives in an environment in which there flows past him the stream of history, a totality of social phenomena which hardly one person in a thousand makes a serious attempt to understand. To this totality of phenomena there are diverse aspects, of these aspects, international relations are one.' Nor was he too troubled by difficulties of definition.

It is no doubt very hard to say what exactly are international relations – or industrial relations, or business relations, or matrimonial relations, or domestic relations. We nevertheless do, if vaguely, know what we mean by international relations, and what we mean by saying we do not understand them.

The starting point for the teacher was then to do

what he can do to assist the student who is seeking after a clearer vision, a less muddled, a better focussed, a less colourblind, a less blindfolded outlook upon that aspect of the social stream of things which I will call international. The point [he went on to stress] is not that this is a bundle of studies. It is a single study, for it is a single urge which we are trying to satisfy [even if] the light for the student must be sought from an infinite variety of sources (2).

It was this recognition and affirmation of international relations as a discipline with a unity and focus of its own that was to be one of Manning's, and the L.S.E.'s most lasting contributions to the development of the subject.

It was, it should be stressed, a subject of which international history formed an integral part. Charles, later Sir Charles, Webster, the first holder of the Stevenson Chair created in 1932, brought to the subject great practical experience (as a participant, for instance, at the Paris Peace Conference), a keen interest in contemporary international diplomacy and organization, and a diplomatic historian's fervent dislike of the sociological patterns of history woven by his predecessor Arnold Toynbee, who had now made his abode at Chatham House as the Stevenson Research Professor of International History. Webster was a devoted and distinguished scholar and an inspiring teacher, who could begin a lecture with a remark such as 'I'll now talk of a clause which I got into the Treaty of Versailles', or enliven a particularly dreary period of nineteenth-century diplomatic history with witty but illuminating anecdotes of 'boudoir diplomacy'.

He and Charles Manning together helped during the 1930s to consolidate the standing of international relations at the School and to secure wider recognition through, for instance, the International Studies Conference of its claims for recognition as a proper subject for undergraduate study. They did not always see eye to eye on how the subject could best be developed or on the stance to be adopted on the burning issues of the day. Manning's penchant for drawing fine distinctions was not always to Webster's or others' taste. Yet Manning was in good company, and was fond of quoting Lord Balfour's reply to a similar charge. 'I am told', Balfour said, 'people complain that I am given to drawing fine distinctions. I am. High policy depends upon fine distinctions; and, if people find they cannot understand them, they should entrust their affairs to those who do' (3). On the whole, however, Manning's more philosophical and analytical approach, the Wittgenstein of international relations, a colleague once called him, neatly complemented Webster's solidly based diplomatic history; and both were keenly sensitive to young people's desire to find their bearings in the increasingly complex and threatening world of the 1930s, a world in which optimism about a future co-operative world order steadily gave way to apprehension about an impending world conflict of possibly untold disaster.

Charles Manning was by all accounts something of a sceptic in his attitude towards the League of Nations upon which in the early 1930s so many hopes for a more co-operative world order still rested and he was particularly alert to the difficulties of combining the collective security system of the League, which tended to reinforce the *status quo*, with the need for 'peaceful change'. Yet his scepticism was accompanied by the conviction that international society was far from constituting an international anarchy; that the elements of order to be found in it were neither as fragile nor as precarious as the newly emerging school of 'realists' were apt to make out; and that in a real sense the society of states, though lacking any over-all system of government, did constitute a quasi-community; indeed, he held out the hope, both then and since, that 'some day there . . . may yet be seen the true *Gemeinschaft* of all the human race'. His contribution to the subject attracted a generous offer for the partial endowment of the chair from Sir Montague Burton, who desired thereby 'to further international peace in accordance with the ideals of the Covenant of the League of Nations.' From 1935, the chair became known as the Montague Burton chair of International Relations.

The next decade was first one of consolidation and then of disruption with the advent of the Second World War. But the coming of peace in 1945 marked the start of a period of steady if modest expansion. It was a world very different from that of the early 1920s. The catastrophe of the First World War had been widely ascribed to the breakdown of the traditional diplomatic methods of the previous era. The combatants, it was often said, had tumbled into that war almost by accident. The League would not only prevent that happening again by providing procedures and machinery which could effectively restrain the more bellicose instincts of men; it could also usher in a new era of friendly co-operation between essentially peace-loving democratic states. By 1945, in contrast, international politics of a peculiarly ruthless character had prevailed undisguised for over a decade. Nor did victory bring the tranquillity of the 1920s. For although in many ways, especially technologically, the world has since 1945 become more of 'an interconnected whole and not a mere agglomeration of state units' (3) one major technological innovation, the advent of nuclear weapons, has put into man's hands the means of his self-destruction. Nor has a more closely knit world (as a result of advances, for instance, in the realm of communications) proved a more co-operative world; on the contrary, as in the past, the more contact there is between peoples the more potentialities for friction seem to exist. What the world has needed is not better communications, but more effective shock-absorbers for preventing conflict from spreading. The network of specialized agencies, from the World Health Organization to the

International Civil Aviation Organization, has testified to the greater awareness of the need for modalities of co-operation which could enable states better to meet their daily responsibilities. Yet in practice they have tended to strengthen rather than to erode the sovereignty of their member states (by making it less of an anachronism than it might otherwise be) and they have consequently done little to bring nearer that collaborative world order upon which the early functionalists pinned their hopes.

Moreover, even though technologically the world may have become increasingly one, the collapse of the 'Armed Concert' of Great Powers (which in 1945 was seen as the nub of the future world order) and the demise of Western European overseas empires has made for a degree of political, cultural, and ideological fragmentation which has complicated, if not actively impeded, most efforts at a more co-operative world order. One result has been that, compared with the often millennial or messianic visions of the League, the United Nations has looked less like an embryo world authority and more like a rather cumbersome piece of diplomatic machinery; and one in which Europe's voice has counted for less and less. In 1945 there was 51 original members of the United Nations, of which 19 were European states; by 1972 with the rise of most Asian and African peoples to full statehood membership had risen to 131, of which only 25 were European states. The collapse of European rule has also often left behind situations replete with the ingredients of conflict, the Arab–Israel conflict, the successive Indo–Pakistan wars, the prolonged sanguinary strife in the former Indo-China; while the political atomization of the world has been accompanied by the cultural fragmentation of world society, as indigenous cultural systems have been revived, and by the growth of ideologies whose very doctrinal rigidity is apt to thwart any but the most modest attempts at international co-operation. Indeed, in Communist doctrine international society has usually been seen as essentially an arena of struggle, of the new and progressive against the old and the moribund, not as the seed-bed of an emerging world community. Amongst most militant revolutionists violence, including physical force, has been widely extolled not only as a unifying force, but as a cleansing and purifying force which can help to 'tear the mask of hypocrisy from the face of the enemy'.

This has not, of course, been the whole story. 'Man's peril may yet be man's salvation.' A state of Hobbesian fear appears to have induced a sense of caution and restraint which has issued forth in an acceptance of the need for a measure of coexistence which can not only ensure man's survival but provide a minimal measure of co-operation on a wide range of economic and social issues. Despite its fluctuating fortunes the United Nations and its agencies have reflected, however fitfully, a deep desire to 'save succeeding generations from the scourge of war', or at least of nuclear war; they have expressed the widespread abhorrence of racial discrimination, at least by whites against non-whites; and they have both expressed and evoked a certain sense of responsibility on the part of the rich nations towards the less-developed peoples of the world, and have provided instruments for the exercise of that responsibility.

Nevertheless, the manoeuvrings of the Cold War, followed by the growing incidence of conflict within the so-called Third World, have so exposed the harsh realities of power politics at the international level as to impose a sobriety and realism of thought about international relationships very different from the intellectual optimism of the 1920s. The advent of thermonuclear weapons momentarily sparked off a sharp wave of protest against the gladiatorial posture of the nuclear powers. But generally the mood in this nuclear age, at least at the level of so-called informed opinion, has at worst been marked by a sense of helplessness in the face of what has often seemed to be the sheer perversity of human nature, and at best by a distrust of political panaceas which purport to offer a once-and-for-all change in the quality of international life and a preference for what Herbert Butterfield called 'maxims which accept the fact of human conflict, but seek to prevent the conflict from overturning the whole civilized order of things'.

Happily, the passivity and scepticism, even cynicism, engendered amongst some of their elders by these sobering experiences has been matched by an intense intellectual curiosity among many young people in the universities as to the reasons why the world is in such a sorry mess and about the sources of conflicts which have often seemed to put their very future in jeopardy. Moreover, in addition to the naturally more optimistic, even if

often carefully concealed, outlook of the young many have had a
strong sense of 'the global village' or at least of being involved in a
mankind which they feel to be tied together more than ever before
in 'an intimacy of conduct, an interdependence of welfare, and
a mutuality of vulnerability'. There has therefore been a strong
potential demand in the post-war years for the study of the confusing but challenging world in which they were growing up.

By the end of the 1940s most universities in Britain were open
to graduate work in international relations, but what many
young people sought was the chance to pursue this intellectual
curiosity of theirs at the undergraduate level, not necessarily by
specializing in international relations, but more often by taking
an optional course which could both give them some understanding of the complexities of international life, and perhaps help
them better to see the international political aspects of their own
specialist studies. The L.S.E. already in 1944 provided for a special
subject of international relations in the final two years of the
B.Sc. (Econ.), but in 1949 there was instituted a two-year Part I
course which included, amongst other optional subjects, a new
one entitled 'The Structure of International Society'. Many who
came to take it believing it to be a soft option, remained, swept
by a sense of intellectual exhilaration, to grapple with the rich
fare Charles Manning had to offer. His own Socratic approach,
set out so vividly in his main work *The Nature of International
Society* published in 1962, was too individual to provide an exact
model for the similar optional courses that were beginning to find
a place in many undergraduate social science and politics degrees
in other British universities. Occasionally, indeed, the very richness and subtlety of the imagery he employed provoked a certain
bewilderment, even hostility; but his persistent and tireless
advocacy both of the merits of the subject itself and of the universities' responsibility to help meet their young people's curiosity
about the world around them made an indelible impression on all
those who shared his concerns.

A development of no less note was the introduction by Sir
Charles Webster in 1946 of the study of the international history of the inter-war period. I believe he was the first historian to
do so in any British university. The meetings of his research
seminar on this period at his home will long remain a cherished

memory of those who took part. His successor in 1953, Norton Medlicott, built up the largest graduate school in Britain dealing with nineteenth- and twentieth-century history and introduced international history as a further special subject for under-graduate study.

At this stage it might be as well to summarize the major con-tributions made by the L.S.E. to the study of international relations in the period I have already covered (i.e. up to the early 1950s) and to indicate in outline the major developments since. It will be convenient to do so under three headings: (1) teaching, (2) research, and (3) professional training.

Teaching

In the teaching realm the L.S.E.'s main contribution has been to secure widespread acceptance of international relations, not necessarily as a distinct discipline but as a subject with a distinc-tive concern, namely, political activity at the level of inter-national society, the structure, characteristic features, and forces within that society, and the *complexe* of relationships and modes of behaviour, particularly political behaviour, between its mem-bers (primarily, but not exclusively, states). It is a subject with multidisciplinary taproots; that is, it draws on a wide range of underpinning disciplines (law, economics, geography), but its unity and identity stems from its distinctive concern or focus.

It is also a subject where sociological and historical approaches tend to converge. The sociological assumes that our experience of international life reveals a degree of intelligibility and regularity which enables us to posit general propositions about the develop-ment and characteristic features of international society and about the *complexe* of relations within it. Moreover the socio-logical approach can complement the historical by helping to make more explicit and articulate historians' hypotheses about past causal relationships and so to cultivate in students a capacity for perceiving the general in the particular. But there is a danger. In its preoccupation with structural analysis the sociological tends to focus, as Stephen Toulmin reminds us, on 'synchronic issues and relationships' defined often 'in static, structural, a-historical . . . and wherever possible mathematical terms'. It needs to be complemented, therefore, by a historical analysis, which can impart a sense of movement, of processes of transition from one system to another, of 'diachronic problems of change', The historical, particularly the international history of the last fifty years, also not only provides the raw material for the formulation and testing of more sociological propositions; it gives depth and perspective to more contemporary studies; and above all it can impart that sense of the concrete, of the particular, and the contingent in human affairs which is an enriching experience in itself and a check upon over-ready sociological generalization.

This approach, reflected particularly in studies of the international political system, is also in large measure synoptic, in the sense of seeking to cultivate an aptitude for seeing problems in the round, for perceiving, analysing, and explaining relationships in multidimensional terms, and holistic in the sense of fostering an aptitude for seeing international society as forming a coherent and complex whole which will enable us better to understand the relationship of the parts. More precisely, the aim is to study the origins and development of the modern system of sovereign states and of the political processes operative within it; to examine the consequences of the geographical expansion of the system in terms of its character and functioning; and to identify the sources and modes of discord and collaboration between its leading members and the bases and instruments of such modicum of international order as exists. This is the macro level.

The micro level is the study of the external relationships of the parts, foreign policy analysis: that is, the external needs of states and the goals of state activity; the various external and internal pressures which determine how foreign policy is made and executed, especially amongst the half a dozen or so Great Powers; and the related problems of rationality and choice within the foreign policy process.

At both the macro and micro levels is the study of international institutions, whether as regulating and ordering devices within the international *complexe* or as instruments of the members of that *complexe*, as channels for both co-operation and conflict, and in terms of the factors which make for cohesion and competition within regional subsystems, alliances, and groupings.

The manner in which the subject has developed in universities in this country reflects, of course, the particular circumstances of the many universities where it is now to be found. As is to be expected in a rapidly growing subject in which there is a continuing and lively discussion over problems of scope and methodology, there is a considerable divergence of opinion as to the manner in which it can best be approached. But these three elements, the study of the international political system, of the foreign policies of the powers, and of international institutions, together with that of international history from 1914 to 1956, has from the mid 1960s constituted the main fare for undergraduate specialists in international relations at the L.S.E. And it is on these three elements that many other universities both in Britain and in the Commonwealth now model their own courses, even though the nomenclature and style may differ greatly from one to another.

Around these core elements have developed a number of more specialist studies. The L.S.E. has been a prime mover, for example, in putting strategic studies on the academic map in this country. These studies are directed to the developments in military technology since 1945 and their effect on international relations; to the role, management, and control of military force in human affairs; and to the related body of strategic theory, for example, deterrence theory. These are all matters of vital consequence to the future of mankind. The 'balance of terror' or 'deterrents' may have been the primary guarantee over the last two decades against conflict on a world scale, but it has been a very delicate, precarious balance, the stability of which has been threatened by each new generation of nuclear weapons, by the emergence of China as a nuclear power, by the continued risk of further nuclear proliferation, and by the persistent fear that the nuclear arms race will take on an independent momentum of its own and continue at an accelerating pace unless effectively controlled. The possibilities and modalities of arms control, whether tacit or explicit, are consequently a major preoccupation of scholars in this field. Another is the threat that civil disorder within states has come to pose to international order, and the instrumentalities available to prevent it from exacerbating Great Power relations or infecting neighbouring areas. In all these matters the insistence that strategic studies should form an integral part of the broader study of international relations can provide a healthy check on too technical a 'nuts and bolts' approach and on a tendency, apparent in many American studies in the field, to shy away from a searching examination of the wider moral and political assumptions from which strategic discussions should take their departure.

The study of the politics of international economic relations so well begun under S. H. Bailey in the 1930s, has also become established, and there is a revival of interest in that old-fashioned but increasingly pertinent subject international political economy. The task is not an easy one; it may indeed become increasingly difficult as habits of thought and modes of analysis steadily diverge. The economist is apt to charge the international relations specialist with operating in a conceptual fog using crude analytical tools; to us far too many economists give the impression that they regard 'consorting with other social scientists as a form of intellectual slumming'. There have been some honourable and much appreciated exceptions, such as Lionel Robbins, James Meade, the late Ely Devons, and some of the younger generation of economists. Yet only too often economists 'are blissfully and amazingly unaware of their own lack of judgement and expertise in political analysis, or of any subjective or professional bias that affects them—much more unaware certainly than the [International Relations] teacher is likely to be of his or her own inexpertise in economics' (4). Thus many economists continue to cling to the picture of an increasingly interdependent world economy, when the weight of the evidence would seem to support the view that the partial world economy of the pre-1929 period has been undergoing a steady process of disintegration, sparked off by the breakdown of the 1930s and continuing apace over the last twenty-five years as the counterpart of the political and ideological fragmentation of the international political system. The process has led both to the 'norms and mores of a previously more integrated partial world economy [becoming] . . . permanently destroyed as they were repeatedly disobeyed' (5) and to the emergence of three relatively distinct economic groupings: the market economies of the industrialized West (including Japan); the developing countries of the Third

World; and the centrally planned economies of the socialist system, with, of course, wide variations within each. Economic analysis is apt to focus pretty exclusively on only one or other of these groups; yet to do so is to convey a distorted picture of the international economy as a whole and to neglect the thickening network of relationships which cut across group boundaries.

This is a sad state of affairs which the L.S.E. has a responsibility to remedy. Fortunately there are signs that younger economists and economic historians are ready to come together with their political science or international relations colleagues to explore modes of interdisciplinary studies on such vitally important matters as (i) the political role of international currencies; (ii) the political dimensions of creditor–debtor relations, in the fields both of monetary support and development; and (iii) a politico-economic study of international production which could relate to traditional trade theory the implications of the rise of multinational business companies.

Then there is the sociology of international law, which focuses on the role of international law in international society and on their mutual impact; on the attitudes of states to international law; and on the relations between international law and international order. It thus serves as a valuable complement to the more traditional and technical but essential study of the content of international law. This content, it might be noted *en passant*, has increased greatly over recent years, but this increase has been accompanied by what many would regard as a marked decline in the weight states accord to their legal obligations. In part this may be ascribed to the ultra-positivistic attitude of socialist states towards an international legal system, the permanence of which they question, and to the initial tendency of many newly independent states to see the content of much of present-day international law as the expression of a vanishing order of international relationships which was designed primarily to serve the interests either of European colonial powers or of American economic imperialists. In short, the domain of international law has increased while the deference accorded to international law has decreased. International relations studies need to take account of both tendencies.

In all these aspects of the subject the elements of both

co-operation and conflict in the international system emerge as locked in a continuing process of interaction. Neither one nor the other merits exclusive attention, for it is the tension between them which makes the international order both so fragile and yet so durable.

Research

Turning to research, there are now probably about two hundred graduate students at the L.S.E. engaged in research on some aspect of international relationships. And one notable recent development has been the setting up in 1967, with generous Ford Foundation support, of the Centre for International Studies. The Centre has done much to encourage multidisciplinary graduate research, particularly on the Soviet Union and Eastern Europe, on Communist China, on Asia and the Far East, and in the hitherto neglected but hopefully growing field of European studies.

Only three points as regards graduate research in international relations can be touched upon here. The first is that although what may be called area studies have recently grown in favour among research students, we insist that just as every specialist should be something of a generalist, and vice-versa, so individual areas should be seen in as broad a context as possible and not treated as self-contained islands insulated from the outside world.

The second is that possibly the greatest attraction of the graduate school in international studies, as in the L.S.E. at large, is its cosmopolitan character. Even in the early 1930s, for example, of 67 graduate students, 12 came from China. It is often from the continuing exchange of ideas with fellow students that each can arrive at a deeper appreciation of how different the world can look from the varying national and cultural vantage points.

The third is that in recent years well over a hundred students have gone from the international history and international relations graduate departments into university appointments all over the world. Give the comparatively modest size of these two departments, this is a not unimpressive record. Indeed, were it not for the academic training these young men and women had received at the L.S.E. the growth of international studies in universities both in this country and throughout the Commonwealth would have been greatly handicapped.

Professional training

To turn now to professional training: our main preoccupations at the L.S.E. have been teaching and research; for the most part the study of international relations, especially at the undergraduate level, is intended in Mark Pattison's words 'to cultivate the mind and form the intelligence'. It is rarely seen as a form of vocational training, and rightly so to my mind. But the L.S.E. has from the early years been concerned to assist professional people, including those intent on equipping themselves more thoroughly for a diplomatic or related career. A number of the evening students who have come to the study of international relations or history over the last two generations have done so for professional reasons. And what an inspiring and hardworking lot most of them have been. Their departure from the L.S.E. is a sad loss for both sides.

In 1927 the Diploma in Diplomatic Studies was introduced and was described as specially adapted for students either seeking posts in the diplomatic or consular services or already holding such posts. This was replaced in 1955 by a foreign service course intended to meet the needs of students in these categories. The importance of these courses should not be exaggerated. But they have often brought to the L.S.E. professional people of considerable quality; and it is just possible that their comradeship here may ease the channels of co-operation in their subsequent professional life.

This brief account of the L.S.E.'s contribution would be incomplete were it not to draw attention to some of the more controversial issues confronting teachers in the field. Charles Manning was a consistent advocate of studying international phenomena in a spirit of detachment; he saw the subject as a branch of humanistic studies, but it was one to be studied 'in a scientific spirit'. To which I myself would only add the need to be more self-conscious and explicit about the fundamental presuppositions of our thought, thus helping the student to discern where our inevitable bias lies. Yet I still wonder occasionally whether commitment may not sometimes be more fruitful and revealing than detachment. May not a teacher who feels deeply, *and thinks rigorously*, sometimes be able to shed a more searching light on the inwardness of the human situation than the imperfectly detached social scientist who may only too easily think in rather crude stereotypes?

Another and related question is whether we at the L.S.E. have paid too little attention to the fashions, particularly the behaviouralist fashions, which have reached our shores from the United States though not, happily to my mind, flooded our campus. How far should the subject develop more along 'scientific' lines, modelling itself on recent developments in the study of physical and biological systems? I can only make two brief points here. The first is that the behaviouralist attempt to apply more rigorously scientific methods to the subject matter of international relations has yielded some good work on analyses of the international system and in integration and decision-making theory. And there has been quite a valuable spin-off in that it has impelled many of us traditionalists to be more precise and rigorous in our use of terms and in the enunciation of propositions sufficiently exact and specific to be testable. But I must confess to a considerable sympathy with the criticism I once came across that the scientific rationalist's 'habit of viewing the world as raw material for experiment, observation, and the dispassionate discovery of laws has made him insensitive to those dimensions of nature and man that can only be apprehended as the unique and mysterious *thisness* of each individual which awakens in us an answering response of feeling'. The scientific rationalist far too often acts, I fear, 'as though he had a card file, a calculating machine, a laboratory inside of him, instead of a heart. And he is crazy'.

The second point is that the behaviouralist often urges us to ignore orthodox disciplinary boundaries. It is said, for instance, that we should devote more attention to the new 'science' of 'conflictology', the argument being, if I have understood it correctly, that conflict is a general feature of human relations so that to understand the causes of that most virulent form of conflict, the use of physical violence at the international level, we should examine other forms of conflict, at the level, for instance, of marital or industrial relations, and then use the insights obtained to examine the root causes of war. This approach is certainly not without interest and promise and there are its protagonists within this School. Yet it is rather disturbingly reminiscent of the analogies drawn in the inter-war period between the strike at the industrial level and war at the international level, or the tendency to conceive of the role of law internationally in terms analogous to the rule of law domestically. Analogies of this kind I regard as dangerously misleading. It is the *environment* (the context) in which conflict arises or law operates that is crucial. States coexist in an environment which lacks 'a common power to keep them all in awe'. It is this very structure of international society which produces, as Herbert Butterfield reminds us, the 'situations of Hobbesian fear, of an irreducible conflict of power' and which makes conflict at the international level so intractable a problem. Similarly, the rule of law internationally is so precarious because, perhaps fortunately, there is no ruler. The astonishing thing is, of course, that there is order, and a very resilient and durable order, in international society; but if we are to understand why this is so we need first to appreciate the characteristics of that particular society, not why divorce rates have risen so strikingly or why wild-cat strikes have become such a commonplace. It is the sense of the particularity of international society that we need to acquire, not a miscellaneous ragbag of disconnected conflict situations.

Still these and many other familiar questions will no doubt continue to provoke controversy here as elsewhere. But what a dull subject it would be without such controversy!

REFERENCES

1. WEBSTER, L. C. K., *The Study of International Politics*, p. 23, Inaugural Lecture (Cardiff: The University of Wales Press, 1923).
2. LEAGUE OF NATIONS, International Institute of Intellectual Co-operation, 'The University Teaching of International Relations', Report of a Preliminary Discussion, *Eighth International Studies Conference* (June 1935) (k. 25. 1935).
3. MANNING, C. A. W., *The Nature of International Society* (quoted), pp. 64 and 177 (London: G. Bell & Sons, 1962).

4. STRANGE, Susan, 'International Economics and International Relations: A Case of Mutual Neglect', *International Affairs* (April 1970), p. 307.
5. MYRDAL, Gunnar, *An International Economy*, p. 42 (London: Routledge and Kegan Paul, 1956).

SOCIAL ILLS AND PUBLIC REMEDIES

R. A. PARKER

R. A. PARKER

B.Sc. (Soc.), Ph.D. (Lond.)

Professor of Social Administration
Bristol University

Educated at Erith County Grammar School; graduated in sociology from the London School of Economics in 1953 and later worked for his Ph.D. there. Lecturer in Social Administration at the L.S.E. 1960–9; member of the Seebohm Committee on Local Authority and Allied Personal Services; former member of the Milton Keynes Development Corporation. Chairman, Social Administration Association. His main publications have been in the fields of child care and housing.

SOCIAL ILLS AND
PUBLIC REMEDIES

My lecture is about the study of social ills and public remedies and, more especially, about how and to what effect this study has been pursued within the academic discipline of social administration. It is by no means self-evident that there should be such a separate field of study within the social sciences. Indeed in other countries with no fewer social ills or social services, the subject of social administration does not exist. It is almost entirely a British phenomenon, and that is interesting. I shall use it as my starting point. To appreciate why we have a subject of social administration we must look backwards: in particular to the history of social work education in this country.

I

Courses, aimed at the preparation of social workers were established in a number of British universities at the beginning of this century. At the L.S.E. the social science department was formed in 1912. Similar developments occurred elsewhere at about the same time; for example at Liverpool, Bristol, Leeds, Birmingham, and Edinburgh. These courses were of one or two years' duration and led to the award of a diploma or certificate rather than a degree. Elsewhere in Europe, however, separate and independent schools of social work were established, quite outside the university system, and they have mostly remained so. In the United States training for social work was often associated with the universities, but financial support came mainly from the employing bodies or from those connected with them. These interests exercised a significant influence upon the direction of development. From the beginning, the American courses laid a clear emphasis upon professional training and the acquisition of practical skill.

Although experience in practical work was also an important part of the British courses, it was uneasily combined with the university tradition of a broad, liberal, and eclectic approach; an approach in which both social ills and public remedies were set in the wide context of, for example, economic history or political philosophy. Their university location built into these courses a conflict between this educational ideology and the more immediate aim of equipping students with the practical abilities and knowledge necessary for them to become useful (and employable) social workers. Indeed, an American scholar visiting the social science department at the L.S.E. in the early 1950s concluded that: 'the old unresolved conflict between training for practice and general academic education is still present' (1).

I happen to believe this was a productive conflict. Its existence, throughout the 1920s and the 1930s, endowed pre-war social work training in this country, and especially at the L.S.E., with a distinctive style. Just how distinctive can best be judged from the proceedings of the early international social work conferences. At the 1928 Paris meeting C. M. Lloyd, then head of the L.S.E. department, advanced what, in that gathering, he regarded as a 'heretical view'. It was this: 'that the social worker . . . will be better not only as a man or woman, but as a social worker, with a wide and deep knowledge of history, economics, public administration, social philosophy and the nature of the people with whom he or she has to deal' (2).

Economics was certainly regarded as a closely allied field of study. The attendance of several British academic economists at that same international social work gathering suggests that they took this view as well. Indeed, it was mainly economists who undertook many of the poverty studies which were conducted in the inter-war period. The reading lists of the day also indicate that social studies students were expected to acquaint themselves with the principal works of political philosophy: Plato, Aristotle, Hobbes, Rousseau, Green, and Mill were much in evidence.

As a result of this broadly based pattern of development, instruction in specific social work techniques, and the accumulation of a particular body of social work knowledge and theory, were slow to appear on the British scene. This was in marked contrast to their growth in the United States. Instead, the social studies courses in our universities provided an atmosphere in which both students and teachers could pursue the study of social problems and public policy in as widesweeping a way as they wished. They were concerned with poverty and unemployment; public assistance and the slums; inequality and opportunity. Of course, social studies departments held no monopoly of interest in matters such as these. Most of them were small in size and relied upon the collaboration of colleagues in other related fields. Nevertheless they did bring together, in a university setting, the traditions of empirical social inquiry, social reform, and commitment to personal action.

This particular mixture began to separate out after the last war; and that it did so was largely the consequence of the professionalization of social work and of the particular form which it took. This process of professionalization may be explained partly by the growing influence of American social work, but also by the war and the post-war legislation which generated a more extensive demand for social workers with special competence and skills. As Donnison (3) has noted, for example, the Children Act, 1948, effectively created the profession of child care officer. Emergency courses were established to produce the much needed social work manpower. Teachers to staff the courses were frequently recruited from amongst practitioners. Training for social work began to be special, technical, and separate: to be exclusive rather than inclusive. Gradually the old social studies courses, although they mostly continued in one form or another, were regarded less and less as the prelude to a job in social work but, increasingly, as the initial preparation for further professional training or for posts in other areas of the social services.

The nature of the special competence upon which social work professionalization built is of particular importance in explaining how this general situation, in the early part of the 1950s, led to the growth of social administration as an identifiably separate field of study. The claim of social work to a professional competence derived from psychological disciplines; especially psychoanalysis. It was this which shifted social work education towards questions of individual treatment and adjustment. This coincided with a period when we thought, with the creation of the Welfare State, that we had solved the major social ills of unemployment and poverty. In that context it was understandable that we looked to the individual as the source of social problems.

Social work became immersed in what Professor Miller (4) has termed 'the psychiatric world view'. This close link with psychiatric theory was the key to professional development in social work and although it brought with it certain undoubted advantages, it also began to insulate social work from issues of social reform. It divorced what Wright Mills (5) has called 'personal troubles' (the concern of the new social work profession) from 'public issues'.

Social reform in this country has a long association with social research and inquiry; with the description of social conditions and distress. As social work education moved closer towards the 'psychiatric' position it not only moved away from concern with social issues and social reform, but from social inquiry as well. With a more precise (and inevitably narrower) conception of social work, much of the earlier interest in the modification of social conditions through collective intervention began to disappear from social work education; albeit reappearing again in the last few years.

This interest, however, did not disappear from the social studies departments and it was this established concern with the study of social ills and public remedies which, detached increasingly from social work education, formed the basis for social administration. This field of study, which emerged as a direct descendant of the 'social education' tradition, took as its central concern the study of the social services; how they have developed; how they operate; whether they are adequate; what their effects are and what changes might be made. Gradually it reinvigorated the tradition of social inquiry, particularly in the field of poverty, and extended its interests into many spheres which touched upon, or affected, social policy. Although usually remaining in the same departments, professional social work courses and the teaching of social administration began to drift apart, and it is only in recent years that there is evidence of any real reunification, as social work searches for a wider definition of its role and as social administration becomes more closely involved with the realities of social planning.

Social administration as a field of study has grown rapidly over the past twenty years. In 1950 Richard Titmuss's was, effectively, the first chair; mine, in 1969, was the twenty-fifth, and others have been created since. Nonetheless, when we attend international gatherings we do not meet our counterparts. Those who, in other countries, study issues of social policy, or the administration of the social services, work in departments, or research institutes, concerned with public administration, law, sociology, town planning, demography, public finance, or economics. This difference is usually explained by reference to the creation and development of the welfare state in this country after the last war, and the impetus which this provided for the development of a field of study especially concerned with it. Admittedly we now devote about a quarter of the gross national product to providing a variety of social services, but other countries spend as much; some more. The myth of the unique nature of the British post-war welfare achievement has been sustained partly because comparative studies have been few and far between; those which have been undertaken have usually referred to the United States rather than the rest of Europe and the Commonwealth.

In my view it is not the existence of the 'welfare state' which has created a field of study called social administration but the special nature of the much earlier development of social work education; in particular its location in the universities. Its comparatively late redirection towards specialized professional courses ensured that a tradition of the general study of social conditions and social action had been created. It was this which provided the basis upon which a special area of study could thereafter be built. In addition, of course, the earlier concern of economists in this area had declined, as their studies also became more specialized, theoretical, and technical.

The subsequent growth of social administration as a field of study during the 1950s and 1960s can be attributed, in part, to the fact that the new professional social work courses, such as the Carnegie experiment inaugurated in this School in 1954, were unable to meet the full extent of the demand for social workers. The major contribution of the technical colleges and the polytechnics was not to make its impact until the 1960s, in the wake of the Younghusband report. Thus the old social studies courses (often renamed) continued to attract, in sizeable numbers, students wishing to enter social work directly or to prepare themselves for subsequent professional courses. The study of social administration, at the L.S.E. for example, owes a debt to this enthusiastic and strongly motivated body of students. They made it possible for many of us to teach and to develop this subject; indeed they were partners in that process.

I have, briefly, endeavoured to explain some of the reasons why the study of social administration grew into what the preamble to the new *Journal of Social Policy* is able to describe as 'an intellectual discipline'. I have, especially, wished to show its close relationship to the developments which occurred in social work education. In particular, the establishment of social work courses in British universities, some sixty years ago, was of crucial importance.

II

It is these earlier origins in social work education which help to explain the course taken by the developing subject of social administration over the last twenty years. It helps us to appreciate the particular strengths and some of the apparent weaknesses. Let me try to generalize about the main characteristics and contributions of social administration since, say, 1950.

There has been a continuing concern to discover (sometimes to rediscover) the scale and the extent of social ills, particularly in the field of poverty. For instance, there has been the work of Townsend and Abel-Smith (6) which concluded that in 1960 'nearly 18 per cent of households, containing about 14.2 per cent of the population, had incomes of less than 140 per cent of the basic national assistance scale'. Interest in social ills, however, has been shared by other disciplines, such as sociology, criminology, and public health as well; moreover it has not been the exclusive preserve of the universities. What has particularly characterized social administration as a field of study has been the attention paid to the description and evaluation of existing social services or policies. Their adequacy and performance have been examined against their stated objectives and against measures of prevailing unmet need. The social services, as public remedies, have formed a primary object of study and, indeed, their shortcomings have assumed, in this process, the character of new social ills.

Sometimes specific services or policies have been studied; for instance, old peoples' homes (7), housing needs (8), or provision for the homeless (9). Sometimes more general themes have been selected and carefully analysed, for example, the redistributive consequences of state intervention (10) or regional and local variation in standards of provision (11, 12). The information derived from such studies has often served to challenge existing assumptions about how, and to what effect, our social services work. These kinds of studies enabled students of social administration to describe their subject (on the many occasions on which they were required to explain what it actually was) as essentially 'problem and action orientated'. However, both the problems and the remedial action were fairly closely related to the anchor point of the social services.

Our bookshelves, typically, carry an array of government publications: reports of committees of inquiry, white papers, parliamentary debates, annual reports, and statistical abstracts. The tradition of the Webbs can be discerned. The publication of a new bill on housing, social security, or some other field of social welfare is a predictable stimulus for detailed analysis and critical reviews. This kind of immersion has been of great value; it has invested the subject with authority and created a potential source of influence. Trends have been revealed, implications of policies exposed, and some of the conventional wisdom of social welfare put in question.

Although this critical study of the social services has been a central feature in social administration it has led outwards in several important directions. First, to a concern with other spheres of public intervention which are not usually classified as social services. This has been no idle trespassing in the territory of other subjects. It proved increasingly essential if the role and the effect of the social services were to be understood fully. Take, as one example, taxation. If one studies an issue, such as the subsidization of council housing, it is impossible to ignore the parallel help provided for owner-occupiers through tax relief on mortgage interest. Family allowances have been studied as a means whereby the State shares with parents some of the extra costs of bringing up children; but again, this issue cannot be divorced realistically from the existence of child allowances within the income tax system. Abuse of welfare benefits exists, but it is insignificant placed alongside the public cost of tax evasion. The study of redistributional principles and redistributional effects cannot be satisfactorily restricted to the social services alone. Of course, none of these comments upon the tax system as a necessary part of the study of social policy will seem remarkable to today's student, but it is worth remembering that Donnison (13), reviewing the teaching of social administration a decade ago, found that 'only a minority of . . . examiners ask questions about the tax system'. That this was still the situation in 1961 is an example of the time lag involved before we recognize the impact of social and economic change. The tax system became relevant to the study of certain social services only when the average earner (and below) became a tax payer: that is, during the Second World War.

A second outward movement from a core concern with the operation and the effect of the social services was towards the study of private remedies. There were several reasons why this happened. One was the growth of occupational welfare provisions, particularly with respect to pensions. By the end of the 1950s this was clearly affecting the development of pensions policy in the public sector, and, less obviously, it bore upon conclusions about equity and the distribution of social benefits. Titmuss, early on, drew attention to the fact that it was not 'inappropriate to apply the term "social service" to private pensions schemes' (14). There were other areas too where special benefits of a 'welfare' nature were available by virtue of employment (usually in the higher echelons): preferential rates of interest for house purchase; special health services; full pay in sickness and other provisions, many closely resembling the state social services. These could not be ignored.

Another reason for the growth of greater interest in the study of private remedies is to be found in the prominent position which ideas about 'community care' attained in the 1960s, especially in policies for the mentally disordered. If more partially dependent people were to be cared for by their families and by communities, rather than in residential homes of one kind or another, a range of essentially voluntary and private contributions was required. Any reasonable plan for the extension of such policies implied, therefore, a reassessment and evaluation of the network of private and informal services or supports existing in families and communities. Of course, these have always existed, despite gloomy prognostications about the collapse of family responsibility or the disintegration of the community. Indeed, had they not existed on a substantial scale the whole edifice of public social services would certainly have long since crumbled under the weight of demand. What was rather different, however, was the more deliberate analysis of these systems and their conjunction with formal social service provision.

There was a further, and more general reason, why students of social administration extended their attention to private remedies. As the spate of post-war social legislation aged, the debate about the appropriate and desirable balance between the market and the State in meeting the individual's needs for insurance against adversity, education, or health care, was reopened. Clearly, the study of social policies could not for long look at the formal social services as if this other remedy system did not exist. What happened, or might happen, in one system profoundly affected the other. When, for example, the demand for day nursery provision remained high and public provision was reduced, private, market alternatives of various kinds and quality grew. Since many of the provisions commonly listed under the heading of 'social services' can be obtained in the market place, why is the State also involved, to varying degrees, in their supply? Are there clear demarcating principles?

Conventionally, the answer has been yes: the social services meet certain needs which the market cannot or will not meet or which, because of the price system, it does so only partially and without adequate regard to questions of social justice. We have also added that the hallmark of the social services is their renunciation of the price system as a basis for settling questions of production and distribution; despite, that is, the widespread existence of charges to users and, of course, the payment of wages to social service employees. There is, however, no immutable or clearly discernible dividing line between the preserves of the market and those of the State. In the fields of housing and education, for example, the State intervenes in numerous ways to control and regulate the private sector. Ultimately, preferences for one kind of balance rather than another arise from political conviction. However, the careful study of the alternatives (and of the several positions in between), has begun to clarify the likely consequences, and demonstrate the implications of our preferences. In saying this, I do not imply the elimination of ideological differences, only their clearer exposition.

It has been one of the special contributions of the large department of social administration in this School to have extended and pushed inquiries towards these broader issues. The keen interest of students and others in the 'purposes' and general effects of social welfare programmes is certainly sharpened by this kind of approach. Problems about the wider economic, social, and political implications of different forms of social policy are more likely to be posed. However, it is my view that the field of social administration as a whole has not yet moved very far towards the examination of issues such as these. We are hampered, I venture to think, not by disinclination but by certain gaps in our studies.

III

The first of these gaps is the scarcity of careful and detailed studies of how, and under what circumstances, different social policies were initiated, changed, or developed. Although social ills and public remedies have been studied separately and have been linked together prescriptively ('do this about that'), an adequate study of the interrelationship between ills and remedies as political phenomena has not developed. In the first place there is the perplexing question of how and why certain social situations get defined as problems warranting public intervention. Even more complex is the question of how and why, once so defined, they do or do not lead to particular kinds of solutions or remedies. I think this issue has been unduly simplified or avoided for several reasons.

It has often been assumed that the social remedy (so-called) which we observe has been, or was, introduced to deal with a specific and identifiable social evil: for instance, that family allowances were primarily intended to ameliorate family poverty, or that elementary education was to eradicate ignorance and illiteracy. The realities appear to be more complicated and the association between the remedy and the visible, or proclaimed ill, is often a partial one. For example, the introduction or the modification of social policies often appears to wait upon the convergence of *several* issues, upon all of which one 'remedy' bears. There is, I suspect, an 'economy of remedies'. Similarly, the acknowledged existence of a social problem may not attract any public action until a crisis arises which obliges government to respond, or until some possible means of dealing with it becomes available. Thus the problems, or ills, to which particular remedies relate may be both numerous as well as obscure. Divisions such as those between economic policy and social policy do not help; there are essentially economic problems to which social policies relate, and there are mainly social problems with economic remedies.

The generally accepted (or textbook) history of how and why our social services emerged as and when they did has superimposed an undue degree of rationality, consensus, and inevitability upon an essentially political process. A certain orderliness and planning are often implicitly assumed (whether judged sinister or beneficent) and the Beveridge plan as well as the ideology of post-war reconstruction lent added credibility to this view. Moreover, as Goldthorpe (15) in particular has pointed out, where an explanation of social policy development in general has been sought it has tended to assume the existence of social imperatives. 'Whatever was, was necessary', whether for humanitarian, political, or economic reasons. I suspect that insufficient weight has been placed upon the struggle and the play of the competing interests which surround measures of social amelioration. The fact that in endeavouring to explain the formation and shape of social policy we are concerned with welfare provision may partly account for this; for anyone to be 'against' welfare is rather like being against virtue and hence difficult to contemplate.

Had there been more detailed studies of social policy developments both before and after the last war we might now be in a better position to generalize (or generalize in different ways, which is equally important) about the 'how' of social policy, and thereby begin to explore the 'why'. That this is only recently occurring to any extent in social administration is partly attributable to our social studies origins which tended to focus on contemporary ills and contemporary remedies, albeit in general terms, rather than upon the past. It may also reflect the fact that many academics in social administration (especially at the L.S.E.) have been, and are, involved in the policy-making process of the here and now.

A second gap in our studies has also restricted the process of generalization about the 'why' of social policy. This, in my opinion, is the neglect of comparative studies. It can, perhaps, be accounted for in several ways. First, by the myth of the uniqueness of the British Welfare State which tended to obscure similar developments occurring in other countries. Secondly, by the absence in other countries of special fields of study comparable with ours. Thirdly, and lastly, by the social action orientation of the early social studies courses, which directed attention to the British scene in which most social work students would actually work.

These two gaps are being closed and, as they are, we may gain a better grasp of the relationships between social policy, economic development, political systems, and ideology. In doing so it may be possible to meet objections like that recently advanced by Pinker who claimed : 'the discipline of social administration lacks that body of theoretical material which might give it a greater intellectual unity and perspective' (16). We cannot necessarily extract theory from history, or from international comparison. But we, like all other students, do not use all the facts; they are approached selectively with certain questions in mind. We are guided by both theory and value. Thus our studies of social ills and public remedies, of their relationships and their development, have not been random. They have been influenced by fairly explicit values about the 'good society', they have also been shaped, albeit in a less obvious way, by theories. These have been implied rather than expressly formulated or consciously debated. This is, in part, what Pinker, and others who deplore the 'theoretical poverty' of social administration, are criticizing; but it is only part. If I interpret them correctly they are also directing attention to the potential variety of theory, some of which may

be derived from incursions into other fields, such as political
science or sociology.

There are, of course, dangers in a preoccupation with theory
without a sound empirical basis: for then it easily becomes un-
profitable and sterile. But the well-established practical orientation of social administration surely protects it as well as any of
the social sciences from this risk. We need more acknowledged
and explicit theoretical frameworks to assist with the tasks of
explanation; to simplify, order, and generalize.

IV

My brief discussion of the place of theory has, rather significantly, focused upon the remedies side of our topic. In general
terms the subject might, not unfairly, be characterized as having
been 'remedy orientated'; indeed this has helped to define its
primary field of interest. Needs (or ills) have been studied, but
often with a view to determining their extent as a yardstick
against which to assess the adequacy of services. Questions about
how social problems get so defined; whose problems they are;
what their causes may be or how they can be understood within
particular socio-economic systems have, more frequently, been
the preserve of sociology.

I am not advocating a competitive development of the study of
social problems; rather a greater degree of collaboration with
specialists in other fields. I do not see how, otherwise, social
administration can move with any confidence into the sphere of
social planning. Whether it should do so, and if so how, will
depend upon the way in which the planning process is perceived.

One version of the social planning task can be described in this
way: 'in all countries, even where the building of the welfare
state is most advanced, the architects are continually labouring
with the tasks of simplification, co-ordination, rationalization and
the achievement of efficiency' (17). These labours of administrative reform are important and, indeed, how they are approached,
undertaken, and resolved is of considerable significance to the
users. If, however, these issues are unduly emphasized in our conception of social welfare planning, social administration is likely
to be drawn magnetically towards management studies of one

kind or another. If, on the other hand, social planning is viewed in more fundamental terms, as, for example, being concerned with movement towards social ideals, then it is necessary to go deeper than administrative issues alone. That is no simple task, but it may be eased by striving for a keener and more overall view of the nature and origins of social ills; and by stressing continually the value component in what is seen as a problem and in what kinds of remedies are proposed.

I believe that those who study social administration and social policy should also seek to play a part in the *process* of social planning as well as making it the object of their inquiries. This view should surprise no one who has been acquainted with this field of study. Certainly it has been, and is, a strong L.S.E. tradition. Teachers of social administration have served on committees of inquiry, on advisory committees, on boards, as consultants, worked within the party machinery, and written tracts. As the extent of deliberate and co-ordinated planning increases, and as pressure mounts to make it a more public and participative process, the potential contribution of social administration needs to be reviewed. I do not intend to do that here, but I will emphasize what appear to me to be three of the considerations to be borne in mind.

There is, first, the need to study the process of planning themselves: although we talk easily about the growth of social planning we still know comparatively little about how it is pursued, and what the political and administrative interests and assumptions actually are. There is little point in assembling data; introducing ideas, or making recommendations about what should happen unless we also understand better how and why these are dealt with differently under different circumstances within various administrative and political systems.

Secondly, in the longer term it is obvious that the greatest contribution to social planning will come from today's and tomorrow's students. I have already discussed what we teach (and should be studying), but there are two additional considerations. One is how we teach and the other is who we teach. The planning process will require people with imagination; conviction; sympathy; breadth of approach; scepticism and the capacity to reflect upon what they do and upon the experience they acquire. All the kinds of virtues, in fact, which Whitehead outlines in his *Aims of Education* (18). How we teach bears upon this. If the bureaucratization of welfare planning is to be avoided, these qualities will be urgently required in those whose task this becomes. There is a valuable tradition in social administration of high standards of teaching and tutorial contact which can continue to support and encourage these capacities.

Then there is the question of who we teach; or conversely who chooses to study in this field. As I have pointed out, in the past there has been a heavy concentration of intending social workers. If, however, the social welfare planning movement is, as one hopes, to become a more collaborative enterprise (involving several interests and spanning traditional disciplines), then it would seem increasingly appropriate to include, for example, students of medicine, architecture, education, or housing management. Indeed this is already happening, and the L.S.E. has played an important part in initiating such experiments. But groups other than various professionals have interests in social planning: there are the consumers. The welfare rights movement has attracted, quite naturally, teachers and students of social administration, and many of them have fulfilled, in both formal and informal ways, an extra-mural teaching function.

The third and last consideration which I would select in reassessing the role of social administration in social planning is this: we have seen, and will I am sure continue to see, a remarkable growth in public social data. The recent publication of *Social Trends* (19) is not the culmination of a development but a first step. Increasingly, I believe, both central and local government will collect and analyse the kind of information which students of social policy, of necessity, have hitherto had to discover for themselves. In doing so of course, they sometimes obtained command over data which were superior to those available to government. I am particularly conscious of the work in the late 1950s, of teams like the Rowntree Trust Housing Study in which, with other colleagues at the L.S.E. and elsewhere, I was involved. The improvement in housing statistics of all kinds since those days has been remarkable. The point I am making is that the influence social administrators were, at times, able to exercise over the development of social policies, arose partly from this special command of relevant information : this will become less frequent. In future, command over ideas and the exposition of principles which help to order, interpret, and use the growing social data, may be of greater inportance : for data without questions are dead and, to return to my earlier point, it is the possession of theory (embryonic though it be) which assists in the choice of illuminating and incisive questions. It has been the hallmark of the L.S.E. and of the work of Professor R. M. Titmuss in particular, to have made that special contribution to the advancement of understanding which comes from the ability to formulate and pose penetrating, yet essentially simple questions, about collective social provisions and policies.

V

Why, one might end by asking, has the L.S.E. played such a predominant part in the development of, and contribution to this field of study? Its size and its close connection with the early 'social work education' tradition have been noted, and one must certainly acknowledge the reputation it has derived from the outstanding and widely known work of individual members of staff. There are a number of other facts which should be taken into account as well. It has made good use of research facilities. It has benefited from being close to the seat of government : not merely because of geographical proximity but because of the widespread contact and involvement of its staff with this network. As a result it has developed, over the years, a good sensory system, adapted to its practical field of study. Its sense of timing, and sense of a good question has thereby been sharpened. The widespread and long-standing connection with practitioners through the use of practical placements for students and the association, often because of this, with former students, has added to it. So has a steady flow of distinguished overseas visitors.

All these threads have proved an especially valuable combination in a subject which has been so closely connected with the study of social ills and public remedies.

REFERENCES

1. SMITH, M. J., *Professional Education for Social Work in Britain*, p. 42 (F.W.A., 1952).
2. *First International Conference of Social Work Report*, vol. ii, p. 131 (Paris, 1928).
3. DONNISON, D. V., *Social Policy and Administration* (Allen & Unwin, 1965).
4. MILLER, S. M., and RIESSMAN, F., *Social Class and Social Policy* (Basic Books, 1968).
5. WRIGHT MILLS, C., *The Sociological Imagination* (Oxford University Press, 1959).
6. TOWNSEND, P., and ABEL-SMITH, D., *The Poor and the Poorest*, Occasional Papers on Social Administration, no. 17 (G. Bell & Sons, 1965).
7. TOWNSEND, P., *The Last Refuge* (Routledge & Kegan Paul, 1962).
8. CULLINGWORTH, J. B., *Housing Needs and Planning Policy* (Routledge & Kegan Paul, 1960).
9. GREVE, J., *London's Homeless*, Occasional Papers on Social Administration, no. 10 (G. Bell & Sons, 1964).
10. TITMUSS, R. M., *Income Distribution and Social Change* (Allen & Unwin, 1962).
11. DAVIES, B. P., *Social Needs and Resources in Local Services* (Joseph, 1968).
12. PACKMAN, J., *Child Care: Needs and Numbers* (Allen & Unwin, 1968).
13. DONNISON, D. V., 'The Teaching of Social Administration', *British Journal of Sociology*, **12**, no. 5 (September 1961).
14. TITMUSS, R. M., *Essays on the Welfare State*, p. 68 (Allen & Unwin, 1958).
15. GOLDTHORPE, J. H., 'The Development of Social Policy in England, 1800–1914', *Transactions of the Fifth World Congress of Sociology* (1964).
16. PINKER, R., *Social Theory and Social Policy*, p. 5 (Heinemann, 1971).
17. MYRDAL, G., *Beyond the Welfare State*, p. 45 (Duckworth, 1960).
18. WHITEHEAD, A. N., *The Aims of Education* (Willams and Norgate, 1932).
19. *Social Trends*, C.O. 1 (H.M.S.O., 1970).

MEASUREMENT IN THE STUDY OF SOCIETY

MAURICE G. KENDALL

MAURICE G. KENDALL

M.A., Sc.D. (Cantab.), F.B.A., F.R.S.A.

Chairman of Scicon (Holdings) Ltd.

Formerly head of the Economic Intelligence Branch of the Ministry of Agriculture and Fisheries, and subsequently Statistician of the U.K. Chamber of Shipping. Professor of Statistics at the London School of Economics and Political Science, 1949–61, and is still visiting Professor at the L.S.E. In 1968 he was awarded a Gold Medal by the Royal Statistical Society. He is the author of fourteen books and many scientific papers on statistics and economics.

MEASUREMENT
IN THE STUDY OF
SOCIETY

It is in the spirit of these lectures to look back over the past in order to appreciate the present. That I shall do. But since the subject of this lecture, 'Measurement in the Study of Society', has been revolutionized in almost every respect in the last twenty years and therefore lies mostly in the future, I shall devote a considerable part of the lecture to the work which still remains to be done. The break with tradition in the study of societal organization in the last two decades has been extensive and profound, and somewhat paradoxically perhaps, I must, in order to illustrate the nature of that break, go further back in time and take a longer run at my subject than some of my colleagues in this series.

History never seems to begin in a clean and satisfactory way, but we may perhaps start from a lively figure of the early eighteenth century, John Arbuthnot, mathematician, Doctor of Medicine, Fellow of the Royal Society, satirist (he was the inventor of the character of John Bull), and friend of Pope and Swift, a man of whom Swift said that if there were a dozen like him he could burn *Gulliver's Travels*. Arbuthnot became interested in one of the first sociological laws to be discussed in scientific terms, the constancy of the sex ratio of births and its slight but significant departure from equality. Among other things he was physician to Queen Anne, which unfortunate woman had seventeen children, all of whom died before her accession to the throne. Whether or not this fact stimulated Arbuthnot's interest in the subject I do not know; but he published in 1710 an essay entitled 'An Argument for Divine Providence, taken from the constant regularity observed in the births of both sexes'.

The demographic laws of birth and death are so familiar to us nowadays that we find it hard to imagine how ignorant our fore-fathers were only two or three centuries ago. In the Middle Ages there were, in general, only two reasons for counting anything relating to human society; one was to find out how many men could bear arms, and the other was to ascertain how much money could be levied by way of tax. Apparently it was fourteenth-century Venice which has the credit of first recognizing women and children as possessing human souls which were worth count-ing as members of her community. Even in Elizabethan times there seems to have been doubt whether males and females were born in equal numbers. Arbuthnot's work was therefore far from being the rather slight contribution to knowledge that it may now appear. He was one of the early statisticians, a man who not only observed quantitative phenomena, but applied the laws of chance to them and, in fact, he has an honourable place in the memory of statisticians as the first man to set up a formal test of a statistical hypothesis.

However, it is not his statistical work which I wish to empha-size, but the explanation he gave for his phenomena. He proved that there were more males born than females, in London at least, but that as males were prone to risk in their early days, the sex ratio at the marriageable age was about equal. As the title of his pamphlet indicates, he regarded this admittedly very remarkable fact as due to Divine Providence. This same explanation persisted through a great part of the eighteenth century. Whether one approved of the state of society or not, whether the Supreme Power took an interest in each individual event or merely wound up the universe like a clock and left it to run under predetermined laws, the ultimate outcome was that the arithmetical features of the world were laid firmly at the door of the Almighty. The concept was expanded and developed by a number of people, notably a German pastor, one J. P. Suessmilch, whose book, the *Göttliche Ordnung*, 'Divine Order as proven by birth, death and fertility of the human species', published in 1741, is an early landmark in the sociological interpretation of statistical observa-tion. Suessmilch also was impressed by the fact that the sexes are in balance at the marriageable age; surely a demonstration that the Creator thoroughly approves of a monogamistic reproduction of the species.

The development of political arithmetic during the eighteenth century brought into prominence more and more statistical regularities in human behaviour, in population, in trade, the incidence of disease, and so forth. The statistical accounts of the time read more like a cross between a Baedeker guide and *Whitaker's Almanack* than our current *Statistical Digests*. But more and more material became available in tabular form and social comparisons were possible over an ever-widening geographical domain. Population census were systematically conducted; the first in Britain occurred in 1801, although I think Iceland had one somewhat earlier. Life assurance became a science. Costs of living were measured by means of index numbers. The kind of enumeration and measurement which we should nowadays call descriptive statistics became a recognized part of government duties. But at the same time doubts were raised whether all this could be or should be blamed on to the Almighty. It seemed that social conditions could be altered by man himself, either by slow evolution or by revolution. The degree to which they should be changed and the manner of changing them have generated acute conflicts ever since.

We now enter on a long period during which a succession of men and women were drawn by their sociological interests into the measurement of social phenomena. They came from all kinds of disciplines. Lagrange, who suggested the first sample social survey round about the year 1790, was a mathematician. Quetelet, one of the greatest names in the subject, after a few false starts as painter, poet, and literary critic, succumbed to mathematics and became an astronomer. Le Play was a mining engineer. Charles Booth was a shipowner. Florence Nightingale was a nurse. Patrick Geddes was a botanist. I mention only a few of the formative individuals; it is no part of my present purpose to catalogue them all. But whatever their origins, whatever class of society from which they were drawn, however they acquired an interest in sociological matters, they were all, I think, motivated by two things; one was a profound dissatisfaction with things-as-they-were and a determination to change them; the other was a realization that it was necessary to measure social phenomena in some scientific way in order to clinch their sociological arguments.

Now statistics are well-known, in O. Henry's phrase, to be the lowest grade of information known to exist, and the compilation of statistical facts is often regarded as a necessary kind of drudgery but a drudgery none the less. In its practitioner it requires a degree of dedication that only another statistician could admire or wish to emulate. Down the years there have been continual protests from humanitarians that statistics can be twisted and misinterpreted and in any case give no true insight into the problems of humanity. The statistician, in fact, like the physical scientist, is pictured as a person devoid of human emotion. It may come as a surprise, then, to find that the early social scientists were dominated by an intensity of emotion which puts our current angry brigades in the shade. Florence Nightingale was described by her biographer as a passionate statistician. She had good reason to be, when the mortality of the British Army at the Crimea was 60 per cent per annum and that due to disease alone, apart from casualties due to enemy action. But she was far from being alone in her horror at the appalling social conditions which confronted her or in her determination to study them numerically.

The situation in which the social reformers of the nineteenth century found themselves differs radically from the one which confronts us today. They had no need to set up elaborate sociological hypotheses. All around them were poverty, slums, crime, disease, illiteracy, drunkenness, immorality. As they saw it these things were caused by man and it was man's duty to get rid of them. Social evil was so manifest to the Victorians that diagnosis was hardly necessary; it was the remedies that must be urgently sought. A few dissonant voices, of course, expressed the view that the poor had only themselves to blame, or that they were a regrettable but essential part of society, but the least altruistic men of the time could hardly avoid the mixture of guilt and compassion which was aroused by social studies. Nor, as it seems to me, was there much difference of opinion about the relative priorities of these various aspects of social degradation. The primary target was poverty. If that could be abolished much if not all social evil, crime and disease in particular, would disappear with it. 'I hate the poor,' said Bernard Shaw, 'I hope to live to see them abolished.' It was a holy simplicity of social aim which we can only envy in the light of our current problems.

There were two problems of present relevance which faced the sociologists of the nineteenth century. They are both method-ological. One was to decide what to measure; the other to find some way of measuring it.

In all statistical work there is an important distinction between counting and measuring. It is relatively easy to count births, deaths, the number of tubercular patients, the number of indict-ments for murder, the numbers of persons paying income tax, and so forth. A great deal of sociological data is still based on head-counting, and rightly so. But measurement is a different thing, especially in sociology. We must remember that whereas in the physical sciences everything can be expressed in terms of a few fundamental units, mass, length, time, and electric charge (which, whatever the philosophical problems involved, can in practice be measured with a high degree of precision) the be-havioural sciences are constantly struggling to measure, or at least to express in quantifiable form, concepts which are not directly observable such as utility, welfare, health, moral stand-ards, opinions, and attitudes of mind.

These problems are still with us. They are of three kinds.

1. First of all, it is not obvious that a particular word which we currently use to describe social circumstances corresponds to some-thing which is even theoretically measurable. The fact that we live in a welfare state and spend a lot of effort in maximizing welfare does not mean that we can measure a quantity of welfare.

2. It is therefore often necessary to measure quantities which are known to be associated with these indefinite concepts and are in fact observable. But this raises problems of choosing the right observables, and very often there are too many of them. We are, in fact, only just beginning to learn how to handle these multi-variate complexes.

3. Thirdly our units of measurement have the embarrassing property of being impermanent. The standard case is that of prices. One of the few things that the variables of economics have in common is that of value as expressed in price, and we

know only too well what can happen to prices even over a relatively short period.

The early sociologists saw these difficulties clearly enough and
it is to their credit that they were not thereby deterred from a
quantitative assault on their problems. An early example will
illustrate the nature of the problem and the lines along which
they attempted a solution. Pierre Le Play (1806–82), engineer,
economist, and senator, was one of the earliest sociologists to
insist on empirical studies of the human environment. It was he
who was mainly responsible for the family budget as a social
instrument, and he was in a position to devote considerable
resources to budgetary analysis. The budget, in fact, was to him
a supreme measure of social effects. 'There is nothing,' he says, 'in
the existence of a worker, no sentiment and no action worth
mentioning which does not leave a clear market trace in the
budget.' But Le Play was what might be described as a statistician
malgré lui. He distrusted any kind of generalization which lost
sight of the individual human being. He quantified case studies
but was flatly opposed to statistical summarization. It was Ernst
Engel, another mining engineer by training, who, basing himself
in part on Le Play's data, formulated the well-known law that
the proportion of income spent on food increases as the family
income decreases.

Le Play is, in fact, an interesting example of how a man can
evolve important research techniques on completely false hypotheses about the phenomena which he is studying. He was deeply
concerned with social conditions, but none of the evils which
were so evident to him was attributed to social evolution. As he
saw it some men were evil because they were born that way.
Others were, he believed, corrupted by false ideas, especially those
of Rousseau that man was born good and of Thomas Jefferson
that they had equal rights. Teachers, he maintained, do harm if
they do not consider themselves as supplementary agents of
parental authority; otherwise they disseminate dangerously novel
ideas. It is no surprise to find that Le Play does not figure very
prominently in the sociological syllabus of the L.S.E.[1] And yet

1. I am indebted for this information about Le Play to a comprehensive and
scholarly account by Paul Lazarfeld, 'Notes on the history of quantification in
sociology – trends, sciences, and problems', *Isis* 52 (1961), 277.

the man inspired a very great deal of quantified studies in the sociological field, and he is fairly to be regarded as one of the founding fathers of measurement in the behavioural sciences.

We have now to notice the monumental work of Charles Booth (1840–1916) on the *Life and Labour of the People of London*, the first volume being published in 1889 and the final, seventeenth volume, in 1903. The impact of this work was enormous. It may be fairly regarded as forming the evidence on which a long train of social legislation was to be based. Some of his early work was done in collaboration with Beatrice Potter, who later became Mrs. Sidney Webb, although he was, if anything, a conservative in politics. For our present purposes the importance of his work is not what he revealed but how he revealed it.

Booth's importance in empirical sociology rests on two grounds, his system of classification of the amorphous material which he had to reduce to order, and the fact that his social survey was conducted by sampling. I daresay that a modern purist would be able to fault him on both counts; certainly his sample would not attain the standards laid down by the Market Research Society. But in retrospect none of this matters against the overwhelming force of the numerical evidence which he produced. And all this, by the way, was carried out largely by his own efforts and at his own expense. It is typical that private enterprise led official statistics until quite recently. Like Florence Nightingale, Booth was highly critical of official statistics and his influence did much to improve them.

Booth's work on London was extended and supplemented by Seebohm Rowntree's work at York. Rowntree's report entitled *Poverty: A Study of Town Life*, published in 1901, rivals Booth's in thoroughness. He extended Booth's work by obtaining information more directly from the families themselves and can be regarded as the inventor of the Poverty Line, the standard minimum below which no individual should be allowed to fall if his health and well-being were not to suffer.

There are many distinguished names between Booth and Rowntree and the present day, Sidney Webb, Graham Wallas, Patrick Geddes, Harold Laski, to name only those most closely associated with the L.S.E. It was characteristic of their work, whether in sociology or in economics, that they set up their hypotheses without much statistical help. It was always pleasant, perhaps essential, to be able to adduce statistical information to support their arguments or to rebut those of their opponents. Indeed none of them would have denied the necessity for scientific evidence to support their theses. But I think it is true to say that few lines of sociological thought were derived by an inspection of data which the modern statisticians would regard as a representative sample. They came from the heart, not the head. Measurement was a rather lowly handmaiden whose duty it was to provide corroborative detail, not to throw up laws of behaviour or to discover new social relationships; least of all to suggest social remedies. This attitude is still quite common. In fact only recently have we begun to realize that intuitively based social policies are not only without scientific foundation but may frustrate the objectives of the very people who advocate them.

To the nineteenth-century sociologist, then, statistics as a subject was almost entirely a matter of data collection and validation. The upsurge of interest in statistics as a branch of scientific method occurred elsewhere in a biological context, deriving largely from the work of Galton and Karl Pearson. It was round about 1890 that it first dawned on the world that chance had laws as inexorable as the deterministic laws of physics, although earlier writers, and notably Quetelet, had drawn attention to the fact in the demographic context. This was exciting but not particularly shocking. There was no particular emotional resistance to the discovery that things like height of human beings or the lengths of claws in crabs or barometric heights at Kew had definite frequency distributions which could conveniently be summarized in mathematical form. But there was a good deal of emotional resistance to the assertion that social phenomena were equally subject to law. Although I do not know that anyone put it quite in this way, the general feeling seemed to be that, having taken the control of society out of the realm of Divine Providence and put it into human hands, humanity was not going to see it taken out of human hands and put at the mercy of the laws of chance. The feeling still exists. In consequence statistical theory developed in biology, meteorology, and latterly in psychology alongside the advances in social descriptive statistics, with little more than a distant nodding acquaintance with social theories.

There were exceptions to this general statement, but they serve only to emphasize its general truth. Pareto, for example, called attention to the distribution of incomes which bears his name; and incidentally it is remarkable how stable the shape of the Pareto distribution has been over the past eighty years in spite of all the egalitarian measures which have been introduced to undermine it. Edgeworth, although working mainly as an economist, produced observational patterns in voting behaviour and contributed a good deal to the mathematical theory of frequency distributions. Udny Yule applied correlation theory to studies of pauperism. It was left for one of the most honoured names in the rolls of the L.S.E. to bring together here the mathematical and the socio-economic approach. I refer to Arthur Lyon Bowley, whose work was lineally descended from that of Booth and Rowntree.

As long ago as 1860 Florence Nightingale wanted to found a chair in applied statistics at Oxford. Apparently she discussed the project at some length with Benjamin Jowett, Arthur Balfour, and Francis Galton. However, it seems that our senior universities were still whispering from their towers the last enchantments of the Middle Ages; only in the last few years have they recognized the enchantments of stochastic processes, and after thirty years of effort Florence gave it up. London was more receptive. Karl Pearson became Professor of Statistics at University College in 1911, having held a chair in applied mathematics since 1884. Bowley joined the staff of the L.S.E. when its first session began in 1895 and became its first Professor of Statistics in 1915, retiring in 1936 after forty years of continuous service.

Bowley was by training a mathematician, graduating as a wrangler at Cambridge in 1891. But he was not a creative mathematical mind and never used his mathematics to any effective extent. He was, however, an outstanding practical statistician. His work on livelihood and poverty, on foreign trade, and on wages and incomes formed models of statistical pertinacity and genuine insight which have had a profound effect on both private and official statistics. He wrote extensively on index numbers and helped to make concepts like national income useful by painstaking steps to show exactly how they should be measured. It has always seemed to me that one of his greatest contributions to the behavioural sciences was his insistence on the importance of measurement. Without going as far as Kelvin, who said that if you cannot measure what you are talking about your knowledge is of a meagre and unsatisfactory kind, Bowley made it plain that he had very little use for concepts which were not operationally meaningful. There was never a man over whose eyes one could pull so little wool.

Bowley's second great contribution was his advocacy of the sampling method. He may be fairly regarded as one of the founding fathers of the social survey. Round about the turn of the present century there were some vigorous arguments about the relative merits of complete census and what was then called 'the representative method', namely inquiry by representative sample. Official statisticians were in favour of complete enumeration. Bowley, who was always highly critical of official statistics and had an extensive knowledge of their shortcomings, argued for the representative method. He had no difficulty in convincing theoretical statisticians but it was uphill work in official quarters. And indeed, it was not until the Second World War that the British Government was forced to recognize sample surveys officially. The theory of sampling as we now have it in the social sciences is a much more sophisticated and mathematical subject than when Bowley considered it. But it still rests on the principles on which he insisted, the greater care which could be taken to secure accurate responses with trained interviewers confining their efforts to a moderately sized sample, the importance of avoiding bias, and the ascription of precision in quantified terms to the results.

Under Bowley's successors the statistical work at the L.S.E. has continued and flourished. It may be invidious to mention living individuals by name but I don't mind being invidious enough to call attention to the academic and public work of Sir Roy Allen and the fact that our professor of social statistics, Claus Moser, was chosen to become head of the Central Statistical Office. Wherever I go in the world I encounter students who recollect gratefully the statistical instruction they received here. In fact, from Bowley's time I think we can claim that we have at the L.S.E. one of the most powerful groups in the world of statisticians working in the behavioural sciences. Years ago I myself had some say in what they did. In the meantime the whole situation has changed radically with the advent of the computer. And so, with a complete lack of responsibility and possibly with their cordial disagreement, I want to go and describe what I think they should do next.

As I have already remarked, until a few years ago there were in existence social evils so glaring that no over-all social strategy was required to justify efforts to remove them. But sooner or later it becomes necessary to define what our social objectives are and in some way to quantify benefit or measure of success in attaining them. The nineteenth and the first half of the twentieth centuries paid little attention to this aspect of social organization, and when they did, usually came up with some vague and unsatisfactory criterion. Blake never explained just what kind of Jerusalem he wanted to build in England's green and pleasant land. Bentham's 'greatest happiness of the greatest number', in a period of expanding population, is nonsense. Phrases like 'from each according to his means, to each according to his needs' are not much better as operational criteria. We are now a little more sophisticated but not much. Not long ago I heard a trade unionist declare that his objective was to bring all wages up to the average. We have, in fact, a large set of social objectives, to eliminate infant mortality, to take care of the aged, to provide comprehensive medical care, to provide adequate housing, to ensure ease of transport, to extend educational facilities, and so on. It is obvious enough that limitation of resource prevents our carrying out comprehensive programmes for all of these simultaneously. It is almost equally obvious that a government tends to minimize electoral dissatisfaction rather than maximize social benefit in reconciling demands on those resources. But these are not points which I wish to make. The more important point is that if we pursue these social aims independently we may frustrate even the limited objectives which we set ourselves. In modern terminology, individual sub-optimization in a cybernetic system may be the reverse of optimization for the system as a whole.

An excellent example of this was provided two or three years ago by Professor Jay Forrester of the Massachusetts Institute of Technology in his book on *Urban Dynamics* (1969). A model structure was developed to represent the fundamental urban processes, showing how industry, housing, and people interact with one another as the city grows and decays. It is only by constructing models which reflect the highly interactive nature and the dynamic nature of the system that the consequences of any particular social measure can be followed through. Forrester, by the way, had as his collaborator a former mayor of Boston, Professor Collins, so he can hardly be accused of an uninformed approach. The two examined four common programmes for improving the depressed nature of the central city. One is the creation of jobs by transporting the unemployed by bus to the suburbs, or by governmental jobs as employer of last resort. The second was a training programme to increase the skills of the lowest income group. The third was financial aid from federal funds. The fourth was the construction of low-cost housing. 'All of these', says Forrester, 'are shown to lie between detrimental and neutral almost irrespective of the criteria used for judgement. They range from ineffective to harmful judged either by their effect on the economic health of the city or by their long range effect on the low-income population of the city.'

These conclusions, especially those concerning housing, are so unpalatable that I doubt whether any politician who hopes to retain power dare adopt them or even mention them. But the reasoning is quite clear.

In fact [says Forrester], it emerges that the fundamental cause of depressed areas in the cities comes from *excess* housing in the low-income category rather than the commonly presumed housing shortage. The legal and tax structures have combined to give incentives for keeping old buildings in place. As industrial buildings age the employment opportunities decline. As residential buildings age they are used by the lower income groups who are found to use them at a higher density population. . . . Housing, at the higher population densities, accommodates more low-income urban population than can find jobs. A social trap is created where excess low cost housing beckons low-income people inward. They continue coming to the city until their numbers so far exceed the available income opportunities that the standard of living declines far enough to stop further inflow. Income to the area is then too low to maintain all of the housing. Excess housing falls into disrepair and is abandoned. One can simultaneously have extreme crowding in those buildings that are occupied while other buildings become excess and are abandoned because the economy of the area cannot support all of the residential structures.

Many of you, I suppose, would instinctively repudiate Forrester's conclusions, or would claim that they do not apply to British conditions, although you may perhaps think that some of what he says strikes unpleasant notes of recognition. I adduce the example to show that under analysis by modern methods, intuition, and common sense are not enough. What I do claim is that in a highly interactive social organism simple and obvious remedies for evils in one domain may be entirely deceptive, and that it is essential to consider the organism as a whole.

Let us consider another example of a similar kind, the problem of transport by road. It goes without saying that a large city has traffic problems which will increase in intensity over the next decade at least. It is obvious, then, that we ought to widen our streets where possible, provide good parking facilities and build good access highways from the suburbs. No highway authority would have difficulty in getting approval for a programme along these lines and possibly financial assistance to implement it. But what then happens? The middle income groups move out of the city, to which they can now commute more easily, and abandon the centre to office blocks, expensive flats, and ghettos, and another cycle of social malaise is set up.

I have deviated somewhat from my main line of argument in order to broaden my terms of reference. The word 'measurement' assigned to the title of this lecture is only a part of the quantification which we can now bring to bear on social problems. We must consider it in the broader context of systems analysis, model-building, and simulation on the computer. Technology and political evolution have put at our disposal some new instruments of different orders of magnitude from those of thirty or forty years ago. The theory of social sampling; the generation of social data on regional, national, and international scale; and, of course, the computer itself. At the same time we have social problems of both old and new varieties. We are therefore in a position to consider anew the whole problem of sociological inquiry and to examine the consequences of social progress.

Admittedly the problem of constructing a model of our highly complex society is not an easy one. But it is essential if we are to attain our social goals. There is, after all, nothing new about model-building, and nothing new about building social models. The fact that we think about social organization at all in a logical way is equivalent to building a mental model, however ill-defined and incomplete it may be. It is nearly twenty years since Professor Phillips here constructed a physical model of the financial system, and although nowadays we do our modelling on a digital computer and not by analogue, it is still an instructive teaching instrument. The plain fact is that the unaided human mind is not capable of thinking about a highly interactive system in a quantifiable way. We can only think about it consciously a piece at a time and it is precisely this limitation which renders thinking about the system in its totality something in which we have to call on help from the logician, the mathematician, and the computer.

I take it that I need not describe at any length what the computer can do, but let me remove one or two misconceptions which still linger. The computer cannot think in any constructive way. It merely thinks strictly along lines which have been laid down for it in meticulous detail by a human being. Nor, in our present context, is it to be regarded as an arithmetic engine, a sort of electronic magnification of the desk calculators with which we are all familiar. It can, of course, do arithmetic and indeed all its operations proceed at a speed which even its high priests find astonishing. What makes it important for our purposes is the size of its memory which, if you add peripheral records on magnetic tape, is practically unlimited. This implies that we can write a program for the simulation of a model, however complex (within reason) and, having fed that program of instructions into memory, run the model as often as we like under all kinds of initial assumptions. We are at last able to experiment in the behavioural sciences.

One implication of this is that economics can no longer be left to the economists or sociology to the sociologists. The study of complex interactive systems requires an interactive team, behavioural scientists, mathematicians, statisticians, psychologists, systems analysts, and numerical data handlers. This is what we have, or are capable of having at the L.S.E. here. It is not for me, at least on this occasion, to suggest how such work should be put in hand, what its implication would be on research; or for that matter on the undergraduate syllabus. I am content to call attention to the enormous potential now available for new behavioural studies of an interdisciplinary kind, something which the L.S.E. has successfully done in the past and, I am confident, can equally successfully do in the future.

MODELS OF MAN

EDMUND LEACH

EDMUND LEACH

M.A. (Cantab.), Ph.D. (Lond.)

Provost of King's College, Cambridge

Professor of Social Anthropology, Cambridge University. Educated at Marlborough College; Clare College, Cambridge (Exhib.); served in the Second World War, Burma Army; graduate student L.S.E., 1938–9, 1946–7; Lecturer, later Reader, in Social Anthropology, L.S.E., 1947–53; Lecturer and later Reader, Cambridge, 1953–72; Anthropological Field Research: Formosa, 1937; Kurdistan, 1938; Burma, 1939–45; Borneo, 1947; Ceylon, 1954, 1956. Fellow of King's College, Cambridge, 1960–6; President, Royal Anthropological Institute since 1971; Chairman, Association of Social Anthropologists, 1966–70; Reith Lecturer, 1967. Publications include: *Social and Economic Organisation of the Rowanduz Kurds, Social Science Research in Sarawak, Political Systems of Highland Burma, Pul Eliya: A Village in Ceylon, Rethinking Anthropology, A Runaway World?, Genesis as Myth, Lévi-Strauss.*

MODELS OF MAN

My brief was to 'trace the changing concepts of the nature of man in society held by the corpus of the social sciences during the present century'. That was an impossible assignment. Between the ultra-idealism of Bernard Bosanquet writing in 1895 and the ultra-empiricism of B. F. Skinner writing in 1971 there is room for the whole of Western philosophy. So my approach will be eclectic. I shall use the word 'model' to mean a drastically over-simplified conceptual scheme which serves as an aid to thinking, like a drawing on a blackboard. Freud's description of the human personality as consisting of Super-Ego, Ego, and Id is a case in point. All the major sociological theorists of the past eighty years, Durkheim, Weber, Pareto, Malinowski, Radcliffe-Brown, Parsons, Lévi-Strauss, to name just a few, have been obsessional 'model' builders in this sense. On the present occasion, most of them will get scarcely a mention. But time is short.

As a start, let me draw attention to four particular models which have quite plainly had an influence on the work of the L.S.E. over the past seventy years, even though the models themselves are of much greater antiquity than that.

As I see it, these four models represent different attempts to deal with the same persistent existentialist difficulty. If human beings are not to live in total isolation from one another, then they will be linked in paired relationships which entail dominance and submission. Thus if I claim consciousness and free-will for myself this necessarily denies free-will to others over whom I am dominant. Yet if I recognize some other creature as 'human like myself', then I am asserting that his or her consciousness and free-will is strictly comparable to my own.

I. Descartes

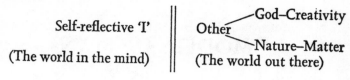

Self-reflective 'I'	Other ⟨ God–Creativity / Nature–Matter
(The world in the mind)	(The world out there)

II. Darwin (Comte) : 'Evolution'

> Similar to Model I but God and Nature are merged
> Nature becomes 'self-creative'

III. Mauss (Malinowski) : 'The Principle of Reciprocity'

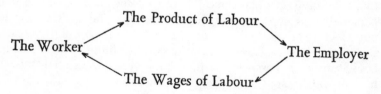

'A'   gift exchange   'B'

IV. The Young Marx : 'Alienated products of work'

The Product of Labour

The Worker   The Employer

The Wages of Labour

FIGURE 1. Four basic models.

Two of my models repudiate free-will. They assume that men are born as separate and individual animals. They can therefore ignore the uncomfortable reality that in paired human relationships one party is *always* dominant over the other. The other two models emphasize connectedness rather than individuality but again fail to come to grips with the fact that interrelationship implies domination.

A passage from de Tocqueville to which the distinguished French social anthropologist Professor Louis Dumont has recently drawn our attention can therefore serve as my text : 'Aristocracy had made a chain of all the members of the community, from the peasant to the King; democracy breaks that chain and severs every link of it.' (1)

My four prototype models are summarized in the diagrams in Figure 1 (p. 152). Let me gloss these diagrams.

Model I. *Descartes*

The Cartesian model polarizes mind and matter, subject and object, culture and nature. Here the self-reflective Ego looks out on to the material world as through a plate-glass window. He assumes, as a matter of faith rather than certain knowledge, that what he observes has reality and that Laws of Nature, as described in mathematics, are 'real' attributes of what goes on on the other side of the glass. The special puzzles of the Cartesian model stem from the artificiality of the separation of subject from object, of observer from observed. In a Cartesian world, natural other can have no will of its own. The state of the machine, as it is now, can only be altered by divine intervention. Hence Cartesian man, considered as object and as part of Nature, is always a man-animal, never a human being.

The Cartesian model is relevant for our discussion because social scientists have quite consciously tried to imitate the natural scientists. Positivistic social science, since Comte, has assumed that social facts exist, out there, as objective entities which are separate and different from the observer. It has been assumed that, as in any other science, these objective social entities are governed by natural laws. The practical dilemma is that, in real *social* situations, observer and observed are of the same human kind. The stuff under observation is capable of acting intentionally; it can tell lies. In such circumstances how can any observer arrive at 'objective truth'?

From this perspective much of the methodology of the social sciences consists of devices designed to separate observer and observed so as to reduce the status of the human beings under observation to that of mechanically controlled natural objects. This applies not only to behaviourist psychology in the style of B. F. Skinner but also to all forms of statistically based macro-economics and much else besides.

Model II. *Darwin (Comte)*

The original Cartesian world was fixed; the Laws of Nature immutable. The idea that there might be meta-Laws of Nature which would of themselves generate change rather than equilibrium only emerged during the nineteenth century. Historically the notion of *social* evolution was antecedent to that of *organic* evolution but, by the time this School was founded in 1895, the two doctrines had become merged in the *Idea of Progress*, of which Professor Ginsberg has written that: 'Despite its vagueness it became part of the general mental outlook and for many it provided a working faith of great vitality' (2). Notice that Professor Ginsberg describes belief in progress as a 'faith'.

Today most of us have become sceptical but earlier in this century there were many social scientists of high repute who believed that social evolution is governed by quite simple natural laws which are open to human discovery. Hobhouse and Westermarck, the first professors of sociology at the L.S.E., both adhered to this doctrine and they have had many successors.

Model III. *Mauss (Malinowski)*

The empiricist version of the Cartesian natural science model and the positivist Comtean model both assume that the goal of all true science must be *objectivity*. The human observer can be, *and should be*, separate from what he observes. The alternative proposition is that, where the stuff under observation consists of the behaviour of *human beings*, 'objectivity' of this Cartesian kind is just nonsense. Human individuals are *not* separable things, like matches in a matchbox. The observer is a participant member of a network of relationships which constitutes the field of his observation.

In that case the real subject matter of *social* investigation is *not* the behaviour of individuals considered as isolate animals, but the nature and content of a set of relationships. This thesis was the dominant doctrine of the functionalist social anthropology that was developed here in the L.S.E. by the pupils of Malinowski and elsewhere by the pupils of Radcliffe-Brown, but its clearest formulation is to be found in Marcel Mauss's *Essai sur le Don* published in 1924. 'I' and 'Other' are here assumed to be human beings of potentially *equal* status. Their mutual relationship is viewed as a *communication* which is manifested as material things which are exchanged between social persons. The 'things' which are exchanged are viewed as symbols rather than artifacts. The crux of this theory is that any gift, considered as object, mediates between Giver and Receiver and specifies by its nature the quality of the relationship between them. For example, a wedding ring is a material object which specifies the nature of the relationship between husband and wife. However, although it is an object, it is not a *separate* object. In a wedding, though the bridegroom gives the ring to his bride, he does not 'give it away'; it is still there within the field of his day-to-day experience, a symbol of the continuing bond, an enduring specification of his role as husband. The reciprocity of obligation between the partners will continue so long as the wife continues to wear her husband's ring. It is not a thing in itself.

So also in the more elaborated case of society conceived of as a total social system. Trobriand Society, as described by Malinowski, or Tikopia Society as described by Firth, was a network of interpersonal rights and obligations, a structure of indebtedness.

Model IV. *The Young Marx*
This model resembles the gift exchange model of Mauss and Malinowski in that it puts the emphasis on the stuff of the relationship rather than on the separate objectivity of individuals, but it also differs in a number of important respects. In the first place 'I' and 'Other' are here assumed from the start to be entities of *unequal* status; the reciprocity can never balance out; consequently relationships are always in a state of flux. Secondly, where the Maussian model sees the objects of exchange as symbols, the Marxist model sees them as artifacts; the material of relationship is the product of 'work'. This work or *praxis* may originate in God (as in Hegel) or in Man (as in Marx) but *work* can never be 'just a symbol'. Work is creativity, it constantly changes the state of the world.

The jargon terms *praxis* and alienation are unlikely to be found in English language sociology much before 1945 (though their German originals were common currency among the young Hegelians a whole century before that); but the model (without the jargon) had great influence upon a number of the most prominent figures in the L.S.E. from quite early days. I have in mind here books such as Harold Laski's *The State in Theory and Practice* (1935) and R. H. Tawney's *The Acquisitive Society* (1921). The latter work expounds the Marxist theory of *praxis* and alienation in its pure form without ever using these particular words.

Notice both the similarity and the difference between my Model III and my Model IV. In Model III the customary gifts exchanged between the two social persons A and B symbolize the social relationship existing between them. Up to a point Model IV might be considered just a special case of Model III. Worker and employer are two social persons. The worker gives the product of his labour to the employer; the employer gives back wages in exchange. Taken together, the exchange of wages for product 'symbolizes' the relationship of employer to worker. This is the schema of Model III. But, if this were an *adequate* description of the facts then, on Maussian theory, the work situation would constitute a bond of affection between the worker and his employer. It is thus significant that we encounter versions of functionalist sociology which manage to pretend that, in a well-managed firm, industrial relationships are cohesive in just this sense. Indeed Marx himself, in his youth, described an imaginary 'free' (i.e. non-capitalistic) industrial system which would operate in just this fashion. The products of labour would serve as symbols of the bond of affection between individual human beings.

But in capitalist industrial society as we actually know it, the situation is quite different. The worker in a factory who exchanges the product of his labour for money wages engages in a once-for-all transaction. He has not 'made a gift' of his labour product, he has *sold it*, like a commodity in the market, and thus lost all control of it. Instead of two social persons linked by a relationship expressed as a material bond, we now have three *separate* entities: Worker–Employer–Product. The product becomes a 'thing in itself'. To use Marx's own formula: 'The product of man is not his own but turns into a hostile power that dominates him.'

I propose now to go back to the beginning and show how these four models fit in with the existentialist dilemma of free-will.

The ambivalence of attitude which most of us feel towards the four models corresponds to our uncertainty about how social science may be distinguished from natural science. Everything that is taught here in the L.S.E. centres round the behaviour of culturally conditioned human beings. But what do we mean by that? Where do we locate the humanity as opposed to the animality of Man? Where do we draw the line between Man and non-Man?

In its most general form this is not just a problem for academics, it is a fundamental issue of philosophy and religion. If 'we' are *human*, what is it that makes us so? And how do we characterize those 'others' who seem to us either *less than human* (and therefore 'bestial') or *more than human* (and therefore 'divine')?

For those who work here in the L.S.E. the problem is especially intractable. Is it possible in social science to distinguish subject from object? Can a *scientific* observer accept the proposition that, if any 'individual other' is *human*, then he or she must have at least as much freedom of decision as I have myself?

In practice, we approach or avoid this problem in different ways according to the traditions of our respective academic disciplines. In the process some of us study the behaviour of *individuals*, others study the *networks of interaction between* individuals, others again discourse about *collectivities* (such as 'the working class' or 'the bourgeoisie') *as if* they were individuals, and yet others, including those who are the most prestigious, prefer to couch their arguments in charts and diagrams and mathematical equations and keep the human individuals out of sight altogether. So let me be strictly personal. How do I see the problem?

'We are all conscious human beings.' That statement implies much more than Descartes' self-reflective *cogito*. It means that if I am conscious, so are you. And it is *this* that constitutes *my* fundamental definition of humanity. All over the world men take it for granted that if 'I' can carry on a meaningful conversation with another creature, then that creature is 'like me' and my moral attitudes are adjusted accordingly. The rules which govern my behaviour towards *human* beings are often the exact converse of those which govern my behaviour towards *non*-human beings; but the distinction between human and non-human is conventional not absolute. For example, in peacetime in England, it is legitimate to kill (and even to eat) most animals other than man, but it is a major crime to kill any member of the species *Homo sapiens*. Yet, under conditions of warfare, when the boundaries of the group of people whom I am prepared to recognize as 'human like myself' becomes suddenly constricted, it becomes my moral duty to kill those who are sociologically inhuman even though they are still members of my own species *Homo sapiens*.

In this complex area of shifting moral values comparative ethnography suggests four generalizations. First: sharply polarized and superficially exhaustive distinctions of the kind 'people like us' *versus* 'people not like us' seem to be universally important elements in human thinking. Second: the boundaries between such categories vary with time and context. Third: the intermediate category which is neither one thing nor the other is always just as significant as the initially polarized opposition. Fourth: the intermediate category itself tends to expand regressively into a series. For example, in Roman Catholic theology, Jesus Christ mediates between the polar categories Man and God; the Virgin Mary then mediates between Man and Christ; and various saints mediate between Man and the Virgin Mary. The general point is that whatever it is that is made to serve as a link between 'I' and 'Other' will, in turn, come to be seen as 'Other' and call for further mediation. In this way the single binary opposition I/Other constantly generates *new* discriminations. With such qualifications in mind let us consider the major polarization, *Culture* versus *Nature*, where Culture is to be read as: 'People-like-us who are genuinely civilized, together with all the material products of our civilization' and Nature is to be read as: 'everything else'.

Because of the prejudices which have been built into my thinking through the circumstances of my own cultural background, I assume that the peculiarity of Man-in-Culture is that he can make conscious choices so as to alter the state of his surroundings.

By this reckoning, a human being, as distinct from an animal, is a creature that engages in purposive goal-directed activity, the outcome of which is made manifest in the products of work, or *praxis*. That is the operational definition which I myself employ in my day-to-day assumptions about my fellow human beings and their relationships to their environment.

Aristotle said something of the same kind but, in the form in which I have presented it, this is very much a modern Western man's view, which depends on the prior Cartesian assumption that Nature 'out there' is governed by mechanical laws and is incapable of acting intentionally. At most periods in history, in most parts of the world, men have made the opposite assumption, namely that intentionality is just as much an attribute of Nature as it is of ourselves and that, as a general rule, Nature is dominant over Culture rather than the other way about.

But in any case, for most of us, a category of Nature which is simply 'everything that is other than Culture' seems too broad to be useful. In practice, most people split this 'other' into two, as in Model I :

(*a*) Things and creatures and powers which are superior to us . . . the sphere of the *superhuman* or *supernatural*.

(*b*) Things and creatures and powers which are inferior to us . . . the sphere of the *subhuman* or physical.

The *subhuman* then embraces the physical world of material things and non-human living creatures and even the physical

Model IA

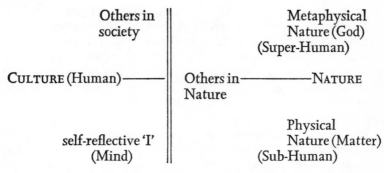

FIGURE 2. Generalized 'I'/'Other'–Culture/Nature schema.

substance of 'men like us' . . . in short, the whole range of stuff
which is the subject matter of the *natural sciences*. The *superhuman* is the domain of metaphysics and theology . . . the locus
of postulated 'supernatural power' . . . in one word, God.

We can readily put this elaboration of my original Model I onto a four-square diagram (Figure 2, Model IA, p. 159), but you
must appreciate that all sorts of further elaborations may arise
from the fact that the self-reflective 'I' sees himself not only as
'other than' Nature and 'other than' God, but also as 'other than'
Society. This last relationship may then be seen as one of encom-
passing hierarchy (for example, Ego is part of a family which is
part of a community, which is part of a society) or as one of
segmentary opposition. For example, Ego is a member of the
working class engaged in perpetual struggle against the ruling
class and so on.

But it is time that I tried to show how these very general statements and diagrams link up with the ancestors of sociology and
political thought. Let us start with Thomas Hobbes.

Hobbesian man belongs to my Model IA. He is a separated
individual living out there in Nature in a state of pre-culture.
In that condition he is governed by primal selfishness which leads
to a ruthless war of all against all. The transformation of animality to humanity, from Nature to Culture, then consists in a
voluntary agreement among individual men to live together
under the man-made rules of a sovereign power.

Hobbes saw the surrender of individual freedom as a conscious
act designed for the mutual benefit of all. By choice, man-in-
culture voluntarily lives under the constraints imposed upon him
by the sovereign acting on behalf of society (the Commonwealth),
but his selfish private 'nature' is unchanged. Considered as object,
the Hobbesian individual is part of sub-human Nature. He is only
dragged into civilization by the coercion of 'Others in Society'. If
we ignore such constraints, it is a Law of Nature that every individual will constantly act in such a way as to maximize his
private self-interests and satisfactions as he judges them to be.

This model is still very relevant. It lies at the base of even the
most respected economic theory; it is the justification for
behaviourist psychology of the Skinner type; it even forms part
of Durkheimian sociology, for Durkheim supposed that the

individual, who is constrained by the jural authority and religious ideology of Society, is in himself a Hobbesian selfish man.

Moreover, theory apart, the whole structure of the English penal system is built up around the proposition that the criminal is a Hobbesian selfish man on whom the normal constraints of society have failed to operate. Granted this assumption, it becomes self-evident that the rational reaction to any rise in the crime rate must always be 'to strengthen the forces of law and order'.

Writing in 1650 Hobbes assumed that the social constraints on the individual are consciously created institutions. One hundred and twenty years later but still 120 years before the publication of Durkheim's *Suicide,* Adam Smith came to recognize that the individual acts of men, when considered statistically, contain patterns which have nothing to do with conscious intentions. To use my Marxist jargon, he recognized that the *selfish* acts of individuals might result in a collective *praxis* of an altruistic kind. In particular, he held that when nations become wealthy it is because the selfish individual 'is led by an invisible hand to promote an end which is not part of his intention'.

Hegel, who was a close reader of Adam Smith, took this metaphor quite literally and recast my generalized Model IA roughly on the lines of Model IB (Figure 3). The paired dichotomies are the same as before but they are no longer separate. The emphasis is now upon relationships rather than isolates; on the process which drives the 'system as a whole' rather than on the objectivity of its component parts. Thus Model IB is also a version of Model IV.

Model IB/IVA

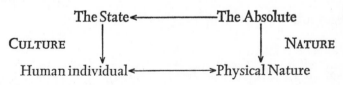

FIGURE 3. The 'I'/'Other' schema as implied by Hegelian dialectic. The emphasis in this case is not on the polarized categories but on the interaction (dialectic) which is generated between them.

For Hegel, the ultimate generative force (creativity) is the metaphysical Absolute (Spirit). The State is then the objectification of Spirit in the world, the *praxis* or 'self-alienation' of God. The State is thus the invisible hand of God promoting God's will in a mysterious way by patterning the sum total of the individual acts of selfish men so that all is in conformity with God's great design.

Around 1844 Feuerbach took Hegel's model and turned it back to front. In effect he maintained that the starting-point of Model IB should be *not* the abstract metaphysical First Cause in the top right hand corner but the self-conscious individual in the bottom left-hand corner. God is a figment of the human imagination; the State and its institutions are the products of *human* creativity.

The young Marx and Engels in the 1844–8 period then pressed the same argument a stage further. We delude ourselves when we postulate a self conscious 'I' which is 'other than' a non-conscious world of Nature. 'Reality' consists in the interaction between the creativity of man and his surroundings. Reality is thus *praxis*, the productivity of man in the world, and *praxis* is the 'objectivization' or 'alienation' of human creativity.[1]

If we use the terminology in this way it becomes part of the definition of *praxis* that it is constantly altering the state of the world: not only the natural physical world external to man but also the social environment of man himself, including the theoretical ideas in terms of which men perceive their historical situation.

In these terms, modern industrial society is the outcome of the evolution of past *praxis*; which is much the same as saying that it is the consequence of the history of technology. However, according to Marxist theory, wage/labour relationships, as we encounter them in industrial society, represent a radical break with the past. This is because *industrial* man's behaviour is based on Model I *individualistic* assumptions, whereas *pre-industrial* man operated with Model III *reciprocity* assumptions. We have come to think of individuals as separate from each other and from the things that they make, whereas formerly human products had

---

1. Marx uses the two words objectivization (*Entäusserung*) and alienation (*Entfremdung*) interchangeably. Engels makes a subtle distinction between the two. See reference 3.

always served to express continuing relationships. This is the point of the De Tocqueville quotation which I cited right at the beginning (p. 152).

This classical Marxist argument entails a restructuring of the categories on the left-hand side of Model IB. Instead of the State we now have the Capitalist Ruling Class and instead of the Human Individual we have the Working Class. The process of alienation through wage labour is such that the worker's creativity is separated from him in material form and converted into the 'surplus value' which becomes the profit of the capitalist and the means by which the capitalist controls 'the means of production'.

The moral crux of the argument is that the surplus value which is the instrument of the labourer's exploitation originates as the labourer's own divinity: his uniquely *human* power to alter the state of the world. 'What is God?', wrote Engels in an early euphoric moment, 'God is man' (4).

At this point, let us go back to the beginning of this century and the beginnings of the L.S.E. When sociology was added to the curriculum in 1904, Hegelian dialectic was going out of fashion and the latest up-to-date model of Man entailed an optimistic belief in progress of the kind which I referred to earlier when I quoted from Professor Ginsberg. It was this positivist progressive climate of opinion which produced, as one of its earliest and most enduring products, Professor Hobhouse's *Morals in Evolution*, the first edition of which appeared in 1906.

One striking characteristic which this book shares with a number of other L.S.E. productions of the same period, and in particular with the works of Professor Westermarck, is that although Hobhouse and Westermarck were both professors of sociology the data that they used was exclusively anthropological. This superficially surprising fact is entirely consistent with the point that I have already made, namely that the social scientists of that day had come to believe that in order to be *truly scientific* it was necessary to adopt some version of my Model I or IA. Although the subject matter of social science was man, the observer needed to separate himself from his subject matter; objectivity necessitated an attitude of impersonality and social distance. Hobhouse and his colleagues showed no interest at all in the lives of individual members of the 'simpler societies'; they were concerned only with 'varieties of custom', 'varieties of social rule', 'varieties of forms of organization'. Human beings, as such, did not enter into their discussions. It is thus understandable that the very 'personal' kind of social anthropology introduced by Malinowski after the First World War, which was based on my Model III, filled them with revulsion.

It needs to be remembered too that because social evolution was at this date being discussed in a Darwinian climate it was thought of as an extremely slow process which was quite compatible with attitudes of extreme conservatism.

In 1909, outside a narrow circle of intellectuals, the prevailing model of Man was still both Protestant and medieval. The Protestant element emphasized the possibility of individual redemption . . . the industrious apprentice could hope to make a personal fortune, the benevolent millionaire could hope to save his own soul. But conversely, the medieval element emphasized the inevitability of the *status quo* and the immobility of the social system considered as a whole. Each individual human being had been born into his proper station; the qualities needed by members of the ruling class were above all, matters of *breed*. It was part of God's great design that the enlightened Europeans should conquer the world so that Christian missionaries might bring the light of the true faith to benighted savages beyond the pale. But although their *souls* were to be saved, their destiny was to be servants.

And even here in the L.S.E., where advanced ideas were being discussed and the general temper was egalitarian and anti-imperialist (at least to the extent that the *possibility* of working-class participation in government was supposed to be taken quite seriously), the general style was Fabian and genteel. In its L.S.E. context, the theme of progress was in no way *revolutionary*, it was simply the very long term consequence of a kind of natural law of historical development. The evidence of comparative ethnography was treated as the prehistoric archaeology of 'modern' society. The Australian aborigines deserved study because they were a kind of living fossil; they exhibited to the close observer what our own civilization had been like before the dawn of *true* history. They belonged to a different epoch of evolutionary development. They were not people-like-us. They were scarcely human.

Why the Australian aborigines? Well, they wore no clothes and were a long way off in space, so they could be thought of as a long way off in time.

Social evolution was assumed to be something which happened to whole societies in the course of millennia. It was something that had happened in the past and no doubt it would happen in the future. But it was remote. It was something about which one could feel detached and scientific.

We are here back at the issue I raised earlier on. If our practical use of the category 'humanity' is that it means 'people like us', where do we draw the boundary between ourselves and the other? Alternatively, since a human being, thus defined, is a creature that can tell lies, how can the student of human beings *ever* hope to arrive at 'objective' truth?

Historically, the social scientists have tried to escape from this dilemma in a variety of ways. The first of these, in terms of chronological development, was to treat cultural difference as if it were species difference.

This general style of thinking goes back a long way and it can be used either to belittle or to enlarge the cultural implications of racial difference. For example, the liberally inclined Rousseau argued at length that on the evidence available, *he* had no grounds for thinking that the physical difference between men and apes was any greater than that between different varieties of Man. But such variations of appearance are differences of *kind* not of *superiority*. If we now observe as we do that men treat one another as superior and inferior, owners and slaves, *these* are differences of *status, not* of kind. *Inequality of status is a product of culture not of nature.* But Rousseau's less sophisticated followers saw the matter in simpler terms. If, as Rousseau claimed, some savages are indistinguishable from apes, then this clearly implies that they are *innately* inferior to ourselves, particularly in regard to morality and intelligence. This self-evident fact could then be used as a justification for the institution of slavery, or, if need be, for genocide.

Such problems are still with us even in Wolverhampton and Notting Hill. Thirty years ago the English professed to be deeply shocked when Hitler decided to exterminate the Jews and the gypsies on the grounds of their racial inferiority but, only a century earlier, British settlers in Tasmania had successfully eliminated the local inhabitants on the grounds that they were vermin. Throughout the nineteenth century the most hotly debated issue among anthropologists was whether the 'living races of mankind' were to be regarded as a single species with a common ancestry or as a hybridization of several originally distinct animals.

Incidentally, in liberal circles, the bias has now gone so far the other way that the doctrine of the universal brotherhood of mankind has assumed the status of an unquestionable religious dogma. It has thus become impossible for anyone to attempt a serious study of racial difference without being accused of racial prejudice even before he has started!

However, the point I want to emphasize in the present context is simply that, when the L.S.E. was first founded, a 'racialist' attitude was more or less taken for granted.

One of the characteristics which was universally attributed to the 'other', 'lower', races was that they were 'slaves to custom' to an extent that we ourselves are not. It was precisely because primitive customs were axiomatically known to be stable and invariant that savages could be observed scientifically and objectively, much as one might study the behaviour of rats or baboons.

This belief has shown extraordinary persistence. In the contemporary literature relating to the 'development' of the countries of the Third World, there is still a widespread tendency to polarize 'modern' society with 'traditional' society. 'Traditional' society is timeless; it is what was there before the Europeans came along; it is imagined as a changeless state of stability. By implication, culture change of any kind is an *abnormality*, which has to be explained as a response to some special *abnormal* cause, namely the 'impact' of progressive 'modern' society. This mode of thinking, I regret to say, was at one time taken for granted here in this School and was vigorously supported by Malinowski himself.

It should be noticed that all such theories which postulate the 'impact' of one cultural system upon another require the assumption that any alien culture is an 'objective' phenomenon of material Nature. Cultures are seen as *things* 'out there', like billiard balls. This is the logical outcome of trying to force social data into the Cartesian mould of the natural sciences. The necessary consequence is that man in 'traditional' societies comes to be treated as an animal rather than as a human being.

This essentially positivist position stands in sharp contrast to the Hegelian derived theory of *praxis* which takes it as axiomatic that it is in the nature of human beings that they should be constantly generating change in their environment, including the culture of their own society.

Over the past twenty years, as a result of the influence of French Structuralism and New Left versions of Marxism, Hegelian models have been coming back into fashion and most of us now take it for granted that human societies are *normally* in a state of flux rather than normally in a state of stability. Consequently it is easy to forget how very 'original' this point of view appeared to be when, in defiance of their master, it was first tentatively formalized here in the L.S.E. by some of Malinowski's pupils in the period 1936–8.

In this connection historians of social anthropology need to remember that when Malinowski undertook his own fieldwork at the time of the First World War and for a long while afterwards, he himself fully accepted the prevailing convention that the Trobrianders were to be regarded as living fossils who lacked the kind of free-will which we habitually claim for ourselves.

Since I was myself for a while a pupil of Malinowski, I should perhaps say something very briefly about that remarkable man. The major innovation which Malinowski introduced into social anthropology was the proposition that the social anthropologist is concerned with the social behaviour of human *individuals* in their face-to-face interactions rather than with 'the customs of primitive peoples'. In my original diagram I have put Malinowski alongside Mauss as the upholder of Model III. But this is an oversimplification. Despite his emphasis on 'the principle of reciprocity' some features of Malinowski's model were distinctly Hobbesian. He assumed that each individual is constantly seeking to operate the prevailing social conventions so as to maximize his private satisfactions. 'Malinowskian man' is thus a pragmatic politician who has an innate understanding of the powerful coercions which he can impose upon his fellows by putting them under social obligation to himself.

Any such game of personal politics is played out within the matrix of an established culture, but, for Malinowski, established culture was by definition stable and self-consistent. Hence the different aspects of customary behaviour (economic, legal, religious, political, and so on) could always be treated as mutually supporting frameworks for a system of reciprocal obligations deriving from the basic kinship organization of the society under examination. In its day, this kind of Malinowskian functionalism seemed to bring new life and realism to the dry as dust conventions of orthodox ethnography but, in retrospect, most of it seems to carry quite preposterously conservative implications. Against the backdrop axiom of 'a functionally integrated cultural whole', any conceivable kind of social development is bound to appear abnormal, pathological, and self-destructive.

But all that was an elaboration of the theme that we can avoid the existentialist dilemma by treating cultural difference as species difference.

A second line of escape which many social scientists have adopted has been to invent the figment of statistical man. The origins of this model go back at least as far as Adam Smith and Ricardo for the economists, to Edward Tylor for the social anthropologists, and to Durkheim for the sociologists, but in these modern days of databanks and computers the faceless monster of the 'average man' needs rather close inspection.

The idea is simple enough: there is safety in numbers. Individuals may cheat and change their minds and tell lies, but if the numerical scale is large enough, such 'errors' will cancel out. Provided the sample is sufficiently random the figures are bound to reveal 'the truth', or at any rate some sort of truth. But what sort of truth? Once again the search is for laws of Nature appropriate to a Cartesian world.

At the back of all forms of statistically based social science is the belief that resort to numbers, probability coefficients, and so on, will lead to truths which are scientific and objective *in the same sense* as are the discoveries of the hard scientists (such as the physicists, the chemists, and the astronomers). They will be facts which are governed by 'mathematical laws' which somehow exist, like the law of gravity, independently of any human intention. In the pay-off, things do not seem to work out like that; the calculations of the astronomers and the physicists will safely take you to the moon and back; the calculations of the economists cannot even tell you what your pound sterling will be worth in German deutschmark by this time tomorrow morning.

I suspect that nearly all of us are rather ambivalent about this anomaly. We will recognize the existence of Adam Smith's 'invisible hand' which promotes ends which are no part of the individual's intention and we would all like to believe that the mysterious operations of this invisible hand could somehow be shown to conform to some kind of scientific 'natural law'. If the subtle procedures of the statisticians, many of which were invented here in the L.S.E. by Professor Bowley and his very distinguished successors, *could* be made to reveal such laws we should all applaud. On the other hand, most of us derived considerable private enjoyment from the signal failure of the opinion pollsters to predict the outcome of the last General Election. All the same, if that imaginary character 'the average man in the street' can exhibit a will of his own in this way, it is a serious matter for everyone who professes to be engaged in social *science*.

I am well aware that I have skirted round large parts of my assignment. I have said nothing of Freud, whose model of man, whatever its limitations, has had enormous influence on the development of all varieties of social theory. I have said nothing of Weber, whose concept of rational–legal bureaucracy can be put alongside the regularities of primitive custom and the regularities of statistical behaviour as a third kind of *predictable social behaviour*. And finally I have said nothing of that version of my Model I which led Durkheim to conceive of society as a kind of superman with the attributes of God. But I warned you from the start that I intended to be eclectic. So let me sum up.

The main point that I have been trying to make in this lecture is double-sided. First of all, any kind of discourse in the social sciences presupposes a model which specifies the basic relationship of human beings to their environment. This is true even when the details of the model are not spelled out.

But these ideas are matters of fashion rather than of fact.

Consequently, models which seem at first sight to be diametrically opposed, such as that of Karl Marx when compared with that of Auguste Comte, turn out on closer inspection simply to be transformations of a single theme.

I have exemplified this transformation thesis by reference to four particular models. I have also made the point that *because* all those who work here in the L.S.E. think of themselves as social *scientists* they tend to be biased towards my Models I and II which are the prototype models of *natural* science. Anyone who is inclined this way is liable to be embarrassed by the intrusion of my Models III and IV which come respectively from social anthropology and left-wing political theory. By special pleading I have been suggesting that, if anything, your bias *ought* to go the other way. I am suggesting that ever since the beginning of the century we have been much too ready to assume that Cartesian models appropriate to the natural sciences *must* be applicable to the social sciences also. We have taken it for granted that a value-free sociology is a possibility and that the attainment of value-free objectivity is the primary justification for all social science methodology. We ought to be more open-minded. The boundary between the human and the non-human is more obscure than has sometimes been supposed. It may or may not be the case that there is an area of *human* science to which the principles of non-human science *cannot* be applied. On that issue I am uncommitted. All I am saying is that, as social scientists, we do not have to take it for granted that in order to be scientific we *must* imitate the natural scientists all along the line.

The issue is all the more acute for us because the boundaries between Culture and Nature are becoming very blurred. Up to now the limits of the problem have seemed fairly simple. We may not be too willing to concede that all men are brothers, but at least, for the past two centuries, we in the Western world have been prepared to let the zoologists set the boundaries. *Homo sapiens* is different. *Language*, we claim, provides mankind with a special kind of consciousness which is *not* shared by other animals. But now even that prop to our vanity is becoming insecure. Jane Goodall's chimpanzees are seen to have individual personalities; robots in California display 'human' cleverness. We need to go back and think out once more just what *we* really are. Do we claim that mind is *uniquely* a quality of man? Are we prepared to attribute mind-like qualities to collectivities of men? If logic machines do *not* possess minds, by what criteria do we make the distinction? Questions of this sort are not just word play. They have real importance for all social scientists. I do not believe that any of us can provide confident answers, but we need to be on our guard lest in our future model-making we once again forget that man as human being is something other than *either* an animal *or* a machine.

REFERENCES

1. DE TOCQUEVILLE, A., *Democracy in America*, vol. ii, part 2, chap 2, p. 92 (Paris: Gallimard, 1961), 2 vols.
2. GINSBERG, M., *The Idea of Progress: A Revaluation*, p. 2 (London: Methuen, 1953).
3. LICHTHEIM, George, *Marxism*, p. 49 n. (London: Routledge & Kegan Paul, 1961).
4. TUCKER, R., *Philosophy and Myth in Karl Marx*, p. 73 (Cambridge, at the University Press, 1964).

SOCIAL KNOWLEDGE
AND THE
PUBLIC INTEREST

JOHN W. N. WATKINS

JOHN W. N. WATKINS

B.Sc. (Econ.), M.A. (Yale)
Professor of Philosophy
The London School of Economics
and Political Science

He abandoned a naval career to enrol as a student at the L.S.E. in 1946. He taught political thought there from 1950 until 1957, when he joined Professor (now Sir Karl) Popper's department. He is the author of a book on Hobbes and of numerous papers in the fields of philosophy of science, political philosophy, philosophy of history, social theory, and practical reason.

SOCIAL KNOWLEDGE AND
THE PUBLIC INTEREST

I

The first prospectus of the London School of Economics, in 1895, stated that training would be provided in the methods of scientific investigation (1). Scientific method was to be cultivated, and not just left to take care of itself.

Sidney and Beatrice Webb each had their reasons for endowing scientific method with high importance. In Sidney's case, the reason was, ultimately, political. His founding of the L.S.E. was connected with his long-term political programme, namely, the gradual, but systematic and unremitting, collectivization of British society. This process of gradual collectivization would require a lot of new social knowledge which would have to be gained through systematic research. In September 1894, after the Hutchinson bequest, Beatrice wrote in her diary that they did not want to spend the money on 'mere propaganda of the shibolleths of collectivism . . . Reform will not be brought about by shouting. What is needed is *hard thinking* . . . So Sidney has been planning to persuade the other trustees to devote the greater part of the money to encouraging *research* and economic study. His vision is to found, slowly and quietly, a London School of Economics and Political Science' (2a).

If the L.S.E. was to assist, albeit in an indirect way, the process of gradual collectivization, should it not be staffed by people sympathetic to collectivism? Sidney's answer to this was unequivocal. The knowledge needed for reforming society must be genuinely scientific knowledge. The L.S.E. must therefore be an independent academic institution with no political bias imposed upon it. It did not matter what political views its members held *so long as they believed in and practised the methods of scientific research.*

The reason why Beatrice attached a high value to scientific method was more romantic. She had a religious temperament; but she was not a believer. I get the impression that the vacuum was at least partially filled by a fierce belief in scientific method as an austere code demanding self-abnegation and humility before the facts. Scientific method was a lifelong concern of hers. In 1889 she had written in her diary of 'the advancement of society on the one [and] only basis that can bring with it virtue and happiness—scientific method' (3a). In 1923 she and Sidney declared that 'without the application of the scientific method to social organization the crucial problem of democracy . . . cannot be solved' (4a). In 1932 they published a book on scientific method. It would not be difficult to poke a little gentle fun at this book: for instance, at its 'recipe for scientific note-taking in sociology' (each separate fact, relating to one time and place, to be recorded on a separate sheet of large quarto paper [5]). There is not much philosophizing about social knowledge in this book; it is more a manual of practical advice about the scientific investigation of institutions and social problems.

But down-to-earth thinking does not always stay down. (Geometry *began* as land-measurement.) You may try to avoid abstract methodology and confine yourself to practical ways of advancing your science. But the questions unavoidably arise: Towards *what* do we want our science to advance? And what should be the general method of its advance? In 1906 Beatrice gave an address at the L.S.E. which opened with a brisk answer to the last question:

What we have to do in social science is to apply the scientific method to the facts of social life. There is only one scientific method— that used in physical science. It consists of three parts—observation, conjecture as to the cause and effect of the facts observed, and after-wards verification by renewed observation. That is the scientific method (6).

Some answers seem to be begging to be turned back into questions. Do we have to apply in social science the same method that is used in physical science? Does this method consist of observation, conjecture, and verification? Indeed, is there really such a thing as 'the' scientific method?

No very striking answers to questions like these came out of the L.S.E. before the 1930s. Abraham Wolf was an excellent historian of science (7) and he did valuable scholarly work on Spinoza (8, 9). But he was an old-style logician and his textbook on scientific method (10) is little more than a rehash of Mill's canons of induction. Graham Wallas was, by all accounts, a wonderful teacher (11); but he did rather bumble on about the psychology of scientific thinking, endlessly intoning the magic formula 'Preparation, incubation, illumination, verification' (12). (In preparing this talk I seized on a lecture by Wallas entitled 'Physical and Social Science' [13], expecting some methodological discussion; but the conclusion to which it cautiously proceeds is that London University should modify its arrangements for post-graduate registration!)

However, from the early 1930s on, a powerful and distinctive methodological tradition developed at the L.S.E. This was, to begin with, the achievement of certain economists reflecting on their own science. What might be called the Venetian view of economics—that economics is a beautiful structure and none the worse for resting on rotten foundations (14)—has never been popular here. To straighten out and clarify the content and status of certain key assumptions and concepts at the basis of economics was an aim common to Robbins (15a), to Hicks and Allen (16), and to Hutchison (17). Hayek, from his familiarity with the methods of economic analysis, went on to develop a general methodology of social knowledge. His famous series of papers, 'Scientism and the Study of Society', appeared in *Economica* during 1942–4 (18) at around the same time as another famous series of papers, Popper's 'The Poverty of Historicism' (19a). The methodological tradition at the L.S.E. was, of course, powerfully reinforced by the arrival of this man, whom Medawar has called, uncontentiously, 'our foremost methodologist of science' (20).

It is this methodological tradition that I want to discuss. But it is too big for me to attempt a general survey of it. I need a principle of selection.

It sometimes happens that a line of inquiry, or a 'research-programme' as Lakatos called it (21), throws up results that rebound against the hopes that originally inspired it. For example, James I ordered John Selden to refute the Puritan claim that Jesus was not born on 25 December. But Selden's researches revealed that changes in the Jewish calendar system made it 'impossible for us to know when our Saviour was born' (22). A more modern example: the old hope of finding a set of axioms from which all mathematical statements could be proved if true, or disproved if false, led eventually to Gödel's famous proof that for *any* consistent set of axioms there are mathematical statements that are neither provable nor disprovable. Or consider an example nearer home: the hope of replacing the crude maxim of classical utilitarianism by a formally consistent and ethically adequate social welfare-function led eventually to Arrow's famous Impossibility-Theorem, about which I shall say something later.

I thought that it might help to give some shape to my lecture if I asked whether anything similar has happened in our own case. Has our methodological tradition produced results which rebounded (in an objective and impersonal way) against the gradualist collectivism which originally inspired the creation of the School and the conscious cultivation of scientific method within it?

II

Well, there is surely no conflict between the gradualist aspect of Webbian collectivism and our methodological tradition. On the contrary, this fits in well with Popper's idea of piecemeal engineering, which explicitly included 'the possibility that a series of piecemeal reforms might be inspired by one general tendency' (19b). Since it is still resisted in some quarters, I would like to pause, for a moment, to restate the argument for piecemeal engineering in four easy steps.

First, any deliberate political reform relies on certain sociological hypotheses; at the very least, on the hypothesis that the proposed measure, call it A, will in fact lead to the desired result, say B.

Secondly, there being no infallible sociological knowledge, it is possible that these hypotheses are either false (A will not lead to B) or seriously incomplete (A will lead to B but also to C, where C may be an unintended result such that the reformer would rather forgo B than have B together with C).

Thirdly, if political reform is to be a rational process, and not a blind gambling with people's lives, political reformers should be in a position to learn from their more serious mistakes, and to correct them.

Fourthly, it will, however, be practically impossible to identify specific mistakes during a sweeping transformation of society. In a massive upheaval, we can hardly ascribe any particular result to any particular measure (any more than we could pinpoint the specific source of the trouble if a powerhouse blew up after some nut-case got in and started throwing all the switches).

It should be remembered that when Popper was developing this argument a lot of influential intellectuals *were* calling for a total remodelling of our society: utopian engineering, as he called it, was in the air. (I may mention in parenthesis that his attack has proved effective in one rather unexpected quarter: nowadays, those intellectuals who despise piecemeal engineering, and who engage in wholesale condemnation of Western society, have mostly lost interest in utopian engineering too. 'The critical theory of society possesses no concepts which could bridge the gap between the present and its future [I am quoting Marcuse, who ought to know] . . . it remains negative' (23). It is as if the cry of the French Revolution, *Tout détruire, puisque tout est à recréer!*, had been shortened to *Tout détruire!*)

Critics have asked: how large does a reform have to be for it to cease being a 'piecemeal' reform? But it is not just a question of size. The question is whether the measure is carried out in a way that allows us to keep track of its main effects, intended and unintended, and to change it if it goes wrong. The eighteenth amendment to the American Constitution, introducing Prohibition, was quite a large-scale experiment, and one partly inspired by a certain moral utopianism; but that did not lift it out of the category of piecemeal engineering. It was based, among other things, on the hypothesis that prohibition of the sale of alcohol would lead to a big reduction in crime. It led instead to a big refutation of that hypothesis; and it was repealed.

III

I turn now to the more controversial question of the bearing of our methodological tradition on the collectivism of the Webbs. As a first step, let me distinguish three main kinds of collectivism, namely: *ethical* collectivism, *sociological* collectivism and *political* collectivism. I will try to elucidate these terms later. But first I want to mention some evidence which suggests to me that the Webbs may have been, at least in their 'Sunday-thinking', collectivists in all three senses.

In a Fabian Tract of 1896 Sidney introduced the concept of *social health*; this, he wrote, 'is something apart from and above the separate interests of individuals, requiring to be consciously pursued as an end in itself' (24). That sounds like ethical collectivism to me; and it appears to presuppose some kind of sociological collectivism: social health is, presumably, the health of something collective. The Webbs liked to talk about 'the social organism'. Mrs. Letwin (3b) has shown that social organicism was a significant tendency in their social philosophizing. They seem to have regarded capitalist civilization as a giant collective which is sick and, indeed, doomed to extinction (4b); and they came to regard Soviet Communism as another giant collective—which, however, enjoys rude health and will survive (25). As to their political collectivism, we might summarize it (no doubt unfairly) thus: the economic life of society will be increasingly organized and controlled until state and society merge into one vast public enterprise.

After this rather perfunctory exegesis I shall now cut adrift from the Webbs and leave myself free to put more definite interpretations on the three kinds of collectivism I mentioned.

IV

I begin with *sociological* collectivism. A full-blooded version of it would run something like this: Sociology is concerned with social collectives, whether these be actual institutions (trade unions, churches, governments) or looser social systems (a caste-system, an industry, a primitive culture). A social collective is more than the sum of its individual members and their relations to one another. A social collective may allow considerable *spielraum* to its members. Nevertheless, they are caught up, whether tightly or loosely, in a network which has tendencies of its own, tendencies which may be resisted for a time but which will prevail in the end. Of course, the sociologist has to observe how individuals function within the collective. But this is subsidiary to his main interest which is to penetrate behind the human detail to the structure of the collective itself and to discover its underlying law of development.

This view has not gone wholly unrepresented at the L.S.E.; but the methodological tradition I have singled out was strongly opposed to this sort of collectivism. A systematic case against it was put by Hayek (18), with acknowledgements to Carl Menger. Hayek accepted one negative thesis from sociological collectivism, namely, that social formations (he preferred this term to 'social collectives') are seldom products of conscious design. True, some institutions have been deliberately instituted; but they have almost invariably developed in ways unforeseen by their instituters (as the Webbs would no doubt acknowledge if they could return to the L.S.E. today). And some of the most ubiquitous 'institutions' (money, for instance, and language) never were *instituted*. But the fact that a social formation is not the result of human design by no means implies that it has an independent existence: it may be the unintended result of human activities. Consider a market. For a given individual, the market exists 'out there'. It has something like the objective reality of Durkheim's *choses sociales*. But it exists as a result of the activities of countless people participating in it.

According to Hayek, the only way to discover something of the structure and working of a social formation is to investigate it from the inside. We have to try to reconstruct it from our knowledge of the participating individuals, and from an understanding of the ways in which they interact and thereby engender unintended social regularities. Hayek called this the 'compositive method'.

It may be asked how the social scientist could know beforehand which individual activities are relevant for the reconstruction of a social formation if he can form no idea of the social formation until he has first reconstructed it from a knowledge of individuals The answer is that he starts, not from scratch, but from some earlier and cruder individualistic model of it.

According to this individualistic approach, social qualities are attitude-dependent: a piece of paper is a pound note only because it is regarded as a pound note, and a man in a dark blue uniform is a policeman only because he is regarded as a policeman. I believe, however, that this approach can take us a long way towards Durkheim's idea of the hard, obstinate, thing-like nature of social phenomena. Take a republican in eighteenth-century France who wants to abolish the monarchy. Now the present view does, admittedly, have the following implication. If this man could have dropped tablets into the municipal water-supply which would have induced remarkable changes in people's attitudes, so that Queen Marie-Antoinette might start saying to her ladies-in-waiting things like, 'Well, girls, who's for a picnic?' and get replies like, 'Sorry Marie, I'm reading *Emile* and I just can't put it down'; *if* such a solvent of attitudes had been available, then the monarchy might have evaporated without any help from the guillotine. But in a tolerably stable and non-totalitarian society, people's attitudes are not so easily modified, and the social qualities they sustain are not so easily destroyed.

And what alternative is there to this individualistic approach? If a sociologist grows impatient with the painstaking method of studying social formations from the inside, and seeks instead to observe a social collective, as such, from the outside, then nothing will present itself for his inspection. Sociological collectivism is not a method, only a metaphysic. The Webbs' book on scientific method has a chapter entitled 'Watching the Institution at Work'; but what it describes is, of course, how to watch *members of* the institution at work.

V

I now turn, without enthusiasm, to *ethical* collectivism. In our methodological tradition, Robbins and Popper have particularly insisted that moral and political evaluations should be frankly avowed as such, and not insinuated surreptitiously in the form of pseudo-scientific statements. The concept of *social health* sounds clinical; but it is, of course, a pseudo-scientific concept: you cannot take a society's pulse or tap its chest. And even if this concept had been given an avowedly normative character, I would still feel uneasy about the claim that the state should aim at 'something apart from and above the separate interests of individuals'. An innocent interpretation could be put on this. Whatever it may be, the public interest surely is not the sum of all private interests; for one thing, private interests often conflict. And since it is, presumably, part of the public interest that conflicts of private interests should be resolved peaceably, one could say that to this extent, at least, the public interest is 'something apart from and above the separate interests of individuals'.

But this phrase could also be interpreted in a more sinister way, to mean that the state should serve an end altogether distinct from the interests of individuals, namely the interest of some reified, and possibly deified, collective, whether tribe, *polis*, or nation. And we know from Popper's famous attack on Platonic justice (26a) that *this* idea provides a pseudo-ethical justification (for there is pseudo-ethics as well as pseudo-science) for treating mere *people immorally*.

VI

I turn now to *political* collectivism. This can be discussed at various levels. Hobhouse, surveying the evolution of mankind from a lofty vantage-point, observed that 'there arises by degrees the ideal of collective humanity, self-determining in its progress' (27). Echoing Hobhouse, Ginsberg urged that the ultimate object of sociology is to investigate this new 'conception of a self-directed humanity' (28). But, being only a philosopher and not a sociologist, I prefer to discuss it in a more mundane form. I shall take the core of political collectivism to be the doctrine that economic processes, no less than military ones, ought to be under direct collective control.

I will not invoke any economic or political arguments against political collectivism. I shall assume, for the sake of argument, that a collectivized society is possible in which it is the *best* who get to the top (29), and in which the political problem posed by the old poser, 'Who plans the planners?', has been happily and democratically solved. I shall assume that the central planning authority aims at nothing other than the public interest or general welfare, and that it interprets this, not in a bad ethically collectivist way, but as some function of the interests of the individual people in the society.

In a polycentric society, to borrow Polanyi's term (30), there are many decision-making centres, each making its decisions in the light of its aims and its appraisal of its local situation. Suppose that a central planning authority of the kind we are imagining is now set up. The old centres no longer make decisions. Instead, they feed their situational appraisals to the central body, which collates them, and which then transmits instructions to the sub-ordinate centres, which they faithfully execute.

It might seem that this collectivized system should certainly serve society better than the old polycentric system. Does not the new central authority possess *all* the information previously dispersed among the old centres; and does it not put all this information together into a unified appraisal of the *total* situation; and does it not use all this knowledge in the *public* interest, whereas they exploited their partial knowledge for their sectional interests?

This sanguine judgement overlooks a main thesis of Hayek's (he first stated it in 1935; see reference [31]): namely, that the knowledge dispersed among the decision-makers in a polycentric society cannot be centralized. Once stated, this thesis seems rather obvious. It can be supported by a variety of arguments. One is this. Presumably, only articulated knowledge could be transmitted to the centre. But we are conscious, at any one time, of only a fragment of the system of beliefs on which we rely in the practical conduct of our lives. You presumably believe that the roof of this theatre will not collapse and that there is no time-bomb ticking away in it. Otherwise you would not stay here. But I daresay that you would not have consciously attended to this belief if I had not drawn it to your attention.

Oakeshott held that explicit, formulated knowledge is not only less extensive but also inferior to the inexplicit, traditional know-how from which it has been extracted, rather as the technical knowledge presented in a cookery book is inferior to the rich cookery know-how from which it was extracted (32). I always felt uneasy about this addition (33). I am ready to concede that it holds for all cookery books, even for *Larousse Gastronomique;* but does it still hold when we substitute the ancient art of land-measurement for cooking, and Euclid's *Elements* for *Larousse Gastronomique?* Anyway, with or without this addition, Oakeshott's thesis entails that very little of our collective practical know-how could be put at the disposal of the central authority.

Another argument for this thesis is that a decision-maker may be responding successfully to a situation which, however, is too complex, and changing too variously, for any verbal description of it to keep pace with it. Moreover, when someone acts according to his appraisal of his situation, he explores that situation further and thereby modifies his appraisal of it. He can put his appraisal in aspic and serve it cold only when the action is over.

Recently, Hayek has provided yet another argument for this thesis (34). Baldly summarized, it is this: anyone attempting to describe fully what he is doing must leave one thing undescribed, namely, the rules with which he conforms in the process of describing what he is doing; he may take the process of conscious articulation further and further; but however far he takes it, there will be something that eludes it, something that is 'meta-conscious'.

But perhaps all these arguments are redundant. Is it not in any case obvious that a central authority could acquire only a tiny part of the knowledge dispersed among a polycentric society?

VII

Let us now look into the claim that the central authority could promote the best interest of the whole society. The claim is not just that it can promote whatever it may happen to regard as the best interest, but that the central authority can *discover* what is in the best interest of a society (from its knowledge of individual wants or preferences), and promote *that.* In other words, its policy decisions could be governed by some suitable maximizing or optimizing rule.

So the question is: could there be such a maximizing or optimizing rule?

Classical utilitarianism tried to provide one. In the last forty years utilitarianism has suffered a series of body-blows. I will briefly recount the familiar story, beginning with Bentham's original formula (as given on the opening page of A *Fragment of Government*): *the greatest happiness of the greatest number.* ('For Bentham', Beatrice Webb remarked, 'was certainly Sidney's intellectual godfather' [2b].)

One basic (and well-known) trouble with this formula can be brought out by an analogy. The engineer in charge of a hotel's heating can measure the rise and fall of a room's temperature, and he can compare the temperature of different rooms. But if he is instructed to promote the greatest warmth of the greatest number of rooms, he will scratch his head. He might concentrate the heating in one room and maximize its temperature; or he might disperse the heat through all the rooms. But he cannot fulfil the double requirement. As Von Neumann and Morgenstern put it: 'A guiding principle cannot be formulated by the requirement of maximizing two (or more) functions at once' (35a).

So the split nature of Bentham's original principle had to be resolved one way or the other. Either one could retain 'the greatest number' principle, and merely hope that the level of uniform happiness would not be too low; or one could retain 'the greatest happiness' principle, and merely hope that its distribution would not be too unfair. This second alternative was generally preferred. (Bentham himself, in his later work, *The Principles of Morals and Legislation*, stated that the 'general object which all laws . . . ought to have . . . is to augment *the total happiness of the community*' [italics added].)

Most reforms involve some cost to someone. When such a reform is proposed, a utilitarian will want to know whether the net effect, utility-wise, would be positive or negative. For it to be in principle possible to know this, at least two things are necessary. First, it must in principle be possible to estimate, for each individual, *how much* utility he would gain or lose by the reform: there must be some sort of cardinal utility-scale for each individual. Second, their respective cardinal utility-scales must be commensurable, so that we can *aggregate* the various positive and negative changes.

Now the first of these two conditions could be met if the doctrine of expected utility were satisfactory. Put in a nutshell, this doctrine says that if in my left hand I hold a ticket entitling the purchaser to a certain prize, and in my right hand a ticket entitling him only to a certain chance, say one-half, of getting that prize, then the value to anyone of the ticket in my right hand is exactly one-half the value to him of the ticket in my left hand. Given this doctrine of expected utility, we can extract cardinal values from a subject's ordinal comparisons in the way suggested by von Neumann and Morgenstern (35b).

I have argued elsewhere (36) that the doctrine of expected utility is false if taken as a description of how people do evaluate risks, and unreasonable if taken as a prescription as to how they ought to evaluate risks. To hide its weaknesses its adherents, who seem to include almost everyone except Shackle (37) and myself, have resorted to what I can only describe as a shocking maltreatment of the good doctrine of diminishing marginal utlity.

Fortunately, there is no need for me to repeat these arguments here. For even if we could have cardinality we could not have commensurability. In 1932 Robbins showed the illegitimacy of the kind of interpersonal comparisons we would need if we were to be in a position to say that one man's utility-gain outweighs another man's utility-loss (15b). Later, I will say something about other kinds of interpersonal comparison. In the meanwhile I will recount the final body-blow.

After Robbins, the problem became to define social welfare simply as a function of the individuals' separate and incommensurable rankings of the choices before them, each individual ranking to count for one and none for more than one. Certain formal requirements were laid down. One was that the social preferences yielded by the individual rankings must be transitive: if 'society' prefers x to y and y to z, then 'society' must prefer x to z. Another was that every configuration of individuals' rankings should yield a determinate social preference (ties being permitted). Also, the Pareto-principle was generally accepted. This says that if some people prefer x to y while the others are indifferent between x and y, then 'society' should prefer x to y.

The problem in this new form proved unexpectedly difficult. At the L.S.E. Kaldor (38) tackled it by adding to the old Pareto principle a new compensation principle, which gained some notoriety. It is not obvious that society should move from state x to state y if, in doing so, it will make poor people somewhat poorer and rich people so much richer that they could, though they won't, compensate the losers and still remain gainers. In any case, it was soon shown (39) that the compensation principle can lead to inconsistent results: x may be Kaldor-preferable to y because a hypothetical compensation would turn x into z which is Pareto-preferable to y; and at the same time y may be Kaldor-preferable to x because a *different* hypothetical compensation would turn y into w which is Pareto-preferable to x.

Why the problem of defining social welfare had been proving so intractable was explained in 1950, when Arrow proved that, if the two formal requirements I mentioned just now, transitivity and determinacy, are accepted, and if there is a choice among more than two alternatives, then there cannot be a social welfare function that simultaneously satisfies a few seemingly minimal adequacy requirements (40).

His adequacy requirements (which included the Pareto-principle in a weaker formulation than I gave just now) have come under minute examination, in the hope that, weak though they already are, some further weakening could be justified that would render them mutually consistent. I am inclined to think that someone who wants to evade Arrow's result should rather follow up Sen's suggestion (41) that the trouble may lie with the formal requirement that the social welfare function be determinate for all configurations of preferences.

But I see no good reason for wanting to evade Arrow's result. With hindsight we can see, I believe, that Arrow proved to be impossible something that we ought in any case to have suspected of being impossible. For compare what was expected to come out of the sought-after social welfare function with what was allowed to go into it. What could go into it was nothing but individual preference-systems, no restriction being placed on these other than internal consistency. They could be a-social or anti-social. No matter: the social welfare function, being determinate for all configurations, will amalgamate them into one *social* preference-schedule! Interpersonal comparisons are excluded; each person's preference-system is in a world of its own. Yet these isolated and autarkic preference-systems were to yield, collectively, 'society's' preference-system, 'society' being just an assemblage of individuals with incommensurable wants. Trying to construct a social welfare function out of these materials is like trying to construct from statistics about plumbers, an average plumber who will actually go round mending the nation's pipes.

We have been witnessing the death-rattle of classical utilitarianism. Despite its basic individualism, classical utilitarianism fell into a kind of ethical collectivism with its idea of maximizing the 'total' or *net* happiness in the community. When net happiness turned out to be a pseudo-aggregate, the ideal of some sort of quantitative maximization was replaced by the ideal of some sort of qualitative optimization. The problem became to determine, in a general way, what social state accords best with everybody's preferences. And this problem proved insoluble.

Thus political collectivism, as I have depicted it, is knocked out on two counts. The central authority could not have the requisite knowledge. And even if, *per impossible*, it could, its decisions (which control the economic life of the community) could not be guided by any principle or rule that was both adequate (in the sense of Arrow's adequacy-requirements) and determinate: either all its decisions would be rule-bound, but bound by an inadequate rule; or at least some of them would not be rule-bound, i.e. would be arbitrary.

I said that I would not bring any political arguments against political collectivism, and I do not think that I have done so. Admittedly, my conclusion fits in with my political bias, which is that of an old-fashioned liberal with conservative tendencies. I never was in love with the idea that the government should try to run society like some vast public enterprise. But the arguments on which I have drawn have all been impossibility-arguments. The case for political collectivism has been undermined, but no case has been made for any alternative.

VIII

Can anything be retrieved from the wreckage of classical utilitarianism? More specifically, can the view that has come to be known as 'negative utilitarianism' avoid objections of the kind that wrecked its classical predecessor? I shall argue that, in a modified form, it can.

I should warn you that in this last part of my lecture, in which I am going to try belatedly to turn constructive, certain moral views will obtrude themselves. Indeed, I will disclose the most relevant of these at once. In *The Open Society* Popper expressed a moral view which is at the basis of negative utilitarianism, and which I share:

I believe that there is, from the ethical point of view, no symmetry between suffering and happiness . . . In my opinion . . . human suffering makes a direct moral appeal, namely, the appeal for help, while there is no similar call to increase the happiness of a man who is doing well anyway (26b).

I daresay that no one here would quarrel with that on moral grounds. But are we not bound to have philosophical reservations about it? The statement 'Alf is suffering but Bert is happy' involves an interpersonal comparison of a rather strong kind. It says that Alf is less happy than Bert; and it adds that Alf is on the negative side, and Bert is on the positive side, of some middle or neutral or zero position. In addition to the old problem of interpersonal comparison, it raises a new problem: we seem to need a non-arbitrary zero. An ordinal utility-scale that has no zero, and an interval scale that has an arbitrary zero, seem to leave out something important. If we try to express on either of these two kinds of scale the proposition that torture by rack is even more terrible than torture by thumbscrew, it will come out as something of an understatement, namely: 'the utility of torture by rack is less than the utility of torture by thumbscrew'.

But can we secure a non-arbitrary zero? And have we not in any case banned áll interpersonal comparison?

No; at least, I was careful not to. We have banned the kind of interpersonal comparison exposed by Robbins, namely, the kind involved in the claim that, if the utility to Alf of a marginal unit of his stock of X is low (perhaps because he has plenty of X), whereas the utility to Bert of a marginal unit of X is high (perhaps because he is short of X), then net utility would be increased by transferring a unit of X from Alf to Bert. But this does not mean that we have banned every kind of interpersonal comparison.

I will now offer two examples where, it seems to me, we are entitled both to postulate some kind of natural zero and to make some kind of interpersonal comparison. My examples are rather unexciting. In the first, Alf and Bert are having their hearing tested. They are sitting blindfolded, in a room which is silent, except for a quietly ticking watch which is gradually brought closer to them. At time t_0 neither of them hears anything. At t_1 Alf just discerns the ticking. Bert does not discern it until t_2 by which time Alf can hear it quite loudly. We can certainly say that Alf's aural sensation was stronger than Bert's from t_1 until just before t_2, for Alf was then hearing something while Bert was hearing nothing. And I think that we can add that at t_2 when Alf heard the ticking quite loudly whereas Bert only just discerned it, Alf's aural sensation was stronger than Bert's. After that, we cannot tell: does Bert perhaps make up for his late start by a more rapid increase in subjective intensity? God knows.

This example does not get us far. I used it only as a softener against any total ban on interpersonal comparisons. My second example will get us a little further. It is adapted from Bishop Berkeley. Alf and Bert have come in from the cold, and are holding out their hands to a cheerful fire. Each agrees that it gives him a pleasant sensation of warmth. Then Alf decides to see how close to the red-hot coals he can bear to hold his hands. To Bert, who does not move, he gives this running commentary: 'Warmer, but still quite pleasant . . . Hot, but tolerable . . . Uncomfortably hot . . . Becoming painful . . . Ough !', and whips his hands away. Interpersonal comparison: at that moment, Alf's heat-sensation was negative, hedonically speaking, while Bert's was positive.

Suppose we agree that their sensations were on opposite sides of some dividing-line. But how are we to locate this dividing-line? If we were constructing a scale for greyness, we might attach $+1$ to pure white, and -1 to jet black, and then find a middling grey to which to attach 0. But in the case of pleasure and pain, we cannot proceed to a midpoint from outer limits because outer limits are not given. Then can we *start* with a middle position? I think we can. As the heat increased there presumably came a time when the sensation had just stopped being pleasurable without yet becoming painful; perhaps the stage reported by Alf as 'Hot, but tolerable'. We could make this sound more scientific by saying that the middle zone is subtended between the pleasure-threshold on one side and the pain-threshold on the other.

It is a big leap from this result to the much wider claim that there is a middle or neutral or 'grey' zone between happiness and suffering. But the time has come for me to start leaping to conclusions. That this zone is vague will not matter too much for our purpose, provided we can say with reasonable confidence that someone is well over on the negative side of it. One day last year Mr. Smith read in his newspaper that his Rolls-Royce shares, in which he had invested all his savings, were worth nothing; later, at the office, he was told that his services would not be required after the end of the month. When he got home he found a note from his wife saying that she had left him for another man. Does anyone doubt that he ended that day on the negative side?

If a utility-scale can be bifurcated non-arbitrarily into a positive side and a negative side, a real difference opens up between an *increase of happiness* and a *reduction of suffering*.

When considering what the task of government should be, it is, I think, a mistake to rush in immediately with *de jure* principles. We should begin with a *de facto* classification whose first two categories are: (a) things which can be done *only* by governments; (b) things which can be done *much more effectively* by governments than by private organizations. If you admit that a certain thing, say road-construction, falls under category (a) and, moreover, is needed by society, then you will have to include it in the task of government whatever your moral and political outlook may be; and the compulsion will be almost as strong if it falls under category (b). After this comes category (c): things that we may or may not include in the task of government, according to our political views. Finally, there is category (d): things that cannot be done by governments.

Thus the practical significance of a principle of public policy is partly to help to determine what should be included (c), and partly to regulate the ways in which things are done under (a) and (b). (Roads, yes; but urban motorways?)

Popper proposed that 'Minimize suffering' should replace 'Maximize happiness' as a principle (*not* as *the* principle) of public policy (26*c*). This is what has come to be known as 'negative utilitarianism'.

That governments should aim at reducing suffering, leaving the pursuit of happiness to private initiative, sounds right to me (42). Taken literally, however, this new *minimization* formula would run into the same difficulties over interpersonal comparison and aggregation that beset the old maximization formula. And there is another point. Popper explained later (26*d*) that he had never intended his formula as a *criterion* for public policy. As it stands, however, this formula looks like a would-be criterion. If I flag down a taxi, point at a Daimler car ahead, and say 'Follow that Daimler', I give the tax-driver an effective criterion to drive by. I would not have given him an effective criterion if I had told him to follow the oldest Daimler still on the road in England today. Yet this latter would constitute a 'criterion' which could in principle be acted upon. (It might even become an effective criterion for a police-car controlled by Scotland Yard.) A 'criterion' that *would* be effective *if* we had information that we do not have, may be called a 'criterion in principle'.

'Minimize suffering' obviously is not an effective criterion; but it does look like a criterion in principle. Popper gave it as an abbreviation for 'Aim at the least amount of avoidable suffering for all'. The tell-tale word *least* again suggests a criterion in principle: *if* a government could measure the suffering-reducing effects of each one of all the possible alternatives before it, *then* its proper course would be dictated by this formula.

The situation seems to be this. Popper inverted a pro-happiness formula into an anti-suffering formula. Good. But the old maximization formula looked like a criterion in principle, and this appearance was incidentally inherited by the new minimization formula. This was contrary to Popper's intention, and exposes it to the standard objection about interpersonal comparison and aggregation. So the anti-suffering formula needs to be weakened to something like the following injunction to governments: 'Don't aim at promoting happiness; aim at reducing suffering.' This is manifestly not a criterion; so it is in no danger of falling foul of Arrow's result, which applies only to determinate social welfare functions.

Admittedly, its indeterminacy means that there can be considerable variations (if you like, considerable arbitrariness) in the ways in which different governments might try to implement this weakened principle. One government might give top priority to dealing with a kind of social misery which would seem a much less urgent problem to another government. This, however, is partially off-set by the fact that there may well be considerable agreement about what are the dark areas and black spots in a society: slums, gangsterism, unemployment, mental illness, etc. These provide multiple targets for piecemeal reform. Negative utilitarianism ties in, of course, with piecemeal engineering; instead of one global target, there is an itemized *Agenda* for government action.

I can now bring the two halves of my title together. I remember Stigler saying that the classical economists were at their best when dealing (whether or not on some Royal Commission or investigating committee) with 'issues posed by concrete problems of the day' (43). Social problems, and especially social ills, are a challenge to social science, and important advances in social science have mostly been stimulated by such challenges. An obvious example is Keynesian economics and the 1930s challenge of mass unemployment. By contrast, the dream of building a New Jerusalem has not, so far as I know, inspired any good sociology, and a government that tried to build a New Jerusalem would embark upon its up-hill task in almost total ignorance. But some social knowledge (far from perfect, but considerably better than nothing) should be available to a government that serves the public interest by tackling identified social evils in a piecemeal way.

I will end on a Hobbesian note. Since the breakdown of a democratic society like ours would cause great misery *and* deprive us of the political ability to do anything about it, negative utilitarianism clearly implies that the over-riding task of the government is to *maintain* the system whose defects and weaknesses it is trying to remedy.

REFERENCES

1. CAINE, Sir Sydney, *The History of the Foundation of The London School of Economics and Political Science*, p. 49 (London: Bell, 1963).
2. WEBB, Beatrice, *Our Partnership* (a) p. 85, (b) p. 210, Barbara Drake and Margaret Cole (eds.) (London: Longmans, 1948).
3. LETWIN, Shirley, *The Pursuit of Certainty*, (a) p. 355, (b) pp. 365–9 (Cambridge, at the University Press, 1965).
4. WEBB, Sidney and Beatrice, *The Decay of Capitalist Civilization*, (a) p. 144, (b) *passim* (London: Allen & Unwin, 1923).
5. —— *Methods of Social Study*, pp. 34–35 (London: Longmans, 1932).
6. WEBB, Beatrice, 'Methods of Investigation' in *Sociological Papers*, L. T. Hobhouse et al. (eds.), vol. 3, p. 345 (London: Macmillan, 1907).
7. WOLF, A., *A History of Science, Technology and Philosophy in the 16th and 17th Centuries* (London: Allen & Unwin, 1935; 2nd edition, 1950).
8. —— *Spinoza's Short Treatise on God, Man, and His Well-Being* (London: 1910; reprinted New York: Russell & Russell, 1963).
9. ——*The Correspondence of Spinoza* (London: Allen & Unwin, 1928).
10. —— *Essentials of Scientific Method* (London: Allen & Unwin, 1925).
11. ROBBINS, L., *Autobiography of an Economist*, pp. 86–89 (London: Macmillan, 1971).
12. WALLAS, Graham, *The Art of Thought* (London: Jonathan Cape, 1926).
13. —— 'Physical and Social Science' in *Huxley Memorial Lectures 1925–1932* (London: Macmillan, 1932).
14. FRIEDMAN, M., *Essays in Positive Economics* (Chicago: University of Chicago Press, 1953).
15. ROBBINS, L., *The Nature and Significance of Economic Science* (London: Macmillan, 1932; 2nd edition, 1935), (a) *passim*, (b) chap. 6.
16. HICKS, J. R., and ALLEN, R. G. D., 'A Reconsideration of the Theory of Value', *Economica* (February and May, 1934).
17. HUTCHISON, T. W., *The Significance and Basic Postulates of Economic Theory* (London: Macmillan, 1938).
18. HAYEK, F. A., 'Scientism and the Study of Society', *Economica* (1942–4), reprinted in *The Counter-Revolution of Science* (Illinois: Free Press, 1952).
19. POPPER, K. R., 'The Poverty of Historicism', *Economica* (1944–5), reprinted in revised form as *The Poverty of Historicism*, (a) *passim*, (b) p. 68 (London: Routledge, 1957).
20. MEDAWAR, P. B., *The Art of the Soluble*, p. 11 (London: Methuen, 1967).
21. LAKATOS, I., 'Falsification and the Methodology of Scientific Research Programmes' in *Criticism and the Growth of Knowledge*, I. Lakatos and A. Musgrave (eds.) (Cambridge, at the University Press, 1970).
22. SELDEN, John, *The Table Talk of John Selden*, S. H. Reynolds (ed.), p. 197 (Oxford: Clarendon Press, 1892).
23. MARCUSE, Herbert, *One Dimensional Man*, p. 201 (Sphere Books, 1968).
24. WEBB, Sidney, *The Difficulties of Individualism*, Fabian Tract no. 69, p. 5 (1896).
25. —— and Beatrice, *Soviet Communism* (London: Longmans, 1937).
26. POPPER, K. R., *The Open Society and its Enemies* (London: Routledge, 1945), (a) chap. 6, (b) chap. 9, n. 2, (c) chap. 5, n. 6(2), (d) (4th edition, 1962), vol. 2, p. 386.

27. HOBHOUSE, L. T., *Democracy and Reaction*, p. 108 (London: T. Fisher Unwin, 1904).
28. GINSBERG, M., *Sociology*, p. 244 (London: Oxford University Press, 1934).
29. HAYEK, F. A., *The Road to Serfdom*, chap. 10 (London: Routledge, 1944).
30. POLANYI, M., *The Logic of Liberty*, pp. 170 ff. (London: Routledge, 1951).
31. HAYEK, F. A., *Individualism and Economic Order*, pp. 54, 155 (London: Routledge, 1949).
32. OAKESHOTT, Michael, *Rationalism in Politics and Other Essays* (London: Methuen, 1962).
33. WATKINS, J. W. N., 'Political Tradition and Political Theory', *Philosophical Quarterly*, 2, 9 (October, 1952), 334 ff.
34. HAYEK, F. A., *Studies in Philosophy, Politics and Economics*, chap. 3 (London: Routledge, 1967).
35. VON NEUMANN, J., and MORGENSTERN, O., *Theory of Games and Economic Behaviour*, (a) §2. 2. 3, (b) §3, 3rd edition (Princeton University Press, 1953).
36. WATKINS, J. W. N., 'Imperfect Rationality' in *Explanation in the Behavioural Sciences*, R. Borger and F. Cioffi (eds.), pp. 184 ff. (Cambridge, at the University Press, 1970).
37. SHACKLE, G. L. S., *Decision Order and Time*, p. 178 (Cambridge, at the University Press, 1961).
38. KALDOR, N., 'Welfare Propositions in Economics', *Economic Journal*, **49** (1939).
39. SCITOVSKY, T., 'A Note on Welfare Propositions in Economics', *Revue of Economic Studies*, **9** (November, 1941).
40. ARROW, K., *Social Choice and Individual Values*, chaps. 5 and 8, 2nd edition (New York: John Wiley, 1963).
41. SEN, A. K., *Collective Choice and Social Welfare*, p. 67 (Edinburgh: Oliver & Boyd, 1970).
42. WATKINS, J. W. N., 'Negative Utilitarianism' in *The Aristotelian Society*, Supplementary volume xxxvii (Harrison & Sons, 1963).
43. STIGLER, G. J., *Five Lectures on Economic Problems*, p. 35 (London: Longmans, 1949).

THE
LEGAL FRAMEWORK
OF SOCIETY

OTTO KAHN-FREUND

OTTO KAHN-FREUND

Dr. jur. (Frankfurt),
LL.M. (Lond.), M.A. (Oxon.), F.B.A.
*Formerly Professor of Comparative Law
University of Oxford*

Educated at the Universities of Frankfurt, Heidel-
burg, Leipzig, London; judge in German courts
1928–33; Barrister at Law (Middle Temple); Hon.
Bencher Middle Temple, 1969; Professor of Law
in University of London (London School of
Economics and Political Science), 1951–64; co-
editor, *Modern Law Review*; President, International Society for Labour Law and Social Legislation; Member, Royal Commission on Trade
Unions and Employers' Associations, 1965–8;
Doctor of Laws (H.C.): Bonn, 1968; Stockholm,
1969; Brussels, 1969. Publications include: *Law
of Carriage by Inland Transport*; English edition
of Renner, *Institutions of Private Law and their
Social Functions*; co-author, *The System of Industrial Relations in Great Britain*; co-author, *Matrimonial Property Law*; *The Growth of Interna-
tionalism in English Private International Law*.

THE LEGAL FRAMEWORK
OF SOCIETY

To discuss the development of legal studies in general and at the London School of Economics in particular is impossible unless one faces at the outset two problems linked with the academic pursuit of law and shared by few of the other social sciences.

The first of these problems is inherent in the first sentence I have spoken: I have referred to law and the other social sciences, and thus assumed that the study of the law is part of the study of society; and, moreover, that legal studies share with other social studies the quality of being a 'science', a social science directed towards the elucidation and understanding of social phenomena. This is the assumption, I think, on which this lecture has been included in this course. It is, however, highly controversial. Part of the story I have to tell here is the gradual unfolding of this controversy, the growth, in fact, of the conception that law is a social technique and to be studied as such, and the role which this School has played in this process. The second of the problems I mentioned arises from the need for combining academic studies with a professional education. I shall revert to it presently.

Let me try for a moment, as best as I can, to show the case against legal studies being classified as a social science. Social sciences, you may say, are largely empirical disciplines: they are about facts, about what was, what is, and what can be expected to develop, about how to find out these facts, and how to sharpen the tools of such factual investigation. But, on the view I am now seeking to describe, law, or perhaps better, the study of the law, has nothing to do with social, that is with typical, facts at all. It is not about facts, but about rules, rules of conduct, norms, and rights and obligations created by such norms. Not about what happens in society, but about what ought to happen, not about what people do but about what they should do. The facts to be investigated by the processes of law and thus of interest to its study are not the typical facts of social behaviour but the individual facts of cases in which the norm was not obeyed, and the sanction attached to the norm, that is the facts expected to happen in response to the violation of the norm: punishment, damages, injunction, etc. On this view the study of the law is confined to the analysis and classification of the rules, no matter whether these emerge from legislative enactments or from the precedential force of decisions. The student of law is not concerned with anything else; let him reflect on how these rules would operate in hypothetical marginal cases. This will train his mind and also, a point to which I shall return, prepare him for his professional work. Why the rules are what they are, how far they are in fact obeyed, how much they contribute to the actual organization of society is in no way his concern, nor is it that of his teacher. Do not let him stray beyond the law library, do not let him squint at what economists, political scientists, sociologists, or statisticians are doing. He will not understand it in any event. Justice does not try to look at such facts. She is blind.

I may with the last few words have given a slightly (but only very slightly) exaggerated twist to this approach and to the educational conclusions which are drawn from it. The approach is that of a highly respectable school of legal thought. It is a school of thought which sees law as belonging to the world of the 'ought' and not of the 'is', as a self-sufficient autonomous body of rules whose normative existence is divorced from its factual origin and from its factual effectiveness. A consistent follower of this doctrine would have to urge me now, having said this, to sit down and hold my peace, because there cannot be any fruitful discussion of legal studies in a universe of discourse which comprises sociology and social anthropology, descriptive economics, statistics, political science, geography, and psychology. The legal discipline may by some who take this view be linked with economic analysis in so far as it has a normative content and perhaps with certain branches of philosophy; possibly so, it is a difficult matter which I cannot and need not pursue further.

This sharp antithesis of the norm and the fact, the *Sollen* and the *Sein*, can result from widely differing fundamental attitudes.

It can exist in a neo-Kantian environment, though it must be said that Hans Kelsen always recognized as legitimate a sociological approach to law, provided it was clearly distinguished from the study of the law itself. It can also exist in very different intellectual surroundings. Is it not inherent in the teachings of the Benthamite John Austin? And has this Austinian approach not had a very strong and lasting influence on the teaching of law in this country? I am not trying to say that the propensity to see law and its administration in a self-contained universe and in isolation from their social environment is exclusively or even preponderantly traceable to the influence of Austin's normative jurisprudence. It is favoured by a much more powerful influence, and by another aspect of legal studies and especially of legal education which is far more significant.

It is, and this brings me to my second problem, that law shares with medicine, with engineering, with statistics, with accounting, and possibly now with some branches of economics, the vital characteristic that those who teach it are not only responsible for forming the minds of their students, for widening their horizon and broadening their knowledge, for training their power of judgement, they are also responsible for educating them for a profession. Let me as strongly as I can disclaim any intention of establishing an antithesis between a professional and a liberal education. To insist that there is no such antithesis is a duty one owes in this School to the memory of the late Sir Alexander Carr-Saunders. A law teacher must bear in mind the needs of his students as future solicitors, barristers, legal advisers, civil servants, or judges. But this obligation does not compel him to adopt any particular attitude to law and to legal studies. In particular it does not compel him to see and to teach law as a self-contained universe of discourse, segregated from its origin in, and its effect on, society. This is shown by the recent Ormrod Report on Legal Education (Cmnd. 4595). However, and no one who has ever had anything to do with these things can underestimate the importance of the point, whilst this link of the professional with the academic may not cramp the style of the individual teacher, it does cramp the style of the faculty or board of studies or department which constructs the curriculum. It determines not how subjects are taught, but what subjects are taught; and it leads inevitably to a choice of subjects in the light of the needs of the profession (and, let us be realistic, of candidates for professional examinations), and not in the light of the needs of society. Nor is it so much of importance here what subjects are taught as what subjects are not taught. It is the 'opportunity cost' of the professional requirements that has concerned many of us most. It explains a great deal of what I shall have to say. It explains, at least to a certain extent, why that elementary introduction into the economic and political structure of society which in many foreign countries is a required part of a legal curriculum is conspicuous by its absence in the syllabuses of most, not of all, law faculties in this country.

I have said that there need be no antithesis between a liberal and a professional education, and this elementary insight is gaining ground: the Ormrod Report shows it clearly. The links between academic legal education and the professional requirements have been greatly strengthened since the Second World War, and on both sides of the profession a candidate now gains very real advantages as regards his professional examinations through having obtained a law degree, and on the solicitors' side also as regards the duration of his apprenticeship. This, however, has increased the responsibility of the law faculties towards the professional organizations and made it even more imperative to pay attention to their needs in the shaping of the curriculum. I greatly welcome the enhanced status of the academic law schools in the organization of professional training, but it has its dangers as well as its opportunities.

The attitude of the legal profession towards academic legal education has greatly changed for the better in the last forty years, and even the attitude towards the importance of academic legal scholarship and research may perhaps begin to change, though it is still in many quarters considered as against professional etiquette outside international law to quote a living author in court. This, however, is not the essential point. The essential point is the lack of sympathy of the practising lawyer to the conception of law as a social technique and to legal studies as a discipline designed to study the social origins and effects of the law. He is much concerned with cause and effect, but only in individual cases. He distrusts (there are exceptions) the conception of typical causes and typical effects which (unless I am quite wrong) is the essence of empirical social studies. It is this anti-thesis of attitudes, and by no means an antithesis of academic and professional purposes, which to my mind is the most serious problem confronting academic legal pursuits. It is in the help towards finding a synthesis that I see the most profound contri-bution this School has made towards the study of the legal frame of society in the three-quarters of a century of its existence.

Not as if this antithesis was due to the arbitrary whims or to the prejudices of any individuals, however exalted, or as if this was an exclusively British phenomenon (though owing to the organization of the profession it may be more pronounced here than in many other countries). It is inherent in the professional work of the practising lawyer. Normally he does not go into action unless either things have gone wrong or there is a need for preventing them from going wrong. The litigation lawyer faces the first, the draftsman the second of these situations. The therapy may be curative or preventive, but the diagnosis is always that of an ill, an actual ill to be dealt with or a potential ill to be kept out of the way. The lawyer's mind is focused on the patho-logical, the marginal situation. This is the heart of the matter. How can legal education and legal studies promote the practical application of the law as a response to necessarily abnormal situations without allowing this preoccupation to distort the view of society formed in the minds of the adepts of this discipline, pupils and teachers, research workers and scholars?

This problem, I repeat it is the problem towards whose solution this School has contributed so conspicuously, does not of course exist for those who adhere to the purely normative view of legal studies to which I have referred. It is only if you see in law a technique of social organization or, as the late Dean Roscoe Pound of the Harvard Law School called it, of 'social engineering', that you can see the problem at all. But as soon as you gain the conviction that it is the duty of the legal teacher and scholar to search for the social forces which make the law and for the forma-tive effect of law on society, you face the issue of the quest for the typical: 'what happens normally?', as against the quest for the marginal: 'but what happens if things do not go their normal way?' Both questions have to be asked and (as far as possible) answered. I say again, it is the obligation of academic legal teachers and scholars to combine the two approaches. They owe it to their students and to themselves.

Let me speculate a little on why it was that this School was enabled to do so much for bridging this gulf and to set the pace of developments which are beginning to spread elsewhere, and then let me, somewhat arbitrarily perhaps, give a few illustrations for what I mean by this approach towards a synthesis.

It is the organization and the scope of activities of the L.S.E. which are, I think, decisive. The symbiosis in the L.S.E. of law, and, I will use the word, the other social sciences, is an important element. More important even is the symbiosis of the lawyers, the economists, sociologists, political scientists, and others. Here, and I am now for a moment speaking personally against a background of memory going back for many decades, it is the subjective factor which counts even more than the objective factor. The joint seminar, the formal co-operation between departments: a vital matter. But how much more vital that spontaneous give and take over the lunch table, or the cup of tea in the Senior Common Room. There is something here which I find it so easy to remember and so very difficult to describe: an atmosphere in which one's assumptions as a lawyer were unconsciously questioned by the spontaneous attitudes of one's colleagues, perhaps it was mutual.

However, in another sense the objective factor was determinative. That was in relation to the shaping of the curriculum, of the choice of subjects, and, important, the choice of such subjects as are conducive towards letting students see the function of law as an element of social organization. I am now thinking of the simple fact that all or practically all members of the Law Department of the L.S.E. are spending (and I think have always spent) a very large part of their working time and energy teaching law to economists, to sociologists, to political scientists, to future social workers. This had a powerful effect on the direction of the interests of the members of the Law Department itself. What is more, it had an indirect influence on the curriculum provided for the law students. In an academic institution in which the law teachers have to prepare and to give courses on commercial law and on labour law for non-lawyers, it is easy to introduce these (and not only these) subjects as options for the lawyers too, even though this may be done under different designations such as mercantile or industrial law. And subjects which are largely unknown to many other law schools (the law of banking, maritime law, or, in a different area, social security) are comparatively easy to develop in an environment where there is a demand for them, though that demand may not or not in the first place come from the law students. What is less easy to prove but nevertheless highly probable is that this situation may have directed not only the interests but also the methods of the law teachers. They were and they are facing students, both undergraduate and graduate, who have no professional legal interest, and whose inclination may be (and among the better ones is) to try to establish in their own minds a connection with what they have learned elsewhere about the social, economic, and political institutions in their normal operation and the function of the law in society. I think those who have taught company law to students specializing in applied economics or in business administration will bear out what I have just said. In gauging and in explaining the formative influence which the Law Department of the School has had on legal education and legal studies in many other British universities, one must bear in mind that from the beginning those planning the work of the Law Department were forced to think of the needs of law students and students of other social sciences at the same time.

There is however another factor which has been most influential. It is the role played in this School by graduate studies. I do not know of any academic institution which cultivates graduate studies in law as much as the L.S.E. has done for many years, none which can boast a catalogue of advanced seminars even remotely comparable to that which one finds in the Calendar of the School. This is important in my context because it is so much easier to experiment and to develop new subjects and new methods at graduate than at undergraduate level, and (this may be my prejudice) the best way of promoting research is through teaching. It is at the graduate level for example that the L.S.E. has made its very important contribution to comparative law, in a large number of fields, in constitutional law and in family law, in the conflict of laws, and in criminal law and procedure. It is also here that the teaching of the law of civil procedure has made a hopeful beginning in this School and in other colleges of the University, especially at University College.

The fact is that at all times matters which at best had a peripheral role in the work of many other Universities (if they had any role at all), were of central importance in this institution. Looking back at the history of legal studies in this country in the course of the last three-quarters of a century, I am persuaded that the L.S.E. played a pioneering role in the development of new subjects and that it did so especially at three periods of its existence: the first was right at the beginning, in the 1890s and the first decade of this century, the second was immediately after the First World War, and the third was within the memories of some of us, after the Second World War. The first two of these three crucial periods saw the evolution of commercial law, industrial or labour law, and administrative law, and after 1945 the L.S.E. set the pace for others by developing family law and the law of taxation.

Some members of my audience may find it surprising that I should emphasize this so much. They may think it a matter of course that topics such as, say, company law, or the law governing collective bargaining, or the organization of local government, or the relation of parents and children should of necessity be included in the syllabus of a law school. I agree that they should be, but I have to report that frequently (though less frequently than used to be the case) they are not. The traditional law syllabuses were geared to a teaching of the common law and of equity and eschewed subjects in which statute law was predominant because this was not on the whole considered as 'lawyers' law'; and, moreover, apart from criminal law and procedure the syllabuses were geared towards private law, land law, tort, contract. Today these tendencies are in the course of being overcome. I have said that if this is the case, it has a great deal to do with what happened here at the three periods to which I have referred.

As Professor Wedderburn points out in a contribution to the Congress at Stockholm of the International Society for Labour Law and Social Legislation in 1966, the development to which I am referring began with the foundation of the L.S.E., in 1895, when Mr. R. A. Wright, who later became a judge and Lord Wright, gave a course on commercial law. Eight years later, in 1903, this blossomed into a course on 'industrial and commercial law', and the first part of it was devoted to the law of contract, including such fundamental commercial contracts as sale of goods, and aspects of negotiable instruments, banking, and insurance. Mr. Wright concluded his announcement of this part of the syllabus with a sentence which may have come as a mild shock to some of his less adventurous colleagues: 'This outline is intended to serve as the necessary groundwork for a more detailed treatment of certain legal topics which bear most closely upon economic and social studies.' This illustrates my point that *ab initio* the needs of the non-lawyers for whom this course was intended induced those responsible for teaching to shift the focus towards that which is economically and socially relevant. This is borne out by the second part of the syllabus which was directed towards 'those branches of the law which immediately affect wage earners by laying down conditions of employment and regulating the standard of life', whilst the third part was a perhaps over-ambitious programme covering matters as widely apart as trade union law, marine insurance and patents. These, as Lord Wright told Lady Beveridge many years later, were lectures for evening students who 'were interested in law from the point of view of accountants, estate agents and similar activities'. 'My subjects', he says, 'were dealt with on practical and simple lines, e.g. contract was kept clear of complications, historical or technical' (1).

Even so, the syllabus was clearly overloaded; three years later it was split in two: commercial law and industrial law. This was in 1906, and this, I think, is the birth of commercial law and labour law as academic subjects in England.

It was a modest beginning. The roots had been planted, but the tree began to grow when after the First World War, in 1926, Gutteridge became the first holder of the full-time Cassel Chair of Commercial and Industrial Law. This was three years before the first full-time chair in English Law, that is full-time teaching in connection with the London LL.B. degree, took its start and Edward Jenks became the first holder of that chair (2).

The appointment of Gutteridge to this new chair meant that both commercial and industrial law became subjects for full time teaching. Commercial law was, I think, of central importance for the development of legal studies in this country and for the particular part the L.S.E. was destined to play in that development. It is, of course, of paramount importance to the student of economics, of accounting, of business administration, and for some of these students it was on a specialized level an optional, and on a more general level a required subject. Gutteridge and his successors developed it at various levels for various categories of undergraduate students. This rubbed off on the legal syllabus of the university where it appeared under the name of mercantile law and the law of business association. All this had an important effect on the outlook of the academic lawyers who worked in the L.S.E., especially on the younger generation, and also on the significance of the L.S.E. as an international centre of legal postgraduate education and research.

I have emphasized the link between the development of new subjects and the beginning of a conception of law as a social technique. Commercial law is not a bad example to illustrate the point. As understood here at the L.S.E. commercial law meant and means both the law of commercial transactions and the law of commercial associations. The term 'commercial law' is not, of course, in this country a technical term as it is in France and in Germany. Certain exceptions apart it is not (as it is in those countries) a separate body of rules for business, different from that applied to non-business transactions or associations. There is no special set of principles governing commercial as distinct from non-commercial sales, or commercial as distinct from non-commercial partnerships; in this country the law merchant was naturalized in the common law more than two hundred years ago. From the point of view of legal education and research this means that the teaching and learning of the law of sale, of insurance, of carriage, of negotiable instruments are nothing but a study of the law of contract and to some extent of movable property, 'approfondi' as the French say with an untranslatable word.

'Approfondi', however, in a very special sense. To turn from what is traditionally taught as the law of contract to that which we call commercial or mercantile law is to come down from the abstract principles to the concrete situations, from the abstract

A and B who play out innumerable variations on the abstract theme of offer and acceptance to the finance company, the dealer, and the customer who are engaged in the very serious and concrete business of agreeing on a hire-purchase transaction. This you just cannot discuss or even consider without thinking and speaking about the peculiar needs of finance companies who have to be protected against fraud, and of potential purchasers who have to be protected against the superior bargaining strength of the financier. You can talk about A and B *ad libitum* without considering the social importance of what they are doing. But who can do this when talking about transactions belonging to a particular sphere of economic life? And if you teach sale of goods to students of commerce, you cannot discuss it in the simplistic terms of the Sale of Goods Act. You must speak in terms of sales c.i.f. and f.o.b. and their numerous hybrids, and how can you do this without explaining why these involved and sophisticated types of transaction were invented by businessmen and what they mean in the living law and in the shaping of commerce?

And as with transactions so with forms of association. In the practice of the law problems of company law are handled by specialists, Chancery judges and barristers, who are not normally professionally interested in and concerned with sale of goods, carriage, or insurance, which belong to the domain of the common law side: the Queen's Bench judges and those who practice before them. But functionally, as social institutions, both belong together. The various facets or aspects of the law governing business, whether the accumulation or the utilization of its capital, should be seen together. To see them together sharpens the sense for the social function of legal institutions. No one who has ever considered the impact of the difference in organization between banks and insurance companies on the techniques of contract making in these two branches of business can fail to understand what I mean. Company law was taught at this School very early; at Cambridge it is a recent growth, at Oxford it does not exist yet, but it flourishes at Birmingham, Manchester, and other universities. In the new University of Warwick, for example, it is one of the two required subjects for third-year law students (labour law is the other). Above all company law flourishes in all the law schools of the University of London.

To study the evolution of the commercial law syllabuses in the L.S.E. would I think be a revealing exercise. It would show the unfolding of the functional treatment of the law. I feel this very strongly when I compare the structure of the B.Sc. (Econ.) course as it is today with what it was when I taught the subject about ten years ago. What I find most remarkable is the inclusion in the syllabus of a course on consumer protection and one on taxation. This co-ordination of the law of contract, of company law, of things such as the law of merchandise marks and of tax, this breaking through the established boundaries of legal disciplines carefully kept apart in most seats of legal learning is a conspicuous contribution the L.S.E. has made and obviously continues to make to the treatment of the law in terms of its social purpose rather than its conceptual structure.

The central role played by commercial law, and the same applies to other subjects such as labour law and administrative law, had in this School important repercussions on graduate as well as undergraduate studies. At the graduate level the formal co-operation between representatives of the various disciplines is easier to organize and also particularly promising: the L.S.E. (like other academic institutions such as the University of Oxford) is showing this in the graduate teaching of the law of competition and monopoly. But graduate studies have always had another important feature: the international significance of the L.S.E. as a centre of research does not have to be emphasized by me. One aspect of this is that for years the L.S.E. has been a focal point for the study of maritime law by advanced students from seafaring countries such as Greece and Norway, and, of course, from the United States. Very largely this was due to the international reputation of Lord Chorley as a specialist in this field, and it has been an important factor in the life of the Law Department.

Mutatis mutandis much of what I have said about commercial law applies to labour law as well. For reasons which we all know this is now becoming fashionable among the lawyers, as someone put it to me, it is becoming a legal 'growth area'. It is just as well to remember that when Lord Wright began to teach it here and even when Gutteridge and after him Lord Justice Slesser and Lord McNair (as they afterwards became) and Professor Robson developed it here, it was virtually unknown in other academic centres. An ordinary lawyer might have been able to associate a meaning with the term 'commercial law', but he would have been at sea when asked to say what could possibly be the area covered by something called 'industrial', to say nothing of 'labour' law. Labour law (or industrial law) was not a required subject for any students, but it was a popular option as a special subject. And the constituency was wider in that it included the social work students who thought of specializing in industrial work, the students of the personnel management course, and those of the trade union course. And here too there was this healthy 'osmotic' effect on the law curriculum itself; labour law became a subject for the London LL.B., for many years taught only in the L.S.E. If for a moment I may indulge in a bit of reminiscing, I took this over from Willie Robson at the end of the Second World War and, like him, I taught two courses: one called 'Law of Labour and Social Insurance' for the non-lawyers, and one then called 'Industrial Law' for the lawyers. It was always my endeavour to get the law students to sit in on the course for the non-lawyers, and at least some of the non-lawyers on the legal course. I felt it might do both some good. I think it did. The two courses, under different names, continue to exist.

Labour law had and has in my opinion an especially important role to play in opening the eyes of student and teacher alike to the social effect or non-effect of the law, and in making them see the frontiers of the law, that is the limits set by society to what it can do. Robson had very rightly shifted the emphasis towards collective labour law, trade unions, trade disputes, above all collective bargaining. In the textbooks on the subject published until less than ten years ago one looks in vain for the words 'collective bargaining' in the text or in the index. Here too the L.S.E. did pioneer work. It 'discovered' a whole new area of law, and (this is the importance of it) an area of law one cannot understand without understanding the rules which are not intended to be law at all, and which cannot operate as law, except under difficulties the magnitude of which we shall now very soon discover. Here the law students were and are made to see law as a social technique in competition with other techniques created by the autonomous two sides of industry without the law having any share in them at all. The problem is not new. Long ago it was discussed in the context of the relation of Church and State and to the problem of conformity and toleration. No scholarly study of the law should omit the consideration of its social frontiers; and it is not for nothing that labour law is now taught very intensively throughout the University of London.

What I have called the 'osmotic' effect of the needs of non-law students did not only emanate from economics and its ancillary disciplines, but equally from the study of government and of political science. Public law, that is constitutional, administrative and, very important, international law had to play in the work of the L.S.E. a much greater part than in many other universities outside London. International law has been a respectable academic subject at least since the sixteenth century, and constitutional law was made respectable by Anson and Dicey in the nineteenth, but administrative law was a dirty word until well after the First World War. We can hardly be surprised to find that even in this School (and this means in this country) it was at first not taught in the Law Department, but in the Department of Politics and Public Administration. Harold Laski, who was a close friend of Felix Frankfurter, then Professor of Administrative Law at Harvard, gave a course on the subject in 1926–7, but as from the following session it was taken over by Professor Robson. It was through him and through the late Sir Ivor Jennings that administrative law become a major subject of legal research and of legal education. But even Robson had to give his courses at first in the Department of Government. It was not until 1933, when Robson had been made a Reader in Administrative Law, that law students were allowed to partake of this dangerous nourishment. Today there is, as the Ormrod Report shows, hardly any academic law school in this country in which administrative law is not taught and examined, and the literature has grown to formidable dimensions. This is a conspicuous example to show how the combination of legal studies and studies in political science has enabled the L.S.E. to be a pioneer in the field of public law.

This contact between legal and political studies has, however, also influenced the spirit in which administrative law like other legal subjects has been and is being taught in this School. I fear that, outside London, the emphasis is frequently placed on pathological situations, and this, as I have said, can lead to serious distortions. What I mean is that administrative law sometimes deteriorates into a study of how the individual is to be protected against the administration (an important subject no doubt) and that the student is not directed to concentrate on the normal administrative processes and their legal framework, for example on the organization and the functioning of local authorities. A glance at the School calendars of the late 1920s and early 1930s shows that the L.S.E. did not succumb to this danger. Of the three courses on the subject first given in the Law Department in 1933-4 one dealt with general principles, one with central and local government, and one with public utilities and industry. In each case an analysis of the functions of administrative authorities and of the principles governing their organization is put in the centre. This approach is still visible today in the courses on elements of government for first-year law students, and in those on public law and on local government for those in their second and third years. It is obvious that no course on administrative law can dispense with a discussion of the judicial remedies available to the individual against unlawful administrative action or inaction. But to treat this as the core and essence of administrative law is a sign of that exaggerated interest in the abnormal in society to which I referred earlier on. The difference in this respect between the discipline of administrative law in this country and in the major continental countries is quite remarkable.

Here, in the L.S.E., the fact that the subject had at first to be taught with an eye to the needs of students of government had, I think, a permanent and a wholesome effect on the substance and on the method of its presentation. The presence here of Robson and of Jennings with their keen interest in the processes of government, central and local, was a guarantee that neither constitutional nor administrative law were geared towards a study of procedures against public authorities. But I think that quite apart from their influence, such an outlook could not have been adopted here in view of the proximity of legal and political studies.

It was thus through the direction it gave to the evolution of public law that the L.S.E. made another decisive contribution to the study of the legal framework of society. And in its very different sphere this has been equally true of international law. Here the decisive factor has always been the link with the study of international relations of which the University of London has for many years been and continues to be a centre.

So far I have spoken of the developments which originated before the First World War and during the inter-war period, and I must now say something about the third of these creative periods, the time after 1945.

To anyone who, like myself, approached legal studies and legal education in the British universities in the 1920s and 1930s, one of their astonishing features was the absence of any interest in the most important legal institution of society: no one studied the law of family relations, of marriage, of the parental relationship, of guardianship, etc. Those who studied private international law learned about the recognition of foreign marriages and foreign divorces, but they never heard anything about the English law of marriage and divorce. The reasons are rooted in the structure and inclinations of the legal profession. Divorce law has traditionally been the preserve of a specialized branch of the Bar with a legal training different from that of the common lawyers, and the professional interest was (outside the criminal law and acute issues of the liberty of the subject) always more geared towards problems of property than towards those problems of personal relations which are the core and essence of family law. Shortly after the Second World War family law was introduced into the teaching curricula and opened up as a subject of scholarly legal efforts through the initiative of the L.S.E.

Or rather, the initiative was largely that of Sir David Hughes Parry who succeeded Edward Jenks as the head of the Law Department. It was he who persuaded the University of London to introduce family law as an optional subject for the LL.B. and who co-operated with other colleges of the University, especially King's College, in developing it. But the L.S.E. had a decisive share not only in the impetus, which came from here, but also in the shaping of the curriculum.

Let me say a word about the curriculum in family law because it illustrates my point, which is the role played by the L.S.E. in the evolution of the study of law as a social institution and as a social technique. Before we began to teach family law, bits and pieces of it had appeared at odd places in other subjects: marriage settlements and family trusts in property law, husband and wife as competent or compellable witnesses in the law of evidence, delictual liability between the spouses and of one spouse for the torts of the other. All these, of course, are freakish situations from the social point of view, and when we drafted the syllabus we tried to emphasize the normal law of marriage, the personal and property relations between spouses as they are among the majority of the people, above all the legal relation between parents and children, custody, guardianship, adoption, and the legal principles governing the care of children deprived of a normal home. Does this sound obvious and platitudinous? I can assure you to some people it sounded almost revolutionary. Let me report two conversations I had at that time. One day I discussed the scheme with a very distinguished law teacher who took a keen interest in it. In the course of that conversation I referred to the intention to include the principles of the Children and Young Persons Act, and of the Children Act; this was the time just after the Curtis Report. My interlocutor looked at me with surprise. 'Very important', he said, 'very important, a matter in which I have been deeply interested for many years—as a matter of charity of course, up to this moment I have never thought of this as *law*'. The other conversation was with a practising barrister who stopped me in the Temple and said: 'I hear you are beginning to teach divorce law.' 'No', I said, 'we are introducing the law of marriage, and also of divorce.' 'Is there any law in marriage?' he asked. After many years at the Bar he was unable to see marriage otherwise than in terms of divorce.

Of course divorce law was and is included in the family law syllabus. How can one teach law without going into marginal and pathological situations? But it was combined with an attempt to display the contribution the law has made to the evolution of marriage as a social institution and the reaction of the law towards changing ideas about the relation between the generations. The very understandable reaction of the practitioner reflected the view one must form of family law in the light of legal practice. Even if we had not been determined not to yield to that view and even if it had not been our own resolve to include the law relating to deprived children, dozens of future social workers and sociology students and their teachers would have compelled us to mend our ways. Here too this combination of the various social sciences in this School had a beneficial effect on legal studies.

The example set through the effort of the University of London proved to be most fruitful. Today all academic law schools in the country teach family law; it is a highly popular option. The literature on the subject is growing. The subject is becoming respectable. Yet it was a late-comer among the academic legal disciplines. Its birthplace is in this building.

To a certain extent this can also be said of the other conspicuous post-war development. This was the growth of tax law as a subject of research and, at post-graduate level, of teaching. The L.S.E. was fortunate in being able to secure the help, at first part time, then full time, of one of the foremost experts in tax law, and it is not easy to imagine how the subject could have been developed here if Professor Wheatcroft had not decided to exchange practice for precept. It goes without saying that a legal syllabus which does not include tax law is hopelessly incomplete from every point of view, the professional as well as the purely academic. What I would venture to submit however is that even more important than the teaching of tax law *ex professo* is the infusion of considerations of income tax and death duty into courses on property and succession and company law. How can one understand the social function of these legal institutions if one ignores the influence of tax law on property transactions, on wills, on the formation and organization of commercial companies? To omit the tax point of view (because this is another 'subject') is just as unrealistic as to omit town planning from the teaching and study of land law. Here a lot has already been done in the L.S.E. for example in the course on administration of estates and trusts, and, as I have said, in the course on commercial law for B.Sc. (Econ.) students. Tax law too is now spreading as a (mainly graduate) subject in the universities. Again the development got its principal impetus from here.

At this moment the L.S.E. is, unless I am quite mistaken, on the point of acting once more as a pioneer in the development of legal studies. Perhaps the most glaring gap in academic legal studies in this country up to now has been the absence of any interest in industrial property: patents, design, trade marks, copyright. British universities have simply ignored and continue to ignore these fascinating subjects which are as vital in practice as they are promising to the scholar and the teacher. I should have thought that patent law or copyright law was, even from the most ortho-dox point of view, at least as fruitful a subject for training the students' minds as contingent remainders and the rule against perpetuities. But if you read about international conferences on, for example, copyright law, you will usually find that most countries are represented by academics, and this country by civil servants. I therefore regard Professor Cornish's interest in these matters and the fact that he has started to teach them to LL.M. students as the possible beginning of something important in the study and teaching of the law in Britain.

Up to now I have discussed the evolution of legal studies and the influence the School has had on them in terms of subjects, but I hope I have shown that the shaping of the syllabus impinges upon the method of treating the law as a subject of teaching and scholarship. However, there has been a development in the method of approach apart from the branching out into new areas. The analysis of what are sometimes called 'legal facts' is now beginning to take shape. Research into the actual operation of matrimonial institutions, especially in the magistrates' courts, has been successfully undertaken; research into the jury system has been done in the L.S.E. itself; and, perhaps partly because of the growing pace of law reform and the interest of the Law Com-mission, we can hope for future developments in the areas of the investigation of accident liability, of standard contracts and other matters. But there is one area of the law in which this sociological approach has become customary and almost generally accepted. The only branches of legal sociology which have grown to adult stature are criminology and penology, and those of us who want to see the study of 'legal facts' develop elsewhere (in relation to contracts and to tort liability and to family law) could not wish for anything better than that the work done, not least in this School, in investigating the causes of crime and the effect of punishment was paralleled in other legal fields. The L.S.E. has, of course, for many years been and continues to be a focal point both in criminological and in penological studies, and again its role as a meeting place of social disciplines and as a clearing house of ideas is essential. Both criminology and penology began to blossom during the inter-war period, and this was largely due to the great work done by Dr. Hermann Mannheim, one of the founders of the systematic study of crime and punishment in this country, and of course one of the leading authorities in these subjects.

That the pioneering role of the L.S.E. continues can be seen by anyone who takes the trouble of looking for five minutes at its annual Calendar. In how many universities is there a course on public law which begins with elements of government as its first part? How many curricula contain a course on 'Sentencing and Treatment of Offenders'? And how many law students up and down the country are ever given a chance of even reflecting on 'Law and Social Policy'? How many law schools provide instruction especially on the law relating to civil liberties, and to the international protection of human rights? How many give courses especially devoted to the law relating to housing? And, if one may ask with great respect, how many realize that what they are teaching is (not by design but simply through the role played by law in society) very much the law of the 'privileged'? Is it not clear that in this country the law relating to the under-privileged (on which a course is provided for the law students at the L.S.E.) will have to move into the focus of studies as it has done so very largely in the better law schools in the United States?

What I have said here was very eclectic and the examples I have given were intended to illustrate the fact that over the last three-quarters of a century, but especially since the Second World War, legal studies have taken a new turn in this country and that the L.S.E. has played a major role in promoting this. What I said was perhaps a little too much concentrated on the teaching side of these studies. If I had the time, I could develop this same thought by pointing to the evolution of legal writing and research. I do not know of any other academic institution which has a legal research division. Let me here however make two points: Beveridge had the wisdom not only to get Gutteridge and Jenks to this School but also to initiate the creation of the only chair in English legal history in the country (and with the exception of the one at Harvard, as far as I know, the only one in the English-speaking world). The L.S.E. has become a centre of research in this field which bears so close a relation to the sociological method to which I have referred. And secondly, I think it is clear to any-one interested in the academic pursuit of the law, that few things have done as much for broadening and deepening these legal studies as the foundation of the *Modern Law Review* by Lord Chorley in 1937. The *Modern Law Review* has always had a close association with the School, and the L.S.E. and the *Modern Law Review* have, I think, given a great deal of mutual help to each other. The general purpose of the *Modern Law Review* has always been and, I hope and trust, will always be to stimulate the study of law as a social science and to pay the closest attention to the social forces which make the law and to law itself as a social force.

This, however, is the direction in which legal studies must and will move and are moving in this country as they do in many foreign countries. To have promoted and accelerated the evolution of law as a social science, and to have done so without neglecting the necessary teaching of and research in law as an intellectual and a professional technique, is I think one of the lasting achievements of the London School of Economics.

REFERENCES

1. BEVERIDGE, Janet, *An Epic of Clare Market*, pp. 72–73 (London: G. Bell & Sons, 1960).
2. LORD BEVERIDGE, *The London School of Economics and its Problems, 1919–1937*, pp. 83 ff. (London: Allen & Unwin, 1960).

MAN AND
HIS ENVIRONMENT

M. J. WISE

M. J. WISE

M.C., B.A., Ph.D. (Birmingham)

Professor of Geography
The London School of Economics
and Political Science

After war service, appointed Lecturer in Geography, University of Birmingham, 1945–51; since that time on the staff of the L.S.E. Chairman, Ministry of Agriculture Departmental Committee of Inquiry into Statutory Smallholdings 1963–7. Member, Department of Environment Landscape Advisory Committee on Trunk Roads 1971–. Vice-President, International Geographical Union 1968–. An Honorary Secretary of the Royal Geographical Society since 1963. Honorary Treasurer of the Geographical Association since 1966. President, Section E of the British Association for the Advancement of Science 1965. Vice-President, Institute of British Geographers. Editor of *Birmingham and its Regional Setting* (1951); author of numerous papers on economic geography and regional planning.

MAN AND
HIS ENVIRONMENT

I

In this lecture I attempt to show how in some ways members of the L.S.E., more particularly its geographers, have contributed to the understanding of environmental problems and to the improvement of the environment.

'The study of Geography', declared John Milton, 'is both profitable and delightful.' He also prescribed that, for the instruction of young people in geographical matters, 'prudent and staid guides' should be appointed. I am not sure that I qualify!

This year, 1972, marks the fiftieth aniversary of the founding of the Joint School of Geography at this School and King's College, London; it is thus a point in the history of an academic institution at which one may look back and review the success of the academic explorations of our 'wise and experte travaylers', to use Richard Willes's phrase. The alliance of the two departments was arranged by H. J. (later Sir Halford) Mackinder, then Reader in Geography at the School, and Professor W. T. Gordon, Professor of Geology at King's College (1). It was encouraged by the then Director, Sir William (later Lord) Beveridge and the Principal of King's College, Dr. (later Sir Ernest) Barker, not least as a way of linking teaching and research in the social sciences and the natural sciences. It was, perhaps, the most fruitful of a number of schemes advanced by Beveridge for forming bridges between the social and the natural sciences (2). In part, the object may have been to introduce into the social sciences the methods of the natural sciences; at least equally important was the need to provide for economic and political studies a basis of knowledge of the diverse conditions of human life over the face of the earth and to evaluate the constraints upon human activities inherent in the physical environment.

II

The origins of many of the themes around which the work of geographers in the L.S.E. has been built are to be found in the writings of Halford Mackinder. At the time of his appointment to the L.S.E., in 1895, this remarkable man was Reader in Geography at Oxford and Principal of University College, Reading. He held the three posts simultaneously. Rothenstein's sketch, which hangs in the L.S.E., conveys the often-held image of him as imperialist and geopolitician; more relevant to our present subject were the environmental lessons of his 'New Geography'. This grouping of ideas developed in the course of some six hundred lectures given in towns all over the country for the Oxford University Extension movement (in one period of three years he travelled more than 30,000 miles) found especially appreciative audiences in the industrial districts of the North of England. At the age of 26, in 1887, in an audacious paper 'On the Scope and Methods of Geography', he placed his views squarely before the Royal Geographical Society (3). It was the paper of a young revolutionary attacking the orthodox views of the day on the organization of academic subjects relating to the environment. 'Knowledge', he thundered, 'is one. Its division into subjects is a concession to human weakness.' 'Damned cheek', muttered at one point a worthy admiral from the front row (4). The orthodoxy of the day separated the study of 'scientific' geography (physical geography) from that of human affairs. But, to Mackinder, it was essential to relate human affairs to the stage on which they occurred; the variations in the character of the stage, the locality, and the different relations that were engendered, were the central themes of the new geography. He was not an ally of the geographical determinists, those who saw man as 'a creature of his environment'. Though nature in large measure controlled, it was man who initiated. It was the interaction that mattered; man altered his environment and the influence of that environment on man's future was in consequence changed. Evaluations of location and of resources rested on considerations of history and culture, scientific and technical skills, ability to move about and to communicate. So an understanding of the changes, and of the persistencies, of geographical values and relationships was an essential element in education. Those who had grasped, in their true relations, the factors of environment were 'likely to be fertile in the suggestion of new relations between the environment and man'. Well applied, such a study had practical value for men of business; but more, if wisely used by statesmen, it could promote peace and would prove 'likely to adjust differences without the crude resort to arms'; if applied to the future, it could assist better balanced relationships between societies and environments. Geography, therefore, was a badly needed science. He defined its function as 'to trace the interaction of man in society and so much of his environment as varies locally' (3).

The world as seen by Mackinder had become a closed system. The exploration of the continental interiors from western countries had almost completed the primary task of geographical exploration and discovery; the patterns of empires had been largely mapped out. In the United States of America the frontier of settlement was about to be closed; the Suez Canal had opened shorter sea-routes between east and west; the Trans-Siberian railway was linking the Baltic with the Pacific. Though detailed mapping remained to be done, the shape of the world was known and the interrelationships between its parts were becoming closer; the answers to man's problems were not to be found through territorial extension but through more exact knowledge of the nature of the terrestrial environment. The links between societies and environments were the products of great repositories of culture and experience; they possessed momentum, and the study of past as well as of present conditions was required. So studies of history, politics, and economics could be joined with the sciences of geology, climatology, and botany to focus on the problems of men and environments.

A further principle was the importance of establishing exact geographical distributions. In Britain, geographical prestige had, up to his time, been acquired by adventurous exploration. Mackinder himself established his standing in this sense by making the first ascent of Mount Kenya in 1899; the 'new' exploration involved critical analysis of information and the meticulous mapping of distributions. Geography was a science of distributions, 'the science, that is, which traces the arrangement of things on the earth's surface'. The individual distributions once mapped, had to be correlated, so opening a way to the making of explanatory statements concerning the nature of environments. It was a lesson long delayed in Britain. Humboldt and Ritter had been teaching the science of distributions and relationships in Germany fifty years earlier, but the lesson when it came could hardly have been more vigorously argued or more effective in its effect on environmental education in schools and universities.

In a closing world, the environmental problem had to be studied on a world scale. No area of the earth was wholly self-contained. There was 'no complete geographical region either less than or greater than the whole of the earth'. In his later years he re-emphasized this theme and, writing in 1942 of the conquest of the air, reasserted that 'the habitat of each separate human being is this global earth'. It is a lesson of which we need frequent reminding, preoccupied as we tend to become with local and national affairs. A change in the balance between society and environment in however remote a corner of the globe has reverberations that may be felt in great or small degree all over the world.

At lower levels of scale, he argued for study and analysis by regions. He was one of the first in Britain to argue seriously for the merits of the regional concept, one that has now become so widely adopted in many academic disciplines and in public life. Regions, rather than nations, were the units of study, and regions were definable in terms of environmental characteristics, not merely by political boundaries. His treatment of regions can well be illustrated by reference to his now classic book *Britain and the British Seas* (5), published in 1902. Is there a better interpretation of the time of the emergence of the city region than his account of London : -

The life of the great metropolis at the beginning of the twentieth century exhibits a daily throb as of a huge pulsating heart. Every evening half a million men are sent in quick streams, like corpuscles of blood in the arteries, along the railways and the trunk roads outward to the suburbs. Every morning they return, crowding into the square mile or two wherein the exchanges of the world are finally adjusted.

. . . In a manner all south-eastern England is a single urban community; for steam and electricity are changing our geographical conceptions. A city in an economic sense is no longer an area covered continuously with streets and houses. The wives and children . . . live without—beyond green fields—where the men only sleep and pass the Sabbath. The metropolis in its largest meaning includes all the counties for whose inhabitants London is 'Town', whose men do habitual business there, whose women buy there, whose standard of thought is determined there.

Or again, consider his interpretation of the transformation of values in the industrial age that had led to the emergence of great industrial complexes in hitherto unpeopled districts: the Black Country, for example:

The whole district is one great workshop, both above ground and below. At night it is lurid with the flames of the iron furnaces: by day it appears one vast loosely-knit town of humble homes, arid cinder heaps and fields stripped of vegetation by smoke and fumes.

Concern for the environment had been kept alive in the nineteenth century in the minds of a few. Mackinder, perhaps, was reflecting the awakening of a more vigorous spirit of inquiry. In the 1880s the Royal Geographical Society had conducted its own inquiry into geographical education and had begun vigorous action to sponsor the study of the environment in universities and schools. In the year of the founding of the L.S.E., Patrick Geddes had founded his Outlook Tower in Edinburgh. From the world's first sociological laboratory he applied sociological insight and biological knowledge to cities, conurbations, and regions. He sought 'a cartography of life, mind and society'. The National Trust was founded in 1895. Ebenezer Howard's exposition of the garden city concept appeared in 1898. The theory of the growth of cities and industrial areas was under investigation. Charles Booth's *Survey of Life and Labour* of the people of London was appearing. Action was in train to ameliorate the effect of the city environment upon the health of city-dwellers. The first experiments at replanting trees on the spoilheaps of the coalfields were in progress. Model industrial villages had been built; civic planning was taking its first steps.

This was then a time to capture the minds of men and to turn them towards the use of the earth and the nature of the human habitat. Let Mackinder's successor as Director of the L.S.E. close our chapter. W. Pember Reeves is best known as radical politician, historian, statesman: like Mackinder he was an associate of the Webbs. He was an environmentalist, too: the disaster of the destruction of the native vegetation and the oncoming of soil erosion in his native New Zealand fired his pen, and in 'The Passing of the Forest' he wrote:

> The axe bites deep. The rushing fire streams bright;
>   Swift, beautiful and fierce it speeds for Man,
> Nature's rough-handed foeman, keen to smite
>   And mar the loveliness of ages. Scan
> The blackened forest ruined in a night,
>
>   .   .   .   .   .   .
>
> ... Ah, bitter price to pay
> For Man's dominion – beauty swept away!

III

My next chapter concerns the development of geographical surveys and the application of the findings to problems of public concern and of government. Geography has always had a practical side. In the sixteenth and seventeenth centuries, theoretical geography contributed to practical exploration and navigation; in the eighteenth and nineteenth centuries, its study was seen as essential to success in commerce. In our own day, it has been geography's ability to help in practical affairs concerning the environment, including the use of land, the layout of towns, the conservation of resources, the defining of regions and of local government areas. Inevitably, the theme is bound up with the work of Dudley Stamp whose influence on the study of the environment and on human affairs extended into almost all lands (6).

It may well have been his early training as geologist and botanist that fired Stamp's zeal for the gathering of first-hand evidence in the field. It was also a realization that statistical material, collected as it was by political and administrative units of curious shapes, offered very imperfect evidence for geographical

analysis. The immediate objective of his Land Utilisation Survey of Britain, begun in 1930, was the creation of a record, 'an
historical document of permanent value'. Through the cartographic ordering of fresh evidence, new problems would be exposed for research, particularly concerning the nature of changes
in the use of land and the reasons for change. Within a few years
the Survey had become a great co-operative effort, uniting students
and staff in field mapping, in the analysis of data and the preparation of map sheets for publication, and in writing the county
reports. The project survived financial crises and critical attacks;
the L.S.E. gave official and practical backing and the finished
work, now acquiring enhanced value as a primary document in
our national archives, justified the efforts of the many hundreds
of workers (7). Very quickly it became clear that the maps had
practical as well as academic value. Governments had begun to
take action towards controlling, in the interest of the public good,
the geographical shape of England and Wales. The maps of the
Survey were used as a basis for town-planning schemes. Their
evidence was employed in planning the revival of British agriculture with wartime food production needs in mind, a revival that
has had lasting results. The Survey provided basic evidence for
the work of the Barlow Commission on the Geographical Distribution of the Industrial Population, 1938–40, and for the Scott
Committee on Land Utilization in Rural Areas, 1941–2 (of which
Stamp was Vice-Chairman).

The Scott Committee's report clearly bore the marks of Stamp's
thinking. 'The proper and profitable use of land, measured not
merely in terms of individual man's immediate need but rather in
terms of man's collective need both present and future is of basic
importance to every nation.' Once withdrawn from rural use,
good agricultural land was a lost resource, and the cost of fore-
going it was not reflected in the prices of the land market. It is not
difficult to trace in Stamp's principles of land use the influence
of early writers of the Conservationist school. There was also a
use of 'scientific' methods of data collection and hypothesis formation leading towards a 'public interest' viewpoint which was in
the tradition of the founders of this School. There was the need to
secure 'the right use of every acre of the land surface in the
national interest'; the 56 million acres of the land of Britain

represented only 1 ¼ acres per head of population from which to provide for food and water, houses, work-places, communications, and recreation. For England alone there was less than 1 acre per head. In the national interest, therefore, land should be put to its 'optimum' use and, indeed, wherever possible to 'multiple' use.

Moreover, it was a time of urban expansion. Much of the best agricultural land lay around the edges of the sprawling cities and conurbations. How far should urban sprawl be checked and new city forms designed and introduced? The general declaration by the government that 'it would seek to prevent the diversion of good agricultural land to other uses where there is less productive land that could reasonably be used' led on to the problem of defining land quality, and the scheme of land classification was produced. The methods of land classification, which were at first rough and ready, have since been much refined and are now regularly applied in formulating plans for urban growth. The definition of the 'right' use of land in the public interest brought the geographer squarely into the problem of conflicting claims on land and resources. Stamp's response was through the construction of the Potential Production Unit and the Standard Nutrition Unit, essentially attempts at quantification, at placing on a more calculated basis the geographer's value judgements of the environment. It is an area of study that, over thirty years later, still remains open, for our progress in cost–benefit analysis has served to reveal even more clearly the difficulty of establishing arguments on grounds of environmental quality when weighed in the scale against considerations that can more readily be valued in monetary terms. Even in such difficulties, as Stamp found, the man who is the master of the surveyed facts is in a strong position.

As one observer remarked, the test of Stamp's work is 'to be seen around us in the well-ordered growth of towns and villages since 1945 as contrasted with the inter-war years' sprawl' (8). He was a major contributor to the system of land use planning for town and country in Britain that became, in 1947, a practical product of wartime idealism. Other instances of the practical application to public problems of scientific surveys come to mind from the same period. It was S. W. Wooldridge, of King's College, founder of modern British geomorphology, with his unrivalled knowledge of the land forms, and of the Tertiary and Quaternary deposits, of the London region who was able to estimate the scale of the sand and gravel resources available and urgently required for the post-war rebuilding and New Towns programmes (9). It was S. H. Beaver who carried out the first pioneer surveys of the derelict land problem in industrial areas, and who began a modern process of discovery that has led not only to an awareness of the problem of dereliction, but to the reclamation of many thousands of acres of industrial waste land and the transformation of landscapes in many industrial districts (10).

Geographical exploration, to use Stamp's own words, had become 'intensive rather than extensive: it has become especially an assessment of natural resources'. Such exploration had to be conducted on a world scale. There were rich nations using land resources unproductively while poor nations went hungry, often for lack of knowledge of the resource base (11). A 'World Land Use Survey' could at least bring to light new facts and relationships; to what extent were constraints on economic development inherent in the physical environment, or how far were they products of misuse of the environment?

Much was achieved using ground survey and air photographs: geologists, hydrologists and agronomists were asked to think with social scientists about the nature of environmental change and about the future welfare of communities. In the light of the current controversy on the future of mankind and its environment, it is interesting to look back on a view that Stamp expressed in 1964.

There are in the world today [he said] the pessimists who see starvation for man and the exhaustion of resources in the near future . . . we range ourselves rather with those who see in the study of the earth's riches and the ecology of man a challenge to a fuller understanding that can but lead to the betterment of mankind (12).

This was not simply the optimistic spirit of the man expressing itself: it was the view of a scientist whose experience gained through survey was that great resources remained to be realized, that given interdisciplinary co-operation and the effective formulation and practice of wise policies for resource management, there were answers within the range of human ingenuity to the problems of resource evaluation, maldistribution, under-development.

But Stamp's definition of the role of the modern geographical explorer was still too narrow to reflect the width of his own interests or those of his colleagues, for example of Ll. Rodwell Jones (13), for long his chief. It failed to include the distribution of human resources. The changing distribution of population remained a central theme in human geography. The emphasis, in the main, was on the process of differentiation of areas. With the movement of people across, say, North America and the emergence of an economy of sub-continental scale or, as R. O. Buchanan showed (14), with the colonization of the lands of the southern hemisphere and the opening of trade, local and regional differences emerged, expressing themselves in regional and local crop associations, settlement forms, regional consciousness; the products of evaluations of climate, terrain and location. The growth of science and technology led societies not to a mastery over nature but to the fashioning of more intimate adjustments demanding ever more precise study of actual and potential resources.

There was, too, the question of the effect of environment upon man himself. The earlier determinists had discredited their school not so much through choice of hypothesis but from premature generalization and exaggerated example. What light could now be thrown on environment and variations in human skill and effort, in health? Accurate mapping of the distribution of disease could pose questions leading to the formation of hypotheses for further testing. Had not Dr. Snow used this method in linking the incidence of cholera in London with an infected source of drinking water? Similar methods could be applied to the relationships between air pollution and acute bronchitis, soil and certain forms of cancer, diet and deficiency diseases (15). The tradition continues: the London Expedition, recently formed by a group of graduate students, is seeking evidence on possible relationships between environment and educational opportunities and learning skills. They should make a contribution to a field in which there is still too little firm evidence.

It will be seen that the developing tradition was an applied one. Another field in which work continues to the present day concerns the rise and fall of industrial regions and the incidence of opportunities for individuals and groups (16). As societies and economies change, so do their geographical shapes. Discussions of methods for influencing regional economic futures were a response to the appearance of localized unemployment in the 1930s. The Barlow Commission in 1938 met a dearth of information on the exact location of industry in Britain and sent out a call for maps. These were provided and the review of their evidence led on to the discussion of public policy. What, if any, was the duty of the state to intervene in the reshaping of regional environments? Was its duty limited only to relieving the immediate symptoms of human distress, such as unemployment? Was there a wider role, not only to promote in distressed areas the location of new enterprise and to assist the adaptation of physical forms to economic and social changes, but also to stimulate and to apply thinking on new shapes for cities and industrial regions, to inspire models for change. In an age, and in a country, in which government policy and action have become probably the most important agents of geographical change, it is not surprising that such questions have remained focal points of discussion. Argument from the L.S.E., it may be claimed, has been influential in focusing political opinion upon the need for co-ordinated action by the various government departments upon environmental questions. The hypothesis that investment in environmental improvement can greatly assist the solution of regional problems is now being tested in action.

A salient advantage of life in this School has been the ability to engage in interdisciplinary studies of such questions. It would be remiss if, in this series of lectures, no mention were to be made of the work of the Greater London Group (17), a research organization of economists, lawyers, geographers, and members of the departments of government and social administration, inspired from the outset by Professor W. A. Robson. Not the least of its tasks has been that of devising possible new structures and areas for local government to meet the changed requirements of the geography of the modern city. Similar motives have inspired the introduction of interdisciplinary courses of study in the social sciences for urban and regional planners. The production of the *Atlas of London* (18) has given us a set of new maps but also a host of new questions; and in an age of urban redevelopment those concerning the links between the lives of individuals and of communities and the physical structures of the city are amongst the most important. Have we not sometimes been quick to seize on opportunities for physical redevelopment without considering whether social and community relationships were being destroyed? What are the forces, different from area to area as they may be, that bind men and women to particular places? How different are individual and group perceptions of local environments from those of the academic or the planner? What desirable goals can we set for the rebuilding of the urban environment and for the best use of the rural environment of Britain in what remains of this century?

If any be in doubt of the importance of these issues, let them go out from Houghton Street into the inner areas of London and examine the quality of the environment that we offer. Or let them consider the implications of the growing city region of London with its radius of perhaps 50 miles from Charing Cross; Mackinder's model greatly intensified in the scale of activity. Or let them consider the possible tendencies towards a giant megalopolis extending from the Ribble and the Tees southwards to the English Channel. As Mr. Goldbury remarked in *Utopia Limited*, 'We haven't come to that exactly but we're tending rapidly in that direction. The date's not distant.'

The lessons are that through disciplined study of environmental characteristics and change, through a fuller understanding of the links between social life and its physical surroundings, influence may be brought to bear on individual action and on public policy; that, if we are to improve environments, we have first to persuade men's minds that the long-term benefits that may accrue exceed the costs of the expenditure and restraints that may be necessary; and that in these matters the role open to geography and to other disciplines within the L.S.E. involved in the study of environmental questions is one strategic in national life. The achievements of the past provide the example. Can we exceed those achievements in the future?

IV

Once again, man–environmental relationships are a subject of major controversy. There is again widespread consciousness of the earth as a closing system. Realization of the earth's limited size has come partly from the way in which rapid transport and communication has, at least for some of us, reduced the scale of the earth; dramatically, also, from man's success in breaking out of the earth system with satellites and space-craft and the resultant awareness of the earth's limits as a home for mankind. Within a thin envelope around the globe is supported, to use J. W. MacNeill's words, 'a hierarchy of plant and animal species, including man, all interconnected and dependent upon one another for life support. It is this living system that is threatened by environmental degradation' (19). Evidence of damage to the system, or of its imperfections, is found in the pollution of Lake Erie, in the environmental effects of great engineering schemes, such as the impact of the hydro-electric and irrigation schemes on the Caspian and Aral Seas, in pollution by oil, in the envelopment of great cities by smoke, in soil erosion, in city slums, in the pressures on land and resources from an increasing population. There is anxiety, if yet little firm evidence, that the energy released into the atmosphere from the burning of fossil fuels may, within a century, have significant effects on climatic conditions. Attention has been alerted to the consequences of technical change, arising not only from the production of pollutants but from the spill-over effects: congestion, noise, lost opportunities for the use of resources.

It has been argued recently that 'if current trends are allowed to persist, the breakdown of society and the irreversible disruption of the life-support systems on this planet, possibly by the end of the century, certainly within the life times of our children, are inevitable' (20). The Secretary-General of the United Nations has stated that nations have perhaps ten years left 'in which to subordinate their ancient quarrels and launch a global partnership to curb the arms race, to improve the human environment, to de-fuse the population explosion and to supply the required momentum to world development efforts'. From a report of the

U.S.S.R. Committee of the Council of Ministers for Science and Technology (21) has come the statement that it is 'necessary for the very existence of mankind that its further progress requires a rational system of the use and conservation of biosphere resources to be put into practice everywhere'.

Not all is gloom. The extent of public awareness and of increasing willingness to pay the costs of environmental improvement is a gain. Efforts have been, or are being, made by governments in many countries, our own, Canada, U.S.S.R., U.S.A., and elsewhere, to control environmental pollution and to evolve machinery for environmental planning. A number of international scientific programmes have thrown new light on the problems of the biosphere. Governments are preparing for an international conference on the environment to be held in Stockholm later this year. The record of achievement in our own School, a few aspects of which we have noted, gives real cause for the expectation that, through well-applied scientific studies and the use of foresight, answers may continue to be found to environmental questions. Indeed a large number of former students of the Joint School are now fully occupied in various aspects of environmental planning; and the products of their work, in the form of improvements to environment and prevention of misuse, are to be seen in countries all over the world.

So it is not necessary to share the views of the gloomiest observers, or to employ forecasts based on exponential growth of population against a concept of finite resources, to be aware of environmental problems at all scales from the global downwards. Just as we reviewed some response to earlier appreciations of environmental problems, so we should consider how well related is our present work to the environmental problems of the time.

During the last decade there has been a new revolution in geographical studies in the universities of Britain, not least in our Joint School. In part, it has been associated with an expansion of the scale of activity that would surely astonish Mackinder, could he be aware of the fruitfulness of the efforts of his group of 'revolutionaries'. The increase in scale of activity has permitted both intensification and diversification of effort.

The physical environment is itself by no means a static one. In our Joint School we can record many achievements: for

example, in the study of the processes of erosion and sedimenta-
tion that shape our physical world and in the analysis of change
in plant communities. The work of scientific exploration of little
known and relatively underdeveloped parts of the earth continues. One of our number, for example, took an active part in
the recent Royal Society–Royal Geographical Society interdisciplinary scientific expedition to the Mato Grosso which threw
new light on the physical processes at work in a hitherto unin-
vestigated area. Well-tried, yet still developing, methods of study
continue to bring important results in application to problems of
development in Ceylon, India, West Africa, Latin America, or to
landscape conflicts in our own countryside. The Second Land
Utilization Survey of Great Britain, directed by Dr. Alice Coleman, from King's College, has yielded fuller information than its
pioneer predecessor.

In some respects there has been a movement away from Mackinder's regional principle. While, it is true, he recognized the
interest of studying the regularities of phenomena over the earth's
surface and the lure of the search for statistical generalizations,
for him it was the differences between places that were important,
and regional synthesis was the final product. Mackinder, of
course, recognized the difficulty that his own advocacy of a
holistic approach was likely to create: that of a conflict between,
on the one hand, the desire to study in depth the distribution of
individual phenomena (for example, land forms, urban growth,
mineral resources) and, on the other, the 'crying need of
humanity' for synthetic studies of society–environment relationships by areas or regions. The recent trend has seemed to emphasize systematic studies, and this may seem paradoxical at a time
when the regional concept has acquired public favour and application. However the paradox may be more apparent than real. It
is perhaps not so much the regional concept that is out of favour
amongst modern geographers as the use of an older stereotyped
regional method. The present search is not only for generalizations on, for example, the relative spacing of cities and towns; it
is also for improved approaches to the study of interactions within and between areas that will produce both better descriptions of
regions and a fuller understanding of how and why they change
shape, rise, or decline.

The emphasis on systematic studies has been greatly encouraged by the introduction of more refined statistical techniques and by improvement in our capacity to measure and to correlate distribution patterns. Kendall's paper of 1939 on the geography of crop productivity was a notable landmark in the application of statistical methods to geographical problems (22). Other statisticians have moved in this direction and geographers have responded rapidly in the last fifteen years to employ the techniques which the advance of statistical methods has placed within their grasp. From the outset of their studies, undergraduate students now acquire a familiarity with statistical and computational methods, in addition to the more traditional cartographic techniques. While the range of available data is still far from adequate, especially in regional statistics, the coming of the computer has opened new avenues for the exploration of geographical data.

Further, the emergence of computergraphics is placing in our hands a new tool for the rapid production of maps of changing geographical situations; it gives clear possibilities for application in regional planning. Change can be monitored, plans adjusted; the forecasting of future geographies is now an active study.

The development of forecasting techniques is of especial importance in application to the problems of city growth. The adoption into geographical theory of concepts derived from the physical sciences has provided opportunities for simulation studies, and for the building of models against which actual change can be measured. The theoretical basis of the subject (though not an aspect, we must probably admit, in which the L.S.E. can claim a large number of original contributions) has certainly been strengthened in recent years. The testing of central place theories and of theories of the location of economic activity has further stimulated understanding of city systems, though models based on assumptions of economic efficiency are tending to prove less attractive than those employing other assumptions about human behaviour. New techniques have been devised for the study of the spatial organization of society. Thus, again, it is in the light of urgent public problems of city and regional planning that we seek ways of breaking into fuller understanding of the relationships within cities between land uses and the traffic that they generate; the functions of city centres and the patterns of movement of people, ideas, goods, and services; service centres and their hinterlands. How far are new trends in personal mobility reshaping both city and countryside? How far will new techniques of communication encourage the decentralization of activities from crowded city centres? At what points in the urban system, and through what mechanisms, can controls and stimuli best be applied? How, in matters of city growth and redevelopment, can the public interest be defined? At this point in our work, Mackinder's voice may be heard again. Scientific research is capable of explosive discoveries but it must always, as he reminded us, keep a true sense of ethical values, of what he called 'the mind of the world' (23). The minds and hearts of people should not be far from our minds in our scientific examinations of cities and their futures.

Modern geography in our Joint School has continued its traditional role of acting as one of many possible bridges between the natural and the social sciences. One example must suffice. The concept of ecology, first evolved a century ago and successfully applied fifty years ago in the biological sciences, was introduced into both geography and sociology. In geography, the modern revival of interest which has related ecological principles to the concepts of systems analysis, has been a powerful organizing force in research and teaching. Human communities whether urban or rural, industrial or agricultural, may be viewed as elements within ecosystems interacting with their fellow human beings and engaging in activities that influence plant and animal communities as well as the resources of the earth itself. To an understanding of the ways in which ecosystems change, and of their constructive and destructive tendencies, an understanding of the motives and reasons for decisions by the human actors is indispensable. Here lies one reason for current interest in research designed to obtain a fuller understanding of the decision-making processes of farmers, industrialists, mineral extractors, governments.

It is also possible, one hopes probable, that the development of the ecosystem concept, coupled with a more complete understanding of the interactions within systems, may open new doors to the solution of problems of managing our environment, of selecting appropriate geographical scales for management, of selecting appropriate points for control and for retrieval of past mistakes, for encouraging activities that are likely to promote the health of the system and to discourage the harmful.

The new technology of satellites and spacecraft should, if wisely used, enable us to watch the effects of man's interference with natural systems, to develop resources, to correct mistakes. Already, remote sensing has had fruitful applications to land use problems, both agricultural and urban. Within a few years it should be possible to call up, as and when it is needed, information on the state of, say, a particular crop on a world scale. The possibilities are great. If they are to be employed efficiently in the interests of achieving a more equitable distribution of resources and of conserving the environment, new links will need to be forged between institutions like ours, concerned with the social sciences, and those whose work lies in the scientific and technical aspects of space systems and information retrieval.

I have indicated only a few current trends; but enough, perhaps, to show that the tradition of interest in, and concern for, man's environment continues undiminished in strength. One would wish for more resources, for more energy, in relation to the size of the tasks. Environments appropriate to their own day have outlived the values of their age; they are with us still and must be adapted and redeveloped. There is the task of measuring current change, observing the effect of current actions, recommending correctives. If the attack on the environmental problem is to succeed, the needs of the future must, to the best of our ability, be foreseen. The tradition that we possess is to maintain a critical watch on the environment of our time and on the processes of environmental change and, through our teaching, to strive for a higher standard of commitment by individuals to environmental values. It is a tradition that involves us in accurate survey and analysis of geographical change, in reviewing the implications of discovered change, in projecting forward observed trends. It charges us to recommend constructive changes in public policy and institutions.

I would wish to focus a still greater share of the resources of the L.S.E. on environmental questions. The environmental problems of our day present a challenge to the social sciences.

The problem of making wise choices, wise resource allocation decisions, within a spatial or geographical frame of reference, is one that, to an extent, involves all the disciplines that are studied here: history, economics, sociology, social administration, social anthropology, government, social psychology, law, all have very clear relevance. There are some encouraging signs: the success of our interdisciplinary master's degree in urban and regional planning is one; the establishment of the Centre for Urban Economics with a commitment to interdisciplinary work is a second. There are many others. The opportunities for combining our disciplines in studies of selected environmental problems are great. Looking back, we can certainly claim that, since its foundation, members of the L.S.E. have contributed towards a fuller understanding of the relationships between societies and environments and to the formation of public policies for environmental management. We can also claim that our Joint School has indeed formed a bridge, opening to students of the geographical environment a very much wider range of experience than is possible in one school or college. At one time the task was to arouse public interest. With this now awakening, the challenge to the social sciences is thereby increased to undertake critical studies of environmental change, to develop environmental values, to lead towards that environmental planning on a world scale which Halford Mackinder saw as an ultimate goal for geographical study and action (24).

Thus not only has the disciplined study of the earth as the home of man proved its place and its value as an educational instrument but, in the words of Percy Maude Roxby (25), 'also through the programme of constructive work which it advocates can it contribute to the realization of "unity in diversity", and that seems the only possible ideal for the life of humanity on a planet, which, however small applied science may make it, will always retain its infinite variety'. To these words we may add only some by the late David Linton (26), one of the most brilliant students and teachers in the history of the Joint School. 'Geographers', he wrote, must surely see in the purpose of their work 'some relation to the current goals of human endeavour and must relate its practice to the needs of the times'.

REFERENCES

1. STAMP, L. D., and WOOLDRIDGE, S. W. (eds.), *London Essays in Geography*, Rodwell Jones Memorial Volume, p. ix (London: L.S.E. and Longmans, Green & Co. Ltd., 1951; reprinted by Books for Libraries, 1969).

2. BEVERIDGE, Lord, *The London School of Economics and its problems 1919–1937*, pp. 88–89 (London: George Allen & Unwin, 1960).

3. MACKINDER, H. J., 'On the Scope and Methods of Geography', *Proceedings of the Royal Geographical Society*, 9 (1887), 141–60.

4. GILBERT, E. W., *Sir Halford Mackinder 1861–1947: An Appreciation of his Life and Work* (London: L.S.E. and G. Bell & Sons, Ltd., 1961), also *Sir Halford J. Mackinder, The Scope and Methods of Geography and the Geographical Pivot of History* (London: Royal Geographical Society, 1951).

5. MACKINDER, H. J., *Britain and the British Seas* (London: Heinemann, 1902).

6. INSTITUTE OF BRITISH GEOGRAPHERS, *Land Use and Resources: Studies in Applied Geography*, A memorial volume to Sir Dudley Stamp (London: 1968).

7. STAMP, L. D., *The Land of Britain: Its Use and Misuse* (London: Longmans, Green & Co. Ltd., 1948).

8. WILDE, G. L., 'Sir Dudley Stamp 1898–1966', *Agriculture*, 73, no. 12 (1966).

9. WOOLDRIDGE, S. W., and BEAVER, S. H., 'The Working of Sand and Gravel in Great Britain: A Problem in Land Use', *Geographical Journal*, 115 (1950), 42–57.

10. BEAVER, S. H., *Report on Derelict Land in the Black Country* (Ministry of Town and Country Planning, 1946).

11. STAMP, L. D., *Our Underdeveloped World* (London: Faber and Faber, 1953).

12. —— Opening Address to the 20th International Geographical Congress, London, 1964, in J. Wreford Watson (ed.), *Congress Proceedings* (Nelson, 1967).

13. JONES, Ll. Rodwell, and BRYAN, P. W., *North America* (London: Methuen, 1924).

14. BUCHANAN, R. Ogilvie, *The Pastoral Industries of New Zealand*, Publications of the Institute of British Geographers, 2 (London: Philip, 1935).

15. STAMP, L. D., *Some Aspects of Medical Geography*, University of London Heath Clark Lectures 1962 (London: Athlone Press, 1964).

16. WILLATTS, E. C., Planning and Geography in the last Three Decades', *Geographical Journal*, 137 (September, 1971).

17. GREATER LONDON GROUP, *Greater London Papers* and other books and papers on local government reform (L.S.E.).

18. JONES, Emrys, and SINCLAIR, D. J., *Atlas of London* (Oxford: Pergamon Press, 1968).

19. MACNEILL, J. W., *Environmental Management*, Constitutional Study prepared for the Government of Canada (Ottawa, 1971).

20. *Ecologist*, 2, no. 1 (1972).

21. STATE COMMITTEE OF U.S.S.R. COUNCIL OF MINISTERS FOR SCIENCE AND TECHNOLOGY, *Resources of Biosphere on the Territory of the U.S.S.R., Scientific Principles of Rational Use and Conservation*, Report for International Conference on the Resources of the Biosphere (Unesco, 1968).

22. KENDALL, M. G., 'Geographical Distribution of Crop Productivity in England', *Journal of the Royal Statistical Society*, 102 (1939), 21–62.

23. MACKINDER, H. J., 'Progress of Geography in the field and in the study during the reign of His Majesty King George the Fifth', *Geographical Journal*, **86** (July, 1935).
24. MACKINDER, H. J., *The Human Habitat*, Presidential Address to Section E, British Association for the Advancement of Science, 1931.
25. ROXBY, P. M., *The Scope and Aims of Human Geography*, Presidential Address to Section E, British Association for the Advancement of Science, 1930.
26. LINTON, D. L., 'Geography and the Social Revolution', *Geography*, **42** (1957), 13–24.

AFFLUENCE
AND DISRUPTION

B. C. ROBERTS

B. C. ROBERTS

M.A. (Oxon.)

Professor of Industrial Relations
The London School of Economics
and Political Science

He is a former President of the British Universities Industrial Relations Association and currently President of the International Industrial Relations Association. He has been Visiting Professor at the Universities of Princeton, M.I.T., Berkeley, and U.C.L.A. and has travelled widely. He is a consultant to the I.L.O. and O.E.C.D. He is Editor of the *British Journal of Industrial Relations* and has published a large number of books and articles on industrial relations, trade unions, etc. He is at present engaged in research on international collective bargaining and the implications of the development of multi-national corporations.

AFFLUENCE
AND DISRUPTION

This lecture is in no sense intended to wind up the series. It is simply the last lecture and it is going to be about industrial relations as a subject of academic concern. The stuff of industrial relations is, as the title suggests, the distribution of affluence and the disruption that occurs in the process of deciding how this is to be achieved. No area of human activity is more important; most men and a large proportion of women spend half their waking time for five days a week, for most weeks of the year, and for most years of their lives in gainful employment. How they behave at work and in connection with it is of fundamental importance to the welfare of mankind and it raises issues about men and society that extend far beyond the concerns of this lecture.

The Industrial Relations Department is the youngest in the L.S.E. That this should be the case may strike you as odd since the founders of the L.S.E., Sidney and Beatrice Webb, were also the pioneers of the systematic study of trade unions and their relations with employers. The London School of Economics and Political Science was in fact founded in between the publication of the *History of Trade Unionism* in 1894, which was the first fruit of their partnership, and the publication in January 1898 of *Industrial Democracy*, the Webbs' general theory of industrial relations.

It has always seemed to me rather curious, that in spite of having the Webbs as its founders, the L.S.E. gave no particular emphasis to the study of trade unions or the broader field of industrial relations until after the Second World War. There have, of course, always been distinguished members of the staff who were deeply concerned with aspects of labour problems. But the Webbs themselves never seem to have given a lecture course on their original field of interest. In the early years of the L.S.E. Sidney Webb lectured on municipal administration as an aspect of sociology. In those days of Westermarck and Hobhouse I think that it must have been under Webb's influence that the calendar recommended sociology as a suitable academic discipline for scripture readers, rent collectors, poor law guardians, members of committees of philanthropic societies, borough councillors, district visitors, workshop and factory inspectors, and trade-union officials. Surprisingly there seems to have been no interest in the history of labour organizations, though there was a course on the history of London guilds and livery companies, which the Webbs had attempted to prove in their history had no lineal connection with the trade unions. The great figures of the L.S.E. mainly concentrated their attention on other areas of social behaviour. Graham Wallas certainly knew a good deal about the early history of trade unions, having written the life of Francis Place and also revised the first chapter of the Webbs' History at their request; but as Professor of Political Science his main interests lay elsewhere.

The reason for this lack of interest in labour problems in the early days of the L.S.E. was primarily due, I suspect, to the Webbs themselves and to their concept of the L.S.E. as an academic institution. Although the Webbs may properly be regarded as the first great British scholars, along with Alfred Marshall at Cambridge, to apply the methods of the social sciences to the history and role of organized labour, they did not inspire many others to follow immediately the trail they had so remarkably blazed. After they had completed their massive works on organized labour the Webbs quickly turned their attention to local government and social administration, which was, I think, the truly great love of their lives. Though they continued to retain an interest in the role of the trade unions and they made one major revision of their History, they became less and less certain of the social effectiveness and value of labour organizations.

This change of attitude may have been due in part to the rather hostile reception trade-union leaders gave to the History and to Industrial Democracy. The unions deeply resented the way in which the Webbs had clinically exposed their administrative and political inadequacies. This hostility may have been made worse by an instinctive realization that the Webbs were not basically sympathetic to many of the characteristic features of working-class behaviour. If Beatrice conveyed a fraction of the contempt for some of the union leaders and the 'sensual working man' expressed in her diary, it is perhaps not surprising that even a decade later she recorded that the 'Parliamentary Committee of the T.U.C. has never forgiven us our scathing criticism of them and their doings in Industrial Democracy' (*Our Partnership*, p. 268).

When Sidney Webb was invited to serve on the Royal Commission on Trade Disputes in 1903, to consider the implications of the Taff Vale decision, Beatrice noted that it would provide them with an opportunity of re-establishing favourable relations with the trade unions. In the event, it did not turn out that way. Sidney Webb could not be persuaded that the Taff Vale decision was altogether bad law, or that it was right that the unions should be given the complete immunities they demanded from any action for damages when they committed a breach of contract. If the recommendations of the Royal Commission had been carried out, the fundamental assumptions of the 1871 Act would have been changed in 1906, instead of, as we know, being reinforced by the Liberal Government. Our industrial relations system would have developed in the way that is only now contemplated: unions would have become fully corporate bodies, the right to strike would have been positively protected except when it was in breach of contract; and Section 4 of the Trade Union Act, 1871, would have been repealed so as to allow unions to enter into enforceable agreements with other organizations and their own members. It has taken sixty-five years to put these changes into effect with the Industrial Relations Act of 1971. Sidney Webb was, in fact, not satisfied that the majority had gone far enough. He added his own characteristic postscript, which challenged the validity of the right to strike, questioned the social values of collective bargaining, and proposed as an alternative a system of national arbitration. Hardly surprisingly the Webbs did not achieve the rehabilitation with the unions for which they had hoped.

The Webbs had another opportunity of re-establishing themselves with the unions when Beatrice was appointed to the Royal Commission on the Poor Law, but again they ran into difficulties with them in spite of the fact that the T.U.C.'s nominee was persuaded to sign Beatrice's radical minority report. Unfortunately for the Webbs, their proposals could have had an adverse effect on the mutual insurance functions of the unions, which they themselves had stressed as a vital element in the unions' bargaining power. Lloyd George's alternative proposals, borrowed from Germany and enthusiastically recommended by the German unions, to whom it gave a beneficial role, proved much more attractive to the British unions than the more ambitious but more bureaucratic state-sponsored schemes of the Webbs. It is again ironic that in 1971 with Robert Carr's massive scheme for retraining the unemployed it is a Conservative who is implementing another basic idea first put forward by the Webbs in 1909.

Apart from the Webbs' disenchantment with the unions, there was another and perhaps more important reason why the L.S.E. did not become a main centre for the study of labour questions before the First World War. It was their desire to create a general school of the social sciences which had no ideological bias in its curriculum or tendency towards their own political point of view. They wanted to establish a centre for the teaching of economics, administration and sociology. Even so, had the Webbs thought it to be sufficiently important, I feel they would have somehow succeeded in making the L.S.E. a great centre of labour studies.

The failure of the Webbs to stimulate the establishment of a strong school of labour studies contrasts with the achievement of John R. Commons and his associates at the University of Wisconsin in the United States. When the first volume of Commons's great *History of Labour in America* appeared in 1917, Wisconsin had already become known as the leading centre of research into labour history in the United States. Robert F. Hoxie at Chicago, Carter Goodrich at Amhurst and later Columbia, were also making a powerful contribution, but without the concentration of resources existing at Wisconsin. By the time the last two volumes of the Commons' *History* appeared in 1935, labour studies were well established in many universities in the United States, and provided a foundation for the later widespread development of industrial relations departments.

The success of Commons at Wisconsin was due to the eminence

of Commons himself as a historian. It was also due to factors in the social history of the State. Heavily populated by Germans, who were strongly socialist in their fundamental political beliefs, the State tended to lean towards radical leadership. The trade union movement, which was strong and politically influential, found the interpretation of Commons and his associates sympathetic and understanding. Thus Commons was assured of strong local support, which was of vital importance in a State university like Wisconsin.

The Webbs did not enjoy the same degree of trade union and academic appreciation as Commons until relatively many years later. In the period until the end of the First World War when the Webbs were exercising their greatest influence on the organization and political philosophy of the Labour Party, they were completely out of sympathy with both the older union leaders and the younger generation of union militants, and also with radical intellectuals both inside and out of the universities.

Much more in harmony with the new radicalism in the trade unions, which had been responsible for the creation of the first industrial union, the National Union of Railwaymen, the Triple Alliance and, during the First World War, the shop stewards movement, was G. D. H. Cole, who, as arrogantly certain of the validity of his own prescription for the new society as the Webbs were of theirs, came into sharp conflict with them. The Webbs scorned the impracticality of the syndicalist ideas of the militants, which excited Cole and led him to develop that peculiarly British Utopian compound of medievalism and the Clydeside shop steward concept of workers control: Guild Socialism. After leading a breakaway from the Fabian Society, and setting up the Labour Research Department to assist the unions, Cole returned to Oxford, where for the next thirty-odd years he turned out a stream of labour histories and political briefs for the times.

Cole's tractarianism had less of an immediate impact on Oxford than Newman's. He did, however, succeed in securing a paper on Labour Movements in the P.P.E. degree and one might say he saw the establishment of his own Keeble College in the foundation of Nuffield, which, since the war, has become a leading centre for the study of industrial relations and labour history. Perhaps his major contribution, however, was his coterie of students, the

Cole group, who were invited to his lunch club and to his weekly devotions in his rooms. Regrettably, since some of it was very good, Cole's work was not taken seriously by the historians, economists, or philosophers who dominated social science at Oxford. The study of organized labour was regarded by most dons as academically perverse, and mainly inspired by political doctrine. What was true of Oxford was also true of elsewhere. Apart from Henry Clay at Manchester, who, in the tradition of Marshall, lectured on the economics of industry, and occasional lectures at the L.S.E., there was relatively little academic interest in the systematic study of trade unions and their impact upon industrial relations until the 1930s.

The General Strike of 1926, though it was a miserable fiasco, confirmed the fears of a very large number of British employers and provided university students with an opportunity of demonstrating their belief in law and order. However, those who looked to the Government for strong legislation to curb the power of the unions were disappointed by Baldwin. The 1927 Trades Disputes Act was bitterly resented by the trade unions, but it made little difference to their bargaining strength and gave employers little more than a token satisfaction. Memory of this Act and its eventual repeal, is I think, having some effect on current union attitudes.

Recognition that they were vulnerable to militant union tactics and afraid that unless they developed a more constructive relationship, they might be faced by a long period of destructive conflict, persuaded a group of large-scale employers, led by Sir Alfred Mond, the Chairman of I.C.I., to seek discussions with the T.U.C. These talks produced a constructive set of proposals for the restructuring of the industrial relations system; but unfortunately they eventually foundered on the reluctance of the majority of employers and left-wing union militants to accept what was explicit in the Mond–Turner proposals, namely that the unions should be fully recognized as equal and responsible partners in a system of industrial democracy.

The General Strike, the failure of the Mond–Turner talks, followed by the great depression, made the labour question a matter which deeply troubled the social conscience of some industrialists and it stirred Montague Burton, the well-known clothing manufacturer, to press his own solutions. In the mind of Burton the dangers were clear and present. He saw the conflicts between labour and capital as not totally dissimilar to the conflicts between states. Industrial conflicts and international conflicts had their roots in social injustice and they could only be solved by the adoption of an appropriate code of international and industrial ethics. Burton's ideas were very similar to those which had been advanced by Albert Thomas, Harold Butler, and Sam Gompers at the peace conference in 1919 and had led to the establishment of the I.L.O. Burton believed that industrial conflict could be eliminated if employers provided high standards of welfare and good wages; he was a strong believer in collective bargaining, but like Sidney Webb he did not think that strikes were desirable and wanted to see compulsory arbitration introduced.

Burton, whose first ambition had been to become an academic rather than an industrialist, was concerned to find that international and industrial relations were relatively little developed as subjects of academic study in the universities. This led him to decide in the early 1930s to found a number of chairs in international relations and in industrial relations. He believed that the universities could build up through research a body of knowledge and through teaching a body of people, who would be able to provide the professional advice and expert administration that was urgently needed to develop and run effective international and industrial peace-keeping systems.

Burton found that not every university he approached was ready to accept his ideas or his money. In the event it was Cambridge, Cardiff, and Leeds, where Burton had his factory, which agreed to establish chairs in industrial relations. Whether the L.S.E. was ever considered and contacted, I do not know; but in 1934 Burton agreed to provide an endowment to secure the continued existence of the Chair in International Relations, which had been founded at the L.S.E. in 1924.

Although universities inspire radical ideas, they tend to be conservative institutions and established faculties are generally reluctant to admit new areas of study to academic grace. Burton's beneficence had been accepted under the pressure of events outside the universities, but the new chairs did not arouse great enthusiasm from the established disciplines. Neither international relations nor industrial relations were thought by many academics to be respectable university subjects.

Although there was no one on the staff of the L.S.E. in the 1930s who was mainly concerned with the industrial relations field, there was some interest in the Department of Social Administration with the low-paid worker; and its head C. M. Lloyd had written a book and given some lectures on trade unions based on the work of the Webbs. The Law Department had developed an active interest in industrial law, a field which had been pioneered at the L.S.E. under Professor Gutteridge, Sir Henry Slesser, and W. A. Robson. This development has been dealt with at some length by Professor Kahn-Freund in an earlier lecture, and I shall not discuss it further except to say that after the Second World War Professor Kahn-Freund made the L.S.E. famous throughout the world as a centre for the study of labour law.

Whilst it could not be said that labour statistics were an innovation of the L.S.E., first Bowley, then Roy Allen, developed the techniques and methods of presenting a series of price and wage indices which were the essential tools of the labour economist. Labour economics was not a recognized branch of economics before the Second World War but it was a focal point of interest and there were a number of members of the economics department who were acutely aware of the need to develop more effective theories of wages and employment. Apart from Lionel Robbins who was deeply concerned about central economic and political issues arising out of the wages question, there were others who were even more directly interested in developing an understanding of the economics of the labour market. One of these was J. R. (now Sir John) Hicks, who, in 1931, gave a course of lectures on the Economic Problems of Industrial Relations; although this course was not repeated in the following years, it was, I suspect, the foundation of his work on the theory of wages. From 1932 E. F. M. Durbin lectured on the theory and practice of the labour market; and in 1936 Brinley Thomas began lecturing on trade unions and labour mobility, pioneering what is now the fashionable field of manpower studies.

The interest in labour problems shown by the Departments of Econnomics, Law and Social Administration was rather surprisingly not equally shared by those who were directly responsible for preparing students for a career in business management. The L.S.E. had been a pioneer of business education with the establishment of the B.Sc.(Econ.) in 1900 and the commerce degree in 1919, and at the postgraduate level from 1932 with the Diploma in Business Administration. Looking back through the syllabus of these courses it is clear that labour problems were virtually ignored. The D.B.A. course included an item called Personnel, but this was limited to such matters as work measurement, selection, training and promotion, welfare work, incentives, and psychoneuroses in industry. The role of unions was not mentioned, collective bargaining and industrial conflict were not touched upon; shop stewards apparently did not exist.

The syllabus reflected a view of the role of organized labour which was derived from the belief that the activities of unions were to be deplored, since they served only to frustrate the beneficence of the market by restricting the optimum utilization of labour. By keeping wages up and production down, unemployment was increased and real wages were lower than they might otherwise have been. All this may have been true, but it was not a good reason for excluding industrial relations as a field of study since it created managers who were to get industry into deep trouble through their lack of knowledge and understanding of labour problems.

Whatever degree of scepticism there was before the Second World War about the need to study industrial relations, this has now given way to a recognition in universities all over the world that it is an area of human activity which is of fundamental importance to the welfare of mankind.

The great growth of interest in industrial relations has been brought about by three main factors. The first was the general acceptance after the Second World War that trade unions were not only a legitimate form of social organization, but had become under modern technological, economic, and social conditions immensely powerful and, therefore, immensely significant in their ability to influence public welfare. The second factor was the growth of professional personnel management and with it a recognition that manpower was an extremely expensive resource that required at least as much specialized concern as any other aspect of management. The third factor lay in the development of the analytical foundations of the subject itself. I propose to look at the impact of each of these factors, first with reference to developments at the L.S.E.

The L.S.E. recognized the new significance of the trade unions when in 1945 it established a one-year course in Trade Union Studies. The idea of establishing this course originated with R. H. Tawney. During the war Tawney, together with Isaiah Berlin, had been the brilliant, but rather eccentric choice of some innocent mind in the Ministry of Labour, to go to Washington to keep Winston Churchill and Ernest Bevin informed on the attitudes of the American trade unions, who Churchill had been told exercised a good deal of influence over Roosevelt. The dispatches of these labour attachés-extraordinary on the doings of the Irish, Italian, and Jewish labour leaders were apparently so entertaining they had a priority position on top of the Prime Minister's daily reading file. Tawney's proposals to establish the course owed something to his American experience, as well as to his life-long interest in the Workers' Educational Association and his famous adult class of Lancashire textile workers. With the support of Lance Beales, Harold Laski, and Carr-Saunders, it was agreed that the L.S.E., which had long provided expert training for future managers, should also help to train future trade-union leaders. When Tawney put the idea of the course to Sir Walter Citrine, who was then General Secretary of the T.U.C., he at once grasped its significance. Citrine was well aware that if trade-union leaders were to play a much larger and more responsible role under post-war conditions than they had done in the past, they would have to be adequately trained and supported by their own experts. A one-year intensive course in the social sciences and their application to the economic and social problems faced by the unions, seemed exactly what was required. It so happened that the means had just become available through the establishment of the T.U.C. Educational Trust, financed astonishingly from the wartime profits of the *Daily Herald*, which was then half-owned by the T.U.C.

Ever since 1945 to this day the T.U.C. Educational Trust, which is now financed by direct subvention from main funds, has provided scholarships and bursaries for the course. Further scholarships have been provided by individual unions, in particular by the Transport and General Workers' Union.

The question must be asked: has the course succeeded? I believe that it has. Former members of the course now hold high positions in the trade unions, many are district and local officials, others are in research posts. Five are present Members of Parliament and one, Roy Mason, was a senior Minister in the last Labour Government. Two former members of the course are now professors and others hold a wide range of teaching posts in industrial relations and related fields. Some have gone into personnel management with considerable success. One has recently been appointed to what is probably the most sensitive and most significant position in contemporary industrial relations, namely, the Chairmanship of the Commission on Industrial Relations. If I were asked to say what the total impact has been on British industrial relations, I would, however, be compelled to say that judging by current problems it has not been great enough.

The Trade Union Studies course has been of considerable importance at the L.S.E. in other respects. It attracted the interest of distinguished teachers such as Evan Durbin and Reg Bassett and some of the most eminent members of many departments of the L.S.E., and it provided the foundation stone of the Department of Industrial Relations.

Alongside the Trade Union Studies course, but administered quite separately from it, for reasons that have been of considerable significance in the evolution of industrial relations in Britain, was the Personnel Management course. Personnel management in the form of factory welfare had been taught in the L.S.E. as part of social administration since the First World War. During the Second World War the Ministry of Labour asked the L.S.E. to provide an emergency training course for personnel officers, who were urgently needed for Royal Ordnance Factories. This work was undertaken by Janet Kydd, who after the war was responsible for the establishment of a one-year postgraduate diploma course for students who wished to make personnel management a career. This course is today probably the best known in Britain and has been immensely successful in producing men and women who now occupy many of the most important personnel posts in private and public enterprise.

The evolution of the teaching of personnel management reflects the changes that have occurred in British industrial relations over the past fifty years. In its origins personnel management stemmed from the two roots I have mentioned earlier. One was the belief that good industrial relations could be created by management who concerned themselves with the social welfare of their employees. The other root was the development of techniques of scientific management, with their concern for the measurement of performance, payment by results, job evaluation, selection, training, and promotion, which were also being taught to D.B.A. students.

The advocates of both types of managerial activity saw the unions as political organizations which served to produce bad relations between workers and employers and to reduce the efficiency of management. For a long time personnel management sought to advance the welfare of workers and to improve the technical efficiency of personnel management with the minimum involvement in the conflict between unions and employers. Dealing with the unions was generally left to employers' associations and it was the foreman's or works manager's job to deal with the stewards. Where no unions existed, and even where they did, it was not uncommon for personnel management to promote a works council or consultative committee as an alternative means of consultation to collective bargaining.

Since the Second World War, with the spread of trade unionism and the growth of plant and company bargaining, the function of personnel management has changed. The senior personnel manager is now generally responsible for advising the board on every aspect of personnel management, including negotiations with the unions and with servicing the line managers in the carrying out of their personnel duties.

The teaching of personnel management, which twenty years ago virtually ignored the existence of unions and emphasized the importance of good human relations between worker and manager, now takes much more fully into account the importance of collective bargaining and the wider context of industrial relations.

The development of modern personnel management has been clearly related to the professionalization of management as a whole, a process in which the L.S.E. has played an important part by its contribution to the advancement of modern business practice through the teaching of accounting, finance, business administration, commercial and industrial law, and personnel management. In this respect it was a rather short-sighted decision for the L.S.E. to abandon the D.B.A., and to do this just when the need for integrated courses in business education had been recognized all over the world, instead of developing it into a high-grade department of business studies, analogous to the Sloan School of Business Management at M.I.T. I am glad to say that to some small extent we have begun to retrace our steps with the recent establishment of the M.Sc. in management studies on an interdepartmental basis; this degree allows a student to specialize in his chosen area of management interest, but compels him to learn something of both the human and organizational aspects of management as well as the numerate techniques.

But let me return to labour studies. The decision by the Department of Economics in 1947 to establish a chair in labour economics was an important recognition of the significance of this field. The eventual choice of Henry Phelps Brown was a brilliant inspiration. His qualifications for the post were at first sight not entirely convincing, since his main published work was a study of the framework of the pricing system. Phelps Brown combined a knowledge of modern economics with a deep understanding of social history and of the forces that moved work people to organize and to go on strike. He illuminated meticulous research into the facts of wage, price, and productivity changes with a penetrating insight into the workings of the labour market. When he retired three years ago it could be said, without challenge that he had made the chair of labour economics at the L.S.E. the most distinguished of its kind throughout the world.

By the early 1960s it was apparent that interest in industrial relations was growing considerably and the number of graduate students was steadily increasing. I became convinced that we needed a department to co-ordinate our interdisciplinary activities more effectively and in 1964 I was able to persuade my colleagues that this step should be taken.

Today the Department has a teaching staff of six and over eighty students. If the Personnel Management course (which for historical reasons remains outside the Department, though intimately linked with it) were included, total teaching staff would be eight, research staff eight, and students over one hundred. Interest in labour and management studies is, of course, not restricted to the Department of Industrial Relations and the Personnel Management course. We are immensely fortunate in the extent to which there is an interest in these fields in the Departments of Economics, History, Law, Politics, Psychology, Sociology, and Statistics; I should also mention the Higher Education Research Unit and the Institute of Manpower Studies, whose fields of interest are close to ours. There can be little doubt that the L.S.E. now has greater staff resources, and probably more students, in the general field of industrial relations than any other university in Britain.

Outside of the L.S.E industrial relations as a university concern has greatly developed over the past twenty years. Today, apart from the three Montague Burton Chairs at Cambridge, Cardiff and Leeds, and the L.S.E. chair, there are chairs at Glasgow and Manchester and three at Warwick; there are a good many readerships and lectureships, and many holders of chairs in the social sciences who have their main interest in industrial relations.

Some indication of the strength of the subject can be gained from the membership of the British Universities Industrial Relations Association, which is now about two hundred strong. The Association was founded at a meeting in Manchester in 1951, at which the hosts were two former L.S.E. students: one of them was also a former staff member, Professor Arthur Lewis; the other, H. A. Turner, now holds the Chair of Industrial Relations at Cambridge.

Another landmark in the evolution of the subject was the establishment in 1963 at the L.S.E. of the *British Journal of Industrial Relations*. The *Journal* now has a world-wide circulation and is recognized as one of the most authoritative publications in this field.

The inquiry by the Donovan Commission and its subsequent report gave a considerable fillip to the study of industrial relations. The present Government's Industrial Relations Act has carried this a stage further. And one of the most important outcomes of the public recognition of the need for more research into industrial relations was the decision by the Social Science

Research Council to establish its own Industrial Relations Research Unit.

The expansion of interest in industrial relations in Britain has been matched by developments in the world at large. The most extensive developments have been in the United States, where the subject is taught at every major university. Important research and teaching institutes exist at Berkeley, M.I.T., Illinois, Cornell, Michigan, Chicago, Princeton, U.C.L.A., and Minneapolis. There are important centres of teaching and research in Australia, Canada, and New Zealand, and during the past decade there has been a remarkable development of interest in most European countries. The countries of Africa, Asia, and Latin America have also established the subject in their universities. There has moreover been a significant development of interest in the Soviet Union and the socialist countries of Eastern Europe. This upsurge of interest encouraged me in 1967 to persuade the British and American Industrial Relations Associations and the Japanese Institute of Labour Studies to institute an International Industrial Relations Association. Over twenty countries now have associations affiliated to the I.I.R.A. and there are individual members and affiliated institutes in about sixty countries. The Third World Congress of the Association will be held at the L.S.E. in 1973. Over five hundred participants are expected from all parts of the world.

Industrial relations as an academic subject has developed to its present level of activity for two reasons. One is because it has become overwhelmingly apparent during the past fifty years that industrial relations have become of major importance to the social stability and welfare of man in contemporary society. It has therefore become increasingly necessary for society to have a greater understanding of the factors that determine the pattern of industrial relations, and a greater capacity to regulate and control the industrial relations system so that it satisfies the social goals of society. The role of the academic is in this respect no different from that which he plays in relation to other areas of human activity, such as law, politics, and international relations.

A second reason for the growth of the subject has been the need to develop specialized knowledge and analytical techniques. It had become increasingly apparent that none of the branches of the social sciences (history, economics, politics, psychology, sociology, or law) could alone provide an adequate understanding of the developments that were taking place in industrial relations. A more unified interdisciplinary approach was a necessary development.

The term industrial relations is itself ambiguous. As a description of an area of human activity that is also now the special concern of a branch of academic study, it is not limited simply to the relations between trade unions and employers. Industrial relations, as an academic subject, is generally understood in a much broader sense, covering in fact every aspect of the behaviour of men and women in their roles as workers and managers, trade unionists and employers. *Industrial* includes not just industry, but every situation where anyone is employed to produce some good or a service for a reward. *Relations* embrace the personal and collective, formal and informal, contractual and conventional, within and related to the environment of work.

Before the Second World War the study of industrial relations was confined mainly to the study of labour history, the economics and statistics of the labour market, and the role of the law. In the United States social psychologists, such as Elton Mayo, Roethlisberger, and Kurt Lewin, were seeking to explain the behaviour of workers in terms of their need to satisfy individual and group imperatives. Since the Second World War the conceptual ideas and methodology of the sociologists have had a significant influence. In this country one is bound to mention the disciples of Lewin at the Tavistock Institute and those university sociologists who have been concerned with the effects of social class and organizational structures on attitudes and behaviour.

In this respect, Joe Goldstein's study of the Transport and General Workers' Union made at the L.S.E. was a seminal work, though I should add that it was not done in the Department of Sociology, which has until recently taken more interest in the wider aspects of industrial society than in industrial relations. Using interview and survey methods and a theory of bureaucracy based on the long-forgotten Michels's 'Iron Law of Oligarchy', Goldstein broke completely from the traditional historical method to show that union government in practice was sometimes very different from that suggested simply by an examination of the rule-book. I was able to follow up Goldstein's work on a broader scale and V. L. Allen, a student of Phelps Brown, Hugh Clegg, H. A. Turner, Seymour Lipset in the United States, and many others, as well as the courts of law and committees of investigation in Britain and America, have since given us a much greater insight into the processes of trade-union government and administration.

In my opinion, without doubt the most important study in the field since the Second World War has been John Dunlop's *Industrial Relations Systems*. Dunlop, a Harvard economist, had first sought to develop a model of a trade union as a wage and employment maximizing institution. This economic analysis did not explain trade-union behaviour to the satisfaction of Lloyd Fisher, Clark Kerr and Arthur Ross, at Berkeley, who produced an alternative model of the union as a political institution, in which survival power and the interest of dominant groups were as important as the labour market in their influence on union policies. The debate on the nature of the union has had many parallels with the economic and sociological arguments about the nature of the firm.

In 1956 Dunlop, influenced by his sociologist colleague at Harvard, Talcott Parsons, put forward the notion that industrial relations could best be understood as a social system. The system consisted of four elements: the actors, the rules, certain contexts such as the economic and technological environment, and an ideology binding the system together. The actors in the system were the workers and managers and the institutions to which they belonged, namely the private and public enterprises, the trade unions and the various other associations of employees and employers. Since there were differences of interest arising out of the sharing of the product of the joint activities of the actors, it was necessary to formulate rules and institutions whereby the conflicts could be regulated and resolved. These rules and institutions might be arrived at voluntarily through the collective bargaining process, or imposed by law. The matters at issue between the actors were mainly generated by changes in the technological, economic, and political environmental contexts.

Although there have been many criticisms of the systems model, it has had considerable influence on academic thought and practical action in Britain, especially through the work of Allan Flanders.

Flanders and his followers have sought to develop the systems model into a sophisticated theory which not only explains the rules and processes of the collective bargaining system, but which also provides the basis for a moral commitment to the preservation of trade-union bargaining, and its concomitant industrial conflict, as an essential feature of a pluralist society.

The inevitability of conflict and the desirability of strong, independent trade unions are central assumptions of Flanders's theory of industrial relations. In Flander's view collective bargaining is not an economic process of buying and selling labour, as the Webbs suggested, but a political process through which unions and employers agree on rules through which they can mutually regulate the employment relationship. The negotiation itself is akin to the diplomatic exercise of power; when negotiations break down this is analogous to war. Strikes, like wars, eventually come to an end, but for stability to be achieved the conflict must be concluded with an agreement that consolidates peace.

Flanders's attempt to create a theory of collective bargaining is open to criticism at a number of points; in particular the transition from analysis of fact to normative statements gives rise to doubts. The evidence suggests that some system of collective negotiation is an inevitable consequence of the growth of organizations employing large numbers of workers in all types of societies. In pluralist countries there has been a strong tendency for collective associations of workers to take the form of trade unions, but this is not an inevitable process, as we know from British experience, where never more than half of the employed labour force has joined trade unions. The figure is much lower in many countries. There are numerous firms in Britain which are not unionized, but which successfully settle issues of conflict between managers and workers without recourse to the methods of collective bargaining. Flanders recognizes that collective bargaining can never be entirely 'free', and he extends his concept of the process to include the role of the state and its agencies as essential elements in the enforcement of rules and norms. Unfortunately Flanders's model of the collective bargaining system does not provide any guidance as to where the line should be drawn between legal regulation and administrative control on the one hand, and the autonomous activity of employers and unions on the other; as a matter of empirical fact it varies from country to country and has changed considerably over time.

Whatever the limitations of Flanders's theory of collective bargaining, there can be no doubt that his practical proposals for the reform of British industrial relations at the plant and company level, although they came long after Phelps Brown, the late Donald Robertson, and others had drawn attention to the breakdown of nationwide bargaining, were highly influential. His emphasis on the need to develop agreed normative systems at the plant and company level through the bargaining process was given immense significance by his justly famous study of the Esso Fawley productivity agreements, which had a considerable effect on employer opinion and encouraged unions to seek similar benefits elsewhere.

The Donovan Commission was greatly influenced by the analysis of the problems and proposals for reform presented by Flanders and his associate, Hugh Clegg, who, together with their followers at Oxford, virtually monopolized the research and strongly influenced the writing of the Report. The essence of the Donovan Commission's proposals was that the existing system was fundamentally sound; needed reform, but not basic change. Underlying this view was a deep moral and political commitment to the existing system, which was based on the belief that conflict between workers and managers was both inevitable and desirable; that trade unions and the collective bargaining process were essential to a pluralist society, and to be preferred to any alternative types of institutions or means of resolving conflicts that might be inherent in the relations of workers and managers in the running of industry and in the sharing of its products; and that reform could be achieved without major change in the law, by putting pressure on the employer rather than on the unions. It was an unstated assumption of the report that union behaviour was mainly a response to the power that was in the hands of the employers. A minority report by Andrew Shonfield, with which I did not entirely agree, though I must confess I was glad he wrote it, challenged some of the assumptions which underlay the majority Report and made alternative proposals. I will indicate why I think this analysis and the Donovan proposals were in important respects inadequate, but I will also acknowledge that they have played an important part in shaping the rapidly changing institutional patterns of industrial relations during the past few years.

In the period which followed the Great Depression, labour and management conflict steadily declined in the industrialized democracies. In 1960 Ross and Hartmann, after examining experience in twelve countries, concluded that the strike was tending to wither away. Other writers supported this contention and found a plausible explanation in the maintenance of full employment, rising standards of living, a greater degree of social security, the advance of social democracy, and the acceptance of trade unions as legitimate and responsible organizations ready to consider the welfare of the community as well as the interests of their members.

Although all these factors are even more significant today than they were a decade ago, the situation has greatly changed. Industrial conflict has been on the increase in all the pluralist states. During the past quinquennium it has reached levels not seen since the 1920s. This growth of strife has probably been due to the very factors believed to have been the cause of the diminution of industrial conflict. The rise of living standards has led to expectations beyond the ability of the economy to fulfil. Long-established patterns of employment have been drastically changed and traditional hierarchies of status and power have been distorted and sometimes completely overthrown. Above all during the past few years, establishments and authorities have been challenged and often found to lack substance. In a world of crumbling certainties, opportunism is invited and its advantages are confirmed when at the highest levels of political and social leadership principles and promises come to be seen as readily abandoned under the pressure of vested interests. Strikes and the threat of strikes have succeeded, in terms of securing rapidly rising money wages, but this gain has been achieved at a cost to society that has been heavy and may yet end in social disaster.

Under conditions of advanced technology involving high capital – labour ratios, low levels of intermediate stocks, and ever more closely integrated production and distributive processes, the balance of bargaining power has tipped in favour of groups who are prepared to exploit this critical strategic situation. Social security policies designed to help those in need from temporary loss of income have further enhanced the willingness of workers to strike. Most important of all, a determination to promote high levels of employment and economic growth has created labour and product market situations in which both unions and employers have gained mutual benefit from raising pay and prices above levels that would have been dictated by other factors alone.

Taken together all of these elements have shifted the Phillips curve, which was noted by Professor Johnson at the first lecture in this series as a major L.S.E. contribution to labour economics, and they are changing the debate about inflation, industrial conflict, and employment.

As a method of resolving differences of interest between different groups, collective bargaining has the merit of legitimizing decisions and thus making them acceptable to those directly involved. Unfortunately it is a method that advances the interest of the strong much better than it protects the weak. The inflationary rates of pay increase have often been not at the expense of employers, but at the expense of the old-age pensioner and the fixed-income groups. Collective bargaining has failed to change significantly the broad distribution of income. The low paid are relatively as badly off as ever they were. It has taken an Act of Parliament to bring about an improvement in the relative pay of women. Industrial conflict, which has grown steadily over the past twenty years, has brought no general gain in real wages to workers over that which can be attributed to increases in productivity; but the nation as a result of strikes and resistance to change is almost certainly worse off from the loss of production and the discouragement of innovation. Unfortunately it is not possible to say who bears the cost of strikes. What is morally unsatisfactory is that it is often the innocent who are compelled to pay tribute, suffer loss of income, bear the costs of frustrated holidays, unheated rooms, delayed deliveries, and deprivation of essential services.

In short, the classic system of power bargaining, based upon the *laissez-faire* theory that what is good for General Motors or the Transport and General Workers' Union, must automatically be good for society, is ceasing to be valid. The limiting conditions under which the ultra-pluralism of competitive liberalism would effectively ensure in the field of industrial relations that justice would be done have largely disappeared, and I cannot see how they can ever be effectively recreated, or indeed that they ought to be recreated. The Galbraithan solution to the equation created by the multi-national corporation faced by massive trade union strength cannot be achieved, as he now recognizes, by the method of each exercising countervailing power. It is too costly to the community.

In this respect I would like to quote from Sidney Webb's addendum to the Royal Commission on Trade Disputes of 1903–6 that I mentioned early in this lecture:

I cannot accept the assumption underlying the Report that a system of organized struggles between employers and workmen, leading inevitably now and again to strikes and lockouts—though it is from the standpoint of the community as a whole, an improvement on individual bargaining—represents the only method or even a desirable method by which to settle the conditions of employment. A strike or a lockout which is not only lawful, but under existing circumstances as a measure of legitimate defence against economic aggression, may be sometimes even laudable—necessarily involves so much individual suffering, so much injury to third parties and so much national loss, that it cannot, in my opinion be accepted as the normal way of settling an intractable dispute. Moreover from the standpoint of the community, such a method has the drawback that it affords no security— and even no prescription—that the resultant conditions of employment will be such as not to be gravely injurious to the community as a whole; I cannot believe that a civilised community will permanently continue to abandon the adjustment of industrial disputes—and incidentally the regulation of the conditions of life of the mass of the people—to what is, in reality the arbitrament of war.

I would echo every word that Sidney Webb wrote as even more valid than when it was published sixty-five years ago. To say this, however, at the present moment is to invite condemnation and derision. We are living through a period when every form of violence has its intellectual defenders, and enjoys a high degree of social tolerance.

Violence is, of course, not a new phenomenon in industrial

relations. In many countries strikes have resulted in the shooting down of demonstrating strikers and serious damage to property. Fear that strikes may be a prelude to political anarchy and revolution has led to the right to strike being virtually abolished in a large part of the world. This danger may seem remote in Britain, but social order is always a matter of precarious balance in a pluralist democracy. For this reason the strict limitation of the role of picketing to one of conveying information is an essential protection of the right to strike itself.

Nevertheless the problem of collective bargaining as a method of pay determination goes far deeper than the present ugly but still relatively slight tarnish of violence. The really critical question is can society stand the strain of the extension of uninhibited collective bargaining. Over the next decade it is likely to extend to every section of the community as technical, professional, and administrative employees up to the highest level organize and turn to the methods employed by the other trade unions to protect their occupational and social interests. We have already had an indication from Sweden that these groups are prepared to bring the economy to a halt when they feel their rightful status and salary positions are being destroyed by the activities of other social groups. It has been strongly argued, and there is much evidence to support the view, that men are more deeply moved to act militantly by a sense of relative deprivation of past superiority than by any other factor. Unfortunately one man's equity is another man's injustice. The establishment of equity in the rewards for work clearly cannot be solved simply by eliminating lower levels of pay, since that can only be achieved by paying all men the same. This would be manifestly inequitable.

I can see no escape from this situation through collective bargaining, but unless we do escape from it the cost will be extremely high in social dislocation, inequity, and perhaps even a much greater degree of state control than known hitherto. I feel sure that before the turn of the century we will have moved closer to some more rational and objective means of determining the broad structure of incomes rather than relying on the crude exercise of power bargaining based upon the capricious ability to inflict damage on industry and the community. The last twenty-five years of world experience has shown that some form of national incomes policy and new institutions to regulate collective bargaining are probably inescapable, in spite of the fact, as I have shown myself, that the ones tried have not so far worked for longer than a short period.

Collective bargaining as we have known it in the past will also have to be changed in character for another reason. It is becoming increasingly clear that as organizations grow larger, more complex and technologically dominated, traditional patterns of authoritarian management become less and less effective. As social values change and educational levels rise, management in the future will have to find legitimacy for its authority in the acceptance of its rationale from the bottom as well as the top of the organization. In organizational terms final responsibility for ultimate decisions may remain with management, but the authority of management to act will necessarily involve a greater degree of participation at all levels. The trend towards the establishment of a socially recognized right of workers to participate in decision-making processes, and along with it a right to share in the profits of the enterprise, is already well established in Europe. With Britain's entry into the E.E.C. and the advent of a European company law, this is bound to have a major influence on British company organization and the pattern of management.

This trend may also be influenced by the growth of multi-national corporations. There are indications that workers and managers of these corporations may well develop special relations that cut across national boundaries. At present we are witnessing the early stages of an expansion of the collective bargaining system from the national to the international level. How this will ultimately develop it is at present impossible to predict, but it may well result in an important challenge to national patterns of industrial relations, creating conflicts of equity, imposing considerable social strains and bringing about new regulatory institutions.

All of these developments are out of harmony with the underlying philosophy of the traditional British collective bargaining model with its emphasis on uninhibited conflict between trade unions and employers. Technological, economic, and social changes will, in spite of current appearances to the contrary, push the structure of British industrial relations in the direction of a unitary frame of reference for the enterprise. We are moving I believe, towards a system of industrial relations which will be closer in many respects to the German model, perhaps even to the Yugoslavian. This does not mean a total abandonment of pluralist values, nor the end of managerial authority, but a change in structures and limitations on the exercise of bargaining power that will involve the development of new procedures of social control. These will be arrived at both by the process of adaptation to change by management and unions and by the reshaping of the legal framework and the establishment of new institutions.

The Industrial Relations Act of 1971 is an attempt to create a more appropriate pattern of social control of employers and unions by making them conform to certain standards of behaviour by using the law to regulate themselves. In this respect the Act tries to maintain the basic concept of employer and union autonomy, but supported by such agencies as the C.I.R. and the National Industrial Relations Court. Whatever happens to this Act, it points inexorably to the way in which I believe we will have to go given contemporary technological, economic, and social trends. No matter how much union leaders and some politicians and managers may protest at the passing of *laissez-faire* collective bargaining, I cannot believe that this sentiment will stop the movement towards a tripartite system of industrial relations in which conflicts that cannot be reconciled within the enterprise are settled with aid of new agencies which provide effective alternatives to strikes.

Although there has been much criticism of the 1971 Industrial Relations Act, which has changed the law more radically than Donovan proposed, on the grounds that industrial relations cannot be reformed by law, I think that it is important to point out that all major changes in industrial relations systems have been accompanied by major changes in legal frameworks. One might cite, as examples of reforms brought about by legislative intervention, the Swedish Collective Bargaining Act of 1928, the German Works Councils Act of 1920, and in the United States the National Labour Relations Act of 1935. In every case the institutional and behavioural adjustments which were required to establish a new equilibrium in the system could not be achieved by the self-regulation of employers and trade unions. In this context there was nothing historically unusual about the passing of the 1971 British Industrial Relations Act.

In indicating my view of current trends I would like to make clear my belief that no framework of law, regulatory agency, or enlightened management policy can guarantee good industrial relations. The concept of good industrial relations is itself an ambiguous notion, but it can be reasonably defined for practical purposes as a situation where conflicts of interest are resolved with the maximum gain and minimum damage to all concerned. It is a situation where conflict only becomes a constructive factor leading to the mutual satisfaction of competing goals if it is constrained by the adoption of appropriate rules, attitudes, and institutions.

We are, I think, only at the beginning of a massive process of change in institutions and procedures which will greatly alter both the role of trade unions and methods of management; and this will make industrial relations a challenging and exciting area of public concern and academic study in the future.

INDEX

War:
 and the study of international
 relations, xxi, 91–94, 97–99, 109.
Webb, Sidney and Beatrice, xviii,
 xxvii, 33, 50, 86, 119, 139, 175, 180–2,
 186, 228, 247–51, 268.
Weber, Max, 30, 31, 45, 47, 49, 50, 51,
 56, 151, 169.
Webster, Charles, xxvii, 34, 93, 95, 96,
 100.
Weldon, T. H., 65.
Welfare benefits, 120.
Welfare economics, 12, 15–17, 21.
Welfare state, xv, 116, 117.
Westermarck, Edward, 34, 41, 45, 52,
 154, 163, 248.
Wheatcroft, George S.A., 216.
Wheeler, G. C. W. C., 52.
Whitehead, A. N., 127.

Wicksell, Knut, 14.
Willis, Richard, 223.
Wise, M. J., xix, xx.
Wolf, Abraham, 177.
Wooldridge, S. W., 230.
World Health Organization, 97.
Workers' Education Association, 256.
Wright, Lord Robert A., 207, 210.
Wright-Mills, C., 116.

Young, Allyn, 15, 33.
Younghusband Report on Social
 Workers in the Local Authority
 Health and Welfare Services, 118.
Yule, Udny, 141.

Zimmern, Sir Alfred, 95.

World Wisdom
The Library of Perennial Philosophy

The Library of Perennial Philosophy is dedicated to the exposition of the timeless Truth underlying the diverse religions. This Truth, often referred to as the *Sophia Perennis*—or Perennial Wisdom—finds its expression in the revealed Scriptures as well as the writings of the great sages and the artistic creations of the traditional worlds.

Living in Two Worlds: The American Indian Experience appears as one of our selections in the American Indian Traditions series.

American Indian Traditions Series

This award-winning series celebrates the unique cultural, spiritual, and artistic genius of the Indians of North America. Classic and contemporary works of scholarship stand alongside collections of the writings and recorded statements of America's first inhabitants. These writings, together with diverse illustrations, testify to an enduring and living legacy.

"The contribution of the American Indian, though considerable from any point of view, is not to be measured by material acquirement. Its greatest worth is spiritual and philosophical. He will live, not only in the splendor of his past, the poetry of his legends and his art, not only in the interfusion of his blood with yours, and his faithful adherence to the new ideals of American citizenship, but in the living thought of the nation."

CHARLES EASTMAN

This book is dedicated to all American Indian people

All royalties from this book will be used to support the Sun Dance religion of various Plains Indian tribes or to purchase copies of this book for distribution to American Indian readers.

LIVING IN TWO WORLDS

THE AMERICAN INDIAN EXPERIENCE

ILLUSTRATED

BY

CHARLES ALEXANDER EASTMAN (OHIYESA)

INCLUDING CONTRIBUTIONS BY OTHER NOTABLE INDIAN LEADERS

EDITED BY

MICHAEL OREN FITZGERALD

FOREWORD BY

JAMES TROSPER

World Wisdom

Book design by Susana Marín

Library of Congress Cataloging-in-Publication Data

Eastman, Charles Alexander, 1858-1939.
  Living in two worlds : the American Indian experience illustrated / by Charles Alexander Eastman
(Ohiyesa) ; including contributions by other notable Indian leaders ; edited by Michael Oren
Fitzgerald ; foreword by James Trosper.
      p. cm. — (Library of perennial philosophy. American Indian traditions series)
  Includes bibliographical references and index.
  ISBN 978-1-933316-76-5 (pbk. : alk. paper) 1. Eastman, Charles Alexander, 1858-1939. 2. Santee
Indians—Biography. 3. Indian physicians—Great Plains—Biography. 4. Lobbyists—Washington
(D.C.)—Biography. 5. Indians of North America—Ethnic identity. 6. Indians of North America—
History—Sources. 7. Indians of North America—History—Pictorial works. 8. Indian philosophy. 9.
Indian leadership. 10. Indians of North America—Biography. I. Fitzgerald, Michael Oren, 1949- II.
Title.
  E99.S22E1844 2009
  970.004'97--dc22
  [B]

                                                                              2009033128

Printed on acid-free paper in South Korea.

For information address World Wisdom, Inc.
P.O. Box 2682, Bloomington, Indiana 47402-2682
www.worldwisdom.com

CONTENTS

EDITOR'S PREFACE

Charles Eastman was born in a buffalo hide tipi in 1858 and raised in a traditional way of life that existed before Europeans came to this continent. He was then catapulted into the industrialized world of the time, where he first qualified as a medical doctor and later went on to become the preeminent spokesman for all American Indians during the first decades of the twentieth century. His words present the essential story of his Sioux people and, by extension, all the Plains Indians of North America. In many important respects, his narrative paints a portrait of the American Indian experience over the last four centuries.

It is impossible to chronicle the saga of all Native Americans in any one account, just as it is impossible to detail the many differences in the beliefs and traditions of the more than 500 original tribes. But few will deny that there are recurring themes in the history of almost every tribe and in the cultures of a majority of the tribes. Who is better qualified to provide an overview of the essential historical facts and recurring cultural themes than Charles Alexander Eastman, a Santee Sioux? His contributions to our understanding of the life ways and philosophy of the First Peoples in North America are so significant that Eastman was presented a special medal at the 1933 Chicago World's Fair honoring the most distinguished achievements by an American Indian in the previous fifty years.[1]

His penetrating insights on various tribes and some of the greatest native leaders in history are not just the result of scholarly study; he personally knew paragons of his race that included Red Cloud, Sitting Bull, and Chief Joseph, and met with official delegations from many tribes when he was a lobbyist for the Sioux tribe in Washington, D.C. at the end of the nineteenth century. Eastman not only studied history; he was part of such key events as the 1890 massacre at Wounded Knee.[2] More importantly, he did not just research the nomadic pre-reservation culture of his ancestors, he lived it.

Eastman was born in the winter of 1858 near Redwood Falls, Minnesota, and in

---

[1] The term "First Peoples" is frequently used in Canada to refer to their indigenous peoples. The term "Native Americans" was first coined by anthropologists to avoid confusion between "*American* Indians" and "*Asian* Indians"—those tracing their origins to the Indian sub-continent. A 1995 U.S. Census Bureau survey found that more American Indians in the United States prefer the term "American Indian" to "Native American." Eastman often uses the term "red man" or "red people" and "white man" or "whites," following the prevailing practice used until the past few decades when some chose to avoid these terms because they thought they were pejorative or confrontational. I believe it is appropriate, indeed sometimes necessary, to use terms that accurately present facts of existence when discussing the perplexing issues of historic and current inter-race relations.

[2] The 2007 HBO film entitled "Bury My Heart at Wounded Knee" used Eastman, played by Adam Beach, as its main protagonist. The film provides a very basic history lesson, although it is not historically accurate in a number of respects.

his youth received the traditional name of Ohiyesa ("the winner"). During his youth he thought his father had been killed by the U.S. government in the so-called "Sioux Uprising of 1862." Ohiyesa's uncle and grandmother taught the youth all of the secrets of virgin nature necessary to carry on the nomadic tribal life. The young man was instilled with the spiritual philosophy of his ancestors and a hatred of the white race that he thought had killed his father. What Ohiyesa did not know was that his father had been pardoned by President Lincoln and had embraced Christianity after his release from prison. In 1873 his father returned to bring his fifteen year old son to live in the civilized world of his day.

Eastman eventually received his undergraduate degree from Dartmouth and obtained his medical degree at Boston College. His first position was on the Pine Ridge Reservation in South Dakota as the government physician for the Lakota Sioux tribe.[3] He was at Pine Ridge before, during, and after the "Ghost Dance" rebellion of 1890-91, and he cared for the wounded Indians after the massacre at Wounded Knee. In 1892 the corrupt Indian agent forced Eastman to resign from his job at the agency in retaliation for Eastman's attempt to help the Sioux prove crimes against the agent and the agent's white friends. In 1893 he accepted a position as field secretary for the International Committee of the YMCA, and for three years traveled extensively throughout the United States and Canada visiting many Indian tribes in an attempt to start new YMCA's in those areas.

In 1897 and '98 Dr. Eastman lived in Washington D.C. as the legal representative and lobbyist for the Sioux tribe. During these years he met leaders from tribes around the country. He explained: "Nearly every Indian delegation that came to the capital in those days—and they were many—appealed to me for advice, and often had me go over their business with them before presenting it." Starting in 1903, as an employee of the Indian Bureau, he spent over six years giving permanent English family names to the Sioux. In the process of creating both English names and family lineage records he met and interviewed almost every living member of the Sioux tribe. His extensive meetings with members of his own tribe and the leaders of numerous tribes throughout North America gave him invaluable insights into the different traditional Indian cultures.

Charles Eastman was the first great American Indian author, publishing the first of his eleven books in 1902.[4] Eastman's writings are often studied not only for their remarkable insights into native culture, but also because they are among the finest examples of American Indian literature. After the success and notoriety of his earliest books, he spent the majority of his adult life lecturing and working in various ways to help all native people and to promote a better understanding of the culture and character of North

---

[3] There are three main divisions of what is known as the great Sioux Nation: the Lakota, Dakota, and Nakota peoples.

[4] A bibliography with publication information is included in the end matter.

America's First Peoples.[5] Ohiyesa said of his life's work: "My chief object has been, not to entertain, but to present the American Indian in his true character before Americans.... Really it was a campaign of education on the Indian and his true place in American history." In the last decade of his life he practiced, so to speak, what he preached and retired to live in a primitive cabin on the shores of a remote lake in Canada. He died in 1939 at the age of eighty.

Living in Two Worlds: The American Indian Experience is divided into six parts. The framework for Part I, "Life in the Deep Woods," is provided by Eastman's first autobiographical book, *Indian Boyhood* (1902), which begins with the events surrounding his birth and continues with his recollections of traditional nomadic life until age 15, in 1873. His second autobiographical book, *From the Deep Woods to Civilization* (1916), concerns his life in the industrialized world of his day from 1873 to 1916 and is the foundation for Part II, "Cultures in Collision." The autobiographical framework for Parts I and II provides a more or less chronological progression through Eastman's life. Selections from three of his other books are interspersed within these parts to provide additional details and observations.[6] The result is an overview of the traditional nomadic life of the Plains Indians and their early reservation experiences until around 1915.

I have tried to rely on other Indian voices when it seemed necessary to clarify points that Eastman did not experience or did not address in sufficient detail, such as life in government boarding schools during the early reservation period.[7] As he explains: "Happily, I had missed the demoralizing influences of reservation life, and had been mainly thrown in with the best class of Christian white people." The most prominent Indian

---

[5] Additional biographical information is presented in Part IV, the section entitled "Late in Eastman's Life He Practiced What He Preached."

[6] Almost all of Eastman's words are excerpted from the award-winning book, *The Essential Charles Eastman (Ohiyesa)* (Bloomington, IN: World Wisdom, 2007), which includes selections from his four most important books: *The Soul of the Indian* (1911), *The Indian Today* (1915), and his two autobiographical books. *The Essential Charles Eastman (Ohiyesa)* is used on dozens of college campuses—both in courses on American Indian culture and American Indian literature—and provides a more comprehensive view of his life and thought. *Living in Two Worlds: The American Indian Experience* also includes excerpts from *Indian Heroes and Great Chieftains* (1918) to detail facts about Red Cloud, Sitting Bull, and Chief Joseph. Selections from all five of Eastman's books have been rearranged in order to consolidate information dealing with the same subject. For example, many of his observations about early reservation life come from *The Indian Today*, which is now out of print. In a number of instances the result is a vignette with an illustration and text, thus allowing the reader to move in and out of the chronological autobiographical narrative to read other information of interest.

[7] My editor's comments are presented in italics to provide context for this rapid journey through four hundred years of history. I have also composed all the captions for the book, which are presented in roman font.

voice, other than Eastman, is that of Joe Medicine Crow, now 96 years of age and the recipient of the Presidential Medal of Freedom, the highest civilian honor given by the United States. Joe Medicine Crow is the Crow tribal historian and the last traditional war chief of the Crow tribe. He was born when government boarding schools were still in existence on the Crow Reservation and recalls some of his family's personal experiences during this deplorable chapter of U. S. history. Medicine Crow's voice is also heard in the Preface and in Part I, Part II, and Part IV of the book.

In Part III, "The Soul of the Indian," we hear of the beliefs, cultural values, and recurring themes of American Indian philosophy through excerpts from Eastman's book of the same name (1911). He was to write of this work: "This book is as true as I can make it to my childhood teaching and ancestral ideals." At various places in Eastman's account of his life and traditional native philosophy it is as if we are sitting around a campfire listening to the wisdom of his forefathers.

Part IV, "Eastman in Later Life," provides a postscript on later events in Eastman's life. Part V, "Other Indian Voices," brings us up to the present day through the words of other American Indian leaders, including information about the on-going cultural renewal that began in the 1940s and '50s. The "Contemporary Indian Voices" are all transcriptions from interviews I conducted over a period of more than twenty years. These leaders echo Eastman's metaphor of simultaneously living between two worlds: the world represented by their traditional ancestral culture and the modern industrial world.

The last section, Part VI, "Historical Timeline," presents a chronological outline of selected key events in four centuries of the American Indian experience of United States history, including all of the important circumstances in Eastman's narrative and events after 1915. On the one hand, many of these facts pertain to one or another specific tribe; on the other hand, every Indian nation has suffered through a variation of these same circumstances, some faring better, some faring worse. The situations presented here are therefore representative of the entire American Indian experience.

In the Appendix, we present the entire text of an apology by the Bureau of Indian Affairs given in the year 2000 to all American Indians on the occasion of the 175th anniversary of the founding of that agency. A section entitled, "Free Supplementary Study Materials," provides a partial list of materials that are available on the publisher's Internet site for teachers and those interested in further study. These materials include a number of thought-provoking discussion questions, some of which are interspersed throughout the book and highlighted with this symbol ☞.[8]

An understanding of the American Indian experience is incomplete without recognizing the current status of life on the Indian reservations. I am often asked whether

---

[8] My thanks to Richard Battersby and Richard Davies at Culver Academies, Mark Bell at St. Paul's School, and Judith Antell at the University of Wyoming for their assistance in formulating discussion questions.

the traditional cultural values described by Eastman still exist amidst the very difficult conditions in contemporary native communities. I concur with the native voices presented on these pages, namely, that the on-going cultural renewal in Indian communities is growing, although it is evident that not everyone lives up to the traditional standards or embraces this cultural revitalization. At the same time, everyone who spends time on Indian reservations comes face to face with the desperate living conditions and health problems that are summarized in the "Timeline of American Indian History: 1620-2009" in Part VI. The vivid descriptions by native authors in contemporary books have done the great service of bringing some of these pressing problems to the attention of others; we thus only present summary information and questions for reflection.[9]

More than 250 photographs and paintings from the end of the nineteenth century help bring the narrative to life. Except where noted, all of the handcrafts are of Sioux origin. Illustrations of activities were selected to best portray the situation described by Eastman, and thus a greater number show members of tribes other than the Sioux. Some of these vintage photographs were staged so as to recreate recurring circumstances in olden-day Plains Indian life. Some today argue that such photographs present a romanticized vision of their nomadic life, but most will agree that these compositions, created with the cooperation of olden-day nomads, more accurately portray the reality of tradi-

Left: Chief Medicine Crow, c. 1880; *Right*: photograph by Edward Curtis of Crow men that includes Chief Medicine Crow. A vignette in Part II includes Joe Medicine Crow's recollections of events in the life of Chief Medicine Crow

---

[9] Some popular works by contemporary Indian authors emphasize the desperation on reservations that gives rise to widespread alcohol and drug use. Almost everyone who spends time on a reservation will recognize people they know who correspond with many fictional characters and situations. However, some of these books allow readers to form mistaken opinions because they fail to note the on-going cultural revival and the fact that the excessive use of intoxicants on reservations—both alcohol and drugs—is almost universally considered to be a pernicious disease. Most natives who fall into these traps do not celebrate their own status during their lucid periods. The American Indian experience includes many different facets.

tional Plains life than photographs of living conditions in the early reservation period. Joe Medicine Crow spoke about the arranged photographs taken by Edward S. Curtis, who photographed his famous grandfather, Chief Medicine Crow: "Today [Curtis] is best known for his beautiful photographs because they capture the spirit of the olden-days when the Indians roamed free…. The old-timers only saw the photographs many years later. Most of them did not remember Curtis because he only spoke through an interpreter, but they really enjoyed seeing the photographs."[10]

Eastman was the first American Indian to write of the idea of living in two conflicting worlds: one represented by the traditional cultural ideals of his ancestors and the other by the modern industrialized world. He was accepted around traditional American Indian campfires and in the elite circles of the white establishment; and, in turn, he tried to get them to accept each other. Eastman rejected the government's policy of trying to completely assimilate all First Peoples into the melting pot of the dominant white civilization. He favored a type of cultural pluralism in which Indians would interact with the dominant society while still retaining their native identity, including many of their traditional beliefs and customs. Eastman also believed that the teachings and spirit of his adopted religion of Christianity and the traditional Indian spiritual beliefs were essentially the same, and that both religions are irreconcilable with the prevailing norms in our technological world. He also pointed out many ways that modern civilization can benefit from the study of traditional American Indian customs. His views are as thought-provoking today as they were one hundred years ago.

The cumulative impact of these native voices, past and present, transcends Sioux culture and history to provide remarkable insights into the life of not only Plains Indians, but all First Peoples. We pause at key events in United States history and learn of recurring themes and ideals in traditional native culture; yet the insights on these pages are not limited to native peoples alone: time and again we hear insights about life in our modern industrialized world from those who walk in two worlds, and we are left to reflect on the extent to which anyone attempting to live according to a universal spiritual and moral philosophy must also live in two worlds. Charles Eastman's words teach us about the American Indian experience, and, in the process, they help each of us to find our way in today's fast-paced world.

MICHAEL FITZGERALD
August, 2009
Bloomington, Indiana

---

[10] Joe Medicine Crow, "Foreword," in *The Image Taker: The Selected Stories and Photographs of Edward S. Curtis* (Bloomington, IN: World Wisdom, 2009), p. vii.

FOREWORD

Charles Eastman (Ohiyesa) is uniquely qualified to provide an introduction to the American Indian experience, including our history and culture. He lived in two worlds: being raised to manhood in the nomadic pre-reservation life of his ancestors and spending his later life in the ruling white society of his time. Eastman was directly involved in important historical events and he knew the leaders of dozens of tribes from across the country. Ohiyesa spent a large part of his later life as a tireless advocate for our race and was arguably the most important spokesperson for all First Peoples during the early twentieth century. Learning from Eastman is learning from the source.

At one time or another every Indian tribe lived through the same pattern of events with the Europeans who came to our shores over a period of four hundred years—beginning in the late sixteenth century. And, while there are many differences between the cultures of the diverse tribes, there are certain ideas that are held in common among many First Peoples. Therefore, even though Eastman's narrative is centered on his life as a Plains Indian, his remarkable insights into the history and culture of other tribes makes *Living in Two Worlds* an overview of the entire American Indian experience. The editor, Michael Fitzgerald, draws upon other native voices to complement Eastman's voice whenever it is necessary to provide additional information or clarity about important moments in American Indian history. The hundreds of carefully selected photographs, illustrations, and maps bring his words to life.

Living in Two Worlds also provides a helpful historical prologue and ends with a historical timeline that takes the reader from about 1916, when Eastman's narrative ends, to our current day. A series of Fitzgerald's interviews with contemporary Indian leaders illustrates the fact that American Indians who want to retain their native identity are obliged to live in two worlds. Each reader is left to ponder his or her own circumstances because anyone trying to live according to traditional ways will have difficulty in today's technological civilization.

Living in Two Worlds is an important addition to the list of books and documentary films produced by Michael Fitzgerald, which present our history and culture to non-Indians and preserve and perpetuate our traditional ways for our Indian people. Some non-Indians have a romanticized view of our Indian way of life, but Fitzgerald has a realistic understanding of the everyday lives of our people because he has stayed for extended periods of time on reservations for almost forty years. His deep appreciation of who we are and the challenges we face is the result of learning about the troubles of our youth as well as the wisdom of our tribal elders. When most non-Indians speak about American Indian history and culture they are on the outside looking in and trying to interpret what they think has happened. Michael Fitzgerald speaks about our Indian ways from the inside looking out because his knowledge is gained by personal experiences and by the way he lives.

This work will instantly become essential reading for anyone who wants to learn about the American Indian experience of the past four hundred years. Readers of all ages and all ethnic backgrounds will gain a deeper understanding of what it means to live between two worlds.

JAMES TROSPER, Shoshone Sun Dance Chief and
Trustee of the University of Wyoming
June, 2009
Fort Washakie, Wyoming

Michael Fitzgerald and James Trosper at the summit of the Grand Teton mountain range

HISTORICAL PROLOGUE

Chronology: 13,000 B.C.E.-1500 C.E.

13,000 B.C.E.   People present in Americas
9,000 B.C.E.   Paleo-Indians established throughout Western Hemisphere
5,000 B.C.E.   First domesticated crops grown
2,500 B.C.E.   First maize (corn) cultivated in Mesoamerica
1492 C.E.   Christopher Columbus reaches Western Hemisphere

Before the Arrival of the Europeans

⬦ Between 45 to 70 million indigenous people live in the Western Hemisphere
  ⬦ The great majority live in South America and Mesoamerica
⬦ Between 5 to 10 million Indians live in North America (U.S. & Canada)
⬦ The population density in continental U.S. is approximately 1 person for every 350 acres
⬦ 30 million bison (buffalo) roam throughout much of the U.S.
⬦ There are over 550 different tribes of American Indians
⬦ There are more than 30 major language families with hundreds of different dialects

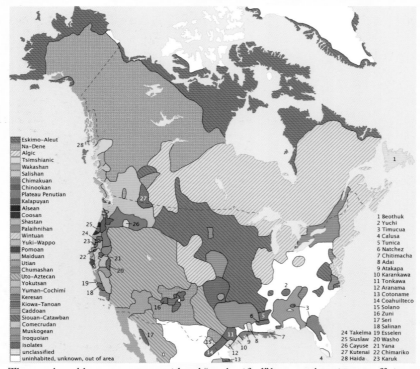

The numbered languages are considered "unclassified" because there is not sufficient
information to determine their genealogical relationship

In 1500 C.E.

✧ Native people are hunter-gatherers, with agriculture and aquaculture in fairer climates
✧ Most are nomadic or semi-nomadic; only sedentary where there is intense agriculture
✧ Epidemic diseases are unknown; there is no resistance to European diseases
✧ Daily time needed to provide material needs for most of the year: 33% to 60%
✧ A life harmonized with nature—punctuated by the intense hardships that nature can impose

Ancestral homelands:

Above: Ancestral homelands of various tribes, including the nine identifiable regions throughout North America
Following pages: Albert Bierstadt, *Indian Encampment in the Rocky Mountains*

PART I: LIFE IN THE DEEP WOODS

INTRODUCTION

What boy would not be an Indian for a while when he thinks of the freest life in the world? This life was mine. Every day there was a real hunt. There was real game. Occasionally there was a medicine dance away off in the woods where no one could disturb us, in which the boys impersonated their elders.

We were close students of nature. We studied the habits of animals just as you study your books. We watched the men of our people and represented them in our play; then tried to equal or excel them in our lives.

No people have a better use of their five senses than the children of the wilderness. We could smell as well as hear and see. We could feel and taste as well as we could see and hear. Nowhere has the memory been more fully developed than in the wild life, and I can still see that I owe much to my early training.

THE YOUNG BABE LOSES HIS MOTHER

I was so unfortunate as to be the youngest of five children who, soon after I was born, were left motherless. I had to bear the humiliating name "Hakadah," meaning "the pitiful last," until I should earn a more dignified and appropriate name.

The babe was done up as usual in a movable cradle made from an oak board two and a half feet long and one and a half feet wide. On one side of it was nailed with brass-headed tacks the richly-embroidered

Among the Sioux it was originally held that children should not be born into a family more often than once in three years, and no woman was expected to bear more than five children, for whom both masculine and feminine names were provided to indicate the order of their birth. —Charles Eastman

Family of Running Owl, Blackfeet

sack, which was open in front and laced up and down with buckskin strings. Over the arms of the infant was a wooden bow, the ends of which were firmly attached to the board, so that if the cradle should fall the child's head and face would be protected. On this bow were hung curious play-things—strings of artistically carved bones and hoofs of deer, which rattled when the little hands moved them.

In this upright cradle I lived, played, and slept the greater part of the time during the first few months of my life. Whether I was made to lean against a lodge pole or was

Unknown Cheyenne

Unknown Bannock

suspended from a bough of a tree, while my grandmother cut wood, or whether I was carried on her back, or conveniently balanced by another child in a similar cradle hung on the opposite side of a pony, I was still in my oaken bed.

After his mother's death Hakadah was raised by his grandmother.

My grandmother, who had already lived through sixty years of hardships, was a wonder to the young maidens of the tribe. She showed no less enthusiasm over Hakadah than she had done when she held her first-born, the boy's father, in her arms. Every little attention that is due to a loved child she performed with much skill and devotion.

Uncheedah (grandmother) was a great singer. Sometimes, when Hakadah wakened too early in the morning, she would sing to him something like the following lullaby:

> Sleep, sleep, my boy, our enemies
> Are far away—are far away.
> Sleep, sleep, my child, while still
> 'tis night;
> Then bravely wake—then bravely
> wake!

Assiniboine mother and child

Scarcely was the embryo warrior ushered into the world, when he was met by lullabies that speak of wonderful exploits in hunting and war. Those ideas which so fully occupied his mother's mind before his birth are now put into words by all about the child, who is as yet quite unresponsive to their appeals to his honor and ambition. He is called the future defender of his people, whose lives may depend upon his courage and skill. If the child is a girl, she is at once addressed as the future mother of a noble race.

—Charles Eastman

Apsaroke mother and child

"Remember that your children are not your own, but are lent to you by the Creator."

—Mohawk proverb

Bear Woman, Southern Cheyenne

5

THE INDIAN MOTHER

The Indian woman has always been the silent but telling power behind life's activities. At the same time she shared equally with her mate in the arduous duties of primitive society. Possessed of true feminine dignity and modesty, she was expected to be his equal in physical endurance and skill, but his superior in spiritual insight. She was looked to for the endowment of her child with nature's gifts and powers, and no woman of any race has ever come closer to universal motherhood.

The Indian was religious from his mother's womb. From the moment of her recognition of the fact of conception to the end of the second year of life, which was the ordinary duration of lactation, it was supposed by us that the mother's spiritual influence counted for most. Her attitude and secret meditations must be such as to instill into the receptive soul of the unborn child the love of the "Great Mystery" and a sense of brotherhood with all creation. Silence and isolation are the rule of life for the expectant mother. She wanders prayerful in the stillness of great woods, or on the bosom of the vast prairie, and to her poetic mind the immanent birth of her child prefigures the advent of a master-man—a hero, or the mother of heroes—a thought conceived in the virgin breast of primeval nature, and dreamed out in a hush that is only broken by the sighing of the pine tree or the thrilling orchestra of a distant waterfall.

And when the day of days in her life dawns—the day in which there is to be a new life, the miracle of whose making has been entrusted to her, she seeks no human aid. She has been trained and prepared in body and mind for this her holiest duty, ever since she can remember. The ordeal is best met alone, where no curious or pitying eyes embarrass her; where all nature says to her spirit: "'Tis love! 'tis love! the fulfilling of life!" When a sacred voice comes to her out of the silence, and a pair of eyes open upon her in the wilderness, she knows with joy that she has borne well her part in the great song of creation!

Presently she returns to the camp, carrying the mysterious, the holy, the dearest bundle! She feels the endearing warmth of it and hears its soft breathing. It is still a part of herself, since both are nourished by the same mouthful, and no look of a lover could be sweeter than its deep, trusting gaze.

She continues her spiritual teaching, at first silently—a mere pointing of the index finger to nature; then in whispered songs, bird-like, at morning and evening. To her and to the child the birds are real people, who live very close to the "Great Mystery"; the murmuring trees breathe His presence; the falling waters chant His praise.

If the child should chance to be fretful, the mother raises her hand. "Hush! hush!" she cautions it tenderly, "the spirits may be disturbed!" She bids it be still and listen to the silver voice of the aspen, or the clashing cymbals of the birch; and at night she points to the heavenly, blazed trail, through nature's galaxy of splendor to nature's God. Silence, love, reverence—this is the trinity of first lessons; and to these she later adds generosity, courage, and chastity.

In the old days, our mothers were single-minded to the trust imposed upon them. A noted chief of our people said:

Daughter of American Horse, Oglala Lakota

"Men may slay one another, but they can never overcome the woman, for in the quiet of her lap lies the child! You may destroy him once and again, but he issues as often from that same gentle lap—a gift of the Great Good to the race, in which man is only an accomplice!"

Many Horses (daughter of Sitting Bull), with son, Hunkpapa Lakota tribe

GRANDMOTHER'S TEACHINGS

The Dakota women were obliged to cut and bring their fuel from the woods and, in fact, to perform most of the drudgery of the camp. This of necessity fell to their lot, because the men must hunt the game during the day. Very often my grandmother carried me with her on these excursions; and while she worked it was her habit to suspend me from a wild grape vine or a springy bough, so that the least breeze would swing the cradle to and fro.

After I left my cradle, my grandmother then began calling my attention to natural objects. Whenever I heard the song of a bird, she would tell me what bird it came from, something after this fashion:

"Hakadah, listen to *Shechoka* (the robin) calling his mate. He says he has just found something good to eat." Or "Listen to *Oopehanska* (the thrush); he is singing for his little wife. He will sing his best."

Indian children were trained so that they hardly ever cried much in the night. This was very expedient and necessary in their exposed life. In my infancy it was my grandmother's custom to put me to sleep, as she said, with the birds, and to waken me with them, until it became a habit. She did this with an object in view. An Indian must always rise early. In the first place, as a hunter, he finds his game best at daybreak. Secondly, other tribes, when on the warpath, usually make their attack very early in the morning. Even when our people are

A winter day, Apsaroke

Unknown family, Southern Cheyenne

moving about leisurely, we like to rise before daybreak, in order to travel when the air is cool, and unobserved, perchance, by our enemies.

As a little child, it was instilled into me to be silent and slow to speak. This was one of the most important traits to form in the character of the Indian. As a hunter and warrior it was considered absolutely nec-

essary to him, and was thought to lay the foundations of patience and self-control. There are times when boisterous mirth is indulged in by our people, but the rule is gravity and decorum.

After all, my babyhood was full of interest and the beginnings of life's realities. The spirit of daring was already whispered into my ears.

EARLY HARDSHIPS

The travois consisted of a set of rawhide strips securely lashed to the tent-poles, which were harnessed to the sides of the animal as if he stood between shafts, while the free ends were allowed to drag on the ground. Both ponies and large dogs were used as beasts of burden, and they carried in this way the smaller children as well as the baggage.

This mode of traveling for children was possible only in the summer, and as the dogs were sometimes unreliable, the little ones were exposed to a certain amount of danger. For instance, whenever a train of dogs had been traveling for a long time, almost perishing with the heat and their heavy loads, a glimpse of water would cause them to forget all their responsibilities. Some of them, in spite of the screams of the women, would swim with their burdens into the cooling stream, and I was thus, on more than one occasion, made to partake of an unwilling bath.

Left: Atsina horse travois
Top right: Sioux dog travois
Bottom right: Cheyenne dog travois

Blackfeet horse travois

Piegan traveling on horse travois

FLIGHT TO CANADA

I was a little over four years old at the time of the "Sioux massacre" in Minnesota. In the general turmoil, we took flight into Canada, and the journey is still vividly remembered by all our family.

The summer after the "Minnesota massacre," General Sibley pursued our people

Above: Two Hidatsa women construct a bull boat by stretching the heavy, tough hide of a male buffalo over a willow grame
Left: Mandan bull boat
Below: Carl Bodmer, *Bull Boats*, c. 1840

across this river. Now the Missouri is considered one of the most treacherous rivers in the world. Even a good modern boat is not safe upon its uncertain current. We were forced to cross in buffalo-skin boats—as round as tubs!

The *Washechu* (white men) were coming in great numbers with their big guns, and while most of our men were fighting them to gain time, the women and the old men made and equipped the temporary boats, braced with ribs of willow. Some of these were towed by two or three women or men swimming in the water and some by ponies. It was not an easy matter to keep them right side up, with their helpless freight of little children and such goods as we possessed.

Now we were compelled to trespass upon the country of hostile tribes and were harassed by them almost daily and nightly. Only the strictest vigilance saved us.

THE INDIAN'S WILD LIFE

I was now an exile as well as motherless; yet I was not unhappy. Our wanderings from place to place afforded us many pleasant experiences and quite as many hardships and misfortunes. There were times of plenty and times of scarcity, and we had several narrow escapes from death. In savage life, the early spring is the most trying time and almost all the famines occurred at this period of the year.

The Indians are a patient and a clannish people; their love for one another is stronger than that of any civilized people I know.

In times of famine, the adults often denied themselves in order to make the food last as long as possible for the children, who were not able to bear hunger as well as the old. As a people, they can live without food much longer than any other nation.

I once passed through one of these hard springs when we had nothing to eat for several days. Soon after this, we came into a region where buffaloes were plenty, and hunger and scarcity were forgotten.

Such was the Indian's wild life! When game was to be had and the sun shone, they easily forgot the bitter experiences of the winter before. Little preparation was made for the future. They are children of Nature, and occasionally she whips them with the

A Sioux woman scrapes an elk hide using a tool typically made from an elk horn

Jerking meat, Flathead

Crow summer camp

Apsaroke winter camp, c. 1908

lashes of experience, yet they are forgetful and careless.

During the summer, when Nature is at her best, and provides abundantly for the savage, it seems to me that no life is happier than his! Food is free—lodging free—everything free! All were alike rich in the summer, and, again, all were alike poor in the winter and early spring. However, their diseases were fewer and not so destructive as now, and the Indian's health was generally good. The Indian boy enjoyed such a life as almost all boys dream of and would choose for themselves if they were permitted to do so.

The frail teepee pitched anywhere, in the winter as well as in the summer, and was all the protection that we had against cold and storms. I can recall times when we were snowed in and it was very difficult to get fuel. We were once three days without much fire and all of this time it stormed violently. There seemed to be no special anxiety on the part of our people; they rather looked upon all this as a matter of course, knowing that the storm would cease when the time came.

Even if there was plenty to eat, it was thought better for us to practice fasting sometimes; and hard exercise was kept up continually, both for the sake of health and to prepare the body for the extraordinary exertions that it might, at any moment, be required to undergo. In my own remembrance, my uncle used often to bring home a deer on his shoulder. The distance was sometimes considerable; yet he did not consider it any sort of a feat.

LOSS OF MY FATHER

The second winter after the massacre, my father and my two older brothers, with several others, were betrayed to the United States authorities. As I was then living with my uncle in another part of the country, I became separated from them for ten years. During all this time we believed that they had been killed by the whites, and I was taught that I must avenge their deaths as soon as I was able to go upon the war-path.

Unknown Lakota

With a carrying bag about her waist, this woman
digs up the earth with a root stick

Great Mystery will disclose only to the most worthy. Only those who seek him fasting and in solitude will receive his signs."

With this and many similar explanations she wrought in my soul wonderful and lively conceptions of the "Great Mystery" and of the effects of prayer and solitude.

As a motherless child, I always regarded my good grandmother as the wisest of guides and the best of protectors. Her observations in practice were all preserved in her mind for reference, as systematically as if they had been written upon the pages of a note-book.

I distinctly recall one occasion when she took me with her into the woods in search of certain medicinal roots.

"Why do you not use all kinds of roots for medicines?" said I.

"Because," she replied, in her quick, characteristic manner, "the Great Mystery does not will us to find things too easily. In that case everybody would be a medicine-giver, and Ohiyesa must learn that there are many secrets which the

Woman using a woven seed beater to collect
seeds into a burden basket

Wife of Yellowhair, Brule Lakota

Unknown, Oglala Lakota

Wife of Old Crow, Cheyenne

A MIDSUMMER FEAST

It was midsummer. Everything that the Santee Sioux had undertaken during the year had been unusually successful. The *Wahpetonwan* band of Sioux, the "Dwellers among the Leaves," were fully awakened to the fact that it was almost time for the midsummer festivities of the old, wild days.

There were to be many different kinds of athletic games; indeed, the festival was something like a State fair, in that there were many side shows and competitive events.

But the one all-important event of the occasion was the lacrosse game, for which it had been customary to select those two bands which could boast the greater number of fast runners.

The *Wahpetonwan* village on the banks of the Minnesota river was alive with the newly-arrived guests and the preparations for the coming event. Meat of wild game had been put away with much care during the previous fall in anticipation of this feast. There was wild rice and the choicest of dried venison that had been kept all winter, as well as freshly dug turnips, ripe berries, and an abundance of fresh meat.

Along the edge of the woods the teepees were pitched in groups or semi-circles, each band distinct from the others.

Piegan encampment, 1900

INDIAN NAMES

Indian names were either characteristic nicknames given in a playful spirit, deed names, birth names, or such as have a religious and symbolic meaning. It has been said that when a child is born, some accident or unusual appearance determines his name. This is sometimes the case, but is not the rule. A man of forcible character, with a fine war record, usually bears the name of the buffalo or bear, lightning or some dread natural force. Another of more peaceful nature may be called Swift Bird or Blue Sky. A woman's name usually suggested something about the home, often with the adjective "pretty" or "good," and a feminine termination. Names of any dignity or importance must be conferred by the old men, and especially so if they have any spiritual significance, as Sacred Cloud, Mysterious Night, Spirit Woman, and the like. Such a name was sometimes borne by three generations, but each individual must prove that he is worthy of it.

—Charles Eastman

A meeting was held to appoint some "medicine man" to make the balls that were to be used in the lacrosse contest; and presently the herald announced that this honor had been conferred upon old Chankpee-yuhah, or "Keeps the Club." Towards evening he appeared in the circle, leading by the hand a boy about four years old. The boy was painted according to the fashion of the age. He held in his hands a miniature bow and arrows.

The medicine man drew himself up in an admirable attitude, and proceeded to make his short speech:

"I wish to announce that if the *Wahpetonwan*s should win, this little warrior shall bear the name Ohiyesa (the winner) through life; but if the Light Lodges should win, let the name be given to any child appointed by them."

George Catlin, *Ah-Nó-Je-Nahge, He Who Stands on Both Sides, a distinguished ball player*, 1835

Lacrosse stick of wood and rawhide. Probably Eastern Sioux/Dakota, c. 1830s

The lacrosse game continued for a long time. First one side, then the other would gain an advantage, and then it was lost, until the herald proclaimed that it was time to change the ball. No victory was in sight for either side.

Suddenly a warrior shot out of the throng like the ball itself! Such a speed! *Eastman's band of Sioux won the day.*

The day had been a perfect one. Every event had been a success; and, as a matter of course, the old people were happy, for they largely profited by these occasions. In memory of this victory, the medicine man, proceeded to confer the name on the young boy.

"Ohiyesa shall be thy name henceforth. Be brave, be patient and thou shalt always win! Thy name is Ohiyesa."

In this way the boy who had been Haka-dah became Ohiyesa—the winner.

Lacrosse was a physical game that included no-holds-barred scuffling and wrestling as players struggled for the ball. George Catlin, *Ball-Play of the Choctaw*, c. 1843

THE GRANDPARENTS TEACH THE YOUNG CHILDREN

It is commonly supposed that there is no systematic education of their children among the aborigines of this country. Nothing could be farther from the truth. All the customs of this primitive people were held to be divinely instituted, and those in connection with the training of children were scrupulously adhered to and transmitted from one generation to another.

Very early, the Indian boy assumed the task of preserving and transmitting the legends of his ancestors and his race.

Almost every evening a myth, or a true story of some deed done in the past, was narrated by one of the parents or grandparents, while the boy listened with parted lips and glistening eyes. On the following evening, he was usually required to repeat it. As a rule, the Indian boy is a good listener and has a good memory, so that the stories were tolerably well mastered. The household became his audience, by which he was alternately criticized and applauded.

This sort of teaching at once enlightens the boy's mind and stimulates his ambition. His conception of his own future career becomes a vivid and irresistible force. Whatever there is for him to learn must be

A Tale of the Tribe, c. 1909, Taos Pueblo; *Opposite*: Storytelling among the Pikuni Blackfeet

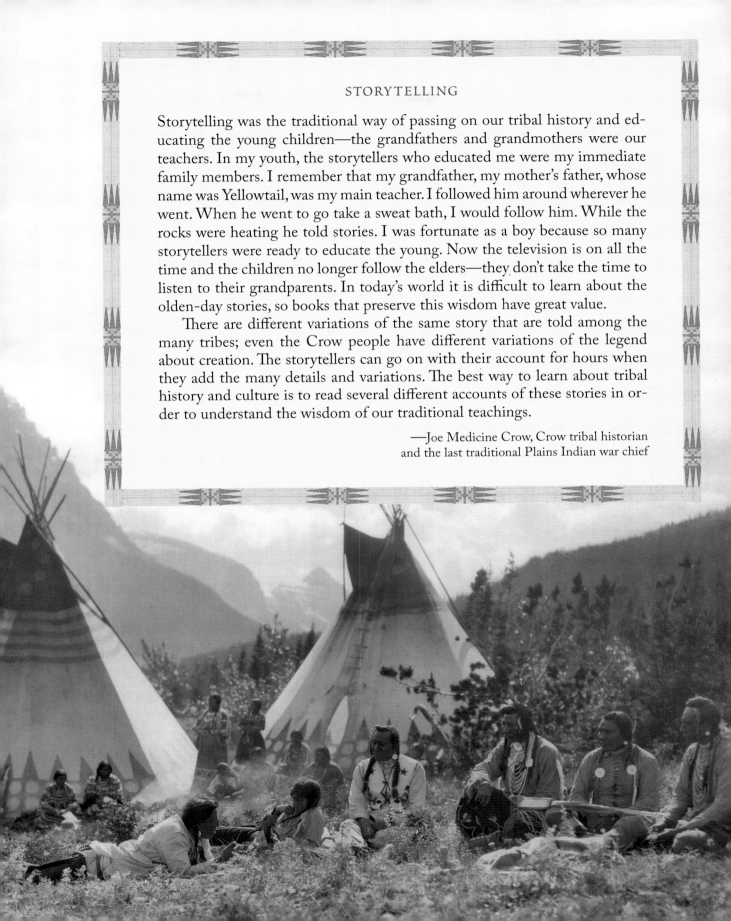

STORYTELLING

Storytelling was the traditional way of passing on our tribal history and educating the young children—the grandfathers and grandmothers were our teachers. In my youth, the storytellers who educated me were my immediate family members. I remember that my grandfather, my mother's father, whose name was Yellowtail, was my main teacher. I followed him around wherever he went. When he went to go take a sweat bath, I would follow him. While the rocks were heating he told stories. I was fortunate as a boy because so many storytellers were ready to educate the young. Now the television is on all the time and the children no longer follow the elders—they don't take the time to listen to their grandparents. In today's world it is difficult to learn about the olden-day stories, so books that preserve this wisdom have great value.

There are different variations of the same story that are told among the many tribes; even the Crow people have different variations of the legend about creation. The storytellers can go on with their account for hours when they add the many details and variations. The best way to learn about tribal history and culture is to read several different accounts of these stories in order to understand the wisdom of our traditional teachings.

—Joe Medicine Crow, Crow tribal historian
and the last traditional Plains Indian war chief

A Brule Sioux medicine man is adding the symbol for the year just past onto a "winter count" hide that
preserves the main event for each year in the tribe's history over a period of more than a century.
This type of record allowed the elders to accurately recite generations of history to their grandchildren.

learned; whatever qualifications are necessary to a truly great man he must seek at any expense of danger and hardship. Such was the feeling of the imaginative and brave young Indian. It became apparent to him in early life that he must accustom himself to rove alone and not to fear or dislike the impression of solitude.

Indeed, the distinctive work of both grandparents is that of acquainting the youth with the national traditions and beliefs. It is reserved for them to repeat the time-hallowed tales with dignity and authority, so as to lead him into his inheritance in the stored-up wisdom and experience of the race. The old are dedicated to the service of the young, as their teachers and advisers, and the young in turn regard them with love and reverence.

A PURE DEMOCRACY

In the first place, the American Indian is free born, hence a free thinker. His government is a pure democracy, based solidly upon intrinsic right and justice, which governs, in his conception, the play of life. I use the word "play" rather than a more pretentious term, as better expressing the trend of his philosophy. He stands naked and upright, both literally and symbolically, before his "Great Mystery." When he fails in obedience, either to natural law (which is supreme law), or to the simple code of his brother man, he will not excuse himself upon a technicality or lie to save his miserable body. He comes to trial and punishment, even to death, if need be, unattended, and as cheerfully as to a council or feast.

What does the original American contribute, in the final summing up, to the country of his birth and his adoption? After all, is there not something worthy of perpetuation in the spirit of his democracy—the very essence of patriotism and justice between man and man? Silently, by example only, in wordless patience, he holds stoutly to his native vision. We must admit that the tacit influence of his philosophy has been felt at last, and a self-seeking world has paused in its mad rush to pay him a tribute.

The government of most tribes was a true democracy. Long council meetings allowed a forum for many speakers and continued until a consensus was achieved. Those who did not agree with the decisions were free to leave and form their own band. Chiefs had prestige only to the extent they demonstrated bravery and honor. Every person considered the impact of their decisions on future generations. The phrase, "the 7th generation," is based upon the traditional Indian teachings that actions of today will affect the future, up to and including the 7th generation to come.

IROQUOIS CONSTITUTION

In 2004 the U.S. State Department acknowledged that the U.S. Constitution was based in part on the Iroquois Constitution. It is a historical fact that there are many striking similarities between these two documents and many founding fathers, including Benjamin Franklin and Thomas Jefferson, had extensive contact with the "Five Nations" of the Iroquois confederacy. One of the main differences is in the important role of women in the Iroquois constitution. These are excerpts from the Iroquois Constitution:

CLANS AND CONSANGUINITY

The lineal descent of the people of the Five Nations shall run in the female line. Women shall be considered the progenitors of the Nation. They shall own the land and the soil.

The women, heirs of the Lordship[1] titles, shall, should it be necessary, correct and admonish the holders of their titles.

When a Lordship title becomes vacant through death or other cause, the women of the clan in which the title is hereditary shall hold a council and shall choose one from among their sons to fill the office made vacant.

RIGHTS OF THE PEOPLE OF THE FIVE NATIONS

The women of every clan of the Five Nations shall have a Council Fire ever burning in readiness for a council of the clan. When in their opinion it seems necessary for the interest of the people they shall hold a council and their decisions and recommendations shall be introduced before the Council of the Lords by the War Chief for its consideration.

RIGHTS, DUTIES, AND QUALIFICATIONS OF LORDS

Wampum strings shall be given to each of the female families in which the Lordship titles are vested. The right of bestowing the title shall be hereditary in the family of the females legally possessing the bunch of shell strings and the strings shall be the token that the females of the family have the proprietary right to the Lordship title for all time to come.

---

[1] The terms "Lord" and "Lordship" are translations of the Iroquois word "sachem", which is a title of leadership. The "great chief", *massasoit sachem*, of the Wampanoag Indians who welcomed the first Pilgrims to Plymouth, Massachusetts in 1620 is remembered today simply as Massasoit. See "King Philip's War", pp. 108-109.

If at any time it shall be manifest that a Confederate Lord has not in mind the welfare of the people or disobeys the rules of this Great Law ... the War Chiefs shall then divest the erring Lord of his title by order of the women in whom the titleship is vested. The women will then select another of their sons as a candidate and the Lords shall elect him. When a Lord is to be deposed, his War Chief shall address him as follows:

"So you disregard and set at naught the warnings of your women relatives. So you fling the warnings over your shoulder to cast them behind you.

"Behold the brightness of the Sun and in the brightness of the Sun's light I depose you of your title and remove the sacred emblem of your Lordship title."

The War Chief shall now address the women of the deposed Lord and say:

"Mothers, as I have now deposed your Lord, I now return to you the emblem and the title of Lordship."

Considerations and Questions

☞ Consider the consequences of living under the Iroquois Constitution, where only women can vote and only men can sit in the council.

☞ Does the Iroquois system provide a check and balance that will force elected officials to give more consideration to the needs of future generations?

Wampum strings

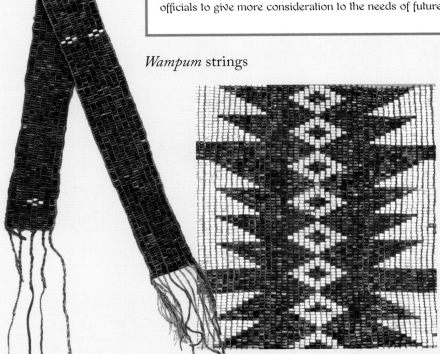

Each knot and beaded design on the wampum belt had a symbolic meaning that mnemonically chronicled different tribal stories, legends, and treaties that included the Iroquois Constitution

AN INDIAN BOY'S TRAINING

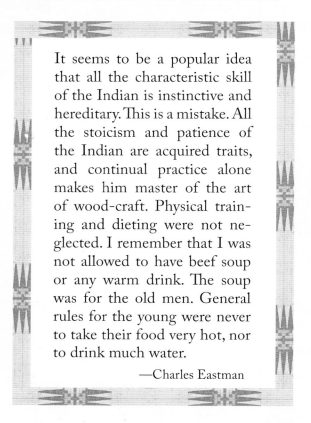

It seems to be a popular idea that all the characteristic skill of the Indian is instinctive and hereditary. This is a mistake. All the stoicism and patience of the Indian are acquired traits, and continual practice alone makes him master of the art of wood-craft. Physical training and dieting were not neglected. I remember that I was not allowed to have beef soup or any warm drink. The soup was for the old men. General rules for the young were never to take their food very hot, nor to drink much water.

—Charles Eastman

At the age of about eight years, if the child is a boy, his mother turns him over to his father for more Spartan training.

My uncle, who educated me up to the age of fifteen years, was a strict disciplinarian and a good teacher. When I left the tee-pee in the morning, he would say: "Hakadah, look closely to everything you see"; and at evening, on my return, he used often to catechize me for an hour or so.

"On which side of the trees is the lighter-colored bark? On which side do they have most regular branches?"

It was his custom to let me name all the new birds that I had seen during the day. I would name them according to the color or the shape of the bill or their song or the ap-pearance and locality of the nest—in fact, anything about the bird that impressed me as characteristic. I made many ridiculous errors, I must admit. He then usually informed me of the correct name. Occasionally I made a hit and this he would warmly commend.

He went much deeper into this science when I was a little older, that is, about the age of eight or nine years. He would say, for instance:

"How do you know that there are fish in yonder lake?"

"Because they jump out of the water for flies at mid-day."

He would smile at my prompt but superficial reply.

"What do you think of the little pebbles grouped together under the shallow water? and what made the pretty curved marks in the sandy bottom and the little sand-banks? Where do you find the fish-eating birds? Have the inlet and the outlet of a lake anything to do with the question?"

He did not expect a correct reply at once to all the voluminous questions that he put to me on these occasions, but he meant to make me observant and a good student of nature.

"Hakadah," he would say to me, "you ought to follow the example of the *shunktokecha* (wolf). Even when he is surprised and runs for his life, he will pause to take one more look at you before he enters his final retreat. So you must take a second look at everything you see."

"In hunting," he would resume, "you will be guided by the habits of the animal you seek. Remember that a moose stays in swampy or low land or between high mountains near a spring or lake, for thirty to sixty days at a time. Most large game moves about continually, except the doe in the spring; it is then a very easy matter to find her with the fawn. Conceal yourself in a convenient place as soon as you observe any signs of the presence of either, and then call with your birchen doe-caller.

"When you have any difficulty with a bear or a wild-cat—that is, if the creature shows signs of attacking you—you must make him fully understand that you have seen him and are aware of his intentions. If you are not well equipped for a pitched battle, the only way to make him retreat is to take a long sharp-pointed pole for a spear and rush toward him. No wild beast will face this unless he is cornered and already wounded. These fierce beasts are gen-

erally afraid of the common weapon of the larger animals—the horns, and if these are very long and sharp, they dare not risk an open fight."

All boys were expected to endure hardship without complaint. In savage warfare, a young man must, of course, be an athlete and used to undergoing all sorts of privations. He must be able to go without food and water for two or three days without displaying any weakness, or to run for a day and a night without any rest. He must be able to traverse a pathless and wild country without losing his way either in the day or night time. He cannot refuse to do any of these things if he aspires to be a warrior.

Sometimes my uncle would wake me very early in the morning and challenge

Unknown Cheyenne boy

me to fast with him all day. I had to accept the challenge. We blackened our faces with charcoal, so that every boy in the village would know that I was fasting for the day. Then the little tempters would make my life a misery until the merciful sun hid behind the western hills.

I can scarcely recall the time when my stern teacher began to give sudden war-whoops over my head in the morning while I was sound asleep. He expected me to leap up with perfect presence of mind, always ready to grasp a weapon of some sort and to give a shrill whoop in reply. If I was sleepy or startled and hardly knew what I was about, he would ridicule me and say that I need never expect to sell my scalp dear. Often he would vary these tactics by shooting off his gun just outside of the lodge while I was yet asleep, at the same time giving blood-curdling yells. After a time I became used to this.

When Indians went upon the war-path, it was their custom to try the new warriors thoroughly before coming to an engagement. For instance, when they were near a hostile camp, they would select the novices to go after the water and make them do all sorts of things to prove their courage. In accordance with this idea, my uncle used to send me off after water when we camped after dark in a strange place. Perhaps the country was full of wild beasts, and, for aught I knew, there might be scouts from hostile bands of Indians lurking in that very neighborhood.

Yet I never objected, for that would show cowardice. I picked my way through the woods, dipped my pail in the water and hurried back, always careful to make as little noise as a cat. Being only a boy, my heart would leap at every crackling of a dry twig or distant hooting of an owl, until, at last, I reached our teepee. Then my uncle would perhaps say: "Ah, Hakadah, you are a thorough warrior," empty out the precious contents of the pail, and order me to go a second time.

With all this, our manners and morals were not neglected. I was made to respect the adults and especially the aged. I was not allowed to join in their discussions, nor

INDIAN ETIQUETTE

No one who is at all acquainted with the Indian in his home can deny that we are a polite people. As a rule, the warrior who inspired the greatest terror in the hearts of his enemies was a man of the most exemplary gentleness, and almost feminine refinement, among his family and friends. A soft, low voice was considered an excellent thing in man, as well as in woman! Indeed, the enforced intimacy of tent life would soon become intolerable, were it not for these instinctive reserves and delicacies, this unfailing respect for the established place and possessions of every other member of the family circle, this habitual quiet, order, and decorum.

even to speak in their presence, unless requested to do so. Indian etiquette was very strict, and among the requirements was that of avoiding the direct address. A term of relationship or some title of courtesy was commonly used instead of the personal name by those who wished to show respect. We were taught generosity to the poor and reverence for the "Great Mystery." Religion was the basis of all Indian training.

I recall to the present day some of the kind warnings and reproofs that my good grandmother was wont to give me. "Be strong of heart—be patient!" she used to say. She told me of a young chief who was noted for his uncontrollable temper. While in one of his rages he attempted to kill a woman, for which he was slain by his own band and left unburied as a mark of disgrace—his body was simply covered with green grass. If I ever lost my temper, she would say:

"Hakadah, control yourself, or you will be like that young man I told you of, and lie under a green blanket!"

In the old days, if a youth should seek a wife before he had reached the age of twenty-two or twenty-three, and been recognized as a brave man, he was sneered at and considered an ill-bred Indian. He must also be a skillful hunter. An Indian cannot be a good husband unless he brings home plenty of game.

These precepts were in the line of our training for the wild life.

GAMES AND SPORTS

The Indian boy was a prince of the wilderness. He had but very little work to do during the period of his boyhood. His principal occupation was the practice of a few simple arts in warfare and the chase. Aside from this, he was master of his time.

Whatever was required of us boys was quickly performed: then the field was clear for our games and plays. There was always keen competition among us. We felt very much as our fathers did in hunting and war —each one strove to excel all the others.

It is true that our savage life was a pre-

Our people, though capable of strong and durable feeling, were not demonstrative in their affection at any time, least of all in the presence of guests or strangers. Only to the aged, who have journeyed far, and are in a manner exempt from ordinary rules, are permitted some playful familiarities with children and grandchildren. Grandparents are the only ones allowed to speak harshly in their criticism. Our old age was in some respects the happiest period of life. Advancing years brought with them much freedom, not only from the burden of laborious and dangerous tasks, but from those restrictions of custom and etiquette which were religiously observed by all others.

—Charles Eastman

shot winter arrows (which were used only in that season), and coasted upon the ribs of animals and buffalo robes.

It was considered out of place to shoot by first sighting the object aimed at. This was usually impracticable in actual life, because the object was almost always in motion, while the hunter himself was often upon the back of a pony at full gallop. Therefore, it was the off-hand shot that the Indian boy sought to master.

Hermon Atkins MacNeil, *The Sun Vow*, 1913

carious one, and full of dreadful catastrophes; however, this never prevented us from enjoying our sports to the fullest extent. As we left our teepees in the morning, we were never sure that our scalps would not dangle from a pole in the afternoon!

Our sports were molded by the life and customs of our people; indeed, we practiced only what we expected to do when grown. Our games were feats with the bow and arrow, foot and pony races, wrestling, swimming and imitation of the customs and habits of our fathers. We had sham fights with mud balls and willow wands; we played lacrosse, made war upon bees,

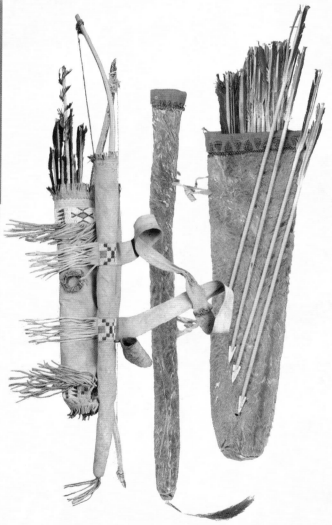

The young boys spent hours practicing to shoot with the bow and arrows

Races were an everyday occurrence. At noon the boys were usually gathered by some pleasant sheet of water and as soon as the ponies were watered, they were allowed to graze for an hour or two, while the boys stripped for their noonday sports.

As soon as the foot race was ended, the pony races followed. All the speedy ponies were picked out and riders chosen. If a boy declined to ride, there would be shouts of derision.

Last of all came the swimming. We loved to play in the water. When we had no ponies, we often had swimming match-

Dakota father teaching a child to shoot with an arrow

Children playing, unknown Cheyenne

es of our own and sometimes made rafts with which we crossed lakes and rivers. It was a common thing to "duck" a young or timid boy or to carry him into deep water to struggle as best he might.

I remember a perilous ride with a companion on an unmanageable log, when we were both less than seven years old. The older boys had put us on this uncertain bark and pushed us out into the swift current of the river. I cannot speak for my comrade in distress, but I can say now that I would rather ride on a swift bronco any day than try to stay on and steady a short log in a river. I never knew how we managed to prevent a shipwreck on that voyage and to reach the shore.

Wrestling was largely indulged in by us all. It may seem odd, but wrestling was done by a great many boys at once—from ten to any number on a side. It was really a battle, in which each one chose his opponent. The rule was that if a boy sat down, he was let alone, but as long as he remained standing within the field, he was open to an attack. No one struck with the hand, but all manner of tripping with legs and feet and butting with the knees was allowed. Altogether it was an exhausting pastime—fully equal to the American game of football and only the young athlete could really enjoy it.

One of our most curious sports was a war upon the nests of wild bees. We imagined ourselves about to make an attack upon the Ojibways or some tribal foe. We all painted and stole cautiously upon the nest; then, with a rush and war whoop, sprang upon the object of our attack and endeavored to destroy it. But it seemed that the bees were always on the alert and never entirely surprised, for they always raised quite as many scalps as did their bold assailants! After the onslaught upon the nest was ended, we usually followed it by a pretended scalp dance.

We had some quiet plays which we alternated with the more severe and warlike ones. Among them were throwing wands and snow-arrows. In the winter we coasted much. We had no "double-rippers" or toboggans, but six or seven of the long ribs of a buffalo, fastened together at the larger end, answered all practical purposes. Sometimes a strip of basswood bark, four feet long and about six inches wide, was used with considerable skill. We stood on one end and held the other, using the slippery inside of the bark for the outside, and thus coasting down long hills with remarkable speed.

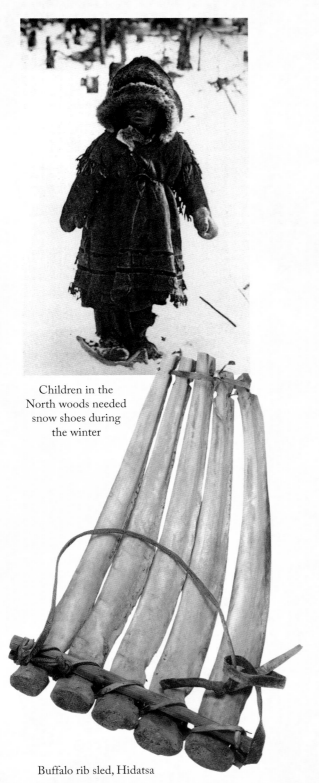

Children in the
North woods needed
snow shoes during
the winter

Buffalo rib sled, Hidatsa

THE BOY HUNTER

It will be no exaggeration to say that the life of the Indian hunter was a life of fascination. From the moment that he lost sight of his rude home in the midst of the forest, his untutored mind lost itself in the myriad beauties and forces of nature. Yet he never forgot his personal danger from some lurking foe or savage beast, however absorbing was his passion for the chase.

The Indian youth was a born hunter. Every motion, every step expressed an inborn dignity and, at the same time, a depth of native caution. His moccasined foot fell like the velvet paw of a cat—noiselessly; his glittering black eyes scanned every object that appeared within their view. Not a bird, not even a chipmunk, escaped their piercing glance.

I was scarcely over three years old when I stood one morning just outside our buffalo-skin teepee, with my little bow and arrows in my hand, and gazed up among the trees. Suddenly the instinct to chase and hunt seized me powerfully. Just then a bird flew over my head and then another caught my eye, as it balanced itself upon a swaying bough. Everything else was forgotten and in that moment I had taken my first step as a hunter.

Our hunting varied with the season of the year, and the nature of the country which was for the time our home. Our chief weapon was the bow and arrows, and perhaps, if we were lucky, a knife was possessed by someone in the crowd. In the olden times, knives and hatchets were made from bone and sharp stones.

For fire we used a flint with a spongy piece of dry wood and a stone to strike

George Catlin, *Buffalo Chase, Upper Missouri*

Snowshoe of wood and rawhide.
Probably Ojibway, c. 1830s

George Catlin, *Buffalo Chase in Snowdrifts, Indians Pursuing on Snowshoes*

John Lone Bull, Dakota

with. Another way of starting fire was for several of the boys to sit down in a circle and rub two pieces of dry, spongy wood together, one after another, until the wood took fire.

We hunted in company a great deal, though it was a common thing for a boy to set out for the woods quite alone, and he usually enjoyed himself fully as much. Our game consisted mainly of small birds, rab-

bits, squirrels and grouse. Fishing, too, oc-cupied much of our time. We hardly ever passed a creek or a pond without search-ing for some signs of fish. When fish were present, we always managed to get some. Fish-lines were made of wild hemp, sin-ew or horse-hair. We either caught fish with lines, snared or speared them, or shot them with bow and arrows. In the fall we charmed them up to the surface by gently tickling them with a stick and quickly threw them out. We have sometimes dammed the brooks and driven the larger fish into a willow basket made for that purpose.

It was part of our hunting to find new and strange things in the woods. We examined the slightest sign of life; and if a bird had scratched the leaves off the ground, or a bear dragged up a root for his morning meal, we stopped to speculate on the time it was done. If we saw a large old tree with some scratches on its bark, we concluded that a bear or some raccoons must be living there. In that case we did not go any nearer than was necessary, but later reported the incident at home. An old deer-track would at once bring on a warm discussion as to whether it was the track of a buck or a doe.

Charles Russell, *Crow Indians Hunting Elk* (detail), c. 1887
Opposite: Roland W. Reed, *The Landmark*, 1912

Whenever, in the course of the daily hunt, the red hunter comes upon a scene that is strikingly beautiful and sublime—a black thunder-cloud with the rainbow's glowing arch above the mountain; a white waterfall in the heart of a green gorge; a vast prairie tinged with the blood-red of sunset— he pauses for an instant in the attitude of worship. He sees no need for setting apart one day in seven as a holy day, since to him all days are God's.

—Charles Eastman

WILDERNESS COOKING

It became a necessary part of our education to learn to prepare a meal while out hunting. It is a fact that most Indians will eat the liver and some other portions of large animals raw, but they do not eat fish or birds uncooked. Neither will they eat a frog, or an eel. On our boyish hunts, we often went on until we found ourselves a long way from our camp, when we would kindle a fire and roast a part of our game.

Generally we broiled our meat over the coals on a stick. We roasted some of it over the open fire. But the best way to cook fish and birds is in the ashes, under a big fire. We take the fish fresh from the creek or lake, have a good fire on the sand, dig in the sandy ashes and bury it deep. The same thing is done in case of a bird, only we wet the feathers first. When it is done, the scales or feathers and skin are stripped off whole, and the delicious meat retains all its juices and flavor. We pulled it off as we ate, leaving the bones undisturbed.

Our people had also a method of boiling without pots or kettles. A large piece of tripe was thoroughly washed and the ends tied, then suspended between four stakes driven into the ground and filled with cold water. The meat was then placed in this novel receptacle and boiled by means of the addition of red-hot stones.

Sioux man cooking meat by throwing heated stones into a buffalo-stomach container

One Bull, Nephew of Sitting Bull Cooking Beef McIntosh S.D.

Above: Blackfoot cookery and smoking meat
Right: Sioux man cooking meat in buffalo-stomach

INTERTRIBAL WARFARE

As regards the original Indian warfare, it was founded upon the principle of manly rivalry in patriotism, bravery, and self-sacrifice. The willingness to risk life for the welfare or honor of the people was the highest test of character. In order that the reputations thus gained might be preserved as an example to the young, a system of decorations was evolved, including the symbolic wearing of certain feathers and skins, especially eagle feathers, and the conferring of "honor names" for special exploits. These distinctions could not be gained unjustly or by favoritism, as is often the case with rank and honors among civilized men, since the deeds claimed must be proved by witnesses before the grand council of war chiefs. If one strikes an enemy in battle, whether he kills him or not, he must announce the fact in a loud voice, so that it may be noted and remembered. The danger and difficulty is regarded above the amount of damage inflicted upon the enemy.

It is easily seen that these intertribal contests were not based upon the same motives nor waged for the same objects as the wars of civilization—namely, for spoil and territorial gain. There was no mass play; army was not pitted against army; individual valor was held in highest regard. It was not usual to take captives, except occasionally of women and children, who were adopted into the tribe and treated with kindness. There was no traffic in the labor or flesh of prisoners. Such warfare, in fact, was scarcely more than a series of duels or irregular skirmishes, engaged in by individuals and small groups, and in many cases was but little rougher than a game of university football. Some were killed because

Charles Russell, *Counting Coup* (detail), c. 1902. The greatest honor for a warrior was to "count coup" on an enemy, based upon the French word "coup," which means "touch." In order to become a "chief," a warrior must accomplish four war deeds: count coup, take an enemy's weapon in hand-to-hand fighting, steal a horse and lead a successful war party. No war honors were given for killing an enemy within many tribes.

Charles Russell, *Return of the Horse Thieves*, 1900

they were caught, or proved weaker and less athletic than their opponents. It was one way of disciplining a man and working off the superfluous energy that might otherwise lead to domestic quarrels. If he met his equal or superior and was slain, fighting bravely to the end, his friends might weep honorable tears.

The slayer of a man in battle was expected to mourn for thirty days, blackening his face and loosening his hair according to the custom. He of course considered it no sin to take the life of an enemy, and this ceremonial mourning was a sign of reverence for the departed spirit.

A scalp might originally be taken by the leader of the war party only, and at that period no other mutilation was practiced. It was a small lock not more than three inches square, which was carried only during the thirty days' celebration of a victory, and afterward given religious burial.

Gros Ventre shield, c. 1860

Coup stick

Crow lance case

Arrows

Bow case
and quiver

Powder Face,
Arapaho chief

Tomahawk

Bow case
and quiver

Lance/coup
stick

Shield

Knife sheath

Cheyenne warrior

Wanton cruelties and the more barbarous customs of war were greatly intensified with the coming of the white man, who brought with him fiery liquor and deadly weapons, aroused the Indian's worst passions, provoking in him revenge and cupidity, and even offered bounties for the scalps of innocent men, women, and children.

AN INDIAN GIRL'S TRAINING

The Indian mother was the spiritual teacher of the child, as well as its tender nurse, and she brought its developing soul before the "Great Mystery" as soon as she was aware of its coming. At the age of five to eight years, she turned her boy over to his father

Beads, Oglala Lakota. The young girls assisted their mothers in all things in order to become the owner of their own homes at the time of their marriages

for manly training, and to the grandparents for traditional instruction, but the girl child remained under her close and thoughtful supervision. She preserved man from soul-killing materialism by herself owning what few possessions they had, and thus branding possession as feminine. The movable home was hers, with all its belongings, and she ruled there unquestioned. She was, in fact, the moral salvation of the race; all virtue was entrusted to her, and her position was recognized by all. It was held in all gentleness and discretion, under the rule that no woman could talk much or loudly until she became a grandmother.

The young maiden has not only the experience of her mother and grandmother, and the accepted rules of her people for a guide, but she humbly seeks to learn a lesson from ants, bees, spiders, beavers, and badgers. She studies the family life of the birds, so exquisite in its emotional intensity and its patient devotion, until she seems to feel the universal mother-heart beating in her own breast. In due time the child takes of his own accord the attitude of prayer, and speaks reverently of the Powers. He thinks that he is a blood brother to all living creatures, and the storm wind is to him a messenger of the "Great Mystery."

Orphans and the aged are invariably cared for, not only by their next of kin, but by the whole clan. It is the loving parent's pride to have his daughters visit the unfortunate and the helpless, carry them food, comb their hair, and mend their garments. A girl who failed in her charitable duties was held to be unworthy of the name.

Oesedah was my beautiful younger cousin. Perhaps none of my early playmates are more vividly remembered than is this

Piegan play tipi

Sioux doll

The way that young girls play with dolls to imitate their mothers has never changed

Katie Blue Thunder, Brule Dakota

Crow girl with doll in cradle board

Girls with toy tipis and dolls, unknown Cheyenne

little maiden. The name given her by a noted medicine-man was Makah-oesetopah-win. It means The-four-corners-of-the-earth. As she was rather small, the abbreviation was considered more appropriate, hence Oesedah became her common name.

Although she had a very good mother, my grandmother, Uncheedah, was her efficient teacher and chaperon. Such knowledge as my grandmother deemed suitable to a maiden was duly impressed upon her susceptible mind. Oesedah was my companion at home; and when I returned from my play at evening, she would have a hundred questions ready for me to answer. Some of these were questions concerning our everyday life, and others were more difficult problems which had suddenly dawned upon her active mind. Whatever had occurred to interest her during the day was immediately repeated for my benefit.

This young maiden carries a spoon made from a buffalo horn in her hand

There were certain questions upon which Oesedah held me to be authority, and asked with the hope of increasing her little store of knowledge. I occasionally referred to little Oesedah in the same manner, and I always accepted her explanation of any matter upon which I had been advised to consult her, because I knew the source of her wisdom. In this simple way we were made to be teachers of one another.

We also had many curious wild pets. There were young foxes, bears, wolves, raccoons, fawns, buffalo calves and birds of all kinds, tamed by various boys. My pets were different at different times.

We were once very short of provisions in the winter time. My uncle, our only means of support, was sick; and besides, we were separated from the rest of the tribe and in a region where there was little game of any

A Sioux woman plucking quills from a porcupine skin. Women softened and dyed the quills before they used them to decorate clothing.

kind. Oesedah had a pet squirrel, and as soon as we began to economize our food she gave portions of her allowance to her pet.

A woman preparing a buffalo hide

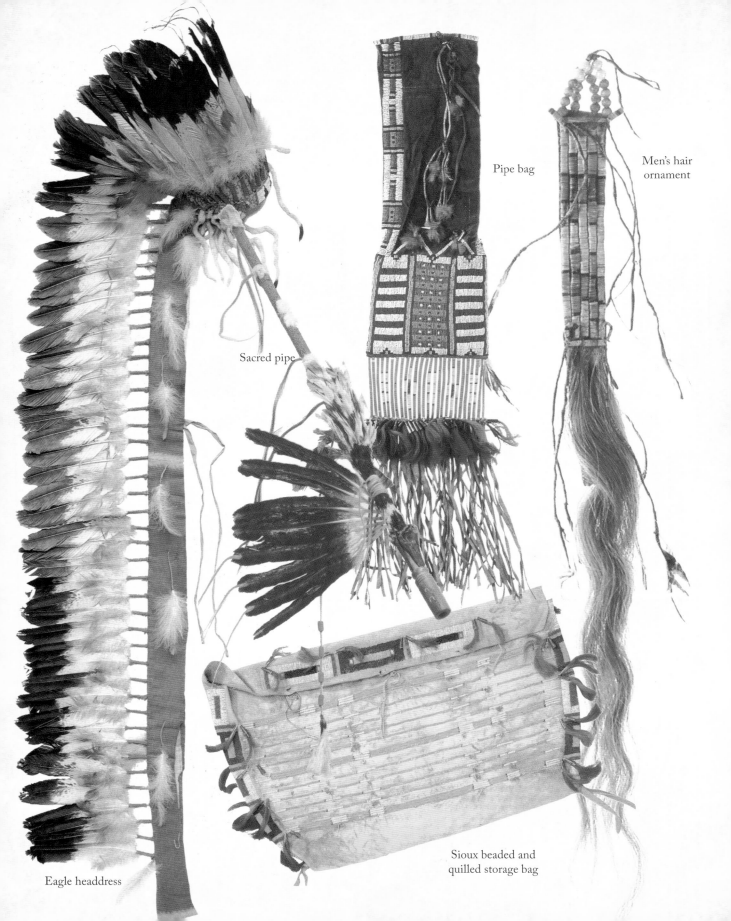

Pipe bag

Men's hair ornament

Sacred pipe

Eagle headdress

Sioux beaded and quilled storage bag

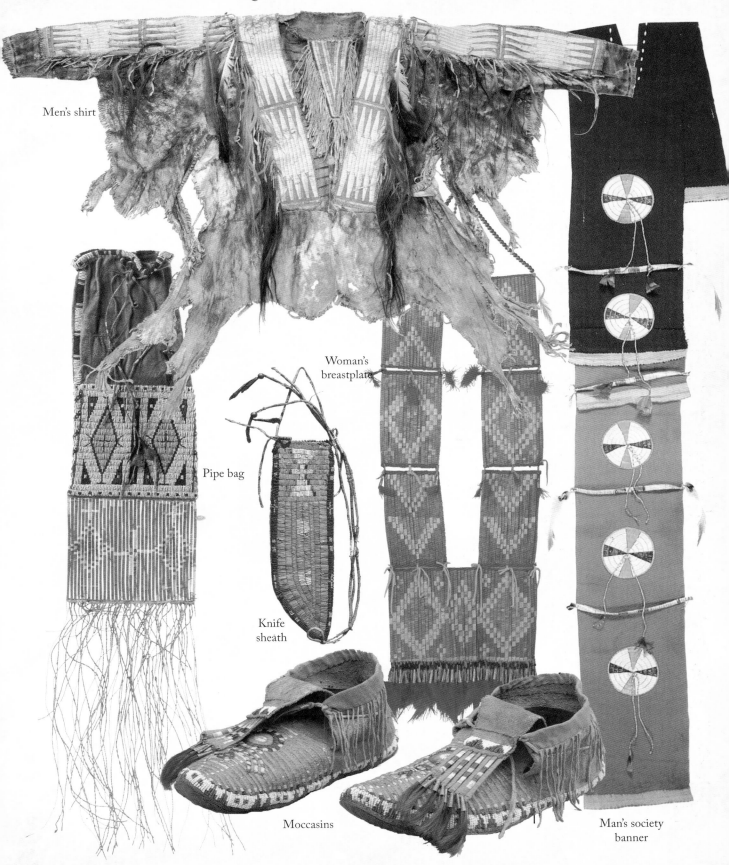

Men's shirt

Pipe bag

Woman's breastplate

Knife sheath

Moccasins

Man's society banner

At last we were reduced very much, and the prospect of obtaining anything soon being gloomy, my grandmother reluctantly suggested that the squirrel should be killed for food. Thereupon my little cousin cried, and said: "Why cannot we all die alike wanting? The squirrel's life is as dear to him as ours to us," and clung to it. Fortunately, relief came in time to save her pet.

INSIGHTS INTO THE DAILY LIFE OF WOMEN

Our native women gathered all the wild rice, roots, berries and fruits which formed an important part of our food. This was distinctively a woman's work. Uncheedah (grandmother) understood these matters perfectly, and it became a kind of instinct with her to know just where to look for each edible variety and at what season of the year. This sort of labor gave the Indian women every opportunity to observe and study Nature after their fashion; and in this Uncheedah was more acute than most of the men. The abilities of her boys were not all inherited from their father; indeed, the stronger family traits came obviously from her. She was a leader among the native women, and they came to her, not only for medical aid, but for advice in all their affairs.

Picking buffalo-berries, Mandan

At the stream collecting water
Opposite: Gathering buffalo-berries

Crow women by the Little Big
Horn river

The young girls assisted their
mothers in many daily tasks

Mother and child collect grains in their canoe

Indian maiden holding rushes

Assembling the tipi.

The women owned the home—the tipi—and all household items in it. They were also responsible for assembling the tipi.

In bravery she equaled any of the men. Once, when we were roaming over a region occupied by other tribes, and on a day when most of the men were out upon the hunt, a party of hostile Indians suddenly appeared. Although there were a few men left at home, they were taken by surprise at first and scarcely knew what to do, when this woman came forward and advanced alone to meet our foes. She had gone some distance when some of the men followed her. She met the strangers and offered her hand to them. They accepted her friendly greeting; and as a result of her brave act we were left unmolested and at peace.

Wife of Slow Bull, Oglala Lakota
Background: Apsaroke on horseback

THE MAIDEN'S FEAST

It was a custom of the Plains Indians to hold peaceful meetings in summer, at which times they would vie with one another in friendliness and generosity. Each family would single out a family of another tribe as special guests of honor. Valuable horses and richly adorned garments were freely given at the feasts and dances. During these intertribal reunions the contests between the tribes were recalled and their events rehearsed, the dead heroes on both sides receiving special tributes of honor.

There were many peculiar customs among the Indians of an earlier period,

some of which tended to strengthen the character of the people and preserve their purity. Perhaps the most unique of these was the annual "feast of maidens." The casual observer would scarcely understand the full force and meaning of this ceremony.

The last one that I ever witnessed was given at Fort Ellis, Manitoba, about the year 1871. In this spot there was a reunion of all the renegade Sioux on the one hand and of the Assiniboines and Crees, the Canadian tribes, on the other. They were friendly. The matter was not formally arranged, but it was usual for all the tribes to meet here in the month of July.

When circumstances are favorable,

Blood, Piegan, and Sarsi encampment, c. 1900

the Indians are the happiest people in the world. There were entertainments every single day, which everybody had the fullest opportunity to see and enjoy. If anything, the poorest profited the most by these occasions, because a feature in each case was the giving away of wealth to the needy in honor of the event. At any public affair, involving the pride and honor of a prominent family, there must always be a distribution of valuable presents.

One bright summer morning, while we were still at our meal of jerked buffalo meat, we heard the herald of the *Wahpeton* band upon his calico pony as he rode around our circle.

"White Eagle's daughter, the maiden Red Star, invites all the maidens of all the tribes to come and partake of her feast. All pure maidens are invited. Red Star also invites the young men to be present, to see

Two Crow girls

that no unworthy maiden should join in the feast."

The herald soon completed the rounds of the different camps, and it was not long before the girls began to gather in great numbers. This particular feast was looked upon as a semi-sacred affair. It would be desecration for any to attend who was not perfectly virtuous. Hence it was regarded as an opportune time for the young men to satisfy themselves as to who were the virtuous maids of the tribe.

There were apt to be surprises before the end of the day. Any young man was permitted to challenge any maiden whom he knew to be unworthy. But woe to him who could not prove his case. It meant little short of death to the man who endeavored to disgrace a woman without cause.

The young boys had a similar feast of their own, in which the eligibles were those who had never spoken to a girl in the way of courtship. It was considered ridiculous so to do before attaining some honor as a warrior, and the novices prided themselves greatly upon their self control.

From the various camps the girls came singly or in groups, dressed in bright-colored calicoes or in heavily fringed and beaded buckskin. Their smooth cheeks and the central part of their glossy hair was touched with vermilion.

The maidens' circle was formed about a cone shaped rock which stood upon its base. This was painted red. Beside it two new arrows were lightly stuck into the ground. This is a sort of altar, to which each maiden comes before taking her assigned place in the circle, and lightly touches first the stone and then the arrows. By this oath she declares her purity.

the chaperons glared at him as if to deter him from his purpose. But with a steady step he passed them by and approached the maidens' circle.

At last he stopped behind a pretty Assiniboine maiden of good family and said:

"I am sorry, but, according to custom, you should not be here."

The girl arose in confusion, but she soon recovered her self-control.

"What do you mean?" she demanded, indignantly. "Three times you have come to court me, but each time I have refused to listen to you. I turned my back upon you.

Twice I was with my friend Mashtinna. She can tell the people that this is true. The third time I had gone for water when you intercepted me and begged me to stop and listen. I refused because I did not know you. My chaperon, Makatopawee, knows that I was gone but a few minutes. I never saw you anywhere else."

The young man was unable to answer this unmistakable statement of facts, and it became apparent that he had sought to revenge himself for her repulse.

"Woo! woo! Carry him out!" was the order of the chief of the Indian police, and the audacious youth was hurried away into the nearest ravine to be chastised.

Lizzie Bear Foot, Dakota

There was never a more gorgeous assembly of the kind than this one. The day was perfect.

The whole population of the region had assembled, and the maidens came shyly into the circle. The simple ceremonies observed prior to the serving of the food were in progress, when among a group of *Wahpeton* Sioux young men there was a stir of excitement. All the maidens glanced nervously toward the scene of the disturbance. Soon a tall youth emerged from the throng of spectators and advanced toward the circle. Every one of

Red Fish's daughter, Sioux

The young woman who had thus established her good name returned to the circle, and the feast was served. The "maidens' song" was sung, and four times they danced in a ring around the altar. Each maid as she departed once more took her oath to remain pure until she should meet her husband.

INDIAN COURTSHIP

Indian courtship is very peculiar in many respects; but when you study their daily life you will see the philosophy of their etiquette of love-making. There was no parlor courtship; the life was largely out-of-doors, which was very favorable to the young men.

In a nomadic life where the female members of the family have entire control of domestic affairs, the work is divided among them all. Very often the bringing of the wood and water devolves upon the

Cutting rushes, Mandan

young maids, and the spring or the woods become the battle-ground of love's warfare. The nearest water may be some distance from the camp, which is all the better. Sometimes, too, there is no wood to be had; and in that case, one would see the young women scattered all over the prairie, gathering buffalo chips for fuel.

This is the way the red men go about to induce the aboriginal maids to listen to their suit. As soon as the youth has returned from the war-path or the chase, he puts on his porcupine-quill embroidered moccasins and leggings, and folds his best robe about him. He brushes his long, glossy hair with a brush made from the tail of the porcupine, perfumes it with scented grass or leaves, then arranges it in two plaits with an otter skin or some other ornament. If he is a warrior, he adds an eagle feather or two.

If he chooses to ride, he takes his best pony. He jumps upon its bare back, simply throwing a part of his robe under him to serve as a saddle, and holding the end of a lariat tied about the animal's neck. He guides him altogether by the motions of his body. These wily ponies seem to enter into the spirit of the occasion, and very often capture the eyes of the maid by their graceful movements, in perfect obedience to their master.

The general custom is for the young men to pull their robes over their heads, leaving only a slit to look through. Sometimes the same is done by the maiden—especially in public courtship.

He approaches the girl while she is coming from the spring. He takes up his position directly in her path. If she is in a hurry or does not care to stop, she goes around him; but if she is willing to stop

Young women collecting herbs

the night. He must be a smart young man to do that undetected, for the grandmother, her chaperon, is usually "all ears."

The night walker, Cheyenne

and listen she puts down on the ground the vessel of water she is carrying.

Very often at the first meeting the maiden does not know who her lover is. He does not introduce himself immediately, but waits until a second meeting. Sometimes she does not see his face at all; and then she will try to find out who he is and what he looks like before they meet again. If he is not a desirable suitor, she will go with her chaperon and end the affair there.

There are times when maidens go in twos, and then there must be two young men to meet them.

There is some courtship in the night time; either in the early part of the evening, on the outskirts of dances and other public affairs, or after everybody is supposed to be asleep. This is the secret courtship. The youth may pull up the tent pins just back of his sweetheart and speak with her during

Elopements are common. There are many reasons for a girl or a youth to defer their wedding. It may be from personal pride of one or both. The well-born are married publicly, and many things are given away in their honor. The maiden may desire to attend a certain number of maidens' feasts before marrying. The youth may be poor, or he may wish to achieve another honor before surrendering to a woman.

When we lived our natural life, there was much singing of war songs, medicine,

Brule serenade

Flute made of wood,
hide, and sinew; probably
Pawnee, c. 1830s

hunting and love songs. Sometimes there were few words or none, but everything was understood by the inflection.

The crude musical instrument of the Sioux, the flute, was made to appeal to the susceptible ears of the maidens late into the night. There comes to me now the picture of two young men with their robes over their heads, and only a portion of the hand-made and carved *chotanka*, the flute, protruding from its folds. I can see all the maidens slyly turn their heads to listen.

MARRIAGE AND FAMILY

There was no religious ceremony connected with marriage among us, while on the other hand the relation between man and woman was regarded as in itself mysterious and holy. It appears that where marriage is solemnized by the church and blessed by the priest, it may at the same time be surrounded with customs and ideas of a frivolous, superficial, and even prurient character. We believed that two who love should be united in secret, before the public acknowledgment of their union, and should taste their apotheosis with nature. The betrothal might or might not be discussed and approved by the parents, but in either case it was customary for the young pair to disappear into the wilderness, there to pass some days or weeks in perfect seclusion and dual solitude, afterward returning to the village as man and wife. An exchange of presents and entertainments between the two families usually followed, but the nuptial blessing was given by the High Priest of God, the most reverend and holy Nature.

The family was not only the social unit, but also the unit of government. The clan is nothing more than a larger family, with its patriarchal chief as the natural head, and the union of several clans by inter-marriage and voluntary connection constitutes the tribe. The very name of our tribe, Dakota, means Allied People. The remoter degrees of kinship were fully recognized, and that not as a matter of form only: first cousins were known as brothers and sisters; the name of "cousin" constituted binding claim,

"The heart of the family is the mother because life comes from her." —Onondaga Proverb

and our rigid morality forbade marriage between cousins in any known degree, or in other words within the clan.

The household proper consisted of a man with one or more wives and their children, all of whom dwelt amicably together, often under one roof, although some men of rank and position provided a separate lodge for each wife. There were, indeed, few plural marriages except among the older and leading men, and plural wives were usually, though not necessarily, sisters. A marriage might honorably be dissolved for cause, but there was very little infidelity or immorality, either open or secret.

It has been said that the position of woman is the test of civilization, and that of our women was secure. In them was vested our standard of morals and the purity of our blood. The wife did not take the name of her husband nor enter his clan, and the children belonged to the clan of the mother. All of the family property was held by her, descent was traced in the maternal line, and the honor of the house was in her hands. Modesty was her chief adornment; hence the younger women were usually silent and retiring: but a woman who had attained to ripeness of years and wisdom, or who had displayed notable courage in some emergency, was sometimes invited to a seat in the council.

THE FALL HUNT

The month of September recalls to every Indian's mind the season of the fall hunt. I remember one such expedition which is typical of many. Our party appeared on the northwestern side of Turtle Mountain; for we had been hunting buffaloes all summer, in the region of the Mouse River, between that mountain and the upper Missouri.

As our cone-shaped teepees rose in clusters along the outskirts of the heavy forest that clothes the sloping side of the mountain, the scene below was gratifying to the eye. The rolling yellow plains were checkered with herds of buffaloes. Along the banks of the streams that ran down from the mountains were also many elk, which usually appear at morning and evening, and disappear into the forest during the warmer part of the day. Deer, too, were plenty, and the brooks were alive with trout. Here and there the streams were dammed by the industrious beaver.

In the interior of the forest there were lakes with many islands, where moose, elk, deer and bears were abundant. The water-fowl were wont to gather here in great numbers, among them the crane, the swan, the loon, and many of the smaller kinds. The forest also was filled with a great variety of birds. Here the partridge drummed his loudest, while the whippoorwill sang with spirit, and the hooting owl reigned in the night.

To me, as a boy, this wilderness was a paradise. It was a land of plenty. To be sure, we did not have any of the luxuries of civilization, but we had every convenience and opportunity and luxury of Nature.

As soon as hunting in the woods began, the customs regulating it were established. The council teepee no longer existed. A hunting bonfire was kindled every morning at daybreak, at which each brave must appear and report. As a rule, the hunters started before sunrise, and the brave who was announced throughout the camp as

Crow archer

the first one to return with a deer on his back, was a man to be envied.

Scarcely had the men disappeared in the woods each morning than all the boys sallied forth, apparently engrossed in their games and sports, but in reality competing actively with one another in quickness of observation. As the day advanced, they all kept the sharpest possible lookout. Suddenly there would come the shrill "*Woo-coo-hoo!*" at the top of a boy's voice, announcing the bringing in of a deer. Immediately all the other boys took up the cry, each one bent on getting ahead of the rest. Now we all saw the brave Wacoota fairly bent over by his burden, a large deer which he carried on his shoulders. His fringed buckskin shirt was besprinkled with blood. He threw down the deer at the door of his wife's mother's home, according to custom, and then walked proudly to his own. At the door of his father's teepee he stood for a moment straight as a pine-tree, and then entered.

When a bear was brought in, a hun-dred or more of these urchins were wont to make the woods resound with their voices: "Wah! wah! wah! Wah! wah! wah! The brave White Rabbit brings a bear! Wah! wah! wah!"

All day these sing-song cheers were kept up, as the game was brought in. At last, toward the close of the afternoon, all the hunters had returned, and happiness and contentment reigned absolute, in a fashion which I have never observed among the white people, even in the best of circumstances. The men were lounging and smoking; the women actively engaged in the preparation of the evening meal, and the care of the meat. The choicest of the game was cooked and offered to the Great Mystery, with all the accompanying ceremonies. This we called the "medicine feast." Even the women, as they lowered the boiling pot, or the fragrant roast of venison ready to serve, would first whisper: "Great Mystery, do thou partake of this venison, and still be gracious!" This was the commonly said "grace."

WILD HARVESTS

When our people lived in Minnesota, a good part of their natural subsistence was furnished by the wild rice, which grew abundantly in all of that region. Around the shores and all over some of the innumerable lakes of the "Land of Sky-blue Water" was this wild cereal found. Indeed, some of the watery fields in those days might be compared in extent and fruitfulness with the fields of wheat on Minnesota's magnificent farms today.

The wild rice harvesters came in groups of fifteen to twenty families to a lake, depending upon the size of the harvest. Some of the Indians hunted buffalo upon the prairie at this season, but there were more who preferred to go to the lakes to gather wild rice, fish, gather berries and hunt the deer. There was an abundance of water-

fowls among the grain; and really no season of the year was happier than this.

The camping-ground was usually an attractive spot, with shade and cool breezes off the water. The people, while they pitched their teepees upon the heights, if possible, for the sake of a good outlook, actually lived in their canoes upon the placid waters. The happiest of all, perhaps, were the young maidens, who were all day long in their canoes, in twos or threes, and when

Seth Eastman, *Harvesting Wild Rice*, 1848

The Rush Gatherer, Kutenai, c. 1906

tired of gathering the wild cereal, would sit in the boats doing their needle-work.

August is the harvest month. There were many preliminary feasts of fish, ducks and venison, and offerings in honor of the "Water Chief," so that there might not be any drowning accident during the harvest. The preparation consisted of a series of feasts and offerings for many days, while women and men were making birch canoes, for nearly every member of the family must be provided with one for this occasion. The blueberry and huckleberry-picking also preceded the rice-gathering.

There were social events which enlivened the camp of the harvesters; such as maidens' feasts, dances and a canoe regatta or two, in which not only the men were participants, but women and young girls as well.

On the appointed day all the canoes were carried to the shore and placed upon the water with prayer and propitiatory offerings. Each family took possession of the allotted field, and tied all the grain in bundles of convenient size, allowing it to stand for a few days. Then they again entered the lake, assigning two persons to each canoe. One manipulated the paddle, while the foremost one gently drew the heads of each bundle toward him and gave it a few strokes with a light rod. This caused the rice to fall into the bottom of the craft. The field was traversed in this manner back and forth until finished.

PREPARING THE RICE FOR USE

Minnesota Ojibway woman drying the rice in the sun on a birch bark mat

A scaffold for drying wild rice over a slow-burning fire to cure the grain

This was the pleasantest and easiest part of the harvest toil. The real work was when they prepared the rice for use. First of all, it must be made perfectly dry. They would spread it upon buffalo robes and mats, and sometimes upon layers of coarse swamp grass, and dry it in the sun. If the time was short, they would make a scaffold and spread upon it a certain thickness of the green grass and afterward the rice. Under this a fire was made, taking care that the grass did not catch fire.

When all the rice is gathered and dried, the hulling begins. A round hole is dug about two feet deep and the same in diameter. Then the rice is heated over a fireplace, and emptied into the hole while it is hot. A young man, having washed his feet and put on a new pair of moccasins, treads upon it until all is hulled. The women then pour it upon a robe and begin to shake it so that the chaff will be separated by the wind. Some of the rice is browned before being hulled.

During the hulling time there were prizes offered to the young men who can hull quickest and best. There were sometimes from twenty to fifty youths dancing with their feet in these holes.

Pretty moccasins were brought by shy maidens to the youths of their choice, asking them to hull rice. There were daily entertainments which deserved some such name as "hulling bee"—at any rate, we all enjoyed them hugely. The girls brought with them plenty of good things to eat.

When all the rice was prepared for the table, the matter of storing it must be determined. Caches were dug by each family in a concealed spot, and carefully lined with dry

Women holding birch bark winnowing trays toss wild rice into the air to let the wind separate the grain from the chaff

grass and bark. Here they left their surplus stores for a time of need. Our people were very ingenious in covering up all traces of the hidden food. A common trick was to build a fire on top of the mound. As much of the rice as could be carried conveniently was packed in parfleches, or cases made of rawhide, and brought back with us to our village.

After all, the wild Indians could not be justly termed improvident, when their manner of life is taken into consideration. They let nothing go to waste, and labored incessantly during the summer and fall to lay up provision for the inclement season. Berries of all kinds were industriously gathered, and dried in the sun. Even the wild cherries were pounded up, stones and all, made into small cakes and dried for use in soups and for mixing with the pounded jerked meat and fat to form a much-prized Indian delicacy.

Cheyenne women pounding cherries
Below: Hanging meat to dry outside a tipi at Fort Belknap, Montana, 1905

Sioux elliptical
case parfleche

Finishing a parfleche

Crow woman decorating a hide

Sioux parfleche envelope

Ojibway woman tapping
maple sap

The art of sugar making from the sap of the hard or sugar maple was first taught by the aborigines to the white settlers. In my day the Sioux used also the box elder for sugar making, and from the birch and ash is made a dark-colored sugar that was used by them as a carrier in medicine. However, none of these yield as freely as the maple. The Ojibways of Minnesota still make and sell delicious maple sugar, put up in "mococks," or birch-bark packages.

A woman and her young helper collect sap from a birch tree in the
North woods

Their wild rice, a native grain of remarkably fine flavor and nutritious qualities, is also in a small way an article of commerce. It really ought to be grown on a large scale and popularized as a package cereal. A large fortune doubtless awaits the lucky exploiter of this distinctive "breakfast food."[1]

In agriculture the achievements of the Indian have probably been underestimated, although it is well known that the Indian corn was the mother of all the choice varieties which today form an important source of food supply for the civilized world. The women cultivated the maize with primitive implements, and prepared it for food in many attractive forms, including hominy and succotash, of which the names, as well as the dishes themselves, are borrowed from the red man. Besides maize and tobacco, some tribes, especially in the South, grew native cotton and a variety of fruits and vegetables.

—Charles Eastman

Apache woman hoeing rows of corn

Mikasuki Seminole women, c. 1895, using a wooden mortar and pestles to grind corn

---

[1] Editor's note: Eastman's prediction was made in 1915, well before these grains were widely used in breakfast foods.

THE INDIAN'S VIEWPOINT ON WORKS OF ART

In his sense of the aesthetic, which is closely akin to religious feeling, the American Indian stands alone. In accord with his nature and beliefs, he does not pretend to imitate the inimitable, or to reproduce exactly the work of the Great Artist. That which is beautiful must not be trafficked with, but must only be reverenced and adored.

It must appear in speech and action. The symmetrical and graceful body must express something of it. Beauty, in our eyes, is always fresh and living, even as God Himself dresses the world anew at each season of the year.

It may be artistic to imitate nature and even try to improve upon her, but we Indians think it very tiresome, especially as one considers the material side of the work—the pigment, the brush, the canvas! There is

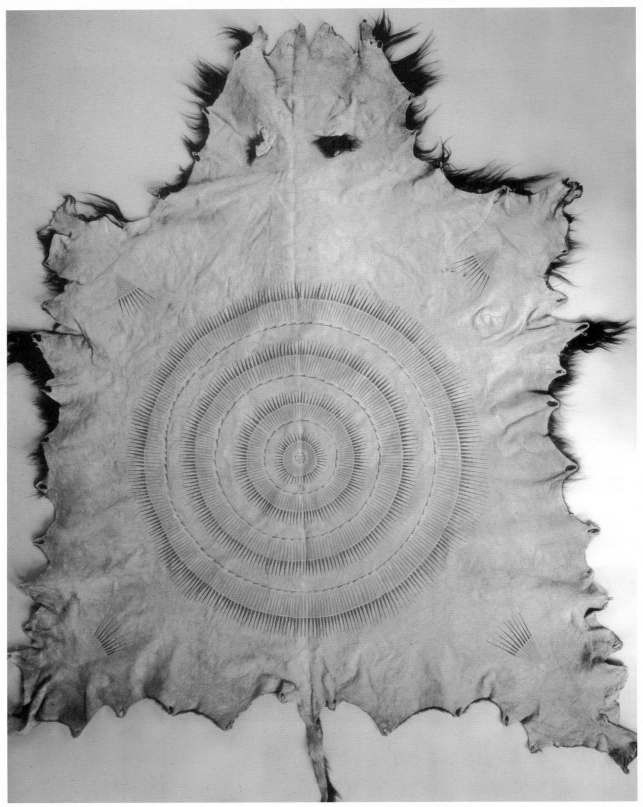

Lakota feathered sun

no mystery there; you know all about them! Worst of all is the commercialization of art. The rudely carved totem pole may appear grotesque to the white man, but it is the sincere expression of the faith and personality of the Indian craftsman, and has never been sold or bartered until it reached civilization.

Now we see at once the root of the red man's failure to approach even distantly the artistic standard of the civilized world. It lies not in the lack of creative imagination—for in this quality he is a born artist—it lies rather in his point of view. I once showed a party of Sioux chiefs the sights of Washington, and endeavored to impress them with the wonderful achievements of civilization. After visiting the Capitol and other famous buildings, we passed through the Corcoran Art Gallery, where I tried to explain how the white man valued this or that painting as a work of genius and a masterpiece of art.

"Ah!" exclaimed an old man, "such is the strange philosophy of the white man! He hews down the forest that has stood for centuries in its pride and grandeur, tears up the bosom of mother earth, and causes the silvery watercourses to waste and vanish away. He ruthlessly disfigures God's own pictures and monuments, and then daubs a flat surface with many colors, and praises his work as a masterpiece!"

This is the spirit of the original American. He holds nature to be the measure of consummate beauty, and its destruction as sacrilege. I have seen in our midsummer celebrations cool arbors built of fresh-cut branches for council and dance halls, while those who attended decked themselves with leafy boughs, carrying shields and fans

of the same, and even making wreaths for their horses' necks. But, strange to say, they seldom made a free use of flowers. I once asked the reason of this.

"Why," said one, "the flowers are for our souls to enjoy; not for our bodies to wear. Leave them alone and they will live out their lives and reproduce themselves as the Great Gardener intended. He planted them: we must not pluck them, for it would be selfish to do so."

The Indian did not paint nature, not because he did not feel it, but because it was sacred to him. He so loved the reality

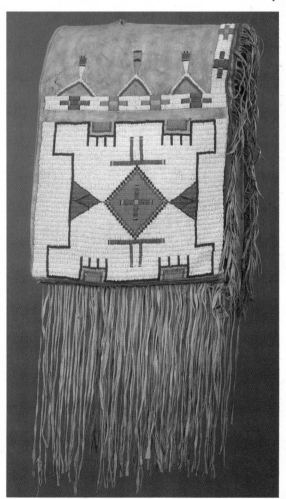

Beaded saddle bag

Sioux beaded bonnet case

that he could not venture upon the imitation. It is now time to unfold the resources of his genius, locked up for untold ages by the usages and philosophy of his people. They held it sacrilege to reproduce the exact likeness of the human form or face. This is the reason that early attempts to paint the natives were attended with difficulty, and there are still Indians who refuse to be photographed.

NATIVE ARTS AND CRAFTS

Indian beadwork in leaf and flower designs is generally modern. The old-time patterns are for the most part simple geometrical figures, which are decorative and emblematic rather than imitative. Shafts of light and shadow alternating or dovetailed represent life, its joys and sorrows. The world is conceived of as rectangular and flat, and is represented by a square. The sky is concave—a hollow sphere. A drawing of the horizon line colored pale yellow stands for dawn; colored red, for sunset. Day is blue, and night black spangled with stars. Lightning, rain, wind, water, mountains, and many other natural features or elements are symbolized rather than copied literally upon many sorts of Indian handiwork. Animal figures are drawn in such a manner as to give expression to the type or spirit of the animal rather than its body, emphasizing the head with the horns, or any distinguishing feature. These designs have a religious significance and furnish the individual with his personal and clan emblem, or coat of arms.

Symbolic decorations are used on blankets, baskets, pottery, and garments of

Sioux man's shirt

ceremony to be worn at rituals and public functions. Sometimes a man's teepee is decorated in accordance with the standing of the owner. Weapons of war are adorned with emblems, and also pipes, or calumets, but not the everyday weapons used in hunting. The war steed is decorated equally with his rider, and sometimes wears the feathers that signify degrees of honor.

In his weaving, painting, and embroidery of beads and quills the red man has shown a marked color sense, and his blending of brilliant hues is subtle and Oriental in effect. The women did most of this work and displayed vast ingenuity in the selection of native materials and dyes. A variety of beautiful grasses, roots, and barks are used for baskets by the different tribes, and some even used gorgeous feathers for extra ornamentation. Each was perfectly adapted in style, size, and form to its intended use.

Pottery was made by the women of the southwest for household furniture and utensils, and their vessels, burned in crude furnaces, were often gracefully shaped and exquisitely decorated. The designs were both imprinted on the soft clay and modeled in relief. The nomadic tribes of the

Unknown beadworker, Apsaroke

Mandan quilled shirt

Comanche moccasins, early 19th century

plains could not well carry these fragile wares with them on their wanderings, and accordingly their dishes were mainly of bark and wood, the latter sometimes carved. Spoons were prettily made of translucent horn. They were fond of painting their rawhide cases in brilliant colors. The most famous blankets are made by the Navajos upon rude hand looms and are wonderfully fine in weave, color, and design.

Sioux woman's dress

This native skill combined with love of the work and perfect sincerity—the qualities which still make the Indian woman's blanket or basket or bowl or moccasins of the old type so highly prized—are among the precious things lost or sacrificed to the advance of an alien civilization. Cheap machine-made garments and utensils, without beauty or durability, have crowded out the old; and where the women still ply their ancient trade, they do it now for money, not for love, and in most cases use modern materials and patterns, even imported yarns and "Diamond dyes"! Genuine curios or antiques are already becoming very rare, except in museums, and sometimes command fabulous prices. As the older generation passes, there is danger of losing altogether the secret of Indian art and craftsmanship.

Navajo weavers

Zuni pottery

Men of all tribes made weapons; men in the southwest were highly skilled in working with silver and turquoise.
Left: Pueblo craftsman making a hole in a piece of turquoise; *Right*: Navajo artisan holding a silver concha belt

INDIAN MUSIC

A form of self-expression which has always been characteristic of my race is found in their music. In music is the very soul of the Indian; yet the civilized nations have but recently discovered that such a thing exists! His chants are simple, expressive, and haunting in quality, and voice his inmost feelings, grave or gay, in every emotion and situation in life. They vary much with tribes and even with individuals. A man often composes his own song, which belongs to him and is deeply imbued with his personality. These songs are frequently without words, the meaning being too profound for words; they are direct emanations of the human spirit. If words are used, they are few and symbolic in character. There is no definite harmony in the songs—only

Left: Middle Woodlands drumstick
Right: Sioux-Cheyenne drum

rhythm and melody, and there are striking variations of time and intonation which render them difficult to the "civilized" ear.

Singing deeds of valor, Dakota

84

Flathead dance

In hunting songs, the leading animals are introduced; they come to the boy to offer their bodies for the sustenance of his tribe. The animals are regarded as his friends, and spoken of almost as tribes of people, or as his cousins, grandfathers and grandmothers.

AN ADVENTUROUS JOURNEY

It must now be about thirty years since our long journey in search of new hunting-grounds, from the Assiniboine River to the Upper Missouri. The buffalo, formerly so abundant between the two rivers, had begun to shun their usual haunts, on account of the first influx of English sportsmen, whose wholesale methods of destruction wrought such havoc with the herds. These

seemingly intelligent animals correctly prophesied to the natives the approach of the pale-face.

As we had anticipated, we found game very scarce as we traveled slowly across the vast plains. There were only herds of antelope and sometimes flocks of waterfowl, with here and there a lonely bull straggling aimlessly along. At first our party was small, but as we proceeded on our way we fell in with some of the western bands of Sioux and Assiniboines, who are close connections.

Each day the camp was raised and marched from ten to twenty miles. One might wonder how such a cavalcade would look in motion. The only vehicles were the primitive travois drawn by ponies and large Esquimaux dogs. These are merely a pair of shafts fastened on either side of the animal, and trailing on the ground behind. A large basket suspended between the poles, just above the ground, supplied a place for goods and a safe nest for the babies, or an occasional helpless old woman. Most of our effects were carried by pack ponies; and an Indian packer excels all others in quickness and dexterity.

The train was nearly a mile long, headed by a number of old warriors on foot, who carried the filled pipe, and decided when and where to stop. A very warm day made much trouble for the women who had charge of the moving household. The pack dogs were especially unmanageable. They would become very thirsty and run into the water with their loads. The scolding of the women, the singing of the old men and the yelps of the Indian dudes made our progress a noisy one, and like that of a town in motion rather than an ordinary company of travelers.

In our nomadic life there were a few unwritten laws by which our people were governed. There was a council, a police force, and an executive officer, who was not always the chief, but a member of the tribe appointed to this position for a given number of days. There were also the wise old men who were constantly in attendance at the council lodge, and acted as judges in the rare event of the commission of a crime.

This simple government of ours was supported by the issue of little sticks about five inches long. There were a hundred or so of these, and

Charles Russell,
The Medicine Man, 1908

Blackfoot travois caravan

they were distributed every few days by the police or soldiers, who kept account of them. Whoever received one of these sticks must return it within five or ten days, with a load of provisions. If one was held beyond the stipulated time the police would call the delinquent warrior to account. In case he did not respond, they could come and destroy his tent or take away his weapons. When all the sticks had been returned, they were reissued to other men; and so the council lodge was supported.

It was the custom that no man who had not distinguished himself upon the warpath could destroy the home of another. This was a necessary qualification for the office of an Indian policeman. These policemen must also oversee the hunt, lest some individuals should be well provided with food while others were in want. No man might hunt independently. The game must be carefully watched by the game scouts, and the discovery of a herd reported at once to the council, after which the time and manner of the hunt were publicly announced.

There were two kinds of scouts, for hunting and for war. In one sense every In-

George Catlin, *Buffalo Hunt under the Wolf-Skin Mask*

dian was a scout; but there were some especially appointed to serve for a certain length of time. An Indian might hunt every day, besides the regularly organized hunt; but he was liable to punishment at any time. If he could kill a solitary buffalo or deer without disturbing the herd, it was allowed. He might also hunt small game.

In the movable town under such a government as this, there was apt to be inconvenience and actual suffering, since a great body of people were supported only by the daily hunt. Hence there was a constant disposition to break up into smaller parties, in order to obtain food more easily and freely. Yet the wise men of the Dakotas would occasionally form large bands of from two to five thousand people, who camped and moved about together for a period of some months. It is apparent that so large a body could not be easily supplied with the nec-

A scout could send a message as far as sixty miles away with a smoke signal

Charles Russell, *The Scouts*, 1902

essaries of life; but, on the other hand, our enemies respected such a gathering! Of course the nomadic government would do its utmost to hold together as long as possible. The police did all they could to keep in check those parties who were intent upon stealing away.

There were many times, however, when individual bands and even families were justified in seeking to separate themselves from the rest, in order to gain a better support. It was chiefly by reason of this food question that the Indians never established permanent towns or organized themselves into a more formidable nation.

THE LAUGHING PHILOSOPHER

There is scarcely anything so exasperating to me as the idea that the natives of this country have no sense of humor and no faculty for mirth. This phase of their character is well understood by those whose fortune or misfortune it has been to live among them day in and day out at their homes. I don't believe I ever heard a real hearty laugh away from the Indians' fireside. I have often spent an entire evening in laughing with them until I could laugh no more. There are evenings when the recognized wit or storyteller of the village gives a free entertainment which keeps the rest of the community in a convulsive state until he leaves them. However, Indian humor consists as much in the gestures and inflections of the voice as in words, and is really untranslatable.

It was a custom with us Indians to joke more particularly with our brothers-and sisters-in-law. But no one ever complained, or resented any of these jokes, however personal they might be. That would be an unpardonable breach of etiquette.

FIRST IMPRESSIONS OF CIVILIZATION

I was scarcely old enough to know anything definite about the "Big Knives," as we called the white men, when the terrible Minnesota massacre broke up our home and I was carried into exile. I have already told how I was adopted into the family of my father's younger brother, when my father was betrayed and imprisoned. We all supposed that he had shared the fate of those who were executed at Mankato, Minnesota.

Now the savage philosophers looked upon vengeance in the field of battle as a lofty virtue. To avenge the death of a relative or of a dear friend was considered a great deed. My uncle, accordingly, had spared no pains to instill into my young mind the obligation to avenge the death of my father and my older brothers. Already I looked eagerly forward to the day when I should find an opportunity to carry out his teachings. Meanwhile, he himself went upon the war-path and returned with scalps every summer. So it may be imagined how I felt toward the Big Knives!

On the other hand, I had heard marvelous things of this people. In some things we despised them; in others we regarded them as *wakan* (mysterious), a race whose power bordered upon the supernatural. I learned that they had made a "fireboat." I could not understand how they could unite two elements which cannot exist together. I thought the water would put out the fire, and the fire would consume the boat if it had the shadow of a chance. This was to me a preposterous thing!

William Cary, *Buffalo Crossing the Missouri*, c. 1890

Train of the Northern Pacific Railway Company

But when I was told that the Big Knives had created a "fire-boat-walks-on-mountains" (a locomotive) it was too much to believe. "Why," declared my informant, "those who saw this monster move said that it flew from mountain to mountain when it seemed to be excited. They said also that they believed it carried a thunder-bird, for they frequently heard his usual war-whoop as the creature sped along!"

Several warriors had observed from a distance one of the first trains on the Northern Pacific, and had gained an exaggerated impression of the wonders of the pale-face. They had seen it go over a bridge that spanned a deep ravine and it seemed to them that it jumped from one bank to the other. I confess that the story almost quenched my ardor and bravery.

Two or three young men were talking together about this fearful invention.

"However," said one, "I understand that this fire-boat-walks-on-mountains cannot move except on the track made for it."

Although a boy is not expected to join in the conversation of his elders, I ventured to ask: "Then it cannot chase us into any rough country?"

"No, it cannot do that," was the reply, which I heard with a great deal of relief.

John Mix Stanley, *Davenport and Rock Island City*, 1855

I had seen guns and various other things brought to us by the French Canadians, so that I had already some notion of the supernatural gifts of the white man; but I had never before heard such tales as I listened to that morning. It was said that they had bridged the Missouri and Mississippi rivers, and that they made immense houses of stone and brick, piled on top of one another until they were as high as high hills. My brain was puzzled with these things for many a day. Finally I asked my uncle why the Great Mystery gave such power to the *Washechu* (the rich)—sometimes we called them by this name—and not to us Dakotas.

"For the same reason," he answered, "that he gave to Duta the skill to make fine bows and arrows, and to Wachesne no skill to make anything."

"Certainly they are a heartless nation. They have made some of their people servants—yes, slaves! We have never believed in keeping slaves, but it seems that these *Washechu* do! It is our belief that they painted their servants black a long time ago, to tell them from the rest, and now the slaves have children born to them of the same color!

"The greatest object of their lives seems to be to acquire possessions—to be rich. They desire to possess the whole world. For thirty years they were trying to entice us to sell them our land. Finally the outbreak gave them all, and we have been driven away from our beautiful country.

"They are a wonderful people. They have divided the day into hours, like the moons of the year. In fact, they measure everything. Not one of them would let so much as a turnip go from his field unless he received full value for it. I understand that their great men make a feast and invite many, but when the feast is over the guests are required to pay for what they have eaten before leaving the house. I myself saw at White Cliff (the name given to St. Paul, Minnesota) a man who kept a brass drum and a bell to call people to his table; but when he got them in he would make them pay for the food!

"I am also informed," said my uncle, "but this I hardly believe, that their Great Chief (President) compels every man to pay him for the land he lives upon and all his personal goods—even for his own existence—every year!" (This was his idea of taxation.) "I am sure we could not live under such a law.

"When the outbreak occurred, we thought that our opportunity had come, for we had learned that the Big Knives were fighting among themselves, on account of a dispute over their slaves. It was said that the Great Chief had allowed slaves in one part of the country and not in another, so there was jealousy, and they had to fight it out. We don't know how true this was.

"There were some praying-men who came to us some time before the trouble arose. They observed every seventh day as a holy day. On that day they met in a house that they had built for that purpose, to sing, pray, and speak of their Great Mystery. I was never in one of these meetings. I understand that they had a large book from which they read. By all accounts they were very different from all other white men we have known, for these never observed any such day, and we never knew them to pray, neither did they ever tell us of their Great Mystery.

"In war they have leaders and war-chiefs of different grades. The common warriors are driven forward like a herd of antelopes to face the foe. It is on account of this manner of fighting—from compulsion and not from personal bravery—that we count no coup on them. A lone warrior can do much harm to a large army of them in a bad country."

It was this talk with my uncle that gave me my first clear idea of the white man.

THE WAY OPENS

I was almost fifteen years old when my uncle presented me with a flint-lock gun. The possession of the "mysterious iron," and the explosive dirt, or "pulverized coal," as it is called, filled me with new thoughts. All the war-songs that I had ever heard from childhood came back to me with their heroes. It seemed as if I were an entirely new being—the boy had become a man!

In the winter and summer of 1872, we drifted toward the southern part of what is now Manitoba. In this wild, rolling country I rapidly matured, and laid, as I supposed, the foundations of my life career, never dreaming of anything beyond this manful and honest, unhampered existence. My horse and my dog were my closest companions. I regarded them as brothers, and if there was a hereafter, I expected to meet them there. With them I went out daily into the wilderness to seek inspiration and store up strength for coming manhood.

"I am now old enough," said I to myself, "and I must beg my uncle to take me with him on his next war-path. I shall soon be able to go among the whites whenever I wish, and to avenge the blood of my father and my brothers." There was one unfortunate thing about my early training; that is, I was taught never to spare a citizen of the United States, although we were on friendly terms with the Canadian white men. The explanation is simple. My people had been turned out of some of the finest country in the world, now forming the great states of Minnesota and Iowa. The Americans pretended to buy the land at ten cents an acre, but never paid the price; the debt stands unpaid to this day. Because they did not pay, the Sioux protested; finally came the outbreak of 1862 in Minnesota, when many settlers were killed, and forthwith our people, such as were left alive, were driven by the troops into exile.

I had already begun to invoke the blessing of the Great Mystery. Scarcely a day passed that I did not offer up some of my game, so that he might not be displeased with me. My people saw very little of me during the day, for in solitude I found the strength I needed. I groped about in the wilderness, and determined to assume my position as a man. My boyish ways were departing, and a sullen dignity and composure was taking their place. I had attained the age of fifteen years and was about to enter into and realize a man's life, as we Indians understood it, when the change came.

One fine September morning as I returned from the daily hunt, there seemed to be an unusual stir and excitement as I approached our camp. My faithful grandmother was on the watch and met me to break the news. "Your father has come—he whom we thought dead at the hands of the white men," she said. He had been imprisoned at Davenport, Iowa, with those who took part in the massacre or in the battles following, and he was taught in prison and converted by the pioneer missionaries. He was under sentence of death, but was among the number against whom no direct evidence was found, and who were finally pardoned by President Lincoln.

One of the first things I observed was my father's reading aloud from a book every morning and evening, followed by a very strange song and a prayer. Although all he said was in Indian, I did not understand it fully. He apparently talked aloud to the "Great Mystery," asking for our safe guidance back to his home in the States. The first reading of this book of which I have any recollection was the twenty-third Psalm, and the first hymn he sang in my presence was to the old tune of Ortonville. It was his Christian faith and devotion which was perhaps the strongest influence toward my change of heart and complete change of my purpose in life.

Many Lightnings, Eastman's father

Assiniboine women and children seated by their tipis, South Dakota

"Modern" Indian home on the reservations, c. 1900

PART II: CULTURES IN COLLISION

MY FIRST SCHOOL DAYS

It was less than a month since I had been a rover and a hunter in the Manitoba wilderness, with no thoughts save those which concern the most free and natural life of an Indian. Now, I found myself standing near a rude log cabin on the edge of a narrow strip of timber, overlooking the fertile basin of the Big Sioux River. As I gazed over the rolling prairie land, all I could see was that it met the sky at the horizon line. It seemed to me vast and vague and endless, as was my conception of the new trail which I had taken and my dream of the far-off goal.

My father's farm of 160 acres, which he had taken up and improved under the United States homestead laws, lay along the north bank of the river. The nearest neighbor lived a mile away, and all had flourishing fields of wheat, Indian corn and potatoes. Some two miles distant, where the Big Sioux doubled upon itself in a swinging loop, rose the mission church and schoolhouse, the only frame building within forty miles.

Our herd of ponies was loose upon the prairie, and it was my first task each morning to bring them into the log corral. On this particular morning I lingered, finding some of them, like myself, who loved their freedom too well and would not come in.

"O-hee-ye-sa! called my father, and I obeyed the call. "It is time for you to go to school, my son," he said, with his usual air of decision. We had spoken of the matter more than once, yet it seemed hard when it came to the actual undertaking.

I remember quite well how I felt as I stood there with eyes fixed upon the ground.

"And what am I to do at the school?" I asked finally, with much embarrassment.

"You will be taught the language of the white man, and also how to count your money and tell the prices of your horses and of your furs. The white teacher will first teach you the signs by which you can make out the words on their books. They call them A, B, C, and so forth. Old as I am, I have learned some of them."

I obeyed my father's wishes, and went regularly to the little day-school, but as yet my mind was in darkness. What has all this talk of books to do with hunting, or even with planting corn? I thought. The subject occupied my thoughts more and more, doubtless owing to my father's decided position on the matter; while, on the other hand, my grandmother's view of this new life was not encouraging.

I took the situation seriously enough, and I remember I went with it where all my people go when they want light—into the thick woods. I needed counsel, and human counsel did not satisfy me. I had been taught to seek the "Great Mystery" in silence, in the deep forest or on the height of the mountain. There were no mountains here, so I retired into the woods. I knew nothing of the white man's religion; I only followed the teaching of my ancestors.

Rev. Alfred L. Riggs, Superintendent of the Santee
Training School

When I came back, my heart was strong. I desired to follow the new trail to the end. I knew that, like the little brook, it must lead to larger and larger ones until it became a resistless river, and I shivered to think of it. But again I recalled the teachings of my people, and determined to imitate their undaunted bravery and stoic resignation.

However, I was far from having realized the long, tedious years of study and confinement before I could begin to achieve what I had planned.

It appears remarkable to me now that my father, thorough Indian as he was, should have had such deep and sound conceptions of a true civilization. But there is the contrast—my father's mother, whose faith in her people's philosophy and train-ing could not be superseded by any other allegiance.

To her such a life as we lead today would be no less than sacrilege. "It is not a true life," she often said. "It is a sham. I cannot bear to see my boy live a made-up life!"

Grandmother! you have forgotten one of the first principles of your own teaching, namely: "When you see a new trail, or a footprint that you do not know, follow it to the point of knowing."

"All I want to say to you," the old grandmother seems to answer, "is this: Do not get lost on this new trail."

"I find," said my father to me, "that the white man has a well-grounded religion, and teaches his children the same virtues that our people taught to theirs. The Great Mystery has shown to the red and white man alike the good and evil, from which to choose. I think the way of the white man is better than ours, because he is able to preserve on paper the things he does not want to forget. He records everything—the sayings of his wise men, the laws enacted by his counselors."

I began to be really interested in this curious scheme of living that my father was gradually unfolding to me out of his limited experience.

"The way of knowledge," he continued, "is like our old way in hunting. You begin with a mere trail—a footprint. If you follow that faithfully, it may lead you to a clearer trail—a track—a road. Later on there will be many tracks, crossing and diverging one from the other. Then you must be careful, for success lies in the choice of the right road. You must be doubly careful, for traps will be laid for you, of which the most dangerous is the spirit-water, that causes a man to forget his self-respect," he added, unwittingly giving to his aged mother material for her argument against civilization.

The general effect upon me of these discussions, which were logical enough on the whole, although almost entirely from the outside, was that I became convinced that my father was right.

My grandmother had to yield at last, and it was settled that I was to go to school at Santee agency, Nebraska, where Dr. Alfred L. Riggs was then fairly started in the work of his great mission school, which has turned out some of the best educated Sioux Indians. It was at that time the Mecca of the Sioux country; even though Sitting Bull and Crazy Horse were still at large, harassing soldiers and emigrants alike, and General Custer had just been placed in military command of the Dakota Territory.

Colonel George Custer

ON THE WHITE MAN'S TRAIL

In the fall of 1874 Charles Eastman began his life at boarding school.

"Remember, my boy, it is the same as if I sent you on your first war-path. I shall expect you to conquer," was my father's farewell. My good grandmother, who had brought me up as a motherless child, bestowed upon me her blessing. "Always remember," said she, "that the Great Mystery is good; evil can come only from ourselves!" Thus I parted with my first teacher—the woman who taught me to pray! *When Ohiyesa parted from his grandmother he said to her,* "Tell my father that I shall not return until I finish my war-path."

The bell of the old chapel at Santee summoned the pupils to class. Our principal read aloud from a large book and offered prayer. I understood that he was praying to the "Great Mystery" that the work of the day might be blessed and their labor be fruitful. A cold sweat came out upon me as I heard him ask the "Great Mystery" to be with us in that day's work in that school building. I thought it was too much to ask of Him. I had been taught that the Supreme Being is only concerned with spirits, and that when one wishes to commune with Him in nature he must be in a spiritual attitude, and must retire from human sound or influence, alone in the wilderness. Here for the first time I heard Him addressed openly in the presence of a house full of young men and young girls!

I hardly think I was ever tired in my life until those first days of boarding-school. All day things seemed to come and pass with a wearisome regularity, like walking railway ties—the step was too short for me. At times I felt something of the fascination of the new life, and again there would arise in me a dogged resistance, and a voice seemed to be saying, "It is cowardly to depart from the old things!"

My father wrote to me in the Dakota language for my encouragement. Dr. Riggs had told him that I was not afraid of books or of work, but rather determined to profit by them. "My son," he wrote, "I believe that

Santee Normal Training School, Santee, Nebraska, c. 1900

Left: Sioux boys, new students at Carlisle, wearing their traditional dress; *Right*: the same boys, three years later, pose in uniform

an Indian can learn all that is in the books of the white man, so that he may be equal to them in the ways of the mind!"

I studied harder than most of the boys. Missionaries were poor, and the government policy of education for the Indian had not then been developed. The white man in general had no use for the Indian. Sitting Bull and the Northern Cheyennes were still fighting in Wyoming and Montana, so that the outlook was not bright for me to pursue my studies among the whites, yet it was now my secret dream and ambition.

Although I could not understand or speak much English, at the end of my second year I could translate every word of my English studies into the native tongue, besides having read all that was then published in the Sioux. I had caught up with boys who had two or three years head start of me, and was now studying elementary algebra and geometry.

One day Dr. Riggs came to me and said that he had a way by which he could send me to Beloit, Wisconsin, to enter the preparatory department of Beloit College. This was a great opportunity, and I grasped it eagerly, though I had not yet lost my old timidity about venturing alone among the white people.

On the eve of departure, I received word from Flandreau that my father was dead, after only two days' illness. He was still in the prime of life and a tireless worker. This was a severe shock to me, but I felt even more strongly that I must carry out his wishes. It was clear that he who had sought me out among the wild tribes at the risk of his life, and set my feet in the new trail, should be obeyed to the end. I did not go back to my home, but in September, 1876,

Sitting Bull, Hunkpapa Lakota

Eastman explains the origin of Sitting Bull's name: It is told that after a buffalo hunt the boys were enjoying a mimic hunt with the calves that had been left behind. A large calf turned viciously on Sitting Bull, whose pony had thrown him, but the alert youth got hold of both ears and struggled until the calf was pushed back into a buffalo wallow in a sitting posture. The boys shouted: "He has subdued the buffalo! He made it sit down!" And from this incident was derived his familiar name of Sitting Bull.

Two Moons, Cheyenne

I started from Santee to Beloit to begin my serious studies.

COLLEGE LIFE IN THE WEST

The journey to Beloit College was an education in itself. At Yankton City I boarded the train for the first time in my life, but not before having made a careful inspection of the locomotive—that fiery monster which had so startled me on my way home from Canada. Every hour brought new discoveries and new thoughts—visions that came and passed like the telegraph poles as we sped by. More and more we seemed to me to be moving upon regions too small for the inhabitants. Towns and villages grew ever larger and nearer together. The streets looked crowded and everybody seemed

to be in the greatest possible hurry. I was struck with the splendor of the shops and the brilliant show windows.

When I reached Beloit on the second day of my pilgrimage, I found it beautifully located on the high, wooded banks of Black Hawk's picturesque Rock River. The college grounds covered the site of an ancient village of mound-builders, which showed to great advantage on the neat campus, where the green grass was evenly cut with lawn.

It must be remembered that this was September, 1876, less than three months after Custer's gallant command was annihilated by the hostile Sioux. I was especially troubled when I learned that my two uncles whom we left in Canada had taken part in this famous fight. People were bitter against the Sioux in those days, and I think it was a local paper that printed the

W. Herbert Dunton, *The Custer Fight*

story that I was a nephew of Sitting Bull, who had sent me there to study the white man's arts so that he might be better able to cope with him. When I went into the town, I was followed on the streets by gangs of little white savages, giving imitation war whoops.

I was now a stranger in a strange country, and deep in a strange life from which I could not retreat. I was like a deaf man with eyes continually on the alert for the expression of faces, and to find them in general friendly toward me was somewhat reassuring. In spite of some nerve-trying moments, I soon recovered my balance and set to work. I absorbed knowledge through every pore. The more I got, the larger my capacity grew, and my appetite increased in proportion. I discovered that my anticipations of this new life were nearly all wrong, and was suddenly confronted with problems entirely foreign to my experience. If I had been told to swim across a lake, or run with a message through an unknown country, I should have had some conception of the task; but the idea of each word as having an office and a place and a specific name, and standing in relation to other words like the bricks in a wall, was almost beyond my grasp. As for history and geography, to me they were legends and traditions, and I soon learned to appreciate the pure logic of mathematics.

At Beloit I spent three years of student life. While in some kinds of knowledge I was the infant of the college, in athletics I did my full share. To keep myself at my best physically, I spent no less than three hours daily in physical exercise, and this habit was kept up throughout my college days.

I found among the students many who were self-supporting, either the sons of poor parents, or self-reliant youth who preferred to earn money for at least a part of their expenses. I soon discovered that these young men were usually among the best students. Since I had no means of my own, and the United States government had not then formulated the policy of Indian education, I was ready for any kind of work, and on Saturdays I usually sawed wood and did other chores for the professors.

Eastman at Knox, 1880

It was here and now that my eyes were opened intelligently to the greatness of Christian civilization, the ideal civilization, as it unfolded itself before my eyes. I saw it as the development of every natural resource; the broad brotherhood of mankind; the blending of all languages and the gathering of all races under one religious faith. There must be no more warfare within our borders; we must quit the forest trail for the breaking-plow, since pastoral life was the next thing for the Indian. I renounced finally my bow and arrows for the spade and the pen; I took off my soft moccasins and put on the heavy and clumsy but durable shoes. Every day of my life I put into use every English word that I knew, and for the first time permitted myself to think and act as a white man.

At the end of three years, Dr. Riggs arranged to transfer me to the preparatory department of Knox College, at Galesburg, Ill., of which he was himself a graduate. Here, again, I was thrown into close contact with the rugged, ambitious sons of western farmers.

As Knox is a co-educational institution, it was here that I mingled for the first time with the pale-face maidens, and as soon as I could shake off my Indian shyness, I found them very winning and companionable. It was through social intercourse with the American college girl that I gained my first conception of the home life and domestic ideals of the white man.

Soon I began to lay definite plans for the future. Happily, I had missed the demoralizing influences of reservation life, and had been mainly thrown in with the best class of Christian white people. With all the strength of a clean young manhood, I set my heart upon the completion of a liberal education.

The next question to decide was what should be my special work in life. It appeared that in civilization one must have a definite occupation—a profession. I wished to share with my people whatever I might attain, and I looked about me for a distinct field of usefulness apart from the ministry, which was the first to be adopted by the educated Sioux.

Gradually my choice narrowed down to law and medicine, for both of which I had a strong taste; but the latter seemed to me to offer a better opportunity of service to my race; therefore I determined upon the study of medicine long before I entered upon college studies. "Hitch your wagon to a star," says the American philosopher, and this was my star!

COLLEGE LIFE IN THE EAST

One summer vacation, at my home in Dakota, Dr. Riggs told me the story of Dartmouth College in New Hampshire, and how it was originally founded as a school

Class photo of Eastman at Dartmouth College

for Indian youth. The news was timely and good news; and yet I hesitated. I dreaded to cut myself off from my people, and in my heart I knew that if I went, I should not return until I had accomplished my purpose. It was a critical moment in my life, but the decision could be only one way. In January, 1882, I set out for the far East, at a period when the government was still at considerable trouble to subdue and settle some of my race upon reservations.

It was a crisp winter morning when the train pulled into Chicago. It seemed to me that we were being drawn into the deep gulches of the Bad Lands as we entered the city. I realized vividly at that moment that the day of the Indian had passed forever.

I was met at the station by friends, who took me to walk upon some of the main streets. I saw a perfect stream of humanity rushing madly along, and noticed with some surprise that the faces of the people were not happy at all. They wore an intensely serious look that to me was appalling.

I was cautioned against trusting strangers, and told that I must look out for pickpockets. Evidently there were some disadvantages connected with this mighty civilization, for we Indians seldom found it necessary to guard our possessions. It seemed to me that the most dignified men on the streets were the policemen, in their long blue coats with brass buttons. They were such a remarkable set of men physically that this of itself was enough to catch my eye.

What is the great difference between these people and my own? I asked myself. Is it not that the one keeps the old things and continually adds to them new improvements, while the other is too well contented

Eastman during college days at Dartmouth College

with the old, and will not change his ways nor seek to improve them?

I went on to Dartmouth College, away up among the granite hills. This was my ambition—that the Sioux should accept civilization before it was too late! I wished that our young men might at once take up the white man's way, and prepare themselves to hold office and wield influence in their native state. Although this hope has not been fully realized, I have the satisfaction of knowing that many Indians now hold positions of trust and exercise some political power.

Athletic Team, Dartmouth College, Eastman, upper left

At Dartmouth College I found the buildings much older and more imposing than any I had seen before. The whole village impressed me as touched with the spirit of learning and refinement. I was a sort of prodigal son of old Dartmouth, and nothing could have exceeded the heartiness of my welcome. Though poor, I was really better off than many of the students, since the old college took care of me under its ancient charter for the benefit of Indians. I was treated with the greatest kindness by the president and faculty, and often encouraged to ask questions and express my own ideas. My uncle's observations in natural history, for which he had a positive genius, the Indian standpoint in sociology and political economy, these were the subject of some protracted discussions in the class room.

For the first time, I became really interested in literature and history. Here it was that civilization began to loom up before me colossal in its greatness, when the fact dawned upon me that nations and tongues, as well as individuals, have lived and died. It was under the Old Pine Tree that the Indians were supposed to have met for the last time to smoke the pipe of peace, and under its shadow every graduating class of my day smoked a parting pipe.

I was very happy when, after my graduation with the class of 1887, it was made possible for me to study medicine at Boston University. The friends who generously assisted me to realize my great ambition were of the type I had dreamed of, and my home influences in their family all that I could have wished for. A high ideal of duty was placed before me, and I was doubly armed in my original purpose to make my education of service to my race. I continued to study the Christ philosophy and loved it for its essential truths, though doctrines and dogmas often puzzled and repelled me.

Eastman in 1890, when he took his Medical Degree at Boston University

At the date of my graduation, in 1890, the government had fully committed itself to the new and permanent plan of educating the young Indians preparatory to admitting them to citizenship. Various philanthropic societies had been formed expressly to help toward this end. These facts gave weight and momentum to my desire to use all that I had learned for their benefit. I soon received my appointment to the position of government physician at Pine Ridge agency in South Dakota, to report October first.

THE HOW AND THE WHY OF THE INDIAN WARS

It is important to understand the underlying causes of Indian wars with the government. There are people today who believe that the Indian likes nothing better than going on the warpath, killing and scalping from sheer native cruelty and lust for blood. His character as a man of peace has not been appreciated. Yet it is a matter of history that the newcomers were welcomed in almost every case with unsuspecting kindness, and in his dealings with the white man the original owner of the soil has been uniformly patient and reasonable, offering resistance only under irresistible provocation.

Whatever may be said for the Indian way of life, its weaknesses are very apparent, and resulted in its early fall when confronted with the complicated system of our so-called modern civilization. With us the individual was supreme; all combination was voluntary in its nature; there was no commerce worthy of the name, no national wealth, no taxation for the support of government, and the chiefs were merely natural leaders with much influence but little authority. The system worked well with men who were all of the same mind, but in the face of a powerful government and an organized army it quickly disintegrated and collapsed. Could the many small tribes and bands have formed a stable combination or league, they might have successfully resisted the invader; but instead they stood separately, though too weak to maintain their dignity by force, and in many cases entered upon a devastating warfare with one another, using the new and more deadly weapons, thus destroying one another. Since there was no central government, but a series of loose confederations of linguistic or allied groups, each of which had its titular head, able to make treaties or to declare war, these bands were met and subdued one at a time.

The transition from their natural life to the artificial life of civilization has been very gradual in most cases, until the last fifty years, when the changes have been more rapid. Those who were first affected were the so-called "Five Civilized Nations" of the South, and the "Six Nations" of New York State, together with some of the now extinct bands in New England, who came in close touch with the early colonists.

One of the first noteworthy Indian wars in the history of America took place in 1675 when King Philip took up arms in Massachusetts. King Philip was the nickname given by the whites to Metacom, the son of the chief who welcomed the Pilgrims in 1620 and helped them survive their first winter in America. A sad feature of this early war was the sufferings of those

Indians who had listened to the preaching of Jesus Christ. In Massachusetts, during King Philip's war, the Christian Indians were treated no better than the "heathen savages." Some were hanged, some imprisoned, and some sold as slaves to the West Indies. At best, they lost their homes and improvements, and nearly perished of cold and hunger.

Thus began a new era in the history of the Indian, inaugurating a kind of warfare that was cruel, relentless, and demoralizing, since it was based upon the desire to conquer and to despoil the conquered of his possessions—a motive unknown to the primitive American.

To be sure the new weapons were more efficient, and therefore more deadly; the new clothing was gayer, but less perfectly adapted to the purposes of primitive life.

1675: KING PHILIP'S WAR

Our "Thanksgiving" holiday commemorates the help the Wampanoag Indians gave to the Pilgrims who arrived at Plymouth, Massachusetts, on the Mayflower in 1620. During the next fifty-five years the English Pilgrims prospered, multiplied and expanded their settlements, while natives were in a slow state of decline from European diseases and loss of tribal lands.

The spark that lit the fire of war arose because English cattle repeatedly trampled Indian corn and the English failed to solve the problem. Members of the Wampanoag tribe then killed

J.L.G. Ferris, *The First Thanksgiving, 1621.* Pilgrims and natives gather to share a meal.

Indeed, the buckskin clothing and moccasins of the Indian were very generally adopted by the white frontiersman. On the other hand, his spiritual and moral loss was great. He who listened to the preaching of the missionaries came to believe that the white man alone has a real God, and that the things he had hitherto held sacred are inventions of the devil. This undermined the foundations of his philosophy, and very

often without substituting for it the Christian philosophy, which the inconsistency of its advocates, rather than any innate quality, made it difficult for him to accept or understand.

A few did, in good faith, accept the white man's God. The black-robed preacher was like the Indian himself in seeking no soft things, and as he followed the fortunes of the tribes in the wilderness,

some English cattle near their camp in what is now Bristol, Rhode Island. A white farmer retaliated by killing an Indian, thus setting in motion a native uprising. After five months of fighting the white settlers launched a surprise attack against a neutral Narragansett camp because the colonists were concerned that the Narragansett might eventually enter the war

> ☛ Consider the validity of this sequence: Contact—Failure to Communicate—European Incursion—Tribal Crisis—Violence—Displacement—Forced Confinement—Forced Assimilation.

on behalf of the other tribes. The colonists massacred the women and children, which enflamed things further. The bitter conflict became a fight to the death on both sides and the Europeans placed "bounties" on American Indians for the first time.

King Philip's War lasted a total of fourteen months and was proportionately one of the bloodiest and costliest wars in American history. More than half of New England's towns were raided by the American Indians and 2,500 (5%) of the colonists were killed. Some 5,000 (more than 50%) of the Indians died and many of those who survived were sent into slavery in the Bahamas, including Metacom's wife and child. Metacom was drawn and quartered and his head was prominently displayed in Plymouth for several years, thus ending the life of the man whose father had welcomed the first colonists to New England. Four native tribes ceased to exist and very few Indians remained in all of southern New England after the war's end.

Capture of Brookfield, Connecticut, during the King Philip's War

the tribesmen learned to trust and to love him. Then came other missionaries who had houses to sleep in, and gardens planted, and who hesitated to sleep in the Indian's wigwam or eat of his wild meat, but for the most part held themselves aloof and urged their own dress and ways upon their converts. These, too, had their following in due time. But in the main it is true that while the Indian eagerly sought guns and gunpowder, knives and whiskey, a few articles of dress, and, later, horses, he did not desire the white man's food, his houses, his books, his government, or his religion.

The two great "civilizers," after all, were whiskey and gunpowder, and from the hour the red man accepted these he had in reality sold his birthright, and all unconsciously consented to his own ruin. Immediately his manhood began to crumble.

This transition period has been a time of stress and suffering for my people. Once they had departed from the broad democracy and pure idealism of their traditions, and undertaken to enter upon the worldwide game of competition, their rudder was unshipped, their compass lost. Then the whirlwind and tempest of materialism and love of conquest tossed them to and fro like leaves in the wind.

Some tribes adopted the customs and civilization of their European conquerors, yet they fared no better. In the early 1800s the Cherokees secured concessions and promises of better treatment from the white men, after which they continued friendly relations and helped in overcoming the Creeks and Seminoles. The Cherokee soon saw the necessity of a stable government and of domestic and agricultural pursuits. They copied the form of their govern-

ment after that of the States. They founded churches, schools, and orphan homes, and upon the whole succeeded remarkably well in their undertaking.

But the white voters wanted their land, thus the policy of removal and concentration of Indians originated early in the nineteenth century, and was carried into effect. "Indian Territory" in Oklahoma was set apart in 1830 as a permanent home for the tribes under the "Indian Removal Act," and the Cherokees and other tribes were removed thither from the Southeastern States. After a terrible journey, in which many died of disease and exhaustion, and one boatload sank in the Mississippi River, those who were left established themselves in the "Promised Land."

Cherokee home

Cherokee homes and farms were in many cases more prosperous than those owned by whites in surrounding areas.

Cherokee school

The Cherokee nation was a long-time ally of the U.S. government. In 1811 the Cherokee refused to join Tecumseh when the Shawnee leader tried to establish an organized alliance of tribes to fight against the white encroachment on Indian land. Instead the Cherokee worked hard to assimilate many aspects of white culture and civilization. They adopted European customs and manners of dress, created a written Cherokee language, published a bilingual newspaper and operated industrial and farm machinery.

The "Five Civilized Tribes" is the term applied to the Cherokee, Chickasaw, Choctaw, Creek, and Seminole tribes, because these tribes adopted many of the colonist's customs and maintained good relationships with their white neighbors.

Cherokee women

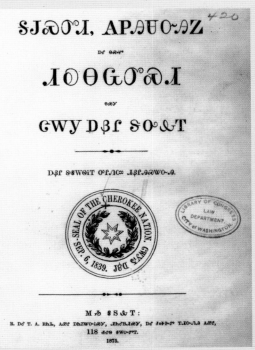

Title page (cover) of the Constitution and laws of the Cherokee Nation published in Cherokee and established in 1827.

Page from the bilingual newspaper *Cherokee Phoenix*

ᏣᎳᎩ ᏗᏐᎢᎦᎢ
CHEROKEE PHŒNIX.

VOL. I. NEW ECHOTA, WEDNESDAY JUNE 4, 1828. **NO. 15.**

EDITED BY ELIAS BOUDINOTT,
PRINTED WEEKLY BY
ISAAC H. HARRIS,
FOR THE CHEROKEE NATION.

At $2.50 if paid in advance, $3 in six months, or $3.50 if paid at the end of the year.

To subscribers who can read only the Cherokee language the price will be $2,00 in advance, or $2,50 to be paid within the year.

Every subscription will be considered as continued unless subscribers give notice to the contrary before the commencement of a new year.

Any person procuring six subscribers, and becoming responsible for the payment, shall receive a seventh gratis.

Advertisements will be inserted at seventy-five cents per square for the first insertion, and thirty-seven and a half cents for each continuance; longer ones in proportion.

All letters addressed to the Editor, post paid, will receive due attention.

of said river opposite to Fort Strother, on said river; all north of said line is the Cherokee lands, all south of said line is the Creek lands.

ARTICLE 2. We the Commissioners, do further agree that all the Creeks that are north of the said line above mentioned shall become subjects to the Cherokee nation.

ARTICLE 3. All Cherokees that are south of the said line shall become subjects of the Creek nation.

ARTICLE 4. If any chief or chiefs of the Cherokees, should fall within the Creek nation, such chief shall be continued as chief of said nation.

ARTICLE 5. If any chief or chiefs of the Creeks, should fall within the Cherokees, that is. north of said line, they shall be continued as chiefs of said nation.

ARTICLE 6. If any subject of the Cherokee nation, should commit murder and run into the Creek nation, the Cherokees will make application to the Creeks to have the murderer killed, and when done; the Cherokee nation will give the man who killed the

William Hambly, (Seal)
his
Big ⊁ Warrior, (Seal)
mark.
WITNESSES.
Major Ridge,
Dan'l. Griffin.
A. M'COY, Clerk N. Com.
JOS. VANN, Cl'k. to the Commissioners.

Be it remembered, This day, that I have approved of the treaty of boundary, concluded on by the Cherokees, east of the Mississippi, and the Creek nation of Indians; on the eleventh day of December, 1821, and with the modifications proposed by the committee and council, on the 28th day of March, in the current year. Given under my hand and seal at Fortville, this 16th day of May, 1822.
CHARLES R. HICKS, (Seal)
WITNESS,
LEONARD HICKS.

Whereas, The treaty concluded between the Cherokees and Creeks, by commissioners duly authorised by the chiefs of their respective na

mitting murder on the subjects of the other, is approved and adopted; but respecting thefts, it is hereby agreed that the following rule be substituted, and adopted; viz: Should the subjects of either nation go over the line and commit theft, and he, she or they be apprehended, they shall be tried and dealt with as the laws of that nation direct, but should the person or persons so offending, make their escape and return to his, her or their nation, then, the person or persons so aggrieved, shall make application to the proper authorities of that nation for redress, and justice shall be rendered as far as practicable, agreeably to proof and law, but in no case shall either nation be accountable.

The 10th article is approved and adopted, and all claims for thefts considered closed by the treaty as stipulated in that article.

The 11th article is approved and adopted, and it is agreed further, the contracting nations will extend their respective laws with equal justice towards the citizens of the other in re

Cherokee National Capitol Building, Tahlequah, Cherokee County

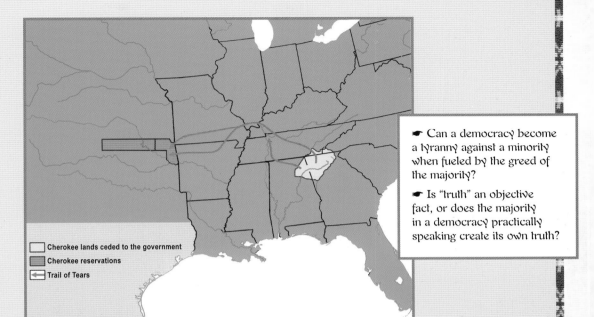

Cherokee lands ceded to the government
Cherokee reservations
Trail of Tears

☞ Can a democracy become a tyranny against a minority when fueled by the greed of the majority?

☞ Is "truth" an objective fact, or does the majority in a democracy practically speaking create its own truth?

Pursuant to the "Indian Removal Act" of 1830, the U.S. government moved all the "Five Civilized Tribes" from their ancestral lands to Oklahoma. In 1838, the military forcibly removed 16,000 Cherokee from their homes in what are now parts of Georgia, Tennessee, North Carolina and Alabama. The families were forced into "concentration camps," the first modern use of concentration camps to imprison an ethnic group. The Cherokee were then marched 1,000 miles to Indian Territory in Oklahoma. As many as 6,000 people, more than one-third of the entire tribe, died in the concentration camps, during and just after that forced march. The Cherokee remember their forced removal as the "Trail of Tears."

Robert Lindneux, *The Trail of Tears*, 1942

FROM NOMADIC LIFE TO RESERVATION LIFE ON THE PLAINS

During a long period the fur trade was an important factor in the world's commerce, and accordingly the friendship and favor of the natives were eagerly sought by the leading nations of Europe. Great use was made of whiskey and gunpowder as articles of trade. Demoralization was rapid. Many tribes were decimated and others wiped out entirely by the ravages of strong drink

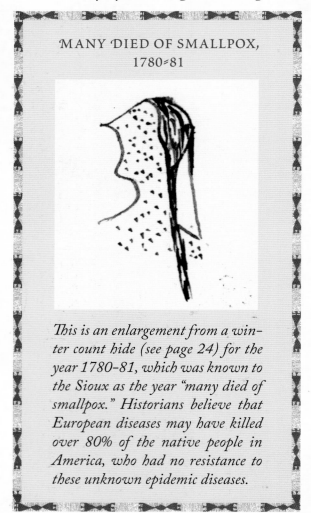

MANY DIED OF SMALLPOX, 1780≠81

This is an enlargement from a winter count hide (see page 24) for the year 1780–81, which was known to the Sioux as the year "many died of smallpox." Historians believe that European diseases may have killed over 80% of the native people in America, who had no resistance to these unknown epidemic diseases.

and disease, especially smallpox and cholera. The former was terribly fatal. The Indians knew nothing of its nature or treatment, and during the nineteenth century the tribes along the Mississippi and Missouri rivers suffered severely. Even in my own day I have seen and talked with the few desolate survivors of a thriving village.

In the decade following 1840, cholera ravaged the tribes dwelling along the great waterways. Venereal disease followed upon the frequent immoralities of white soldiers and frontiersmen. As soon as the Indian came into the reservation and adopted an indoor mode of life, bronchitis and pneumonia worked havoc with him, and that scourge of the present-day red man, tuberculosis, took its rise then in overcrowded log cabins and unsanitary living, together with insufficient and often unwholesome food. During this period there was a rapid decline in the Indian population, leading to the now discredited theory that the race was necessarily "dying out" from contact with civilization.

It must always be borne in mind that the first effect of association with the more advanced race was not improvement but degeneracy. I have no wish to discredit the statements of the early explorers, including the Jesuit priests; but it is evident that in the zeal of the latter to gain honor for their society for saving the souls of the natives it was almost necessary to represent them as godless and murderous savages—otherwise there would be no one to convert!

Of course they were not angels, but I think I have made it clear that they were a God-fearing, clean, and honorable people before the coming of the white man.

In the early 1860s wagon trains were

using the Bozeman Trail through Sioux territory in Wyoming and Montana. The great Sioux Chief Red Cloud led a two year war against the military forts located along the Bozeman Trail. The country was perfectly suited to the guerilla warfare which is characteristic of Indians. Red Cloud would not sign the treaty until he saw forts C. F. Smith and Phil Kearney abandoned. Here is probably the only instance in American history in which a single Indian chief was able to enforce his demands and make a great government back down. At that time it would have cost immense sums of money and many lives to conquer him, and would have retarded the development of the West by many years. Red Cloud's War resulted in the Fort Laramie Treaty of 1868.

RED CLOUD'S WAR & THE FORT LARAMIE TREATY OF 1868

Red Cloud's War was the only major war lost by the U.S. until the military withdrawal from Vietnam in 1975. The Fort Laramie Treaty of 1868 granted permanent ownership of millions of acres of land in South Dakota and Wyoming to the Sioux, including all of the Black Hills. Red Cloud agreed to live in peace at Pine Ridge, South Dakota, on this new Sioux Reservation. The Sioux were also granted the permanent right to camp and hunt on "unceded territory" that includes a large part of what is now Northern Wyoming and Southern Montana.

Sioux met with representatives of the U.S. Army in 1868 prior to the Fort Laramie Treaty

LOCATIONS DESCRIBED BY EASTMAN

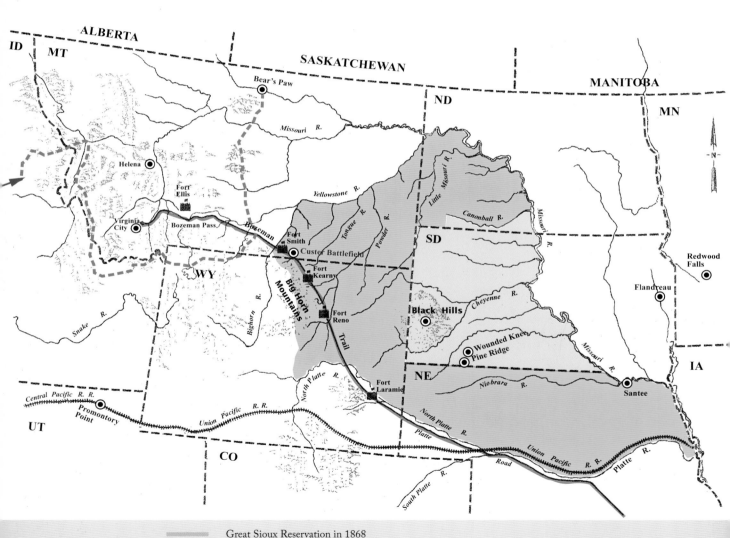

ALBERTA

ID | MT

SASKATCHEWAN

MANITOBA

Bear's Paw

ND

MN

Missouri R.

Helena

Fort
Ellis

Yellowstone R.

Little Missouri R.

Canonball R.

Missouri R.

Redwood
Falls

Virginia
City

Bozeman Pass

Bozeman

Fort
Smith

Tongue R.

Powder R.

SD

Flandreau

WY

Custer Battlefield

Big Horn Mountains

Fort
Kearny

Bighorn R.

Black Hills

Cheyenne R.

Snake R.

Fort
Reno

Trail

Wounded Knee
Pine Ridge

Missouri R.

IA

Central Pacific R. R.

Promontory
Point

Union Pacific R. R.

North Platte R.

Fort
Laramie

NE

Niobrara R.

Santee

UT

North Platte R.

CO

Platte R.

Road

Union Pacific R. R.

Platte R.

South Platte R.

Great Sioux Reservation in 1868
"Unceded Indian territory for hunting buffalo"
Last part of Chief Joseph Trail
Transcontinental railroad
Bozeman Trail
State lines

- BOZEMAN TRAIL was the wagon route through ancestral Sioux territory that was the cause of Red Cloud's War in 1866–68.
- CUSTER BATTLEFIELD is the site of the 1876 battle in which Colonel Custer and 267 troopers and scouts of U. S. 7th Cavalry were killed when they attacked a camp of Sioux and Cheyenne located in the "Unceded Indian Territory."
- CHIEF JOSEPH'S TRAIL is the last part of the 1,700 mile route taken in 1877 by the Nez Perce during their attempt to flee to Canada rather than be relocated to a reservation. They were captured at "Bear's Paw," forty miles from the Canadian border.
- FLANDREAU, SD is the 1870s homestead site of Eastman's father, Many Lightnings.
- FORT LARAMIE, WY is the site where the Fort Laramie Treaty of 1868 was signed.
- FORT SMITH, FORT KEARNEY and FORT RENO were abandoned by the Army under the terms of the Fort Laramie Treaty of 1868.
- GREAT SIOUX RESERVATION under the Fort Laramie Treaty of 1868 was "set apart for the absolute and undisturbed use and occupation of the Indians herein named [the Sioux]." In addition, "the United States now solemnly agrees that no persons except those herein designated and authorized so to do, … shall ever be permitted to pass over, settle upon, or reside in the territory described in this article." Further, "No treaty for the cession of any portion or part of the reservation herein described which may be held in common shall be of any validity or force as against the said Indians, unless executed and signed by at least three-fourths of all the adult male Indians."
- PINE RIDGE, SD is the town on the Sioux reservation where Eastman worked as the government physician in 1890–91.
- PROMONTORY POINT, UT is the site of the 1869 ceremony celebrating the joining of two railroads to complete the transcontinental railroad.
- REDWOOD FALLS, MN is Eastman's 1858 birthplace.
- SANTEE, NE is the site of the mission school attended by Eastman in 1876.
- UNCEDED INDIAN TERRITORY under the Fort Laramie Treaty of 1868 was reserved for Indian hunting and the government "also stipulates and agrees that no white person or persons shall be permitted to settle upon or occupy any portion of the same; or without the consent of the Indians first had and obtained, to pass through the same."
- WOUNDED KNEE, SD is the site of the 1890 massacre of Big Foot's band of Sioux by the U. S. 7th Cavalry.

Chief Red Cloud

good medicine. Our young men herded the horses and made love to the girls. Where the tipi was, there we stayed and no house imprisoned us. No one said, "To this line is my land, to that is yours." In this way our fathers lived and were happy…. Then they sang the Indian songs and would be as the Lakotas were and not as the white men are….

Shadows are long and dark before me. I shall soon lie down to rise no more. While my spirit is with my body the smoke of my breath shall be towards the Sun for he knows all things and knows that I am still true to him….

The Great Mystery is familiar with my spirit and when I die I will go with him. Then I will be with my forefathers. If this is not in the heaven of the white man, I shall be satisfied. The Sun is my father. The God of the white man has overcome him. But I shall remain true to him.

—Red Cloud, Sioux

Years later Red Cloud spoke to his people:

My sun is set. My day is done. Darkness is stealing over me. Before I lie down to rise no more, I will speak to my people.

Hear me, my friends, for it is not the time for me to tell you a lie. The Great Spirit made us, the Indians, and gave us this land we live in. He gave us the buffalo, the antelope, and the deer for food and clothing….

We fought our enemies and feasted our friends. Our braves drove away all who would take our game…. Our children were many and our herds were large. Our old men talked with spirits and made

Chief Red Cloud

118

In 1862 Congress authorized the construction of the transcontinental railroad. The Northern Pacific Railroad started in California and the Union Pacific Railroad started in Omaha, Nebraska. The construction of the railroad started the slaughter of buffalo herds in order to feed the tens of thousands of railroad workers. In 1869 the transcontinental railroad was completed when the two lines met in Promontory Point, Utah.

Joining the tracks for the first transcontinental railroad, Promontory Point, Utah, 1869

The completion of the transcontinental railroad opened the way for a flood of homesteaders, speculators and prospectors to come to the West. The railroad also provided for the transportation of buffalo hides to Eastern markets, thus accelerating the organized slaughter of the buffalo. The railroads represented the final clash of "iron age" machines against the vestiges of the "golden age" culture of traditional indigenous people.

Railroad passengers of the Union Pacific slaughter the bufffalo herds. Painting by Robert Lindneux

THE GOVERNMENT'S SOLUTION: SACRIFICE THE BUFFALO

The Indian race had been an indomitable foe, and occupied a vast region which by 1870 was already beat upon by the tides of settlement. The government determined upon two things: First, the Indians must be induced, bribed, or forced to enter the reservation. Second, they must be trained and persuaded to adopt civilized life, and so saved to the future if he proved to be worth saving, which many doubted. In order to carry out these projects his wild food supply had to be ruthlessly cut off, and the buffalo were of necessity sacrificed. It had been found impossible to conquer the Plains Indians without destroying the buffalo, their main subsistence. Therefore vast herds were ruthlessly destroyed by the United States army, and by 1880 they were practically extinct. Since it was found cheaper to feed Indians than to fight them, the one-time warriors were corralled upon their reservations and kept alive upon government rations.

The buffalo provided all of the needs of the Plains Indians: food, clothing, shelter, and weapons. Black Elk, the famous Sioux holy man, wrote of the sacred significance of the buffalo in Indian culture: "*Tatanka*, the buffalo, is the closest four-legged relative that we have, and they live as a people, as we do. The buffalo represents the people and the universe and should always be treated with respect, for was he not here before the two-legged peoples, and is he not generous in that he gives us our homes and our food? The buffalo is wise in many things, and, thus, we should learn from him and should always be as a relative with him."

At the time the Europeans arrived on the continent there were about thirty million buffalo. By 1880 less than two thousand remained. This virtual extermination was much more than the loss of their main subsistence; for the Indians it was the loss of something that was ineffably sacred—a wound that pierced the heart of every native person.

CHIEF JOSEPH (1840–1904) AND THE NEZ PERCE

Chief Joseph of the Nez Perce tribe, whose Indian name is translated "Thunder Rolling from the Mountains"

In 1877, with 2,000 U.S. soldiers in hot pursuit, Chief Joseph and other Nez Perce chiefs led 800 Nez Perce, fewer than 200 of whom were warriors, toward freedom at the Canadian border rather than submit to relocation onto a reservation. For over three months, the Nez Perce battled and out-maneuvered their pursuers, traveling 1,700 miles across Oregon, Washington, Idaho, Wyoming and Montana. Even the unsympathetic General William Tecumseh Sherman could not help but be impressed with the march, stating that "the Indians throughout displayed a courage and skill that elicited universal praise.... [They] fought with almost scientific skill, using advance and rear guards, skirmish lines, and field fortifications." *The Nez Perce successfully eluded the troops led by General Howard and camped to rest less than 40 miles south of Canada. Unbeknownst to them, a different column of troops led by General Miles came upon their camp from the East. Finally, after a devastating five-day battle with freezing weather conditions and no food or blankets, Chief Joseph negotiated conditions for his tribe's surrender. The battle is remembered in popular history by the words attributed to Chief Joseph at his formal surrender to General Miles.*

I am tired of fighting. Our chiefs are killed … the old men are all dead…. It is cold, and we have no blankets; the little children are freezing to death. My people, some of them, have run away to the hills, and have no blankets, no food. No one knows where they are—perhaps freezing to death. I want to have time to look for my children, and see how many of them I can find. Maybe I shall find them among the dead. Hear me, my chiefs! I am tired; my heart is sick and sad. From where the sun now stands, I will fight no more forever.

—Chief Joseph (Thunder Rolling from the Mountains)

Charles Eastman wrote of this famous escape attempt:

Chief Joseph, who conducted that masterly retreat of seventeen hundred miles, burdened with his women and children, the old men and the wounded, surrendered at last, as he told me in Washington, because he could "bear no longer the sufferings of the innocent." These men were not bloodthirsty or wanton murderers; they were as gentle at home as they were terrific in battle. Chief Joseph never harmed a white woman or child, and more than once helped non-combatants to a place of safety. It is a fact that when Joseph met visitors and travelers in Yellowstone Park, some of whom were women, he allowed them to pass unharmed, and in at least one instance let them have horses. He told me that he gave strict orders to his men not to kill any women or children.

Chief Joseph's own story of the conditions for his surrender was prepared by himself with my help in 1897 when he came to Washington to present his grievances after the government refused to honor the terms of their agreement with the Nez Perce. I sat up with him nearly all of one night; and I may add here that we took the document to General Miles, who was then stationed in Washington, before presenting it to the government. The General said that every word was true. General Miles said to the chief that he had recommended and urged that their agreement be kept, but the politicians and people who occupied the Nez Perce land were afraid if he returned he would break out again and murder innocent white settlers! What irony!

The great Chief Joseph died broken-spirited and broken-hearted. He did not hate the whites, for there was nothing small about him, and when he laid down his weapons he would not fight on. But he was profoundly disappointed in the claims of a Christian civilization. I call him great because he was simple and honest. Without education or special training he outgeneraled the best and most experienced commanders in the army of the United States, although their troops were well provisioned, well armed, and above all unencumbered. He was great finally, because he never boasted of his remarkable feat. I am proud of him, because he was a true American.

Eastman also cited Chief Joseph's explanation to illustrate the manner in which the government "purchased" land from many American Indian tribes:

The famous Nez Perce, Chief Joseph, illustrates his grievance very lucidly in the *North American Review* for April, 1879, in an interview with Bishop Hare of South Dakota.

> "If I ever sold any land to the government," says he, "it was done in this way: Suppose a man comes to me and says: 'Joseph, I want to buy your horse.' I say to him: 'I am satisfied with my horse. I do not wish to sell him at any price.' Then the man goes to my neighbor and says to him: 'I want to buy Joseph's horse, but he would not sell it to me.' My neighbor says: 'If you will buy my horse, I will throw in his horse!' The man buys my neighbor's horse, and then he comes and claims my horse and takes it away. I am under no obligation to my neighbor. He had nothing to do with my horse."

MID-1880s: LARGE PARTS OF THE WEST ARE INDUSTRIALIZED

The famous Anaconda copper smelters and mines, Butte, Montana

Smelters at the base of Anaconda Hill, Butte, Montana

THE FINAL WARFARE ON THE PLAINS

Scarcely was the Fort Laramie Treaty of 1868 completed by which the Sioux ceded a right of way in return for assurances of permanent and absolute possession of other territory, including the Black Hills and Bighorn Mountains, when gold was discovered in these regions. This fact created great excitement and a general determination to dispossess the Sioux of the country just guaranteed to them, which no white man was to enter without the consent of three fourths of the adult men of the tribe.

Public excitement was intense, and the government found itself unable to clear the country of intruders and to protect the rights of the Sioux. It was reported that there were no less than fifteen thou-sand men in the Black Hills district mining and prospecting for the yellow metal. The authority of the United States was defied openly by the frontier press and white people. Then the Indians took matters into their own hands, carried on guerilla warfare against immigrants, and harassed the forts until the army was forced to enter upon a campaign against them.

It is a fact that Sitting Bull was thoroughly opposed to yielding any more territory. No doubt he foresaw the inevitable result. He had taken up the cause of the Eastern Sioux in Minnesota and fought the government in 1862. He had supported Red Cloud in his protests against the establishment of the Bozeman trail, and against the new forts. Unfortunately for him, the other bands of Sioux whom he had helped in their time of need were now all settled

Yellow Shirt, Brule Sioux

upon reservations, so that he had not much support except from Crazy Horse's band, and the so-called "hostiles" of the Western bands. Hostilities began in 1872, culminating in 1876 with the famous "Custer fight," which practically ended the struggle, for after annihilating Custer's command the Indians fled into British America. Four years later Sitting Bull was induced to come in and settle down upon the Sioux reservation.

With Sitting Bull's surrender in 1881, all Indian warfare worthy of the name had now come to an end. There were left Geronimo's small bands of Apaches, who were hunted down in an all but inaccessible country and finally captured and confined in Southern forts. Subsequent "Indian outbreaks," so-called, are usually a mere ruse of the politicians, or are riots caused by the disaffection of a few Indians unjustly treated by their government agents.

American Horse, Oglala Sioux

Geronimo, Apache

SITTING BULL (c.1831–1890)

I met Sitting Bull personally in 1884, and since his death I have gone thoroughly into the details of his life with his relatives and contemporaries. He considered that the life of the white man as he saw it was no life for his people, but hoped by close adherence to the terms of the Fort Laramie Treaty of 1868 to preserve the Big Horn and Black Hills country for a permanent hunting ground. When gold was discovered and the irrepressible gold seekers made their historic dash across the plains into his forbidden paradise, then his faith in the white man's honor was gone forever, and he took his final and most persistent stand in defense of his nation and home. His bitter and at the same time well-grounded and philosophical dislike of the conquering race is well expressed in a speech made before the 1875 Indian council at Powder River. I will give it in brief as it has been several times repeated to me by men who were present.

> Behold, my brothers, the spring has come; the earth has received the embraces of the sun and we shall soon see the results of that love! Every seed is awakened and so has all animal life. It is through this mysterious power that we too have our being and we therefore yield to our neighbors, even our animal neighbors, the same right as ourselves, to inhabit this vast land.
>
> Yet hear me, friends! We have now to deal with another people, small and feeble when our forefathers first met with them, but now great and overbearing. Strangely enough, they have a mind to till the soil, and the love of possessions is a disease in them. These people have made many rules that the rich may break, but the poor may not! They have a religion in which the poor worship, but the rich will not! They claim this mother or ours, the Earth, for their own use, and fence their neighbors away from her, and deface her with their buildings and their refuse. They compel her to produce out of season, and when sterile she is made to take medicine in order to produce again. All this is sacrilege.
>
> This nation is like a spring flood; it overruns its banks and destroys all who are in its path. We cannot dwell side by side. Only seven years ago we made a treaty by which we were assured that the buffalo country should be left to us forever. Now they threaten to take that from us also. My brothers, shall we submit? Or shall we say to them: "First kill me, before you can take possession of my fatherland!"

During the autumn of 1876, after the fall of Custer, Sitting Bull was hunted all through the Yellowstone region by the military. The hostiles were driven about from pillar to post for several years, and finally took refuge across the line in Canada, where Sitting Bull had placed his last hope of justice and freedom for his race. He found that if they had liberty on that side, they had little else; that the Canadian government would give them protection but no food; and that the buffalo had been all but exterminated and his people were starving. He was compelled at last, in 1881, to report to Fort Buford, North Dakota, with his band of hungry, homeless, and discouraged refugees. It was, after all, to hunger and not to the strong arm of the military that he surrendered in the end.

In 1885 Sitting Bull worked in Buffalo Bill's Wild West Show in New York City for four months. He often asked the same question: "How can there be so much poverty in big cities?" Sitting Bull gave away almost all of the money he earned in the Wild West Show to newsboys and hobos. Some of his words were preserved:

All the Indians pray to God for life, and try to find out a good road, and do nothing wrong in this life. This is what we want, and to pray to God. But you did not believe us.

You should say nothing against our religion, for we say nothing against yours. You pray to God. So do all of us Indians, as well as the Whites. We both pray to only one God, who made us all.

—Sitting Bull, Sioux

Sitting Bull and Buffalo Bill Cody

☛ Was there ever any possibility that the Native Peoples could have "won"? If so, what form could this victory have taken? If not, why not?

THE CALAMITY OF EARLY RESERVATION LIFE

The Indian wife ruled undisputed within her own domain, and was to us a tower of moral and spiritual strength, until the coming of the border white man, the soldier and trader, who with strong drink overthrew the honor of the man, and through his power over a worthless husband purchased the virtue of his wife or his daughter. When she fell, the whole race fell with her.

A nation is not conquered until the hearts of its women are on the ground. Then, no matter how brave its warriors nor how strong their weapons, it is done.

—Cheyenne Proverb

Before this calamity came upon us, you could not find anywhere a happier home than that created by the Indian woman. There was nothing of the artificial about her person, and very little disingenuousness in her character. Her early and consistent training, the definiteness of her vocation, and, above all, her profoundly religious attitude gave her a strength and poise that could not be overcome by any ordinary misfortune.

The Indian woman suffered greatly during the transition period of civilization, when men were demoralized by whiskey, and possession became masculine. The division of labor did not readily adjust itself to the change, so that her burdens were multiplied while her influence decreased. Tribe after tribe underwent the catastrophe of a disorganized and disunited family life.

After the destruction of the buffalo the Indians were forced to rely upon the U.S. government for rations of food and clothing. Here Indians are waiting to receive rations.

Typical Indian log cabin, such as Eastman's father lived in at Flandreau, Dakota Territory

As the men have gradually assumed the responsibility of the outdoor toil, cultivating the fields and building the houses, the women have undertaken the complicated housekeeping tasks of their white sisters. It is true that until they understood the civilized way of cooking and the sanitation of stationary homes, the race declined in health and vigor.

Waiting for rations

1884: SECRETARY OF INTERIOR'S ORDER

Many of these demoralizing influences were the result of the Secretary of the Interior's actions in 1884. Dr. Joe Medicine Crow, the Crow tribal historian and the last traditional Crow chief, explains:

In 1884, the Secretary of Interior issued the so-called "Secretary's Order" to "de-tribalize" the Indian people and make them into white men as soon as possible—a unilateral cultural assimilation process. One of the first things they wanted to do was establish a school, a boarding school. The boarding

Nez Perce boy

school was set up about 1890 at Crow Agency with a boy's dormitory, girl's dormitory, the dining room, classrooms, and other facilities. The Crow children were required to be taken to that boarding school and left there, including very young kids, 5, 6, 7 years old. The Indian agent would send out his Indian policemen to collect the children—he had a force of Indian policemen. They were ruthless because they had to try to please the agent and, of course, they get paid, so they were his men, his Gestapo. So, every once in a while they would go out throughout the country and look for kids age 5 and take them away from their parents and bring them to the boarding school. And there they would become like slaves; they were mistreated and some were even killed there. At the boarding school, the children were also forbidden to speak their native language. If they were caught speaking the Crow language they made the children chew a strong soap—it had a terrible taste. The kids also couldn't play any Indian games—they were forbidden to follow anything to do with the traditional culture. If they violated any of these rules they were not allowed to visit with their parents on the weekends or to go home for family visits.

A lot of children died mysteriously. One of my grandfathers, Chief Medicine Crow, took in a little Nez Perce baby boy when the Nez Perce went through Crow country while they were running from the government troops with Chief Joseph. The parents intended to return and pick up the baby after they quit running from the troops, but they never returned. Chief Medicine Crow raised the Nez Perce baby as part of his family. The boy later had to go to government

Girls gathering corn husks to be used as padding in bed mattresses at the St. Francis Mission School on Rosebud, South Dakota, c. 1900

Baking bread at the Willow Creek Boarding School, c. 1907

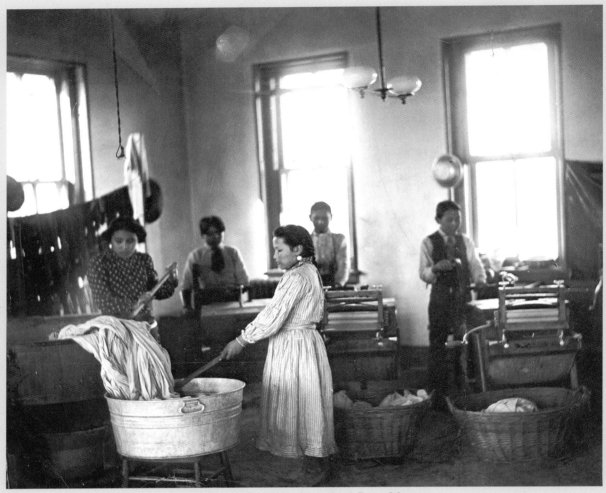

Laundry at the Crow boarding school, Pryor, Montana

boarding school and he died there. No one knows exactly what happened. I think he was punished so hard that he died; this same thing happened to many other children.

When my uncle, Bob Yellowtail, was just five years old, his little old grandmother, her name was Bear Stays by the Side of the Water, took her little tipi and her horses and went to the Wolf Mountains where they hid all summer. But the police found out about it—probably somebody told them. When they found out that he and his grandma were out in the Wolf

Mountains they went out there, looked for them and found them. His father, Yellowtail, followed the police so when they found Yellowtail's mother and his son he rode up and was right there with them. When they took the little boy away from his grandmother they were rough, putting the little boy over the back of the saddle to travel the 35 miles back to Crow Agency. So his father said, "Look he's just a baby. I'll take him to the boarding school tomorrow." The Indian police decided to let the father bring him in, so the next morning they took the little boy to the boarding school at Crow Agency. There are many families that can tell similar stories.

Over time almost every Christian denomination opened churches and schools on the reservation; each family was assigned to become a member of one or another of the churches. The government encouraged this process to help assimilate the Indians because the churches actively tried to convert the Indians away from their traditional ceremonies. Children who went to the church schools were not physically mistreated, so families preferred to send their children to the church schools instead of the government boarding school. By about 1920 the government boarding school at Crow Agency closed because all of the children were going to the church schools. The government thought that if the Indians became Christians then they would turn away from their Crow traditions, and, of course, some Indians did turn away from the traditions; but most Indians embraced Christianity without abandoning their own cultural traditions. There was no problem in the Indian way; everyone had a little different way to pray but everyone was praying to the same, one God, so there was no problem.

The "Secretary's Order of 1884" also prohibited the Indians from practicing all activities related to their culture, including all traditional ceremonies. The reservation police had the power to enforce this Order to prevent any traditional singing and dancing. The Crow people were afraid to even put on their native costumes; they were told to wear overalls, white man's outfits—told to start becoming white men. Our people were forced to become farmers and give up their traditions.

—Joe Medicine Crow,
recipient of the Presidential Medal of Freedom

Boys and girls gardening

A DOCTOR AMONG THE INDIANS

The Pine Ridge Indian agency was a bleak and desolate looking place in those days, more especially in a November dust storm such as that in which I arrived from Boston to take charge of the medical work of the reservation. In 1890 a "white doctor" who was also an Indian was something of a novelty, and I was afterward informed that there were many and diverse speculations abroad as to my success or failure in this new role, but at the time I was unconscious of an audience. I was thirty-two years of age, but appeared much younger, athletic and vigorous, and alive with energy and enthusiasm.

After reporting to the Indian agent, I was shown to my quarters, which consisted of a bedroom, sitting room, office, and dispensary, all in one continuous barrack with the police quarters and the agent's of-

Pine Ridge Agency, 1890

fices. This barrack was a flimsy one-story affair built of warped cottonwood lumber, and the rude prairie winds whistled musically through the cracks. There was no carpet, no furniture save a plain desk and a couple of hard wooden chairs, and everything was coated with a quarter of an inch or so of fine Dakota dust. This did not disconcert me, however, as I myself was originally Dakota dust!

Home of Chief Red Cloud at Pine Ridge Agency, 1891

I had not yet thought seriously of making a life contract with any young woman, and accordingly my place was at the agency mess where the unmarried employees took their meals.

THE "BIG ISSUE"

It so happened that this was the day of the "Big Issue," on which thousands of Indians scattered over a reservation a hundred miles long by fifty wide, came to the agency for a weekly or fortnightly supply of rations, and it was a veritable "Wild West" array that greeted my astonished eyes. The streets and stores were alive with a motley crowd in picturesque garb, for all wore their best on these occasions. Every road leading to the agency was filled with white-topped lumber wagons, with here and there a more primitive travois, and young men and women on ponies' backs were gaily curveting over the hills. The Sioux belle of that period was arrayed in grass-green or bright purple calico, loaded down with beads and bangles, and sat astride a spotted pony, holding over her glossy uncovered braids and vermilion-tinted cheeks a gaily colored silk parasol.

Cheyenne slaughtering cattle, 1901

Toward noon, the whole population moved out two or three miles to a large corral in the midst of a broad prairie, where a herd of beef cattle was held in readiness by the agency cowboys. An Indian with stentorian voice, mounted on a post, announced the names of the group whose steer was to be turned loose. Next moment the flying animal was pursued by two or three swift riders with rifles across their saddles. As the cattle were turned out in quick succession, we soon had a good imitation of the old time buffalo hunt. The galloping, long-horned steers were chased madly in every direction, amid yells and whoops, the firing of guns and clouds of yellow dust, with here and there a puff of smoke and a dull report as one stumbled and fell.

Receiving beef rations, late 1900s

The excitement was soon over, and men of each group were busy skinning the animals, dressing the meat and dividing it among the families interested.

Meanwhile the older women, sack in hand, approached the commissary, where they received their regular dole of flour, bacon, coffee, and sugar. Fires were soon blazing merrily in the various temporary camps scattered over the prairie and in the creek bottoms, and after dinner, horse races and dancing were features of the day. Many white sight-seers from adjoining towns were usually on hand. Before night, most of the people had set off in a cloud of dust for their distant homes.

Crow Indians waiting for rations, c. 1905

Sioux Indians receiving their beef rations, 1893

INTRODUCTION TO THE "GHOST DANCE RELIGION"

Captain Sword, the dignified and intelligent head of the Indian police force, was very friendly, and soon found time to give me a great deal of information about the place and the people. He said finally:

"*Kola* (my friend), the people are very glad that you have come. You have begun well; we Indians are all your friends. But I fear that we are going to have trouble. I must tell you that a new religion has been proclaimed by some Indians in the Rocky Mountain region, and some time ago, Sitting Bull sent several of his men to investigate. We hear that they have come back, saying that they saw the prophet, or Messiah, who told them that he is God's Son whom He has sent into the world a second time. He told them that He had waited nearly two thousand years for the white men to carry out His teachings, but instead they had destroyed helpless small

Sword, Oglala Lakota

nations to satisfy their own selfish greed. Therefore He had come again, this time as a Savior to the red people. If they would follow His instructions exactly, in a little while He would cause the earth to shake and destroy all the cities of the white man, when famine and pestilence would come to finish the work. The Indians must live entirely by themselves in their teepees so that the earthquake would not harm them. They must fast and pray and keep up a holy or spirit dance that He taught them. He also ordered them to give up the white man's clothing and make shirts and dresses in the old style.

Slow Bull, Miniconjou Lakota

Kicking Bear, Miniconjou Lakota

"My friend," Sword went on, "our reservation has been free from this new teaching until the last few weeks. Quite lately this ghost dance was introduced by Slow Bull and Kicking Bear from Rosebud"—a neighboring agency. "It has been rapidly gaining converts in many of the camps. This is what the council today was about. The agent says that the Great Father at Washington wishes it stopped. I fear the people will not stop. I fear trouble, *Kola*."

THE GHOST DANCE

Cheyenne gather for the Ghost Dance ceremony

The Ghost Dance Religion asked the Indians to return to their ancestral traditions and renounce all that came from the white man, including alcohol and violence. Kicking Bear explained: "the Indians who have heard this message and who dance and pray and believe will be taken up in the air and suspended" *during which time the Great Spirit will* "cover the earth with new soil to a depth of five times the height of a man, and under this new soil will be buried all the whites." *After the earth is renewed, those that believe will be* "set down among the ghosts of their ancestors, relatives and friends."

Scenes of Arapaho Ghost Dance
ceremony, 1893

ELAINE GOODALE

Then I met several young ladies, teachers in the boarding school, and a young man or two, and finally Miss Elaine Goodale [from Massachusetts], who was not entirely a stranger, as I had read her articles on Indian education in the *Independent* and elsewhere. Miss Goodale was supervisor of Indian schools in the Dakotas and Nebraska, and she was then at Pine Ridge on a tour of inspection. She was young for such a responsible position, but appeared equal to it in mentality and experience. I thought her very dignified and reserved, but this first evening's acquaintance showed me that she was thoroughly in earnest and absolutely sincere in her work for the Indians. I had laid my plans carefully, and purposed to serve my race for a few years in my profession, after which I would go to some city to practice, and I had decided that it would be wise not to think of marriage for the present. I had not given due weight to the possibility of love.

Events now crowded fast upon one another. It would seem enough that I had at last realized the dream of my life—to be of some service to my people—an ambition implanted by my earlier Indian teachers and fostered by my missionary training. I was really happy in devoting myself mind and body to my hundreds of patients who left me but few leisure moments.

After the second "Big Issue," I had another call from Captain Sword. He began, I believe, by complimenting me upon a very busy day. "Your reputation," he declared, "has already traveled the length and breadth of the reservation. You treat everybody alike, and your directions are under-

Elaine Goodale Eastman

stood by the people. No government doctor has ever gone freely among them before. It is a new order of things. But I fear you have come at a bad time," he added seriously. "The Ghost dancers have not heeded the agent's advice and warning. They pay no attention to us policemen. The craze is spreading like a prairie fire, and the chiefs who are encouraging it do not even come to the agency. They send after their rations and remain at home. It looks bad."

"Do they really mean mischief?" I asked incredulously, for Mr. Cook and I had discussed the matter and agreed in thinking that if the attempt was not made to stop it by force, the craze would die out of itself before long.

THE GHOST DANCE WAR

A religious craze such as that of 1890-91 was a thing foreign to the Indian philosophy. I recalled that a hundred years before, on the overthrow of the Algonquin nations, a somewhat similar faith was evolved by the astute Delaware prophet, brother to Tecumseh. It meant that the last hope of race entity had departed, and my people were groping blindly after spiritual relief in their bewilderment and misery. I believe that the first prophets of the "Red Christ" were innocent enough and that the people generally were sincere, but there were doubtless some who went into it for self-advertisement, and who introduced new and fantastic features to attract the crowd.

I told a visiting government inspector that I still did not believe there was any widespread plot, or deliberate intention to make war upon the whites. In my own mind, I felt sure that the arrival of troops would be construed by the ghost dancers as a threat or a challenge, and would put them at once on the defensive. I was not in favor of that step; neither was Reverend Charles Smith Cook, the Episcopal missionary, who was also called into conference; but the officials evidently feared a general uprising, and argued that it was their duty to safeguard the lives of the employees and others by calling for the soldiers without more delay. As a matter of fact, the agent had telegraphed to Fort Robinson for troops before he made a pretense of consulting us Indians, and they were already on their way to Pine Ridge.

I scarcely knew at the time, but gradually learned afterward, that the Sioux had many grievances and causes for profound discontent, which lay back of and were more or less closely related to the ghost dance craze and the prevailing restlessness and excitement. Rations had been cut from time to time; the people were insufficiently fed, and their protests and appeals were disregarded. Never were more ruthless fraud and graft practiced upon a defenseless people than upon these poor natives by the politicians! Never were there more worthless "scraps of paper" anywhere in the world than many of the Indian treaties and government documents! Sickness was prevalent and the death rate alarming, especially among the children. Trouble from all these causes had for some time been developing, but might have been checked by humane and conciliatory measures. The "Messiah craze" in itself was scarcely a source of danger. Other tribes than the Sioux who adopted the new religion were left alone, and the craze died a natural death in the course of a few months.

At this juncture came the startling news from Fort Yates, some two hundred and fifty miles to the north of us, that Sitting Bull had been killed by Indian police while resisting arrest, and a number of his men with him.

We next heard that the remnant of his band had fled in our direction, and soon afterward, that they had been joined by Big Foot's band from the western part of Cheyenne River agency, which lay directly in their road. United States troops continued to gather at strategic points, and of course the press seized upon the opportunity to enlarge upon the strained situation and predict an "Indian uprising." The reporters were among us, and managed to secure much "news" that no one else ever heard of. Border towns were fortified and cowboys

Indian police reenact the arrest of Hunkpapa Sioux
Chief Sitting Bull at his cabin on the Standing Rock
Reservation, South Dakota, on December 15, 1890

and militia gathered in readiness to protect
them against the "red devils." Certain classes of the frontier population industriously
fomented the excitement for what there
was in it for them, since much money is apt
to be spent at such times. As for the poor
Indians, they were quite as badly scared as
the whites and perhaps with more reason.

During this time of grave anxiety and
nervous tension, the cooler heads among us
went about our business, and still refused to
believe in the tragic possibility of an Indian
war. It may be imagined that I was more
than busy, though I had not such long dis-
tances to cover, for since many Indians accustomed to comfortable log houses were
compelled to pass the winter in tents, there
was even more sickness than usual. I had
access and welcome to the camps of all the
various groups and factions.

Sioux Chief Big Foot's band, later massacred at
Wounded Knee, ready for their Ghost Dance, 1890

WOUNDED KNEE

I had planned to enter upon my life work unhampered by any other ties, and declared that all my love should be vested in my people and my profession. At last, however, I had met a woman whose sincerity was convincing and whose ideals seemed very like my own. She spoke the Sioux language fluently and went among the people with the utmost freedom and confidence. Her methods of work were very simple and direct. I do not know what unseen hand had guided me to her side, but on Christmas day of 1890, Elaine Goodale and I announced our engagement.

Three days later, we learned that Big Foot's band of ghost dancers from the Cheyenne River reservation north of us was approaching the agency, and that Major Whiteside was in command of troops with orders to intercept them. Late that afternoon, the Seventh Cavalry under Colonel Forsythe was called to the saddle and rode off toward Wounded Knee creek, eighteen miles away. The Seventh Cavalry was the same unit that was massacred with Custer at the Battle of the Little Big Horn.

The morning of December 29th was sunny and pleasant. We were all straining our ears toward Wounded Knee, and about the middle of the forenoon we distinctly heard the reports of the Hotchkiss guns. Two hours later, a rider was seen approaching at full speed, and in a few minutes he had dismounted from his exhausted horse and handed his message to General Brooke's orderly. Big Foot's band had been

Burial of the dead after the massacre at Wounded Knee, 1891

Chapel of the Holy Cross, Pine Ridge Agency, used as a hospital for wounded Indians during the "Ghost Dance War"

wiped out by the troops, and reprisals were naturally looked for. The enclosure was not barricaded in any way and we had but a small detachment of troops for our protection. Sentinels were placed, and machine guns trained on the various approaches.

On the day following the Wounded Knee massacre there was a blizzard.

On the third day it cleared, and the ground was covered with an inch or two of fresh snow. We had feared that some of the Indian wounded might have been left on the field, and a number of us volunteered to go and see. I was placed in charge of the expedition of about a hundred civilians.

It took all of my nerve to keep my composure in the face of this spectacle, and of the excitement and grief of my Indian companions, nearly every one of whom was crying aloud or singing his death song. The white men became very nervous, but I set them to examining and uncovering everybody to see if one were living. Although they had been lying untended in the snow and cold for two days and nights, a number had survived.

All this was a severe ordeal for one who

had so lately put all his faith in the Christian love and lofty ideals of the white man. Yet I passed no hasty judgment, and was thankful that I might be of some service and relieve even a small part of the suffering.

In March, all being quiet, Miss Goodale decided to send in her resignation and go East to visit her relatives, and our wedding day was set for the following June.

WAR WITH THE POLITICIANS

I have tried to make it clear that there was no "Indian outbreak" in 1890-91, and that such trouble as we had may justly be charged to the dishonest politicians, who through unfit appointees first robbed the Indians, then bullied them, and finally in a panic called for troops to suppress them. From my first days at Pine Ridge, certain Indians and white people had taken every occasion to whisper into my reluctant ears the tale of wrongs, real or fancied, committed by responsible officials on the reservation, or by their connivance. To me these stories were unbelievable, from the point of view of common decency. I held that a great government such as ours would never condone or permit any such practices, while administering large trust funds and standing in the relation of guardian to a race made helpless by lack of education and of legal safeguards. At that time, I had not dreamed what American politics really is, and I had the most exalted admiration for our noted public men. Accordingly, I dismissed these reports as mere gossip or the inventions of mischief-makers.

In spite of all that I had gone through,

life was not yet a serious matter to me. I had faith in every one, and accepted civilization and Christianity at their face value—a great mistake, as I was to learn later on. I had come back to my people, not to minister to their physical needs alone, but to be a missionary in every sense of the word, and as I was much struck with the loss of manliness and independence in these, the first "reservation Indians" I had ever known, I longed above all things to help them to regain their self-respect.

On June 18, 1891, I was married to Elaine Goodale in New York City.

Our new home was being built when we reached Pine Ridge, and we started life together in the old barracks, while planning the finishing and furnishing of the new.

There was nothing I called my own save my dogs and horses and my medicine bags, yet I was perfectly happy, for I had not only gained the confidence of my people, but that of the white residents, and even the border ranchmen called me in now and

Camp near Pine Ridge, 1891. It stands on the site of the Wounded Knee massacre of December 1890, in which the U.S. Army's 7th Cavalry destroyed Chief Big Foot's band of Miniconjou Sioux, effectively crushing the last vestiges of American Indian morale.

then. I answered every call, and have ridden forty or fifty miles in a blizzard, over dangerous roads, sometimes at night.

Eastman then relates how he obtained personal knowledge of fraud by the Indian agent and his white colleagues against the Sioux. He then attempted to help the Lakota people bring legal proceedings against the Indian agent. As a result:

I was promptly charged with "insubordination" and other things, but my good friend, General Morgan, then Commissioner, declined to entertain the charges. I, on my part, kept up the fight at Washington through influential friends, and made every effort to prove my case, or rather, the case of the people, for I had at no time any personal interest in the payment. The local authorities followed the usual tactics, and undertook to force a resignation by making my position at Pine Ridge intolerable. An Indian agent has almost autocratic power, and the conditions of life on an agency are such as to make every resident largely dependent upon his good will. We soon found ourselves hampered in our work and harassed by every imaginable annoyance. My requisitions were overlooked or "forgotten," and it became difficult to secure the necessaries of life. I would receive a curt written order to proceed without delay to some remote point to visit a certain alleged patient; then, before I had covered the distance, would be overtaken by a mounted policeman with arbitrary orders to return at once to the agency. On driving in rapidly and reporting to the agent's office for details of the supposed emergency, I might be rebuked for overdriving the horses, and charged with neglect of some chronic case of which I had either never been informed, or to which it had been physically impossible for me to give regular attention.

The result of the affair was that I was shortly offered a transfer. The agent could not be dislodged, and my position had become impossible. The superintendent of the boarding school, a clergyman, and one or two others who had fought on our side were also forced to leave. We had many other warm sympathizers who could not speak out without risking their livelihood.

We declined to accept the compromise, being utterly disillusioned and disgusted with these revelations of government mismanagement in the field, and realizing the helplessness of the best-equipped Indians to secure a fair deal for their people. Later experience, both my own and that of others, has confirmed me in this view. Had it not been for strong friends in the East and on the press, and the unusual boldness and disregard of personal considerations with which we had conducted the fight, I could not have lasted a month. All other means failing, these men will not hesitate to manufacture evidence against a man's, or a woman's, personal reputation in order to attain their ends.

It was a great disappointment to us both to give up our plans of work and our first home, to which we had devoted much loving thought and most of our little means; but it seemed to us then the only thing to do. We had not the heart to begin the same thing over again elsewhere. I resigned my position in the Indian service, and removed with my family to the city of St. Paul, where I proposed to enter upon the independent practice of medicine.

CIVILIZATION AS PREACHED AND PRACTICED

After thirty years of exile from the land of my nativity and the home of my ancestors, I came back to Minnesota in 1893. Although a young couple in a strange city, we were cordially received socially, and while seriously handicapped by lack of means, we had determined to win out. I opened an office, hung out my sign, and waited for patients. It was the hardest work I had ever done! Most of the time we were forced to board for the sake of economy, and were hard put to it to meet office rent and our modest living expenses.

To be sure, I had been bitterly disappointed in the character of the United States army and the honor of government officials. Still, I had seen the better side of civilization, and I determined that the good men and women who had helped me should not be betrayed. The Christ ideal might be radical, visionary, even impractical, as judged in the light of my later experiences; it still seemed to me logical, and in line with most of my Indian training.

With all the rest, I was deeply regretful of the work that I had left behind. I could not help thinking that if the President knew, if the good people of this country knew, of the wrong, it would yet be righted. I had not seen half of the savagery of civilization! While I had plenty of leisure, I began to put upon paper some of my earliest recollections, with the thought that our children might someday like to read of that wilderness life. This was the beginning of my first book, *Indian Boyhood*, which was not completed until several years later.

We were slowly gaining ground, when one day a stranger called on me in my office. He was, I learned, one of the field secretaries of the International Committee of Y.M.C.A., and had apparently called to discuss the feasibility of extending this movement among the Indians. *Ohiyesa then accepted the role as the traveling Indian secretary for the Y.M.C.A.*

I traveled over a large part of the western states and in Canada, visiting the mission stations among Indians of all tribes, and organizing young men's associations wherever conditions permitted. I think I organized some forty-three associations. This gave me a fine opportunity to study Protestant missionary effort among Indians. I seriously considered the racial attitude toward God, and almost unconsciously reopened the book of my early religious training, asking myself how it was that our simple lives were so imbued with the spirit of worship, while much church-going among white and nominally Christian Indians led often to such very small results.

I was constantly meeting with groups of young men of the Sioux, Cheyennes, Crees, Ojibways, and others, in log cabins or little frame chapels, and trying to set before them in simple language the life and character of the Man Jesus. I was cordially received everywhere, and always listened to with the closest attention. Curiously enough, even among these men who were seeking light on the white man's ideals, the racial philosophy emerged from time to time.

I remember one old battle-scarred warrior who sat among the young men got up and said, in substance: "Why, we have followed this law you speak of for untold ages!

We owned nothing, because everything is from Him. Food was free, land free as sunshine and rain. Who has changed all this? The white man; and yet he says he is a believer in God! He does not seem to inherit any of the traits of his Father, nor does he follow the example set by his brother Christ."

Ohiyesa ("the Winner")

A TEARFUL FAMILY REUNION

My two uncles who were in the Custer fight lived in Canada from the time of our flight in 1862, and both died there. I was happy to be sent to that part of the country in time to see the elder one alive. He had been a father to me up to the age of fifteen, and I had not seen him for over twenty years. I found him a farmer, living in a Christian community. I had sent word in advance of my coming, and my uncle's family had made of it a great occasion. All of my old playmates were there. My uncle was so happy that tears welled up in his eyes. "When we are old," he smiled, "our hearts are not strong in moments like this. The Great Spirit has been kind to let me see my boy again before I die." The early days were recalled as we feasted together, and all agreed that the chances were I should have been killed before reaching the age of twenty, if I had remained among them; for, said they, I was very anxious to emulate my uncle, who had been a warrior of great reputation. Afterward I visited the grave of my grandmother, whose devotion had meant so much to me as a motherless child. This was one of the great moments of my life.

PUBLIC SPEAKING

Throughout this period of my work I was happy, being unhampered by official red tape in the effort to improve conditions among my people.

Among other duties of my position, I was expected to make occasional speaking trips through the East to arouse inter-

est in the work, and it thus happened that I addressed large audiences in Chicago, New York, Boston, and at Lake Mohonk. I was taken by slum and settlement workers to visit the slums and dives of the cities, which gave another shock to my ideals of "Christian civilization." Of course, I had seen something of the poorer parts of Boston during my medical course, but not at night, and not in a way to realize the horror and wretchedness of it as I did now. To be sure, I had been taught even as a child that there are always some evil minded men in every nation, and we knew well what it is to endure physical hardship, but our poor lost nothing of their self-respect and dignity. Our great men not only divided their last kettle of food with a neighbor, but if great grief should come to them, such as the death of child or wife, they would voluntarily give away their few possessions and begin life over again in token of their sorrow. We could not conceive of the extremes of luxury and misery existing thus side by side, for it was common observation with us that the coarse weeds, if permitted to grow, will choke out the more delicate flowers. These things troubled me very much; yet I still held before my race the highest, and as yet unattained, ideals of the white man.

My effort was to make the Indian feel that Christianity is not at fault for the white man's sins; it is rather the lack of Christianity. And, I freely admitted that this nation is not Christian, but declared that the Christians in it are trying to make it so. I found the facts and the logic of them often hard to dispute, but was partly consoled by the wonderful opportunity to come into close contact with

At his Dartmouth class reunion Eastman provided a striking contrast to many of his classmates

the racial mind, and to refresh my understanding of the philosophy in which I had been trained, but which had been overlaid and superseded by a college education. I do not know how much good I accomplished, but I did my best.

AT THE NATION'S CAPITAL

My work for the International Committee of the Y.M.C.A. brought me into close association with some of the best products of American civilization. Had I not known some of these people, I should long ago have gone back to the woods.

I wished very much to resume my profession of medicine, but I was as far as ever from having the capital for a start, and we had now three children. At this juncture, I was confronted by what seemed a hopeful opportunity. Some of the leading men of the Sioux, among them my own brother, Rev. John Eastman, came to me for a consultation. They argued that I was the man of their tribe best fitted to look after their interests at Washington. Although not a lawyer, they gave me power of attorney to act for them in behalf of these claims, and to appear as their representative before the Indian Bureau, the President, and Congress.

After signing the necessary papers, I went to Washington, where I urged our rights throughout two sessions and most of a third, while during the summers I still traveled among the Sioux. I learned that scarcely one of our treaties with the United States had been carried out in good faith in all of its provisions.

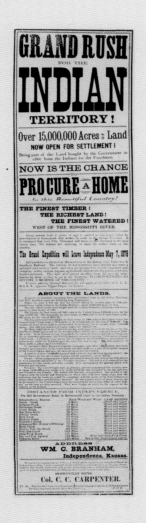

A.B. Cutts, the energetic General Passenger Agent and Ticket Agent for the M&StL, looked forward to a boom in passenger revenues when the government opened the Cheyenne River Reservation.

The Dawes Act split up every reservation into allotments for each tribal member of 160 acres for agricultural use or 80 acres for ranching. Many allotments were not large enough for sustainable ranching or farming, so Indian families were in desperate economic need. For more than forty years the U.S. government ignored the pleas of Eastman and other American Indian leaders and gave or sold millions of acres of so-called "surplus" land on reservations across America to non-Indians under the "Homestead Act." These acts violated the terms of various treaties. LeBeau, South Dakota, is now an abandoned town.

"INDIAN TERRITORY" IN OKLAHOMA IS "FOREVER SECURE" FOR THE TRIBES

During the early and mid-1800s the federal government removed many tribes from their ancestral homelands to reservations in "Indian Territory" in Oklahoma, which the U.S. agreed to "forever secure and guarantee" for these tribes.

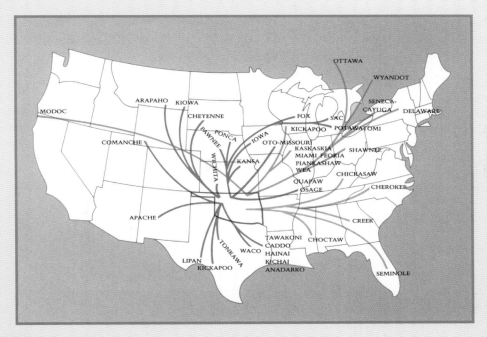

Within two years of the enactment of the Dawes Act, the U.S. began to give away "surplus land" on Indian reservations throughout the country. From 1889-95, seven different "Oklahoma Land Rushes" gave away over 15 million acres of Indian Territory. The largest of these, known as the "Great Oklahoma Land Rush," took place in 1893 and gave away 7 million acres in the "Cherokee Strip" in one day. In the case of the Cherokee, "forever" amounted to 55 years from the time of the Trail of Tears.

Start of the "Great Oklahoma Land Rush" of 1893

Now for the first time I seriously studied the machinery of government, and before I knew it, I was a lobbyist. I came to Washington with a great respect for our public men and institutions. Although I had had some disillusioning experiences with the lower type of political henchmen on the reservations, I reasoned that it was because they were almost beyond the pale of civilization and clothed with supreme authority over a helpless and ignorant people, that they dared do the things they did. Under the very eye of the law and of society, I thought, this could scarcely be tolerated. I was confident that a fair hearing would be granted, and our wrongs corrected without undue delay. I had overmuch faith in the civilized ideal, and I was again disappointed.

The officials received me courteously enough, and assured me that the matters I spoke of should be attended to, but as soon as my back was turned, they pigeonholed them. After waiting patiently, I would resort to the plan of getting one of the Massachusetts Senators, who were my friends, to ask for the papers in the case, and this was generally effective.

I would approach a legislator who was a stranger to me, in the hope of being allowed to explain to him the purpose of our measure. He would listen a while and perhaps refer me to someone else. I would call on the man he named, and to my disgust be met with a demand for a liberal percentage on the whole amount to be recovered. If I refused to listen to this proposal,

Crow delegation to Washington D.C.

I would soon find the legislator in question "drumming up" some objection to the bill, and these tactics would be kept up until we yielded, or made some sort of compromise.

As I have said, nearly every Indian delegation that came to the capital in those days—and they were many—appealed to me for advice, and often had me go over their business with them before presenting it. The old men often amused me by their shrewd comments upon our public men.

An old chief said of President McKinley: "I never knew a white man show so much love for mother and wife." "He has a bigger heart than most white men," declared Little-fish, "and this is unfortunate for him. The white man is a man of business, and has no use for a heart."

One day, I found a number of the chiefs in the Senate gallery. They observed closely the faces and bearing of the legislators and then gave their verdict. One man they compared to a fish. Another had not the attitude of a true man; that is, he held to a pose. Senator Morgan of Alabama they called a great councilor. Senator Hoar they estimated as a patriotic and just statesman. They picked out Senator Platt of Connecticut as being very cautious and a diplomat. They had much difficulty in judging Senator Tillman, but on the whole they considered him to be a fighting man, governed by his emotions rather than his judgment. Senator Turpie of Indiana they took for a preacher, and were pleased with his air of godliness and reverence. Senator Frye of Maine they thought must be a rarity among white men—honest to the core!

Theodore Roosevelt has been well known to the Sioux for over twenty-five years, dating from the years of his ranch life. He was well liked by them as a rule. Spotted Horse said of him, "While he talked, I forgot that he was a white man."

I have been much interested in the point of view of these older Indians. Our younger element has now been so thoroughly drilled in the motives and methods of the white man, at the same time losing the old mother and family training through being placed in boarding school from six years of age onward, that they have really become an entirely different race.

> ☛ What methods did the U.S. government use to subdue and control America Indians?
> ☛ What other challenges did American Indians face?

THE SOUL OF THE WHITE MAN

My last work under the auspices of the government was the revision of the Sioux allotment rolls, including the determination of family groups, and the assignment of surnames when these were lacking. This work occupied me for six years, and gave me insight into the relationships and intimate history of thirty thousand Sioux.

I feel that I was a pioneer in this new line of defense of the native American, not so much of his rights in the land as of his character and religion. I am glad that the drift is now toward a better understanding, and that he is become the acknowledged hero of the Boy Scouts and Camp Fire Girls, as well as of many artists, sculptors, and sincere writers.

I was invited to represent the North American Indian at the First Universal Races Congress in London, England, in

1911. It was a great privilege to attend that gathering of distinguished representatives of 53 different nationalities, come together to mutually acquaint themselves with one another's progress and racial ideals. I was entertained by some well known men, but there was little time for purely social enjoyment. What impressed me most was the perfect equality of the races, which formed the background of all the discussions. It was declared at the outset that there is no superior race, and no inferior, since individuals of all races have proved their innate capacity by their standing in the universities of the world, and it has often happened that men of the undeveloped races have surpassed students of the most advanced races in scholarship and ability.

From the time I first accepted the Christ ideal it has grown upon me steadily, but I also see more and more plainly our modern divergence from that ideal. I confess I have wondered much that Christianity is not practiced by the very people who vouch for that wonderful conception of exemplary living. It appears that they are anxious to pass on their religion to all races of men, but keep very little of it themselves. I have not yet seen the meek inherit the earth, or the peacemakers receive high honor.

Why do we find so much evil and wickedness practiced by the nations composed of professedly "Christian" individuals? The pages of history are full of licensed murder and the plundering of weaker and less developed peoples, and obviously the world today has not outgrown this system.

Behind the material and intellectual splendor of our civilization, primitive savagery and cruelty and lust hold sway, undiminished, and as it seems, unheeded. When I let go of my simple, instinctive nature religion, I hoped to gain something far loftier as well as more satisfying to the reason. Alas! it is also more confusing and contradictory. The higher and spiritual life, though first in theory, is clearly secondary, if not entirely neglected, in actual practice. When I reduce civilization to its lowest terms, it becomes a system of life based upon trade. The dollar is the measure of value, and might still spells right; otherwise, why war?

Yet even in deep jungles God's own sunlight penetrates, and I stand before my own people still as an advocate of civilization. Why? First, because there is no chance for our former simple life anymore; and second, because I realize that the white man's religion is not responsible for his mistakes. There is every evidence that God has given him all the light necessary by which to live in peace and goodwill with his brother; and we also know that many brilliant civilizations have collapsed in physical and moral decadence. It is for us to avoid their fate if we can.

I am an Indian; and while I have learned much from civilization, for which I am grateful, I have never lost my Indian sense of right and justice. I am for development and progress along social and spiritual lines, rather than those of commerce, nationalism, or material efficiency. Nevertheless, so long as I live, I am an American.

PART III: THE SOUL OF THE INDIAN

FOREWORD

The religion of the Indian is the last thing about him that the man of another race will ever understand.

First, the Indian does not speak of these deep matters so long as he believes in them, and when he has ceased to believe he speaks inaccurately and slightingly.

Second, even if he can be induced to speak, the racial and religious prejudice of the other stands in the way of his sympathetic comprehension.

Third, practically all existing studies on this subject have been made during the transition period, when the original beliefs and philosophy of the native American were already undergoing rapid disintegration.

My little book [*The Soul of the Indian*] is as true as I can make it to my childhood teaching and ancestral ideals, but from the human, not the ethnological standpoint. So much as has been written by strangers of our ancient faith and worship treats it chiefly as matter of curiosity. I should like to emphasize its universal quality, its personal appeal!

We know that all religious aspiration, all sincere worship, can have but one source and one goal. We know that the God of the lettered and the unlettered, of the Greek and the barbarian, is after all the same God.

THE GREAT MYSTERY

The original attitude of the American Indian toward the Eternal, the "Great Mystery" that surrounds and embraces us, was as simple as it was exalted. To him it was the supreme conception, bringing with it the fullest measure of joy and satisfaction possible in this life.

The worship of the "Great Mystery" was silent, solitary, free from all self-seek-

Sioux praying with the pipe

ing. It was silent, because all speech is of necessity feeble and imperfect; therefore the souls of my ancestors ascended to God in wordless adoration. It was solitary, because they believed that He is nearer to us in solitude, and there were no priests authorized to come between a man and his Maker. None might exhort or confess or in any way meddle with the religious experience of another. Among us all men were created sons of God and stood erect, as conscious of their divinity. Our faith might not be formulated in creeds, nor forced upon any who were unwilling to receive it; hence there was no preaching, proselyting, nor persecution, neither were there any scoffers or atheists.

Greeting the sun, Dakota

There were no temples or shrines among us save those of nature. Being a natural man, the Indian was intensely poetical. He would deem it sacrilege to build a house for Him who may be met face to face in the mysterious, shadowy aisles of the primeval forest, or on the sunlit bosom of virgin prairies, upon dizzy spires and pinnacles of naked rock, and yonder in the jeweled vault of the night sky! He who enrobes Himself in filmy veils of cloud, there on the rim of the visible world where our Great-Grandfather Sun kindles his evening camp-fire, He who rides upon the rigorous wind of the north, or breathes forth His spirit upon aromatic southern airs, whose war-canoe is launched upon majestic rivers and inland seas—He needs no lesser cathedral!

THE VISION QUEST

That solitary communion with the Unseen which was the highest expression of our religious life is partly described in the word *hambeday*, literally "mysterious feeling," which has been variously translated "fasting" and "dreaming." It may better be interpreted as "consciousness of the divine."

The first *hambeday*, or religious retreat, marked an epoch in the life of the youth, which may be compared to that of confirmation or conversion in Christian experience. Having first prepared himself by means of the purifying sweat lodge, and cast off as far as possible all human fleshly influences, the young man sought out the noblest height, the most commanding summit in all the surrounding region. Knowing that God sets no value upon material things, he took with him no offerings or sacrifices other

Slow Bull, Sioux medicine man

mystic found his highest happiness and the motive power of his existence.

When he returned to the camp, he must remain at a distance until he had again entered the sweat lodge and prepared himself for intercourse with his fellows. Of the vision or sign vouchsafed to him he did not speak, unless it had included some commission which must be publicly fulfilled. Sometimes an old man, standing upon the brink of eternity, might reveal to a chosen few the oracle of his long-past youth.

Hidatsa vision quester in buffalo robe

than symbolic objects, such as paints and tobacco. Wishing to appear before Him in all humility, he wore no clothing save his moccasins and breech-clout. At the solemn hour of sunrise or sunset he took up his position, overlooking the glories of earth and facing the "Great Mystery," and there he remained, naked, erect, silent, and motionless, exposed to the elements and forces of His arming, for a night and a day to two days and nights, but rarely longer. Sometimes he would chant a hymn without words, or offer the ceremonial "filled pipe." In this holy trance or ecstasy the Indian

COMMUNION WITH THE NATURAL WORLD

The elements and majestic forces in nature, Lightning, Wind, Water, Fire, and Frost, were regarded with awe as spiritual powers, but always secondary and intermediate in character. We believed that the spirit pervades all creation and that every creature possesses a soul in some degree, though not necessarily a soul conscious of itself. The tree, the waterfall, the grizzly bear, each is an embodied Force, and as such an object of reverence.

The Indian loved to come into sympathy and spiritual communion with his brothers of the animal kingdom, whose inarticulate souls had for him something of the sinless purity that we attribute to the innocent and irresponsible child. He had faith in their instincts, as in a mysterious wisdom given from above; and while he humbly accepted the supposedly voluntary sacrifice of their bodies to preserve his own, he paid homage to their spirits in prescribed prayers and offerings.

In every religion there is an element of the supernatural, varying with the influence of pure reason over its devotees. The Indian was a logical and clear thinker upon matters within the scope of his understanding, but he had not yet charted the vast field of nature or expressed her wonders in terms of science. With his limited knowledge of cause and effect, he saw miracles on every hand—the miracle of life in seed and egg, the miracle of death in lightning flash and in the swelling deep! Nothing of the marvelous could astonish him; as that a beast should speak, or the sun stand still. The virgin birth would appear scarcely more miraculous than is the birth of every child that comes into the world, or the miracle of the loaves and fishes excite more wonder than the harvest that springs from a single ear of corn.

Who may condemn his superstition? Surely not the devout Catholic, or even Protestant missionary, who teaches Bible miracles as literal fact! The logical man must either deny all miracles or none, and our American Indian myths and hero stories are perhaps, in themselves, quite as credible as those of the Hebrews of old. If we are of the spiritual type of mind, that sees in natural law a majesty and grandeur far more impressive than any solitary infraction of it could possibly be, let us not forget that, after all, science has not explained everything. We have still to face the ultimate miracle—the origin and principle of life! Here is the supreme mystery that is the essence of worship, without which there can be no religion, and in the presence of this mystery our attitude cannot be very unlike that of the natural philosopher, who beholds with awe the Divine in all creation.

It is simple truth that the Indian did not, so long as his native philosophy held sway over his mind, either envy or desire to imitate the splendid achievements of the white man. In his own thought he rose superior to them! He scorned them, even as a lofty spirit absorbed in its stern task rejects the soft beds, the luxurious food, the pleasure-worshiping dalliance of a rich neighbor. It was clear to him that virtue and happiness are independent of these things, if not incompatible with them.

It is my personal belief, after thirty-five years' experience of it, that there is no such thing as "Christian Civilization." I believe that Christianity and modern civilization are opposed and irreconcilable, and that the spirit of Christianity and of our ancient religion is essentially the same.

THE ONE INEVITABLE DUTY

In the life of the Indian there was only one inevitable duty—the duty of prayer—the daily recognition of the Unseen and Eternal. His daily devotions were more necessary to him than daily food. He wakes at daybreak, puts on his moccasins and steps down to the water's edge. Here he throws handfuls of clear, cold water into his face, or plunges in bodily. After the bath, he stands erect before the advancing dawn, facing the sun as it dances upon the horizon, and offers his unspoken orison. His mate may precede or follow him in his devotions, but never accompanies him. Each soul must meet the morning sun, the new, sweet earth, and the Great Silence alone!

Vision quester

Every act of his life is, in a very real sense, a religious act. He recognizes the spirit in all creation, and believes that he draws from it spiritual power. His respect for the immortal part of the animal, his brother, often leads him so far as to lay out the body of his game in state and decorate the head with symbolic paint or feathers. Then he stands before it in the prayer attitude, holding up the filled pipe, in token that he has freed with honor the spirit of his brother, whose body his need compelled him to take to sustain his own life.

Vision quester

When food is taken, the woman murmurs a "grace" as she lowers the kettle; an act so softly and unobtrusively performed that one who does not know the custom usually fails to catch the whisper: "Spirit, partake!" As her husband receives the bowl or plate, he likewise murmurs his invocation to the spirit. When he becomes an old man, he loves to make a notable effort to prove his gratitude. He cuts off the choicest morsel of the meat and casts it into the fire—the purest and most ethereal element.

Friendship is held to be the severest test of character. It is easy, we think, to be loyal to family and clan, whose blood is in our own veins. Love between man and woman is founded on the mating instinct and is not free from desire and self-seeking. But to have a friend, and to be true under any and all trials, is the mark of a man!

The highest type of friendship is the relation of "brother-friend" or "life-and-death friend." This bond is between man and man, is usually formed in early youth, and can only be broken by death. It is the essence of comradeship and fraternal love, without thought of pleasure or gain, but rather for moral support and inspiration. Each is vowed to die for the other, if need be, and nothing denied the brother-friend, but neither is anything required that is not in accord with the highest conceptions of the Indian mind.

THE SUN DANCE

In the old days, when a Sioux warrior found himself in the very jaws of destruction, he might offer a prayer to his father, the Sun, to prolong his life. If rescued from imminent danger, he must acknowledge the divine favor by making a Sun Dance, according to the vow embraced in his prayer, in which he declared that he did not fear torture or death, but asked life only for the sake of those who loved him. Thus the physical ordeal was the fulfillment of a vow, and a sort of atonement for what might otherwise appear to be reprehensible weakness in the face of death. It was in the nature of confession and thank-offering to the "Great Mystery," through the physical parent, the Sun, and did not embrace a prayer for future favors.

The ceremonies usually took place from six months to a year after the making of the vow, in order to admit of suitable preparation; always in midsummer and before a large and imposing gathering. They naturally included the making of a feast, and the giving away of much savage wealth in honor of the occasion, although these were no essential part of the religious rite.

When the day came to procure the pole, it was brought in by a party of warriors, headed by some man of distinction. The tree selected was six to eight inches in diameter at the base, and twenty to twenty-five feet high. It was chosen and felled with some solemnity, including the ceremony of the "filled pipe," and was carried in the fashion of a litter, symbolizing the body of the man who made the dance. A solitary teepee was pitched on a level spot at some distance from the village, and the pole raised near at hand with the same cer-

Sioux Sun Dance, 1910

Sioux Sun Dance center pole, c. 1990

Cheyenne Sun Dance, c. 1910

Crow Sun Dance, 1950s

emony, in the center of a circular enclosure of fresh-cut boughs.

Meanwhile, one of the most noted of our old men had carved out of rawhide, or later of wood, two figures, usually those of a man and a buffalo. Sometimes the figure of a bird, supposed to represent the Thunder, was substituted for the buffalo. It was customary to paint the man red and the animal black, and each was suspended from one end of the cross-bar which was securely tied some two feet from the top of the pole. I have never been able to determine that this cross had any significance; it was probably nothing more than a dramatic co-incidence that surmounted the Sun-Dance pole with the symbol of Christianity.

The paint indicated that the man who was about to give thanks publicly had been potentially dead, but was allowed to live by the mysterious favor and interference of the Giver of Life. The buffalo hung opposite the image of his own body in death, because it was the support of his physical self, and a leading figure in legendary lore. Following the same line of thought, when he emerged from the solitary lodge of preparation, and approached the pole to dance, nude save for his breech-clout and moccasins, his hair loosened and daubed with clay, he must drag after him a buffalo skull, representing the grave from which he had escaped.

The dancer was cut or scarified on the chest, sufficient to draw blood and cause pain, the natural accompaniments of his figurative death. He took his position opposite the singers, facing the pole, and dragging the skull by leather thongs which were merely fastened about his shoulders. During a later period, incisions were made in

Shoshone Sun Dance, 1940s

the breast or back, sometimes both, through which wooden skewers were drawn, and secured by lariats to the pole or to the skulls. Thus he danced without intermission for a day and a night, or even longer, ever gazing at the sun in the daytime, and blowing from time to time a sacred whistle made from the bone of a goose's wing.

INDIAN MEDICINE

There is no doubt that the Indian held medicine close to spiritual things, but in this also he has been much misunderstood; in fact everything that he held sacred is indiscriminately called "medicine," in the sense of mystery or magic. As a doctor he was originally very adroit and often successful. He employed only healing bark, roots, and leaves with whose properties he was familiar, using them in the form of a distillation or tea and always singly. The stomach or internal bath was a valuable discovery of his, and the sweat lodge or Turkish bath was in general use. He could set a broken bone with fair success, but never practiced surgery in any form. In addition to all this, the medicine-man possessed much personal magnetism and authority, and in his treatment often sought to reestablish the equilibrium of the patient through mental or spiritual influences—a sort of primitive psychotherapy.

The Sioux word for the healing art is "*wah-pee-yah*," which literally means readjusting or making anew. "*Pay-jee-hoo-tah*," literally root, means medicine, and "*wakan*" signifies spirit or mystery. Thus the three ideas, while sometimes associated, were carefully distinguished.

It is important to remember that in the old days the "medicine-man" received no payment for his services, which were of the nature of an honorable function or office. When the idea of payment and barter was introduced among us, and valuable presents or fees began to be demanded for treating the sick, the ensuing greed and rivalry led to many demoralizing practices, and in time to the rise of the modern "conjurer," who is generally a fraud and trickster of the grossest kind. It is fortunate that his day is practically over.

Ever seeking to establish spiritual comradeship with the animal creation, the Indian adopted this or that animal as his "totem," the emblematic device of his society, family, or clan. It is probable that the creature chosen was the traditional ancestress, as we are told that the First Man had many wives among the animal people. The sacred beast, bird, or reptile, represented by its stuffed skin, or by a rude painting, was treated with reverence and carried into bat-

tle to insure the guardianship of the spirits. The symbolic attribute of beaver, bear, or tortoise, such as wisdom, cunning, courage, and the like, was supposed to be mysteriously conferred upon the wearer of the badge. The totem or charm used in medicine was ordinarily that of the medicine lodge to which the practitioner belonged, though there were some great men who boasted a special revelation.

Medicine bundles

THE SWEAT LODGE AND CEREMONIAL OF THE PIPE

There are two ceremonial usages which, so far as I have been able to ascertain, were universal among American Indians, and apparently fundamental. These are the "*ini-pi*," or sweat lodge, and the "*chan-du-hu-pah-yu-za-pee*," or ceremonial of the pipe. In our Siouan legends and traditions these two are preeminent, as handed down from the most ancient time and persisting to the last.

In our Creation myth or story of the First Man, the sweat lodge was the magic used by The-one-who-was-First-Created, to give life to the dead bones of his younger brother, who had been slain by the monsters of the deep. Upon the shore of the Great Water he dug two round holes, over one of which he built a low enclosure of fragrant cedar boughs, and here he gathered together the bones of his brother. In the other pit he made a fire and heated four round stones, which he rolled one by one into the lodge of boughs. Having closed every aperture save one, he sang a mystic chant while he thrust in his arm and sprinkled water upon the stones with a bunch of sage. Immediately steam arose, and as the legend says, "there was an appearance of life." A second time he sprinkled water, and the dry bones rattled together. The third time he seemed to hear soft singing from within the lodge; and the fourth time a voice exclaimed: "Brother, let me out!" (It should be noted that the number four is the magic or sacred number of the Indian.)

This story gives the traditional origin of the "*inipi*," which has ever since been deemed essential to the Indian's effort to purify and recreate his spirit. It is used both by the doctor and by his patient. Every man must enter the cleansing bath and take the cold plunge which follows, when preparing for any spiritual crisis, for possible death, or imminent danger.

Not only the "*inipi*" itself, but everything used in connection with the mysterious event, the aromatic cedar and sage, the water, and especially the water-worn boulders, are regarded as sacred, or at the least adapted to a spiritual use. For the rock we have a special reverent name—"*Tunkan*," a contraction of the Sioux word for Grandfather.

The natural boulder enters into many of our solemn ceremonials, such as the "Rain Dance," and the "Feast of Virgins." The lone hunter and warrior reverently holds up his filled pipe to "*Tunkan*," in solitary commemoration of a miracle which to him is as authentic and holy as the raising of Lazarus to the devout Christian.

There is a legend that the First Man fell sick, and was taught by his Elder Brother the ceremonial use of the pipe, in a prayer to the spirits for ease and relief. This simple ceremony is the commonest daily expression of thanks or "grace," as well as an oath of loyalty and good faith when the warrior goes forth upon some perilous enterprise, and it enters even into his "*hambeday*," or solitary prayer, ascending as a rising vapor or incense to the Father of Spirits.

In all the war ceremonies and in medicine a special pipe is used, but at home or on the hunt the warrior employs his own. The pulverized weed is mixed with aromatic bark of the red willow, and pressed lightly into the bowl of the long stone pipe. The worshiper lights it gravely and takes a whiff or two; then, standing erect, he holds it silently toward the Sun, our father, and toward the earth, our mother. There are modern variations, as holding the pipe to the Four Winds, the Fire, Water, Rock, and other elements or objects of reverence.

There are many religious festivals which are local and special in character, embodying a prayer for success in hunting or warfare, or for rain and bountiful harvests, but these two are the sacraments of our religion. For baptism we substitute the "*inipi*," the purification by vapor, and in our holy communion we partake of the soothing incense of tobacco in the stead of bread and wine.

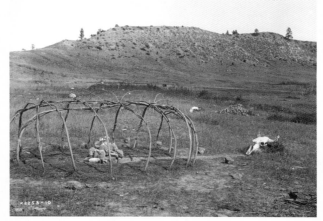

Cheyenne sweat lodge, c. 1910

Shoshone sweat lodge at Fort Washakie, c. 2006

LOVE OF POSSESSIONS IS A WEAKNESS

The native American has been generally despised by his white conquerors for his poverty and simplicity. They forget, perhaps, that his religion forbade the accumulation of wealth and the enjoyment of luxury. To him, as to other single-minded men in every age and race, from Diogenes to the brothers of Saint Francis, from the Montanists to the Shakers, the love of possessions has appeared a snare, and the burdens of a complex society a source of needless peril and temptation. Furthermore, it was the rule of his life to share the fruits of his skill and success with his less fortunate brothers. Thus he kept his spirit free from the clog of pride, cupidity, or envy, and carried out, as he believed, the divine decree— a matter profoundly important to him.

It was not, then, wholly from ignorance or improvidence that he failed to establish permanent towns and to develop a material civilization. To the untutored sage, the concentration of population was the prolific mother of all evils, moral no less than physical. He argued that food is good, while surfeit kills; that love is good, but lust destroys; and not less dreaded than the pestilence following upon crowded and unsanitary dwellings was the loss of spiritual power inseparable from too close contact with one's fellow-men. All who have lived much out of doors know that there is a magnetic and nervous force that accumulates in solitude and that is quickly dissipated by life in a crowd; and even his enemies have recognized the fact that for a certain innate power and self-poise, wholly independent of circumstances, the American Indian is unsurpassed among men.

It was our belief that the love of possessions is a weakness to be overcome. Its appeal is to the material part, and if allowed its way it will in time disturb the spiritual balance of the man. Therefore the child must early learn the beauty of generosity. He is taught to give what he prizes most, and that he may taste the happiness of giving, he is made at an early age the family almoner. If a child is inclined to be grasping, or to cling to any of his little possessions, legends are related to him, telling of the contempt and disgrace falling upon the ungenerous and mean man.

Public giving is a part of every important ceremony. It properly belongs to the celebration of birth, marriage, and death, and is observed whenever it is desired to do special honor to any person or event. Upon such occasions it is common to give to the point of utter impoverishment. The Indian in his simplicity literally gives away all that he has, to relatives, to guests of another tribe or clan, but above all to the poor and the aged, from whom he can hope for no return. Finally, the gift to the "Great Mystery," the religious offering, may be of little value in itself, but to the giver's own thought it should carry the meaning and reward of true sacrifice.

The man who is a skillful hunter, and whose wife is alive to her opportunities makes many feasts, to which he is careful to invite the older men of his clan, recognizing that they have outlived their period of greatest activity, and now love nothing so well as to eat in good company, and to live over the past. The old men, for their part, do their best to requite his liberality with a little speech, in which they are apt to relate the brave and generous deeds of their host's ancestors, finally congratulating him upon being a worthy successor of an honorable line. Thus his reputation is won as a hunter and a feast-maker, and almost as famous in his way as the great warrior is he who has a recognized name and standing as a "man of peace."

The true Indian sets no price upon either his property or his labor. His generosity is only limited by his strength and ability. He regards it as an honor to be selected for a difficult or dangerous service, and would think it shame to ask for any reward, saying rather: "Let him whom I serve express his thanks according to his own bringing up and his sense of honor!"

Nevertheless, he recognizes rights in property. To steal from one of his own tribe would be indeed disgrace if discovered, the name of "*Wamanon*," or Thief, is fixed upon him forever as an unalterable. The only exception to the rule is in the case of food, which is always free to the hungry if there is none by to offer it. Other protection than the moral law there could not be in an Indian community, where there were neither locks nor doors, and everything was open and easy of access to all comers.

The property of the enemy is spoil of war, and it is always allowable to confiscate it if possible. However, in the old days there was not much plunder. Before the coming of the white man, there was in fact little temptation or opportunity to despoil the enemy; but in modern times the practice of "stealing horses" from hostile tribes has become common, and is thought far from dishonorable.

Murder within the tribe was a grave of-fense, to be atoned for as the council might decree, and it often happened that the slayer was called upon to pay the penalty with his own life. He made no attempt to escape or to evade justice. That the crime was committed in the depths of the forest or at dead of night, witnessed by no human eye, made no difference to his mind. He was thoroughly convinced that all is known to the "Great Mystery," and hence did not hesitate to give himself up, to stand his trial by the old and wise men of the victim's clan. His own family and clan might by no means attempt to excuse or to defend him, but his judges took all the known circumstances into consideration, and if it appeared that he slew in self-defense, or that the provocation was severe, he might be set free after a thirty days' period of mourning in solitude. Otherwise the murdered man's next of kin were authorized to take his life; and if they refrained from doing so, as often happened, he remained an outcast from the clan. A willful murder was a rare occurrence before the days of whiskey and drunken rows, for we were not a violent or a quarrelsome people.

It is said that, in the very early days, lying was a capital offense among us. Believing that the deliberate liar is capable of committing any crime behind the screen of cowardly untruth and double-dealing, the destroyer of mutual confidence was summarily put to death, that the evil might go no further.

"Let neither cold, hunger, nor pain, nor the fear of them, neither the bristling teeth of danger nor the very jaws of death itself, prevent you from doing a good deed," said an old chief to a scout who was about to seek the buffalo in midwinter for the relief of a starving people. This was his childlike conception of courage.

THE INDIAN MORAL CODE

Long before I ever heard of Christ, or saw a white man, I had learned from an untutored woman the essence of morality. With the help of dear Nature herself, she taught me things simple but of mighty import. I knew God. I perceived what goodness is. I saw and loved what is really beautiful. Civilization has not taught me anything better!

As a child, I understood how to give; I have forgotten that grace since I became civilized. I lived the natural life, whereas I now live the artificial. Any pretty pebble was valuable to me then; every growing tree an object of reverence. Now I worship with the white man before a painted landscape whose value is estimated in dollars! Thus the Indian is reconstructed, as the natural rocks are ground to powder, and made into artificial blocks which may be built into the walls of modern society.

The first American mingled with his pride a singular humility. Spiritual arrogance was foreign to his nature and teaching. He never claimed that the power of articulate speech was proof of superiority over the dumb creation; on the other hand, it is to him a perilous gift. He believes profoundly in silence—the sign of a perfect equilibrium. Silence is the absolute poise or balance of body, mind, and spirit. The man who preserves his selfhood ever calm and unshaken by the storms of existence—not a leaf, as it were, astir on the tree; not a ripple upon the surface of shining pool—his, in the mind of the unlettered sage, is the ideal attitude and conduct of life.

If you ask him: "What is silence?" he will answer: "It is the Great Mystery!" "The holy silence is His voice!" If you ask: "What are the fruits of silence?" he will say: "They are self-control, true courage or endurance, patience, dignity, and reverence. Silence is the cornerstone of character."

"Guard your tongue in youth," said the old chief, Wabashaw, "and in age you may mature a thought that will be of service to your people!"

The moment that man conceived of a perfect body, supple, symmetrical, graceful, and enduring—in that moment he had laid the foundation of a moral life! No man can hope to maintain such a temple of the spirit beyond the period of adolescence, unless he is able to curb his indulgence in the pleasures of the senses. Upon this truth the Indian built a rigid system of physical training, a social and moral code that was the law of his life.

There was aroused in him as a child a high ideal of manly strength and beauty, the attainment of which must depend upon strict temperance in eating and in the sexual relation, together with severe and persistent exercise. He desired to be a worthy link in the generations, and that he might not destroy by his weakness that vigor and purity of blood which had been achieved at the cost of much self-denial by a long line of ancestors.

He was required to fast from time to time for short periods, and to work off his superfluous energy by means of hard running, swimming, and the sweat lodge. The bodily fatigue thus induced, especially when coupled with a reduced diet, is a reliable cure for undue sexual desires.

Personal modesty was early cultivated as a safeguard, together with a strong self-respect and pride of family and race. This was accomplished in part by keeping the child ever before the public eye, from his birth onward. His entrance into the world, especially in the case of the first-born, was often publicly announced by the herald, accompanied by a distribution of presents to the old and needy. The same thing occurred when he took his first step, when his ears were pierced, and when he shot his first game, so that his childish exploits and progress were known to the whole clan as to a larger family, and he grew into manhood with the saving sense of a reputation to sustain.

The youth was encouraged to enlist early in the public service, and to develop a wholesome ambition for the honors of a leader and feast maker, which can never be his unless he is truthful and generous, as well as brave, and ever mindful of his personal chastity and honor. There were many ceremonial customs which had a distinct moral influence; the woman was rigidly secluded at certain periods, and the young husband was forbidden to approach his own wife when preparing for war or for any religious event. The public or tribal position of the Indian is entirely dependent on his private virtue, and he is never permitted to forget that he does not live to himself alone, but to his tribe and his clan. Thus habits of perfect self-control were early established, and there were no unnatural conditions or complex temptations to beset him until he was met and overthrown by a stronger race.

THE ATTITUDE TOWARD DEATH

The attitude of the Indian toward death, the test and background of life, is entirely consistent with his character and philosophy. Death has no terrors for him; he meets it with simplicity and perfect calm, seeking only an honorable end as his last gift to his family and descendants. Therefore, he courts death in battle; on the other hand, he would regard it as disgraceful to be killed in a private quarrel. If one were dying at home, it is customary to carry his bed out of doors as the end approaches that his spirit may pass under the open sky.

Next to this, the matter that concerns him most is the parting with his dear ones, especially if he has any little children who must be left behind to suffer want. His family affections are strong, and he grieves intensely for the lost, even though he has unbounded faith in a spiritual companionship.

The outward signs of mourning for the dead are far more spontaneous and convincing than is the correct and well-ordered black of civilization. Both men and women among us loosen their hair and cut it according to the degree of relationship or of devotion. Consistent with the idea of sacrificing all personal beauty and adornment, they trim off likewise from the dress its fringes and ornaments, perhaps cut it short, or cut the robe or blanket in two. The men blacken their faces, and widows or bereaved parents sometimes gash their arms and legs till they are covered with blood. Giving themselves up wholly to their grief, they are no longer concerned about any earthly possession, and often give away all that they have to the first comers, even to their beds and their home. Finally, the wailing for the dead is continued night and day to the point of utter voicelessness; a musical, weird, and heart-piercing sound, which has been compared to the "keening" of the Celtic mourner.

The old-time burial of the Plains Indians was upon a scaffold of poles, or a platform among the boughs of a tree—their only means of placing the body out of reach of wild beasts, as they had no implements with which to dig a suitable grave. It was prepared by dressing in the finest clothes, together with some personal possessions and ornaments, wrapped in several robes, and finally in a secure covering of raw-hide. As a special mark of respect, the body of a young woman or a warrior was sometimes laid out in state in a new teepee, with the usual household articles and even with a dish of food left beside it, not that they supposed the spirit could use the implements or eat the food but merely as a last tribute. Then the whole people would break camp and depart to a distance, leaving the dead alone in an honorable solitude.

There was no prescribed ceremony of burial, though the body was carried out with more or less solemnity by selected young men, and sometimes noted warriors were the pall-bearers of a man of distinction. It was usual to choose a prominent hill with a commanding outlook for the last resting-place of our dead. If a man were

> ☛ How and why is the traditional Native attitude toward wealth and material possessions different from today's prevailing values?

Joseph Henry Sharp, *Dividing the Chief's Estate*, c. 1900. It is customary for the family to have a "give-away" ceremony in which all of the possessions of the deceased person are distributed throughout the tribe. The recipients offer prayers for the spirit of the departed person.

slain in battle, it was an old custom to place his body against a tree or rock in a sitting position, always facing the enemy, to indicate his undaunted defiance and bravery, even in death.

I recall a touching custom among us, which was designed to keep the memory of the departed near and warm in the bereaved household. A lock of hair of the beloved dead was wrapped in pretty clothing, such as it was supposed that he or she would like to wear if living. This "spirit bundle," as it was called, was suspended from a tripod, and occupied a certain place in the lodge which was the place of honor. At every meal time, a dish of food was placed under it, and some person of the same sex and age as the one who was gone must afterward be invited in to partake of the food. At the end of a year from the time of death, the relatives made a public feast and gave away the clothing and other gifts, while the lock of hair was interred with appropriate ceremonies.

Certainly the Indian never doubted the immortal nature of the spirit or soul of man, but neither did he care to speculate upon its probable state or condition in a future life. The idea of a "happy hunting-ground" is modern and probably borrowed, or invented by the white man. The primitive Indian was content to believe that the spirit which the "Great Mystery" breathed into man returns to Him who gave it, and

Absaroke burial platform

Blackfoot burial platform, photo by Roland Reed

that after it is freed from the body, it is everywhere and pervades all nature, yet often lingers near the grave or "spirit bundle" for the consolation of friends, and is able to hear prayers. So much of reverence was due the disembodied spirit, that it was not customary with us even to name the dead aloud.

FINAL THOUGHTS

Such are the beliefs in which I was reared—the secret ideals which have nourished in the American Indian a unique character among the peoples of the earth. Its simplicity, its reverence, its bravery and uprightness must be left to make their own appeal to the American of today, who is the inheritor of our homes, our names, and our traditions. Since there is nothing left us

but remembrance, at least let that remembrance be just!

I do not wish to disparage any one, but I do say that the virtues claimed by "Christian civilization" are not peculiar to any culture or religion. My people were very simple and unpractical—the modern obstacle to the fulfillment of the Christ ideal. Their strength lay in self-denial. Not only men, but women of the race have served the nation at most opportune moments in the history of this country.

Best of all, perhaps, we are beginning to recognize the Indian's good sense and sanity in the way of simple living and the mastery of the great out of doors. Like him, the wisest Americans are living, playing, and sleeping in the open for at least a part of the year, receiving the vital benefits of the pure air and sunlight. His deeds are carved upon the very rocks; the names he loved to speak are fastened upon the landscape; and he still lives in spirit, silently leading the multitude, for the new generation have taken him for their hero and model.

I call upon the parents of America to give their fullest support to those great organizations, the Boy Scouts and the Camp Fire Girls. The young people of today are learning through this movement much of the wisdom of the first American. In the mad rush for wealth we have too long overlooked the foundations of our national welfare. The contribution of the American Indian, though considerable from any point of view, is not to be measured by material acquirement. Its greatest worth is spiritual and philosophical. He will live, not only in the splendor of his past, the poetry of his legends and his art, not only in the interfusion of his blood with yours, and his faithful adherence to the new ideals of American citizenship, but in the living thought of the nation.

Eastman in 1916

PART IV: EASTMAN IN LATER LIFE

LATE IN EASTMAN'S LIFE HE PRACTICED WHAT HE PREACHED

The five books that make up Eastman's narrative were first published from 1902 to 1918; thus different parts of his narrative end during these years. Additional information sheds light on the fact that Eastman practiced what he preached throughout the remainder of his life.

In 1910 Eastman began his long association with the Boy Scouts, helping Ernest Thompson Seton establish the Boy Scouts of America, based in large part on the prototype of the American Indian. It was also at about this time that he became in high demand as a lecturer and public speaker, traveling extensively in the U.S. and abroad. Dr. Eastman was chosen to represent the American Indian at the Universal Races Congress in London in 1911. His public speaking continued for the remainder of his life.

Beginning in 1910 and for the rest of his life, Ohiyesa also became involved with many progressive organizations attempting to improve the circumstances of the various Indian tribes. At one time he was president of the Society of American Indians, one prominent organization of that type.

From 1915 to 1920 the Eastman family created and operated a summer camp for girls, Oahe, at Granite Lake, New Hampshire, attempting to teach Indian life-ways and values to young girls.

He and his wife separated in August 1921. While the couple declined to comment on the reason for their separation, their descendants later commented that they believed that the primary reason was the increasing dispute between the couple regarding the best future for the American Indian. Elaine Goodale East-

Eastman in the woods around Camp Oahe, c. 1918

Eastman teaching archery at Camp Oahe

of the American Indians in order to improve their own lives.

In 1928 Ohiyesa purchased land on the north shore of Lake Huron, near Desbarats, Ontario, Canada. For the remainder of his life, in addition to lecturing occasionally, he lived in his remote and primitive cabin in communion with the virgin nature that he loved so dearly. In his last years he spent only the coldest winter months with his son in Detroit, where he died on January 8, 1939, at the age of eighty. For several years toward the end of his life he worked on a major study of the Sioux, but the project was never completed.

man stressed total assimilation of Native Americans into the "melting pot" of the dominant society and she apparently increasingly tried to dominate her husband's views.[1] As already noted, Charles Eastman favored a type of cultural pluralism, or multiculturism, in which Indians would interact with the dominant society while still retaining their native identity, including many of their traditional beliefs and customs. He worked tirelessly to improve the conditions on reservations in the hope that they could become bastions of tribal traditions—in effect cultural homelands. He believed Indians could live between two worlds, so to speak, by successfully assimilating the best aspects of our modern civilization while rejecting those features that are inconsistent with Christian and traditional Indian teachings. Eastman also believed that other races should adopt the best customs and beliefs

---

[1] The interviews on which these conclusions are based are set forth in detail in a biography on his life: Raymond Wilson, *Ohiyesa: Charles Eastman, Santee Sioux* (Urbana: University of Illinois Press, 1983).

Eastman in Sioux regalia on the waterfront of Camp Oahe

Eastman at Rainy Lake, Ontario

Eastman in 1927

PART V: OTHER INDIAN VOICES

ISHI: THE LAST ABORIGINAL INDIAN

Ishi adzing juniper wood for a bow

The last pre-reservation Indian, Ishi, lived in the wild for the first fifty years of his life, emerging from the woods of Northern California in 1911. Ishi was the last of his Yahi tribe, which was the last of four tribes collectively known as the Yana. "Ishi" means "man" in the Yahi dialect of Yana; his real name was never known because it was taboo in Yahi society to say one's own name. As he was the last member of his tribe, his real name and all Yana people disappeared forever when he died of pneumonia in 1916.

Eastman writes in a number of places about the idea of living between two conflicting worlds: one represented by the traditional cultural ideals of his ancestors and the other by the modern technological world. Eastman was the first pre-reservation Indian to present extensive observations about the idea of living between these two worlds. Ishi expressed similar thoughts about the conflict between nomadic life in virgin nature and life in our technological civilization.

The anthropologists with whom Ishi lived for the last years of his life recorded a large amount of information about his life and beliefs, which resulted in a book, Ishi in Two Worlds,[1] *that preserves his penetrating observations about the two conflicting worlds. The story of Ishi's life became prominent in popular culture through an award-winning documentary film, a stage play and two movies, one starring Graham Greene and John Voigt. Those who knew him well in the last years of his life observed,* "Ishi was religious, his mysticism as spontaneous and unstrained as his smile. He believed in the making and peopling of the world by gods and demigods, and in the taboos laid down by the Old Ones. He also believed in a Land of the Dead where the souls of his tribe live." *Ishi found that Christian beliefs were consistent with his ancestral teachings:* "Christian doctrine interested him, and seemed to him for the most part reasonable and understandable."

Regarding the dominant American culture, "He approved of the 'conveniences' and variety of the white man's world." *Ishi concluded,* "the white man is fortunate, inventive, and very, very clever; but childlike and lacking in a desirable reserve, and in a true understanding of Nature—her mystic face; her terrible and her benign power." *Another of his friends observed,* "He looked upon us as sophisticated children—smart, but not wise. We knew many things, and much that is false. He knew nature, which is always true. His were the qualities of character that last forever. He was kind; he had courage and self-restraint, and though all had been taken from him, there was no bitterness in his heart. His soul was that of a child, his mind that of a philosopher." *On his deathbed, just before he passed to the world of spirits, Ishi's last words to his friends were,* "You stay, I go."

Ishi aiming an arrow

---

[1] Theodora Kroeber, *Ishi in Two Worlds* (Berkeley: University of California Press, 1962). All quotations in this section are from *Ishi in Two Worlds*.

CONTEMPORARY INDIAN VOICES

All of the Contemporary Voices consist of excerpts from my interviews with Native leaders of seven different tribes over the past twenty-five years. Their observations provide important insights into the contemporary situation on Indian reservations. Their collective wisdom will also benefit anyone searching to find a balance in today's fast-paced society.

Joe Medicine Crow, Crow

Joe Medicine Crow, recipient of the Presidential Medal of Freedom

In 1934 the Commissioner of Indian Affairs issued a so-called "Indian Re-organization Act" that removed the prohibitions imposed by the "Secretary's Order of 1884." So from that time on the people could do their ceremonials. For fifty years there was a strict period of cultural transition. However, the government could not take away the intangible things; the Crow people still had their values, their traditional religion, and their philosophy—they kept them. During this time they had to go hide and perform some of their rituals—many families tried to keep their spiritual traditions alive in the secrecy of their homes. And, all of the clan rules were kept intact right up to this day, which is a good thing because those are important rules to follow. So we survived with our values and most of our ceremonials. The tribal culture was kept alive.

The powwow is one vehicle that is keeping our children "Indian." Of course they go to school, but during the Crow Fair you'll see even the little kids all dressed up, dancing, parading on horses, going back to the old Indian ways and enjoying themselves. Then they put their Indian costumes away and they go to school. I'm glad to see that they are hanging on to the old ways.

I have lived in two worlds: one is a traditional Crow Indian way—I dance, sing and go to ceremonies and all those things; and at the same time, I lived like a modern American, going to several colleges; I had

Crow boy on horseback

good jobs. I can mix the two, blend the two, get the best from each and enjoy life living in both worlds. When I want to give advice to these young Crow Indian boys and girls I tell them "never forget the old tribal ways, this brings a good life." And I also tell them, "go to school, get a good education and be able to compete in the white man's world in finding jobs, following your profession. You can blend the two and enjoy a good bi-cultural way." It is possible to live in both worlds. That is my advice to these young kids, and they are doing it now.

James Trosper, Arapaho/Shoshone

There are a lot of challenges that our people have faced and a lot of challenges our ancestors had to face throughout history, especially in the last 500 years. When you look at everything that was against them it is really a wonder that our people are still here today—the disease, the government policies.... It was really devastating to our people.

Our people survived all of these challenges because they continued to follow our traditional spiritual teachings; they continued to perform the sacred ceremonies. Without this sacred center I just don't think we could have survived. Now our traditional ways remain strong. I think that our children today need to realize that the traditional ways are good and come from the Creator and that we can be a part of American society but also hold onto our traditional values, still hold onto our traditional teachings.

Our sacred ceremonies not only benefit each individual, they also benefit the

James Trosper, Shoshone/Arapaho, Shoshone Sun Dance chief, Trustee of University of Wyoming

entire tribe, our country and the whole world. For example, in the Sun Dance we pray for the tribe, we pray for our country. Those prayers are really offered for all Indian people, for the whole world, and for the whole universe. We pray for everything. During the Sunrise Ceremony the leaders offer a special prayer and the purpose for that prayer is really a global prayer—we are praying for the whole world and really for the whole universe because everything in the Sun Dance represents a different part of the universe. That sunrise prayer and that time of the day are dedicated to the blessing of the whole world.

We do have to live in today's world, we do have to learn the way that things work

Crow Sun Dance lodge

in today's world. But I don't think that we need to take the attitude of "out with the old, and in with the new." I think that we need to hold onto the old and we need to learn the new. This is important for our people. My advice to anybody is to hold onto the good things, to the old things that the Creator has taught to our people and that have passed down for generations. I tell our youth, or anybody that needs help, that by turning back to our traditional ways, by turning back to the things that the Creator has blessed us with, we can find all the answers to all of the problems and all the challenges that we face today.

☞ Did their traditional values help American Indians overcome the challenges of the past four centuries?

Gordon Tootoosis, Cree

I lost my daughter and her husband, who had four kids. When I became the guardian of my grandchildren I moved from Los Angeles back here to Saskatchewan to raise them on the Poundmaker Reservation—the Poundmaker First Nation. We have the sweat lodge right here; we don't have one in L.A. We have our Sun Dances, we have other sacred ceremonies, we have our drum here, we have our songs, and we have our pipe here. I choose to live here with my relatives, the rest of the Cree, because I feel that my grandchildren need to know who they are. They need to retain their value system, they need to know and retain our belief systems, our world view as Cree, First Nations people here in North America.

There are many sacred ceremonies that

Gordon Tootoosis, Cree, actor

are still alive. When you hear our drum and our singing, our traditional music, you should know that there is no music anywhere in the world like ours. All of these are gifts from the Creator. We have our Sun Dances; as far as I know all of the Plains tribes still have the Sun Dance, although they are done a little differently by each tribe. You can find those ceremonies. Present tobacco or a little offering to the elders and then find out more about the sacred ceremonies.

What is paramount is attaining an education from the educational system from wherever we live, in my case here in Saskatchewan. The educational system is all in the English language so a person can make

Shoshone-Arapaho sweat lodge, c. 2006

a living. That type of education teaches you how to make a living; but to know how to live you need a different learning. Our traditional background as First Nations people teaches us how to live. Both ways are important because to make a living we need schooling, but we must never forget the ways of our ancestors—that is the most important.

Arvol Looking Horse, Sioux

As the Keeper of the Sacred Pipe, as spiritual leader among our people, we have a great concern about the future generations. Our ways of life here on the earth are not good. People use a lot of foul language; people are in a lot of pain—spiritually, physically, mentally. They need to remember our traditional teachings.

Arvol Looking Horse, Sioux, keeper of the original sacred pipe of the Sioux people

Sitting Bull said over 100 years ago, "Take the good and leave the bad." He was saying to the people that you should learn to go to school and get educated. We need to balance ourselves today through education, by going to school, and by also follow-

ing our traditional way of life. We say that the mind, the body, and the spirit can bring wholeness to life—that is what we believe in. Our ceremonies, our songs, our prayers are about life, about how sacred things are, and about trying to live a beautiful sacred way of life.

John Arlee, Salish

John Arlee, Salish, traditional spiritual leader, author

Among Native peoples there is always a tribe somewhere that is praying for the livelihood of all the people, for their crops, for their harvest, their hunting, for a cure to sickness. Everybody is dancing and praying about these things. That's exactly what we do at our [Salish] wintertime ceremony, praying for this coming year, that we'll have a successful year. At the [Crow-Shoshone] Sun Dance they're carrying a heavy load, carrying some responsibility for their tribe—they're sacrificing these three days for themselves and all people. This is exactly what our tribe does in our wintertime ceremony; so in every tribe there is a ceremony that is being held for each season.

This means that one tribe is not carrying the entire load for all the people. Every tribe has a time when they're praying for the world in general.

Janine Pease, Crow/Hidatsa

The Sun Dance is a source of tremendous strength for our people. All across the high plains I see this tradition as being very strong and important for the way in which families carry out their lives. It weaves together several very important spiritual traditions: the sweat lodge, the medicine bundles, and the vision quest. The Sun Dance creates a very vibrant community that is dynamic; it's growing and people are very deeply involved in it—not only the elders but also people in their middle age and young people. I know in my family there are people as young as fifteen and twenty who are taking part in the Sun Dance as a year round spiritual expression.

The commitment that people in the Sun Dance give, the sacrifice they give on behalf of their families, is a great thing. A family member in a Sun Dance involves the entire extended family; so we see people saying, "Well, my auntie went into the Sun Dance because she was devoted to the health and well-being of her niece or nephew who's been ill, or to having her grandchildren in a good healthy home." That prayer, that expression, and that commitment of prayer, is very powerful. It focuses the whole family on the purpose of prayer. There are various gifts the sun dancers can have while they're in the Sun Dance lodge, like the cattails, the mint, and the sage. Big family groups bring those gifts to the dancers to show respect

Janine Pease, Crow/Hidatsa, American Indian Educator of the Year

and share prayers. The interaction of that many people with the Creator is a broad strengthening of the community—it's the talk of the town when there is a Sun Dance on: how many people went in and how long did they stay? All of that is very positive—it's an uplifting spiritual event in the community that is very, very important.

In our American Indian communities, our children are surrounded by wonderful resources, right in your own home sometimes. There are people who know a great deal about our very own tribes, about our land, the language, about traditions. It is so important to learn about ways of living that have sustained our people for thousands of years. When I talk to my nieces and neph-

Bringing cattails to the sun dancers, Crow Sun Dance, 1970s

ews and my grandchildren, I say, "Be daring, turn the TV off. Take a couple of days break from the cable TV and listen to your elders."

These are the things that I say to our youth: follow the traditional ways, the richness of music and dance, the access to spiritual expression in our communities; all of those things, and the values of American Indian living, those are what make an American Indian person who they are.

Inés Talamantez, Apache

You need to exercise, you need to eat good healthy food, and you need to take care of your mind. The way you do that is by studying; even if you're not in school, you can read books and there's a lot you can learn from books. And there's also a lot you can learn from speaking with your elders, if you're in a situation where they are available to you. Begin to respect them because they have a lot of wisdom and they have the solution for us in terms of how to deal with society. You can be a member of this American society, because you are an American, but at the same time you are also a Native person and you can be a part of your Native culture. There are ways of doing that and one of the most important is by trying to learn the language.

Take the time to be quiet and be by yourself and reflect on what your gifts are because there are two ways to go: you can go the good way and live in harmony with nature, which is what our ancestors have always done; or you can go the other way and end up in prison, because you didn't follow the good path, you followed the wrong path.

Inés Talamantez,
Apache, UCSB

Sometimes it seems as though it's easier to go the wrong path, because there are things out there that make you feel good, but it's only temporary. Those things don't make you feel good in your life, and what you need is to figure out what are the things that make you feel good. One of the things that makes you feel good is to get out into nature—go walking, go hiking, go swimming in the ocean, or wherever you live, in a river or a lake, experience the beauty of America, experience how America is such a sacred place. Everywhere you go in this land, our people have been there and they have said, "This place is sacred." We have to return to those ways by being in the natural world. Spend time hiking, walking, swimming, and being in the natural world; and recognize that our elders have always told us that we're connected to the natural world, that we have an obligation to it, to protect it.

> ☞ Consider the validity of the stereotype that today's reservation culture approves of the excessive use of intoxicants, including alcohol and drugs.

Tantoo Cardinal, Métis/Cree

The people who came to America wanted to weaken us and make us ineffectual in standing up for who we are as human beings. Their most powerful weapon was to try to take our spirituality, our cultural base, our language, our songs—all of that. For generations and generations we've been getting misinformation put into every aspect of our being. Anything you can do to learn something of your language, of your culture and your spiritual ways will be strengthening and clarifying because that's what was taken away from us. There is an incredible wealth of knowledge about who you are as an individual, a family, a culture, all out there.

Tantoo Cardinal, Métis/Cree, actress

I came through a rather poor education system, and the images of who I was were not very good; a lot of those things are changing. I always feel it is important to learn from the walking encyclopedias and the walking museums—the elders around you. Pick their brains, get to know their hearts and their souls; and also, *read, read, read.* Always keep in touch with your inner heart and inner mind. Go into those places that are not comfortable, places you don't want to look at, especially places that should be sorted out. If you can talk about things or think about them out loud, then that gives them a chance to come out to the open. Be objective with yourself and objective with other people, because it is our journey to know who we are and why we are here. It takes a lot of courage to be an upstanding human being, to know yourself, a lot of courage.

Thomas Yellowtail, Crow

Everyone can see how things have changed from the olden times, when sacred values were at the center of our life, up to the present day, when our society does not seem to have a sense of the sacred. If people continue on their present course, with no prayer and no respect for sacred things, then things will get worse and worse for everyone.

Many young people wonder what may happen to this world that we are in, and what they should do if they want to follow a spiritual path. They may think, "Do I have an opportunity to lead a life in accordance with the traditional ways?" It is important for the young people to understand their traditional religion. Each man will pass from this earth in his own time. We have to make a choice, each one of us must choose at this present moment which path to follow.

There is nothing more I can say except to raise my voice in prayer:

"All the people should unite and pray

bad things about other ways that they don't know about. There should be no hard feelings about someone else if he is following a way that leads to You. Help us to see this wisdom. *Aho, Aho!*"

Thomas Yellowtail, Crow Medicine Man and Sun Dance Chief

together, regardless of their beliefs. You have given different ways to different people all over the world. As we know, this earth is round like a wagon wheel. In a wagon wheel, all the spokes are set into the center. The circle of the wheel is round and all spokes come from the center and the center is You, *Acbadadea*, The Maker of All Things Above. Each spoke can be considered as a different religion of the world which has been given by You to different people and different races. All of the people of the world are on the rim of the wheel and they must follow one of the spokes to the center. The different paths have been given to us but they all lead to the same place. We all pray to the same God, to You. There are different places on the wheel so each way may look strange to someone following a different path. It is easy for people to say that their way is the best if they know all about their faith and it is good for them. But they should refrain from saying

Center Pole, Crow Sun Dance lodge, 1970s

☛ What values do you share with traditional American Indians?

☛ To what extent is each of us living between two worlds if we are trying to maintain traditional values in our daily lives?

PART VI: HISTORICAL TIMELINE

TIMELINE OF AMERICAN INDIAN HISTORY: 1620-2009

1620: Pilgrims arrive on Plymouth Rock, Massachusetts
   ⬧ Our "Thanksgiving" holiday commemorates the help given to the Pilgrims by the Wampanoag Indians

1675: King Philip's War—the bloodiest war in America's history on a per capita basis
   ⬧ About 5% of all colonists are killed; most New England towns are raided
   ⬧ More than 50% of all Indians in New England are killed; captives sent to Bahamas as slaves
   ⬧ A sad way to repay the tribe that welcomed the first Pilgrims

Mid-1700s: Plains Indian horse culture begins with arrival of horses descended from Spanish mounts

1780-81: The first major epidemic comes to the Sioux—the year "Many Died of Smallpox"
   ⬧ European diseases killed over 80% of the native people

1790-1834: "Indian Trade and Intercourse Acts" provide "civilization programs" for Indians, including:
   ⬧ Impartial justice toward Indians   ⬧ Regulated buying of Indian lands
   ⬧ Promotion of commerce   ⬧ Promotion of experiments to civilize tribes ("assimilation")

1811-12: Tecumseh, a Shawnee chief, attempts to organize an alliance of tribes against the government
   ⬧ The alliance is crushed at the Battle of Tippecanoe
   ⬧ This campaign is the closest any Indian comes to forming an organized resistance
   ⬧ The Cherokee stay loyal to the U.S. and refuse to join Tecumseh

1830: "The Indian Removal Act of 1830"
   ⬧ Stated U.S. policy toward Indians remains assimilation into the "melting (smelting) pot"
   ⬧ The Cherokee adopt many aspects of the dominant culture and civilization
   ⬧ But white voters covet the land of the "Five Civilized Tribes"

1830-1880s: U.S. removes dozens of tribes to "Indian Territory" in Oklahoma
   ⬧ Treaties agree to "forever secure and guaranty" this land for the Native peoples

1838: Cherokee "Trail of Tears"—Cherokee herded into "concentration camps"
   ⬧ Up to 8,000—about 33%—of the tribe die before, during, and after 1,000 mile forced march to Oklahoma Territory

1858: Charles Eastman is born in Minnesota

1862: Transcontinental railroad construction starts in Omaha, Nebraska and California
   ⬧ The large scale slaughter of buffalo begins

1866-68: Red Cloud's War and Fort Laramie Treaty of 1868
   ⬧ Sioux win the war and retain much of South Dakota, including all of the Black Hills

✧ Sioux guaranteed the right to hunt in "Unceded Territory" in Wyoming and Montana

1869: Completion of the transcontinental railroad
   ✧ Railroad allows the transportation of buffalo hides to Eastern markets
   ✧ Brings an increasing number of settlers to the West

1874: Gold discovered in the Black Hills of South Dakota
   ✧ Settlers and prospectors invade the Sioux reservation
   ✧ The U.S. violates its treaty obligations with the Sioux

1876: Custer's Last Stand—Sioux and Cheyenne wipe out Custer and troops of U.S. 7th Cavalry
   ✧ Accelerates the policy to exterminate the buffalo to force all Indians onto reservations

1881: Virtual extinction of the buffalo—as few as 2,000 remain in scattered groups
   ✧ Loss of something ineffably sacred to the Indians; a wound in the heart of all Native peoples

1881: Sitting Bull's surrender ends warfare on the Plains

1884: Secretary of Interior creates criminal code that outlaws large community ceremonies and rites
   ✧ Small "social gatherings for amusement" are allowed

1884-1934: Reservation Period of "forced cultural assimilation"
   ✧ Religion: each family arbitrarily assigned to one or another Christian denomination
   ✧ Education: children forcibly taken from homes into boarding schools in deplorable conditions
      ✧ Teaching only goes to 6th grade level in most reservation schools
      ✧ Hair is cut; cast-off clothes worn; use of native language prohibited; harsh punishments

1886: Geronimo's final surrender after numerous captures—end of all Indian warfare

1887: Dawes Act—allots each Indian 160 acres for a farm or 80 acres for a ranch
   ✧ All "excess land" to be sold or given away under the Homestead Act

1889-95: Seven "Oklahoma Land Rushes" give away over 15 million acres of Indian Territory
   ✧ 1893: "Cherokee Strip Land Run" gives away 7 million acres of Cherokee land in one day
   ✧ For the Cherokee, "forever secure" meant 50 years from the time of the Trail of Tears

1890: Wounded Knee Massacre by the U.S. 7th Cavalry crushes last vestiges of Indian morale

1900: Census reports only 237,000 American Indians in the U.S.
   ✧ Less than 5% of the Native population in 1500 C.E.

Early 1900s: Form of today's "powwows" starts to emerge as social gatherings celebrate tribal traditions
   ✧ Derived from the Algonquin word *pawauog*, meaning "medicine man" or "healer"

1910: The Boy Scouts and Camp Fire Girls are founded based on American Indian values:
   ✧ Reverence for nature; individual self-reliance; charity towards one's neighbor

1917: World War I provides an opportunity for Indian patriotism
- 12,000 men volunteer in first six months of the war; 5,000 more serve later in the war
- 10,000 women join the Red Cross
- Native communities buy $25 million of war bonds; $75 for every man, woman and child
- "Paradox of patriotism"—Indians are the most oppressed, yet the most patriotic racial group
- Some Indians move to cities for war-related work and do not return to reservations after war's end

1934: "Indian Reorganization Act"—repeals Dawes Act and Secretary of Interior's Order of 1884
- First Peoples can once again openly practice their traditional culture
- Each reservation can establish its own tribal government, but their powers are limited
- 90 million acres (66%) of Indian land taken away during the 47 years of the Dawes Act

Mid-1930s: considered by many as the low point of American Indian culture and morale
- Loss of many sacred ceremonies
- Intense poverty from loss of land and great economic hardship during the depression years

1939: Charles Eastman dies

1941: World War II again highlights the paradox of patriotism displayed by Indians
- 25,000 serve in the military; and at least twice that many move to work in defense plants
- 400 Navajo "code talkers" create an unbreakable military code
- More natives move to cities for war-related work and do not return to reservations after war's end

1940s-50s: Emergence of cultural revival—winds of renewal blow on many reservations
- World War II ignites interest in traditional sacred ceremonies on many reservations
- Powwows spread throughout the U.S. during these decades

1948-70: Bureau of Indian Affairs (BIA) creates a national program of "relocation" to cities
- Recruiting, travel expenses, job placement and training encourages movement from reservations to cities
- Continuing efforts to assimilate Indians into one "melting pot"
- Program has mixed results, but most stay in the cities

1950s-60s: Native American Church expands its presence to most reservations
- First arrived in Oklahoma from Mesoamerica during World War I
- Peyote ritual with emphasis on moral conduct and abstinence from alcohol
- Many Christian Indians and traditionalists also attend ceremonies

1959-62: U.S. Supreme Court repeatedly supports Native treaty rights, ruling that:
- Tribal courts have "sovereignty" in all matters regarding tribal members except war
- Businesses on reservations not required to collect state sales tax
- Tribal police and courts have jurisdiction over non-Indian owned land on reservations
- These cases encourage litigation based upon treaty rights and past violations

1970s: "Red Power" movement is led primarily by AIM—the American Indian Movement
- 1969: 18 month seizure of Alcatraz Island in San Francisco Bay

- 1972: AIM demands and receives justice for a tribal member in Gordon, Nebraska
- 1972: 6 day occupation of BIA headquarters in Washington, D.C. by AIM
- 1973: AIM occupation at Wounded Knee leads to nine week siege with FBI
- 1978: Red Power draws to an end with 1,000 person march in Washington D.C.
- Red Power raises public awareness of problems and restores Indian pride
- Over 1,000 native newspapers, journals and newsletters come into existence in the 1970s-80s

1970s: Protests mount to improve Indian health care
- Government study documents that 3,406 women (3% of Indian women of child-bearing years) were sterilized in government clinics without their informed consent from 1973-76.

1970s-80s: Explosion of interest in traditional sacred ceremonies among most tribes
- Reservations come to be perceived as cultural homelands
- Multiple Sun Dances take place every week during July and August on each Sioux reservation

1975-90: Congress passes a series of laws that empower Native people, including:
- 1975: Indian Self-Determination and Educational Assistance Act
  - Each tribe can now control its schools, police, courts, tribal housing and health clinics
- 1978: American Indian Religious Freedom Act
  - Guarantees access to sacred sites and the use of sacred objects
- 1978: Tribally Controlled Community College Assistance Act
  - Federal assistance to all tribally chartered post-secondary school institutions
- 1978: American Indian Child Welfare Act
  - Stops the practice of placing welfare children in non-Indian homes off the reservations
  - In 1974 over 25% of all Indian children are in foster care or government boarding schools
- 1990: Native American Graves Protection and Repatriation Act
  - Requires museums to return any of a tribe's human remains, sacred or ceremonial objects

1980: Supreme Court rules that U.S. illegally took Black Hills and awards the Sioux $110 million
- The tribe refuses payment and demands return of the land
- The money remains in an interest-bearing account which now amounts to over $760 million
- This case is only one of scores of litigation throughout the U.S. for past treaty violations

1987: Supreme Court recognizes right of tribes to operate gambling outside state control
- Now 200 tribes operate casinos and bingo parlors generating more than $1 billion in annual profit
- Large majority of the profits are concentrated in a few tribes near metropolitan areas
- Gambling creates addictions among tribal members and is against traditional values
- Gambling creates large problems on remote reservations that cannot attract non-Indian players

1992: Congressional Committee issues "Misplaced Trust: The BIAs Mismanagement of the Indian Trust Fund"
- Report acknowledges the BIA has lost billions of dollars from Indian trust funds for over 100 years
- Auditors note at least $2.4 billion is unaccounted for from just 1973-92
- Billions more untraceable because of questionable nature of government's records
- As of 2009, the problems remain uncorrected and the money unpaid

2000: BIA issues a formal apology to all American Indians (see p. 199)

2009: Circumstances on Indian reservations are complex and multi-dimensional:
- American Indians are proud of their cultural and ethnic heritage
- There is an irreversible movement for traditional cultural renewal
- Many embrace both Christianity and their ancestral traditions
- Each federally recognized tribe is a semi-autonomous "nation" within the U.S.
- There are 310 reservations for 100+ tribes (some tribes have several; many have none)
- 2,800,000 people list their racial identity as American Indian, although most have mixed heritage
  - Another 1.6 million list mixed racial heritage, most without citing any tribal affiliation
- Native health problems:
  - Death rate for ages 15-24 is 60% higher than overall population
  - Death rate for ages 25-44 is 80% higher than overall population
  - Alcoholism, tuberculosis, diabetes, pneumonia and suicides are much higher than the average
- Violent crime on reservations:
  - Violent crime is 250% higher than overall population (Senate Committee on Indian Affairs)
  - 60% of Indian women will become victims of violence during their lifetimes
- Poverty is a recurring problem, with no solution in sight:
  - 26% live below the poverty line—the highest of any racial group (Census Bureau, 2002)
  - Six of the seven counties with the lowest income in the U.S. are on reservations in South and North Dakoka
  - Economic barriers that inhibit employment on reservations include:
    - Remote geographic locations
    - Inadequate education
    - Lack of access to investment capital
    - Traditional custom to "give-away" property
  - Improved mechanization of farm and ranch work create more unemployment

☞ Industrialized nations will struggle over the next century to control the earth's shrinking natural resources.

⬦ What ethical obligations do we owe to underdeveloped nations that are rich in natural resources?

⬦ Will other industrialized countries share our altruism?

⬦ Will the governments of underdeveloped countries recognize the human rights of their indigenous peoples?

⬦ Is there a possibility that history can repeat itself in certain respects?

PRIDE IN THEIR ANCESTRAL HERITAGE
STARTS AT AN EARLY AGE

Powwow dancing

THE "PARADOX OF PATRIOTISM" ENDURES

- ✧ American Indians remain the racial group with the highest rate of volunteer military service
- ✧ Powwows and some sacred rites feature an Indian honor song for the American flag and veterans

The American flag is prominent at most powwows and some sacred rites, including this Crow-Shoshone Sun Dance lodge, c. 1990

☛ Has the U.S. government adequately compensated American Indians for four centuries of injustice? Consider what other actions might be possible or appropriate.

☛ Do whites still consider themselves to be culturally superior to indigenous peoples?

✧ If so, how does it affect the majority view on native culture, land title and "inalienable rights"?

At this powwow the American flag is carried at the front of the grand entry parade, immediately behind the traditional eagle feather coup stick, c. 2006

197

Indian Reservations in the Continental United States

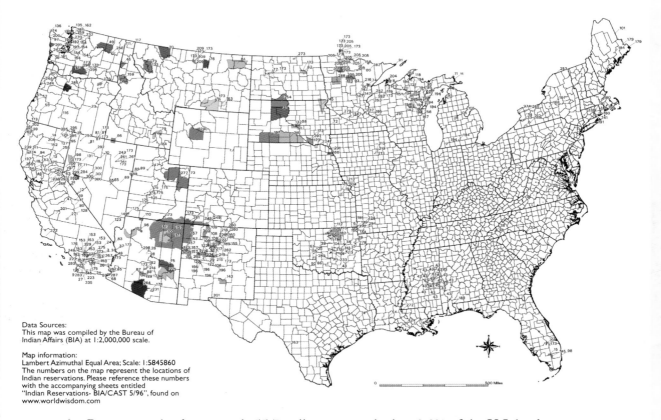

Data Sources:
This map was compiled by the Bureau of
Indian Affairs (BIA) at 1:2,000,000 scale.

Map information:
Lambert Azimuthal Equal Area; Scale: 1:5845860
The numbers on the map represent the locations of
Indian reservations. Please reference these numbers
with the accompanying sheets entitled
"Indian Reservations- BIA/CAST 5/96", found on
www.worldwisdom.com

✦ Reservation land now totals 55.7 million acres, which is 2.3% of the U.S. land area
✦ Financial desperation forced the sale of about 50% of reservation land to non-Indians
✦ Between 1% to 2% of the land in the U.S. remains in Indian ownership

INDIAN RESERVATIONS FORM PART OF A "CULTURAL MOSAIC"

✦ A "cultural mosaic" is based on the belief that a country as a whole becomes stronger by having each different ethnic group retain its unique cultural identity and diversity
✦ The majority of people who consider themselves American Indian live on or near reservations.
  ✦ Over 1,000,000 Indians (40%) live on reservations; about 30% live in nearby cities
  ✦ Many Indians who live in large cities congregate at American Indian centers
  ✦ Explained, in part, by close ties to family and the vitality of traditional Native culture

> ☞ What is a reservation: a sanctuary, or a trap, or both? How has this changed over time?

✦ Most American Indians support the idea of a visible cultural mosaic that allows them to retain their Indian identity and promotes multiculturalism

APPENDIX

Remarks of Kevin Gover, Assistant Secretary-Indian Affairs, Department of the Interior at the Ceremony Acknowledging the 175th Anniversary of the Establishment of the Bureau of Indian Affairs, September 8, 2000

In March of 1824, President James Monroe established the Office of Indian Affairs in the Department of War. Its mission was to conduct the nation's business with regard to Indian affairs. We have come together today to mark the first 175 years of the institution now known as the Bureau of Indian Affairs.

It is appropriate that we do so in the first year of a new century and a new millennium, a time when our leaders are reflecting on what lies ahead and preparing for those challenges. Before looking ahead, though, this institution must first look back and reflect on what it has wrought and, by doing so, come to know that this is no occasion for celebration; rather it is time for reflection and contemplation, a time for sorrowful truths to be spoken, a time for contrition.

We must first reconcile ourselves to the fact that the works of this agency have at various times profoundly harmed the communities it was meant to serve. From the very beginning, the Office of Indian Affairs was an instrument by which the United States enforced its ambition against the Indian nations and Indian people who stood in its path. And so, the first mission of this institution was to execute the removal of the southeastern tribal nations. By threat, deceit, and force, these great tribal nations were made to march 1,000 miles to the west, leaving thousands of their old, their young and their infirm in hasty graves along the Trail of Tears.

As the nation looked to the West for more land, this agency participated in the ethnic cleansing that befell the western tribes. War necessarily begets tragedy; the war for the West was no exception. Yet in these more enlightened times, it must be acknowledged that the deliberate spread of disease, the decimation of the mighty bison herds, the use of the poison alcohol to destroy mind and body, and the cowardly killing of women and children made for tragedy on a scale so ghastly that it cannot be dismissed as merely the inevitable consequence of the clash of competing ways of life. This agency and the good people in it failed in the mission to prevent the devastation. And so great nations of patriot warriors fell. We will never push aside the memory of unnecessary and violent death at places such as Sand Creek, the banks of the Washita River, and Wounded Knee.

Nor did the consequences of war have to include the futile and destructive efforts to annihilate Indian cultures. After the devastation of tribal economies and the deliberate creation of tribal dependence on the services provided by this agency, this agency set out to destroy all things Indian.

This agency forbade the speaking of Indian languages, prohibited the conduct of traditional religious activities, outlawed traditional government, and made Indian people ashamed of who they were. Worst of all, the Bureau of Indian Affairs committed these acts against the children entrusted to its boarding schools, brutalizing them emotionally, psychologically, physically, and spiritually. Even in this era of self-determination, when the Bureau of Indian Affairs is at long last serving as an advocate for Indian people in an atmosphere of mutual respect, the legacy of these misdeeds haunts us. The trauma of shame, fear and anger has passed from one generation to the next, and manifests itself in the rampant alcoholism, drug abuse, and domestic violence that plague Indian country. Many of our people live lives of unrelenting tragedy as Indian families suffer the ruin of lives by alcoholism, suicides made of shame and despair, and violent death at the hands of one another. So many of the maladies suffered today in Indian country result from the failures of this agency. Poverty, ignorance, and disease have been the product of this agency's work.

And so today I stand before you as the leader of an institution that in the past has committed acts so terrible that they infect, diminish, and destroy the lives of Indian people decades later, generations later. These things occurred despite the efforts of many good people with good hearts who sought to prevent them. These wrongs must be acknowledged if the healing is to begin.

I do not speak today for the United States. That is the province of the nation's elected leaders, and I would not presume to speak on their behalf. I am empowered, however, to speak on behalf of this agency, the Bureau of Indian Affairs, and I am quite certain that the words that follow reflect the hearts of its 10,000 employees.

Let us begin by expressing our profound sorrow for what this agency has done in the past. Just like you, when we think of these misdeeds and their tragic consequences, our hearts break and our grief is as pure and complete as yours. We desperately wish that we could change this history, but of course we cannot. On behalf of the Bureau of Indian Affairs, I extend this formal apology to Indian people for the historical conduct of this agency.

And while the BIA employees of today did not commit these wrongs, we acknowledge that the institution we serve did. We accept this inheritance, this legacy of racism and inhumanity. And by accepting this legacy, we accept also the moral responsibility of putting things right.

We therefore begin this important work anew, and make a new commitment to the people and communities that we serve, a commitment born of the dedication we share with you to the cause of renewed hope and prosperity for Indian country. Never again will this agency stand silent when hate and violence are committed against Indians. Never again will we allow policy to proceed from the assumption that Indians possess less human genius than the other races. Never again will we be complicit in the theft of Indian property. Never again will we appoint false leaders who serve purposes other than those of the tribes. Never again will we allow unflattering and stereotypical images of Indian people to deface the halls of government or lead the American people to shallow and ignorant beliefs about Indians. Never again will we attack your religions, your languages, your rituals, or any of your tribal ways. Never again will we seize your children, nor teach them to be ashamed of who they are. Never again.

We cannot yet ask your forgiveness, not while the burdens of this agency's history weigh so heavily on tribal communities. What we do ask is that, together, we allow the healing to begin: As you return to your homes, and as you talk with your people, please tell them that time of dying is at its end. Tell your children that the time of shame and fear is over. Tell your young men and women to replace their anger with hope and love for their people. Together, we must wipe the tears of seven generations. Together, we must allow our broken hearts to mend. Together, we will face a challenging world with confidence and trust. Together, let us resolve that when our future leaders gather to discuss the history of this institution, it will be time to celebrate the rebirth of joy, freedom, and progress for the Indian Nations. The Bureau of Indian Affairs was born in 1824 in a time of war on Indian people. May it live in the year 2000 and beyond as an instrument of their prosperity.

FREE SUPPLEMENTARY STUDY MATERIALS

World Wisdom's Internet site provides many free supplementary materials with numerous illustrations, maps, and films to facilitate classroom and independent study, including:

The webpage for *Living in Two Worlds: The American Indian Experience* containing:
(http://www.worldwisdom.com/livingintwoworlds.aspx)
- ☩ Streaming film of lectures by Michael Fitzgerald given to high school students using a range of photographs, maps, and films
  - ◦ "The American Indian Experience: 1600-2009"
  - ◦ "Living in Two Worlds: Recurring Themes in American Indian Culture"
  - ◦ Each lecture is one hour total viewing time, presented in two parts
- ☩ Streaming film clips from the 2-DVD set entitled *Native Spirit & The Sun Dance Way*, including:
  - ◦ "The Sweat Lodge"
  - ◦ "The Vision Quest"
  - ◦ "Sun Dance Overview"
  - ◦ "Living in Two Worlds: Interviews with Native Elders"
- ☩ A section entitled "Free Teaching Aids" that includes:
  - ◦ "Historical Prologue"
  - ◦ Many maps and illustrations for classrom use
  - ◦ "Does our future hold a 'melting pot' or a 'cultural mosaic', or both?"
- ☩ "Discussion Questions", together with suggestions, that include the following general subject areas:
  - ◦ "Traditional American Indian Culture"
  - ◦ "Ongoing Challenges"
  - ◦ "What does the American Indian experience teach us about democracy?"
  - ◦ "What can we learn from the American Indians?"
  - ◦ "In what ways are each of us Living in Two Worlds?"
  - ◦ "Questions to Ponder"
- ☩ Additional information about the editor, Michael Fitzgerald

"American Indian Resources" that include:
(http://www.worldwisdom.com/aminresources.aspx)
- ☩ More than fifty film clips with Native elders on different topics
- ☩ Slide shows
- ☩ Illustrated flash presentations
- ☩ Online library of articles
- ☩ Free e-products
- ☩ References to facilitate further study

"American Indian Online Image Gallery" that contains:
(http://www.worldwisdom.com/amingallery.aspx)
- ☩ More than 100 vintage and rare photographs and illustrations

"Edward Curtis Resources" that include:
(http://www.worldwisdom.com/curtisresources.aspx)
- ☩ Searchable chapters of Edward S. Curtis' writings on 80 different tribes
- ☩ More than 400 Curtis photographs that can be sorted by tribe and by subjects that include men, women, children, groups, the sacred, camp life, and homes/structures

EASTMAN'S BIBLIOGRAPHY

Charles Eastman's first book, *Indian Boyhood*, was published in 1902. It is the story of his own early life in the wilds of Canada, and it was an immediate public success generating public notoriety and a demand for more of his writings. He wrote a total of eleven books, including *Red Hunters and the Animal People* (1904), *Old Indian Days* (1906), *Wigwam Evenings* (1909), *Smoky Day's Wigwam Evenings: Indian Stories Retold* (1910), *The Soul of the Indian* (1911), *Indian Child Life* (1913), *Indian Scout Talks* (1914), *The Indian Today: The Past and Future of the First American* (1915), *From the Deep Woods to Civilization* (1916), and *Indian Heroes and Great Chieftons* (1918). All of his books were successful, some were used in school editions, and many were translated into French, German, Danish, and Czech languages. He also contributed numerous articles to magazines, reviews, and encyclopedias.

BIOGRAPHICAL NOTES OF OTHER INDIAN VOICES

JOHN ARLEE is a Salish traditional spiritual leader and teaches both the Salish language and Salish tribal history at the Salish Kootenai College in Pablo, MT. He is the author of *Over a Century of Moving to the Drum: Salish Indian Celebrations on the Flathead Reservation*. He has also recorded traditional songs on multiple CDs. He lives on the Salish Flathead Reservation in Arlee, Montana.

BLACK ELK (1863-1950) was a renowned Oglala Sioux spiritual leader and medicine man. He participated in the Battle of the Little Big Horn in 1876, at about the age of twelve, and later toured with Buffalo Bill's Wild West Show in Europe. Black Elk was wounded in the Wounded Knee Massacre in 1890. He became a Catholic in 1903, taking the name Nicholas Black Elk. Later, he told the story of his life to John Neihardt, first published in 1932 as *Black Elk Speaks*, and revealed the sacred rites of the Oglala Lakota to Joseph Epes Brown, first published in 1953 as *The Sacred Pipe: Black Elk's Account of the Seven Rites of the Oglala Sioux*. The commemorative edition of Brown's other classic book, *The Spiritual Legacy of the American Indian: With Letters While Living with Black Elk*, contains previously unpublished correspondence from Brown that sheds new light on the debate on whether Black Elk was a sincere Catholic while at the same time practicing his ancestral spiritual traditions. These letters also record many of Black Elk's observations on modern life and traditional Indian culture.

TANTOO CARDINAL is considered by many as today's most widely recognized American Indian actress. Her film credits include *Dances with Wolves*, *Legends of the Fall* and *Smoke Signals*. A Métis-Cree from Canada, she was raised among her Cree people and speaks her native language.

CHIEF JOSEPH (1840-1904), whose traditional name was Thunder Rolling Down the Mountain, was the chief of a band of the Nez Perce tribe, whose ancestral homeland is the Wallowa Valley of northeastern Oregon. Chief Joseph refused to sign any treaty giving up his ancestral land and in 1873 he negotiated with the federal government to ensure his people could stay in their beloved Wallowa Valley.

In 1877, the government reversed its policy and threatened to force his band onto a reservation in Idaho. Chief Joseph led 800 Nez Perce, mostly women and children, toward freedom at the Canadian border rather than submit to relocation onto a reservation. For over three months, the Nez Perce battled and outmaneuvered their pursuers, traveling 1,700 miles across Oregon, Washington, Idaho, Wyoming, and Montana. The commander of the U.S. cavalry remarked upon the skill with which the Nez Perce fought. Finally, after a devastating five-day battle during freezing weather conditions with no food or blankets, Chief Joseph surrendered less than 40 miles south of Canada. His leadership and wisdom earn him a place as one of the most famous American Indian leaders.

KEVIN GOVER is an author, educator, policy specialist, and an administrator in the public, private, and academic realms. Since 2007, Gover has served as director of the Smithsonian Institution's National Museum of the American Indian. He has also been Professor of Law at Sandra Day O'Connor College of Law at Arizona State University, Tempe. Prof. Gover previously practiced law with various firms, including one which he founded and which grew into one of the largest Indian-owned firms in the country. In 1997, Professor Gover was selected by President Clinton to serve as Assistant Secretary of the Interior for Indian Affairs. He has been widely praised for his reform efforts and for the apology he crafted on behalf of the Bureau of Indian Affairs to the nation's Indian communities for the history of wrongs done to them. (Those remarks can be read on World Wisdom online Library.) Kevin Gover is a member of the Pawnee Tribe of Oklahoma.

THE IROQUOIS CONSTITUTION, also known as the Great Binding Law, was the founding document of the Iroquois Confederacy. Five tribes, the Mohawk, Oneida, Seneca, Cayuga, and Onondaga, initially constituted the confederacy, which was based in what is now the northeastern U.S. Each tribe was allowed a certain number of representatives in a body called the Great Council of Sachems. Each tribe ceded certain powers to the council while reserving the power to handle issues involving the inner workings of its own tribe. The Tuscarora tribe later moved into the area controlled by the Iroquois and became subject to the Iroquois Constitution as a non-voting member. Most scholars have speculated that this constitution was created between the middle fifteenth and early seventeenth centuries. However, recent studies have suggested the accuracy of the account found in Iroquois tradition, which argues that the federation was formed around August 31, 1142, based on a coinciding solar eclipse.

   The precise content of the Iroquois Constitution was preserved over generations by the knots and beaded designs on wampum strings, each of which has a meaning that symbolically chronicles tribal history, legends, and treaties. The first English-language translations of the wampum strings that preserved the Iroquois Constitution were completed years before the U.S. Constitution. In 2004 the U.S. State Department acknowledged that the U.S. Constitution was based in part on the Iroquois Constitution. It is a historical fact that there are many striking similarities between these two documents and that many founding fathers, including Benjamin Franklin and Thomas Jefferson, had extensive contact with the "Five Nations" of the Iroquois Confederacy.

ISHI (d. 1916) was the last pre-reservation Indian. He lived in the wild for the first fifty years of his life, emerging from the woods of Northern California in 1911. Ishi was the last of his Yahi tribe, which was the last of four tribes collectively known as the Yana. "Ishi" means "man" in the Yahi dialect of Yana; his real name was never known because it was taboo in Yahi society to say one's own name. As he was the last member of his tribe, his real name and all Yana people disappeared forever when he died of pneumonia in 1916. The anthropologists with whom Ishi lived for the last years of his life recorded a large amount of information about his life and beliefs, which resulted in a book, *Ishi in Two Worlds*, that preserves his penetrating observations about the conflict between his ancestral traditions and our prevailing societal values. The story of Ishi's life became prominent in popular culture through an award-winning documentary film, a stage play, and two movies, one starring Graham Greene and John Voigt.

KICKING BEAR (1846-1904) was a holy man and band chief of the Minneconjou Lakota Sioux. He fought in many battles with the U.S. Army, including the Battle of the Little Big Horn in 1876. He was active in the Ghost Dance religious movement of 1890 and traveled to visit the movement's leader, Wovoka, a Paiute holy man living in Nevada. Kicking Bear was instrumental in bringing the Ghost Dance to the Sioux in South Dakota. Following the killing of Sitting Bull in December, 1890, Kicking Bear was imprisoned in Illinois. Upon his release in 1891, he joined Buffalo Bill's Wild West Show for a short time. A gifted artist, Kicking Bear painted his account of the Battle of the Little Big Horn at the request of artist Frederic Remington in 1898, more than twenty years after the battle.

ARVOL LOOKING HORSE is the 19th Generation Keeper of the original White Buffalo Calf Pipe, the sacred pipe of the Lakota, Dakota, and Nakota Nations. He is widely recognized as a chief and the spiritual leader of all three branches of the Sioux tribe. He is the author of *White Buffalo Teachings* and a guest columnist for *Indian Country Today*. A tireless advocate of maintaining traditional spiritual practices, Chief Looking Horse is the founder of Big Foot Riders, which memorializes the massacre of Big Foot's band at Wounded Knee, and World Peace Day. His prayers have opened numerous sessions of the United Nations and his many awards include the Juliet Hollister Award from the Temple of Understanding, a Non-Governmental Organization with Consultation Status with the United Nations Economic and Social Council. He lives on the Cheyenne River Reservation in South Dakota.

JOE MEDICINE CROW is a recipient of the Presidential Medal of Freedom, the highest civilian honor given by the United States. The White House press release states: "Dr. Joseph Medicine Crow, the last living Plains Indian war chief, is the author of seminal works in Native American history and culture. He is the last person alive to have received direct oral testimony from a participant in the Battle of the Little Bighorn: his grandfather was a scout for General George Armstrong Custer. A veteran of World War II, Medicine Crow accomplished during the war all of the four tasks required to become a 'war chief', including stealing fifty Nazi SS horses from a German camp. Medicine Crow was the first member of his tribe to attend college, receiving his master's degree in anthropology in 1939, and continues to lecture at universities and notable institutions like the United Nations. His contributions to the preservation of the culture and history of the First Americans are matched only by his importance as a role model to young Native Americans across the country."

JANINE PEASE is the founding president of the Little Big Horn College in Crow Agency Montana, a past president of the American Indian Higher Education Consortium (for two terms), a director of the American Indian College Fund (for seven years), was appointed by President Clinton to the National Advisory Council on Indian Education (for eight years), and currently serves on the Montana Board of Regents Higher Education. She wrote the Introductions for *The Essential Charles Eastman (Ohiyesa)*. Dr. Pease has won several prestigious awards: National Indian Educator of the Year (1990), the MacArthur Fellowship Award (better known as the "Genius Award"), and the ACLU Jeanette Rankin Award. She has been named one of the "One Hundred Montanan's of the Century" by the *Missoulian Magazine* and one of the fourteen most important American Indian leaders of the 20th century in *New Warriors*, by R. David Edmunds (University of Nebraska Press). Janine is a Crow and Hidatsa Indian, enrolled as a Crow. She is currently the Vice President for Academic Affairs at Fort Peck Community College in Poplar, Montana.

RED CLOUD (1822-1909) was a war leader of the Oglala Lakota Sioux. Between 1866 and 1868 he led a successful guerilla war against the military forts located along the Bozeman Trail in northwestern Wyoming and southern Montana that is known as "Red Cloud's War". The Sioux victory resulted in the Fort Laramie Treaty of 1868, which granted large tracts of land to the Sioux tribe, including all of the Black Hills in South Dakota. This treaty stipulated that "no cessation" of land would be valid "unless executed and signed by at least three-fourths of all adult male Indians". Based upon this provision, the U.S. Supreme Court ruled in 1980 that the U.S. illegally took the Black Hills from the Sioux after gold was discovered there in the mid-1870s. Red Cloud's War was the only major war lost by the U.S. until the military withdrawal from Vietnam in 1975.

SITTING BULL (c. 1831-1890) was a Lakota Sioux holy man and one of the most famous American Indians. He had a vision predicting a Native victory over Army soldiers, which became a reality a short time later at the Battle of the Little Big Horn in 1876. He then moved his band of followers to Canada for five years before he was forced to surrender to U.S. forces in order to prevent the starvation of his people. He briefly toured with Buffalo Bill's Wild West Show before returning to the Standing Rock Indian Reservation. He was killed by Indian police during an attempt to arrest him to prevent him from supporting the Ghost Dance Religion. Sitting Bull's death on December 15, 1890 resulted in a panic among his tribe that led to the Wounded Knee Massacre on December 29, 1890, which crushed all remaining American Indian resistance and morale.

INÉS M. TALAMANTEZ is a professor at the University of California, Santa Barbara. Dr. Talamantez is a Mescalero Apache, a graduate of Dartmouth College, and the author of *Teaching Religion and Healing*. She has a book forthcoming on the Apache women's puberty ceremony and has contributed articles to *Native Religions and Cultures of North America: Anthropology of the Sacred and Unspoken Worlds: Women's Religious Lives*. She is the past president of the Indigenous Studies Group at the American Academy of Religion and is one of the most well known American Indian scholars. She has pioneered the creation of a PhD program in religious studies with an emphasis in Native American Religious Traditions at UCSB, awarding PhDs to twenty-six Native American scholars. She and her husband live in Santa Barbara.

GORDON TOOTOOSIS, a veteran of over 40 films, has appeared in *Reindeer Games* (2000) and *Legends of the Fall* (1994) with Brad Pitt and Anthony Hopkins, and then in *Alaska* (1996) with Charlton Heston. He acted the role of Chief Red Cloud in the HBO documentary film entitled *Bury My Heart at Wounded Knee* (2007). Mr. Tootoosis won the Eagle Spirit Award at the American Indian Motion Picture awards in 2001. When Tootoosis became the guardian of his four grandchildren upon the untimely death of his daughter and son-in-law, he and his wife of over 40 years, Irene Seseequasis, moved from Los Angeles back to the Poundmaker Reserve in Saskatchewan Canada to raise their grandchildren. They still reside on the Poundmaker Reserve.

JAMES TROSPER is a Sun Dance chief of the Shoshone tribe on the Wind River Indian Reservation in Wyoming. He is from a long line of Shoshone Sun Dance chiefs that includes John Trehero, the Sun Dance chief who brought the Shoshone Sun Dance to the Crow tribe, and is a direct descendent of Chief Washakie, who is the most important chief of the Shoshone tribe in history. Mr. Trosper is deeply involved in developing and promoting programs to preserve the Shoshone language and cultural heritage. He is also part Arapaho, a director of the Chief Washakie Foundation, a director of the Grand Teton National Park Foundation, and a Trustee of the University of Wyoming. He wrote the Foreword for *Indian Spirit: Revised and Enlarged*. Trosper, his wife, and their two children, live in Fort Washakie, WY.

THOMAS YELLOWTAIL (1903-1993), Crow medicine man and Sun Dance chief, was one of the most admired American Indian spiritual leaders of the last century. As a youth he lived in the presence of old warriors, hunters, and medicine men who knew the freedom and sacred ways of pre-reservation life. In February 1993, when Yellowtail received the Montana Governor's Award for the Arts in recognition of his work in preserving the traditional culture of the Crow tribe, the program for the award ceremony contained the following quotation: "This man is outside of time as we know it, centered in the spiritual world. Thomas Yellowtail has perpetuated the spiritual traditions of his Crow tribe as one of the last living links to pre-reservation days. But his legacy is not limited to Native Americans because his principles and his message benefit anyone searching to find a balance in this fast-paced technological society." His wife, Susie, was the first American Indian Registered Nurse and a tireless advocate for improvement in the health and education of her Crow people. She is enshrined in the Montana Hall of Fame in the State Capital Building in Helena.

The story of Yellowtail's life and his descriptions of the Sun Dance Religion are revealed in the book *Yellowtail: Crow Medicine Man and Sun Dance Chief*, published by the University of Oklahoma Press (1991).

MICHAEL OREN FITZGERALD is an author, editor, and publisher of books on world religions, sacred art, tradition, culture, and philosophy. He has composed over a dozen books that have received more than fifteen prestigious awards. Eight of his books and two documentary films produced by him are used in university classes. Fitzgerald is an acknowledged authority on the religion and culture of the Plains Indians and is also the adopted son of the late Thomas Yellowtail. Fitzgerald has taught Religious Traditions of the North American Indians in the Indiana University Continuing Studies Department at Bloomington, Indiana. He holds a Doctor of Jurisprudence, cum laude, from Indiana University. Michael and his wife, Judith, have spent extended periods of time visiting traditional cultures and attending sacred ceremonies throughout the world. They have an adult son and live in Bloomington, Indiana.

All royalties for Fitzgerald's books and documentary films on American Indians are donated to various American Indian charities, including The American Indian College Fund, Smithsonian's Museum of the American Indian, for the support of Crow, Shoshone and Lakota Sun Dances and to provide books and films to tribal colleges and high schools located on Indian reservations throughout the U.S. and Canada.

Michael and Judith Fitzgerald with Susie and Thomas Yellowtail, Bloomington, Indiana, 1980

INDEX

For a glossary of all key foreign words used in books published by World Wisdom, including metaphysical terms in English, consult: www.DictionaryofSpiritualTerms.org.
This on-line Dictionary of Spiritual Terms provides extensive definitions, examples, and related terms in other languages.

World Wisdom's
Other American Indian Titles

All Our Relatives: Traditional Native American Thoughts about Nature
compiled and illustrated by Paul Goble, 2005

The Cheyenne Indians: Their History and Lifeways
by George Bird Grinnell, edited by Joseph A. Fitzgerald, 2008

The Earth Made New: Plains Indian Stories of Creation
compiled and illustrated by Paul Goble, 2009

The Essential Charles Eastman (Ohiyesa): Light on the Indian World
edited by Michael Oren Fitzgerald, 2007

The Feathered Sun: Plains Indians in Art and Philosophy
by Frithjof Schuon, 1990

The Gospel of the Redman: Commemorative Edition
compiled by Ernest Thompson Seton and Julia M. Seton, 2005

The Image Taker: The Selected Stories and Photographs of Edward S. Curtis
edited by Gerald Hausman and Bob Kapoun, 2009

Indian Spirit: Revised and Enlarged
edited by Judith and Michael Oren Fitzgerald, 2006

Native Spirit: The Sun Dance Way
by Thomas Yellowtail, edited by Michael Oren Fitzgerald, 2007

The Spirit of Indian Women
edited by Judith and Michael Oren Fitzgerald, 2005

The Spiritual Legacy of the American Indian: Commemorative Edition
with Letters While Living with Black Elk
by Joseph Epes Brown, 2007

Tipi: Home of the Nomadic Buffalo Hunters
compiled and illustrated by Paul Goble, 2007

Films about American Indian Culture
by World Wisdom

Native Spirit & The Sun Dance Way
produced by Michael Oren Fitzgerald, directed by Jennifer Casey, 2007